Architecture and Patterns for
IT Service Management, Resource
Planning, and Governance

Making Shoes for the Cobbler's Children

Architecture and Patterns for IT Service Management, Resource Planning, and Governance

Making Shoes for the Cobbler's Children

Charles T. Betz

ELSEVIER

AMSTERDAM • BOSTON • HEIDELBERG
LONDON • NEW YORK • OXFORD
PARIS • SAN DIEGO • SAN FRANCISCO
SINGAPORE • SYDNEY • TOKYO
Morgan Kaufmann is an imprint of Elsevier

MORGAN KAUFMANN PUBLISHERS

Publisher	Diane Cerra
Publishing Services Manager	George Morrison
Senior Project Manager	Brandy Lilly
Assistant Editor	Asma Palmeiro
Cover Design	Cate Barr
Composition	diacriTech
Copyeditor	Graphic World Inc.
Proofreader	Graphic World Inc.
Indexer	Graphic World Inc.
Interior printer	The Maple-Vail Book Manufacturing Group
Cover printer	Phoenix Color

Morgan Kaufmann Publishers is an imprint of Elsevier.
500 Sansome Street, Suite 400, San Francisco, CA 94111

This book is printed on acid-free paper.

Library of Congress Cataloging-in-Publication Data
Application submitted

ISBN-13: 978-0-12-370593-8
ISBN-10: 0-12-370593-2

For information on all Morgan Kaufmann publications,
visit our Web site at *www.mkp.com* or *www.books.elsevier.com*

Printed in the United States of America
06 07 08 09 10   5 4 3 2 1

To Sue, light and love of my life and my best friend: Your patience in the face of my many foibles and your support for my dream chasing means more to me than you can imagine.

To my son Keane: You are precious beyond words.

Contents

Table of Figures

Table of Tables

Foreword

ALTHOUGH WE'VE OFFICIALLY STEPPED INTO the 21st century, we've barely passed over the threshold. For many of us, simply the phrase "the 21st century" conjures up visions of flying cars, vacationing on space stations, and a utopian world where everything is computerized.

These visions haven't quite been fully realized. There are some promising prototypes of flying cars out there. Dr. Paul S. Moller continues to make progress on his skycar, with the possibility of delivery in early 2009! According to a report published by the *Toronto Daily Star,* even Boeing has gotten into the act with the goal of developing a flying car that is quiet, fuel-efficient, and easy to fly and maintain and that costs the same as a luxury vehicle.

Even civilian space travel is beginning to come around. The success of Burt Rutan's SpaceShipOne has fueled imagination and investment in the private aerospace industry. *Business 2.0* featured a cover story about the impact of privatization in the space industry, including enthusiastic predictions of wider access to space travel—even vacations in space—within the next decade!

But of the three visions that define our daydreams of the 21st century, only the third—a completely computerized world—appears already to be a reality. Virtually everything today is computerized in some way, shape, or form. Almost every aspect of science, medicine, entertainment, business, and government relies on computer technology. From new hybrid automobiles to the gas pumps they are designed to shun, computer technology is pervasive and persistent in its proliferation.

But, as Charles Betz's book helps underscore, this situation hardly qualifies as utopian.

In most companies IT has evolved—perhaps it's time to consider intelligent design. This is the value of Charlie's book. Charlie describes a process-based approach coupled with data modeling and metadata concepts, which translate in turn to distributed system architectures: a type of three-legged stool for the purpose of putting more intent into ITSM infrastructure design. I consider him one of the foremost thinkers in the area. He has certainly opened my eyes to the wonders of it all.

This book can both serve as an introduction to these important concepts as well as provide in-depth information about data modeling and the ever-important IT value chain.

Take his advice seriously and put it to work now because as we move further into the 21st century and find ourselves maintaining highways in the sky and managing the reservation system for the newest Space Station Luxury Resort, the role of IT will only become increasingly vital.

Ken Wendle, FISM
ITSM Solution Lead, Hewlett Packard
Co-founder and Past President, itSMF, USA

Boxes and Lines

THIS BOOK HAS LOTS OF boxes and lines. Nevertheless, it is not a technical book per se. It is merely attempting to be precise in describing conceptual relationships.

No particular technical background is required to understand the concepts outlined here; notations are simplified from formal industry standards and clearly described.

Patience and persistence, of course, may be required and hopefully will be well rewarded.

Preface

Technology made large populations possible; large populations now make technology indispensable.

—Joseph Wood Krutch[1]

Technology and information technology (IT) are among the few assets humanity can count on in the face of our myriad challenges. Although technology cannot by itself remedy the human condition, or point the direction toward peace, it has repeatedly shown itself to be a great servant and enabler.

Virtually all organizations—small, medium, and large, across the world—depend to some degree on technology. Software development and systems administration are skills sought worldwide as gateways to greater economic security. And worldwide investment in IT continues apace, into the hundreds of billions and trillions of dollars.

With all this importance and investment, it is ironic that the activity of managing IT itself continues to be one of the most troubled areas in today's large organizations. IT teams and their sponsors rely on rumor, impression, and educated guesses when faced with critical decisions. Project and security failures abound. There is little visibility as to how and where the IT dollar is spent and what (if any) the measurable results are, and there is less understanding of the complex dependencies present in what seem not like engineered systems but like organically grown ecologies of information processing.

Would you trust a banker dressed in shabby clothes? An auto mechanic whose car backfires and emits black smoke? How would you feel if you visited a financial planner's office and saw past-due credit card notices on her desk?

Would you trust a banker dressed in shabby clothes?

Perception is reality. An IT organization that appears to not know what it is managing does not inspire confidence, no matter how resilient the core system operations may be or how pleased individual project sponsors are. Culturally and psychologically, society's expectation is that IT will be organized, rational, and measurable—the dot-com bubble notwithstanding.[2] IT is who society turns to when it needs to organize complexity. If IT cannot solve its own problems, how can it be entrusted with the burdens of its customers?

Of course, this is overgeneralized, unfair, and harsh. That's the brutal reality of perception.

Therefore, the business case for investing in improved management infrastructure for IT is self-evident. The cost of not doing so is simply too high. If the IT organization can no longer support its internal operations with undocumented processes, disparate data, and manual tools, then investments in more robust platforms must be made. The alternative is to be the shabby banker, and although an internal IT organization with a monopoly on IT services may get away with this for some time, in today's fluid business environment with multiple sourcing alternatives it is a risky strategy.

The Internet spreads rumors and urban legends with alarming speed, but it has also proved to be the death of many long-cherished myths. Among these is the old story that a frog placed in slowly heated water will not react and will boil to death.[3]

Myth or not, it's a compelling metaphor for where enterprise IT management finds itself in the early 21st century. Starting in the middle of the last century in the equivalent of cool water—comparatively limited operations, simple technologies, and minimal expectations—IT as an enterprise capability has languished in the increasing heat, not effectively reacting to the gradual but cumulatively dramatic changes in its circumstances. Much analysis has been devoted to why; this book proposes some concrete actions. It's time for a leap.

Why, How, and For Whom This Book Was Written

We always, it seems, are provided with a glut of material on the *next* big thing, and not enough on how to make the *last* big thing actually work.

—Alec Sharp[4]

This book is intended as a bridge between theory and practice in large-scale IT management.

This book is meant to provide a coherent, architectural overview of the enterprise IT landscape, identifying the major aspects of the large IT organization and how they interact—with specific attention to process, data, and enabling systems.

It is intended for computing and information systems professionals working for large corporations. These are professionals employed in IT and information systems as a support function, not as a primary line of business; that is, I am talking not about Intel's microchip engineers or Microsoft's software architects but about the people running those companies' sales, human resources, and accounting systems. Particularly, the book is aimed at the managers and staff of internally facing IT capabilities:

▶ IT strategic planning
▶ Service management and support
▶ Enterprise architecture
▶ IT portfolio management
▶ Project management office

It's also aimed at IT outsourcing firms, whose primary value chain *is* the provision of IT services. (Whether you are an internal or external provider, the book's framework encourages you to think in terms of IT as a coherent business entity.)

This book will be useful to anyone going through ITIL or COBIT training.

It will benefit those concerned with IT governance in its various aspects, especially IT directors and group managers receiving general direction from their senior leadership to "make it so." It will be useful to anyone implementing an Information Technology Infrastructure Library (ITIL)[5] or Control Objectives for Information and related Technology (COBIT)[6] initiative or being trained in those frameworks. (Some familiarity with, and/or access to, these frameworks is recommended to obtain maximum value from this book.) Anyone participating in any form of IT process improvement may find value here.

It will also be of interest to detail-oriented senior executives, who may not read the whole book but can provide it to their staff as evidence that the problem is becoming better understood and some implementation road maps are emerging. The book is a workable template that will help reduce redundancy and increase IT agility and transparency. It can be read cover to cover or be used simply as a desk reference. (We spent quite a bit of time on the index.)

It is a next step book for those saying:

"Okay—let's 'run IT like a business.' Now what?"

The book moves horizontally through the IT value chain and vertically from the high-level objectives of IT governance down to the specific process, data, and system architectures enabling it. It fills the gap between general *guidance* on IT governance and detailed discussions about the specific tools and technologies that *support and enable* IT governance. It is a step toward a more "off-the-shelf" standard set of approaches.

Why Another Book?

In many cases, the I/S [information system] data situation can be compared with the mechanic who never fixes his car because he is too busy servicing others.

—IBM[7]

There is much high-level guidance emerging on the subject of IT governance, but because this guidance comes from a variety of sources and can be highly general, it presents the would-be user with challenges.

This book is a response to the lack of concrete guidance in the major process frameworks, such as ITIL.

Major frameworks such as ITIL, Capability Maturity Model Integration (CMMI), and COBIT require substantial interpretation before implementation and in the United States in particular are still underappreciated. As will be seen, they also are overlapping and inconsistent, and no one framework can claim comprehensive coverage of IT yet.

There is no end of material available from vendors discussing detailed particulars about emerging trends and products, but this material is, of course, written to serve their interests.

Commercial research firms do excellent work but are focused on partitioning and decomposing the IT market—this book is focused on overlaps and synergies across the IT problem domain.

Large consulting firms may have rich and powerful integrated methods, but they are proprietary and expensive. Smaller firms may not have sufficient depth of understanding; this is an active market with many new entrants. *Caveat emptor.*

Finally, many authors are joining the fray, most with fine ideas, but they are often focused on higher-order questions and less concerned with some of the nuts-and-bolts issues encountered when seeking an integrated IT capability and especially in achieving alignment across diverse IT functions.

PowerPoint is not a system of record.

The consequences of this are apparent in most large IT organizations: lack of process understanding that leads to uncoordinated initiatives to purchase tools from vendors who have a strategy of never admitting they compete against one another ("Oh, we don't do what they do; we can interoperate with them."). Redundant IT governance and enablement applications require interfaces that are risky to build and expensive to run, and in many cases such integration is overlooked or bypassed. Consulting firms may be brought in with a variety of approaches, driving further tool acquisitions, or engage in lengthy one-time harvests of data into diagrams and voluminous spreadsheets, promptly turning stale. (PowerPoint is not a system of record.)

If internal IT organizations in particular are to avoid needless outsourcing and prosper, it is important for them to consider the issues outlined herein; they are areas of active research and concern for large IT service providers seeking to take over internal IT development and operations.

An Architecture for IT Itself

And why beholdest thou the mote that is in thy brother's eye, but considerest not the beam that is in thine own eye?

—Matthew 7:3

This book treats ITIL, COBIT, and the rest of the IT literature as a statement of requirements.

The book you are holding is the analysis and high-level design of a logical IT value chain system, a.k.a. "enterprise resource planning for information technology." It is an architecture. It was written through treating ITIL, COBIT, and much other IT literature as an extended *statement of requirements,* filtered through my industry experiences. Process, information, and distributed systems modeling techniques were applied to deriving a unified structure from these requirements in an effort no different from applying those techniques to other business processes.

This book is intended to provide the IT organization with an architectural framework to coordinate IT process renewal activities with acquisitions of IT enablement products and services; counterbalance the claims of vendors, integrators, and consultants; and clarify a confusing and overlapping product and concept landscape.

Don't confuse this work with any of the excellent books on enterprise architecture. This book is an application of enterprise architecture principles (process, data, and systems analysis) upon IT itself (including, paradoxically, the organizations, tools, and processes supporting enterprise architecture in the IT organization).

It is also *not* a book on enterprise resource planning (ERP) systems, such as SAP or Oracle. The "ERP for IT" or "IT resource planning" theme underlying this book is evocative and provocative, but the products are generally immature and it is still early in this particular hype cycle.

Does the world need another book on IT project management or IT operations? It does need more detail on how these areas relate.

Much ink has been spilled on IT. The danger with a broadly scoped book such as this is attempting to boil an ocean. The strategy for counteracting this danger has been a bias toward the difficult. You will not find extended descriptions of well-understood IT functions but rather a focus on cross-functional dynamics in the IT value chain. It's debatable whether the world needs another book on IT project management or IT operations—but it does need more detail on how these two areas relate to each other, beyond accidental integration.

Some will critique any discussion of data and systems as bordering on irrelevant technicalities. "It's all about the process" in this point of view. I do not agree. The reason we care about process, data, *and* system in detail is that the margin for IT enablement is so small that no redundancy or inefficiency can be tolerated. Interfaces in this problem area are complex; maintaining alignment across the high IT functional walls is as difficult as in any other area of the business, and these problems are compounded by the typically limited resources available to spend on enabling a supporting process like IT.

Reading This Book

This book is an application of enterprise architecture principles upon IT itself.

Icons

This book unashamedly borrows from the "For Dummies" and similar types of books in establishing a set of icons:

Vocabulary: especially where terminology is unclear in the industry

Dialog: a hypothetical conversation presented to clarify complex or subtle issues

Case Study: an actual situation relevant to the points being made

Key Point: pay attention here

Food for Thought: interesting stuff to know, historical context, and so on

Author's Note: a personal comment from the author

Structure

The book is written as an analysis of IT domain requirements from an architectural perspective. Establishing "views" on a complex problem is a standard enterprise architecture or software engineering technique used here, with process, data, and application systems being the major perspectives.

Part I has two major sections:

Chapter 1 outlines some of the current problems of IT management and presents a number of loosely defined concepts that have been posed as solutions to IT's management problems. This section can be seen as a high-level problem statement.

Chapter 2 provides a detailed discussion of a value chain–based framework. Most IT organizations are divided along the major functional fault lines of planning and controlling, building, and operating—there is little recognition of IT as an overall supply chain. This section serves as a business process analysis.

Drawing on COBIT, ITIL, and CMMI, the chapter maps IT processes and process areas into a value chain framework, focused on describing the IT activities in terms of their value-adding contributions and handoffs. The value chain discussion remains at a high level (it's not the purpose of this book to dig deeply into the theory of an IT value chain), and the framework is used to structure the functional requirements for comprehensive IT automation. Nonfunctional requirements are also discussed.

Having described the problem in Part I, Part II goes on to describe solutions.

Chapter 3 develops the converse of the process coin: data. Starting with the metrics used for managing and optimizing process, a detailed conceptual data model is described that represents my years of experience in solving internal IT problems.

The IT industry is still wrestling with fundamental concepts and language.[8] The goal of this chapter is to clarify the various casual terms of IT governance into a precise vocabulary represented in a form useful for architectural analysis and mapped to both the IT processes and the IT systems.

Chapter 4 gets into the meat of systems architecture. Based in part on the previous analysis and in part on current real-world vendor trends, a reference inventory of distributed IT enablement systems is proposed and interactions are detailed. This detailing is necessarily incomplete (there are far too many permutations to consider), but this discussion of interactions leads to…

Chapter 5, in which this book borrows the concept of design patterns from software engineering. A pattern is a general solution to a common problem; it is not a completed design that can be directly implemented but rather is a description or template that can be used in various situations. The chapter uses a modified pattern language approach to discuss particular challenges in IT management and detailed responses to them using all tools and methods illustrated to date: process, functional, organizational, data, and systems views.

The book concludes in Chapter 6 with some reflections on current industry challenges. The appendices include methods used in this book, a discussion of IT professionalization, current IT professional organizations, and a glossary (as well as the usual list of references and index).

Where appropriate, chapters contain sections dedicated to making a business case and implementation tips, as well as further reading.

IT Enablement

IT enablement in this book is defined not as the enablement of business processes by IT but as the enablement (often automated) of IT's own business processes.

Gaps and Omissions

This book deliberately avoids much discussion of the following:

▶ Desktop computing
▶ Security
▶ Facilities
▶ IT organizational structure
▶ IT human resources management

More could also be said about IT financial management.

The discussion is broad and cross-disciplinary, and apologies are tendered in advance to any domain experts who feel their subject matter is ill-treated. Please feel free to forward corrections, comments, or criticisms to the publisher.

Acknowledgments

THIS BOOK IS THE RESULT of a journey through IT that started in 1976. As a seventh grader, my junior high had 110-baud teletype access to the Minnesota Educational Computing Consortium time-sharing systems (Univac, Control Data, and Hewlett Packard), where I first was exposed to computer programming (although my interest was more in the online chat capability, known as XTalk, that existed even then).

In 1986, I received as a gift Intel 8088 IBM PC (with *two* floppy drives) from my mother. My journey then proceeded through end user, power user, support staff, programmer of desktop databases, networking, IT manager, enterprise system consultant, software developer, information architect, metadata and configuration manager, and enterprise architect. En route, I passed through the history of modeling and software development, from structured to CASE to OO, and into the emerging subjects of IT portfolio and service management. I picked up enough real computing along the way to land a master of science in software engineering from the University of Minnesota.

While working as a data architect for Target Corporation, my boss dropped by and offered me a chance to lead a project to create a data dictionary integrated from two CASE tools. This introduced me to the world of metadata, a fascinating discipline and perspective, and that experience led to a position leading the Metadata Management Office in Best Buy's cutting-edge integration competency center. One day, my friend (and local ITIL guru) Chris Capadouca came up to me and asked, "What's the difference between a metadata repository and a configuration management database?" Attempting to answer this question started a most interesting journey indeed, one leading to my master's research and culminating in this book.

Academics and technologists often spend their careers learning more and more about less and less. I've been learning a little about a lot. Many people have helped me understand this complex problem domain and build the cross-functional perspective described in this book; I acknowledge some of the key contributors here.

The debt I owe Chris Capadouca is deep and profound—for introducing me to ITIL, for helping coin the term "model-driven configuration management," for producing the first distributed IT reference architecture I have ever seen, and for contributing many other deep insights and challenging conversations. Also for providing fun boat rides.

Curt Abraham, for educating me on what it means to be an enterprise architect.

Jim Holmes, for being my first data modeling mentor. Adrienne Tannenbaum, for showing interest in my writing. Elizabeth Sisely, for being my master's capstone project adviser. Doug Jones, for mentoring and supporting me through some difficult times in my transition to an actual corporation. John Schmidt, for educating me on what it means to be a technologist in a business context. Art Caston, for providing me (through the Best Buy architecture team) with a rigorous foundation as an enterprise architecture practitioner.

John Valente, Tony Briggs, and Larry Coates, for supporting the nascent repository capability at Best Buy. Todd Soller, for posing the tough question, "How are you going to keep this stuff up to date?" That question opened my eyes to the challenges of business process management. Greg Johnson, Mike Harder, Manuel Palacios, and Wendy Filipek, for their hard work in making part of the ERP-IT vision come true.

Pete Rivett and Sandra Foster of Adaptive, for a great partnership in making the capability real. Pete also for his thorough manuscript critiques! Greg Keller of Embarcadero, for his enthusiastic and positive messages of support that have helped keep me going.

Dan Dixon, for critical backing at key points and being an all-around good guy. Brian Raney, for his topnotch technical leadership and references. Brian Duren, for references and support.

Doug Jackson of Dow Chemical, for his ITIL initial data modeling work. Boris Pevzner of Centrata, for the introduction of the idea of a "nonorderable service." Mehmet Orun, for his suggestion that metrics be moved to the start of the data chapter (among other invaluable insights). Bruce Clark and James Sturdevant, for manuscript assistance.

Iris Fliegelman of Shared Insights, for seeing enough merit in my material to justify appearances at the BPM and EA conferences. Tony Shaw of Wilshire Conferences, for giving support and assistance at various points, including key opportunities to speak at DAMA/Wilshire.

Martin Erb, for the opportunity to speak at the national IT Service Management Forum and for ongoing excellent feedback and collegiality. The local DAMA chapter, for speaking opportunities (sorry I haven't been around much lately).

The honors program (in particular Chris Gordon) in the University of Minnesota's College of Liberal Arts—I continue to highly value my *summa* political science B.A.; without it I would probably not be writing this book.

The software engineering program at the University of Minnesota, and in particular my 2003 cohort comrades Sean Goggins, Peggy Dora, Bryan Kamrath, and Rich Davies, for continued amusement, insight, and general troublemaking.

The many readers and correspondents I have gained through my weblog, *www.erp4it.com;* I will be starting to post more now, folks!

To my current colleagues: I have learned so much from so many of you in so many ways and will acknowledge that debt more fully in future works.

My reviewers: Richard Soley, David Pultorak, R. Todd Stephens, Karen Lopez, Dennis Gaughan, Robert Handler, Pete Rivett, Chris Capadouca, Peggy Dora, Rene Aerdts, Mehmet Orun, Matt Machczynski, Sean Goggins, Ian Rowlands, John Schmidt, and Doug McClure. Your comments and critiques have helped make this a far stronger manuscript, and any remaining weaknesses are, of course, my own responsibility.

My editor Diane Cerra, for seeing merit in what must have seemed like a somewhat far-fetched proposal. Asma Stephan, for providing manuscript and editorial assistance. Julie Laing for copyediting.

Finally, my family, Sue and Keane, for tolerating my frequent long sojourns at the silicon altar.

Apologies if I have overlooked anyone else!

IT is by nature led by smart and often introspective people. This book at best is an incremental step forward in the application of IT-based techniques to understanding IT itself. To the extent it contributes anything new, it is through standing on the shoulders of giants. I claim sole credit only for my errors.

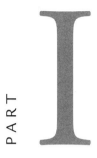

THE IT VALUE CHAIN

For CIOs, it has been like trying to run a business before the invention of bookkeeping.

—Howard Rubin, Meta Group[9]

THIS IS A BOOK ABOUT ENABLING the IT value chain. What is it? What exactly is being enabled? Why is enabling it important?

Part I introduces the endemic problems of enterprise IT, and many proposed solutions, followed by an in-depth discussion of what a large IT organization does, in the form of a systematic framework based on value chain analysis. Part I overall is The Challenge, and Part II is Some Solutions.

chapter 1

Introduction: Shoes for the Cobbler's Child

1.1 The Achievements of IT

In my more than eighteen years at the Federal Reserve, much has surprised me, but nothing more than the remarkable ability of our economy to absorb and recover from the shocks of stock market crashes, credit crunches, terrorism, and hurricanes—blows that would have almost certainly precipitated deep recessions in decades past. This resilience, not evident except in retrospect, owes to a remarkable increase in economic flexibility, partly the consequence of deliberate economic policy and partly the consequence of innovations in information technology.

—Alan Greenspan[10]

BECAUSE THE FIRST PART OF THIS BOOK is going to focus on the problems of IT to a great degree, let's at least glance at the achievements.

IT (arguably) started with the invention of writing and counting. Managing libraries was a problem known to the ancient Egyptians, and the challenges of categorizing, tracking, and deriving useful information from raw data thus date from earliest history to the present. Innovations such as the abacus; decimal arithmetic; dual-entry accounting; the large-scale, professionally managed countinghouse; and modern filing and workflow techniques all predated the electronic automation of information management.

Because the first part of this book is going to focus on the problems of IT to a great degree, let's at least glance at the achievements.

The harnessing of electricity opened up new possibilities in information management, first realized through electromechanical devices and then the vacuum tube, transistor, and integrated circuit. The increases in processing power, communications bandwidth, and data storage over the past 50 years are dramatic:

▶ The fastest transactional systems can process upward of 3 million transactions a minute, enough volume to support a large city's worth of people doing nothing but ordering things.

▶ The largest data warehouses now are 100 terabytes, or 5 times all of the text in the Library of Congress.

▶ The fastest long-distance network links exceed 40 gigabits per second, enough speed to transmit the Library of Congress text in just over 1 hour.

▶ And as Ray Kurzweil notes, "Supercomputers will achieve one human brain capacity by 2010, and personal computers will do so by around 2020. By 2030, it will take a village of human brains (around a thousand) to match $1000 of computing. By 2050, $1000 of computing will equal the processing power of all human brains on Earth."[11]

Enabling technology's effective utilization, especially in the context of large organizations, is the purpose of this book.

However, this technical capacity is meaningless until placed into the service of human desire. Enabling technology's effective utilization, especially in the context of large organizations, is the purpose of this book—and although much improvement is needed, consider again the opening quote from former Federal Reserve Board Chairman Alan Greenspan. The world's aggregate computing capabilities in economic service are now *manifest at the macroeconomic level,* which is quite remarkable if you stop to think about it.

This chapter is a thematic chapter. It discusses at a high level the failures of IT, and some of the proposed solutions, and in so doing sets a conceptual stage for the more detailed, technical analysis to follow.

1.2 The Problems

The problems of enterprise IT have had much ink spilled about them, and I refer you to the pages of the IT trade press for the latest horror stories and tirades.

Generally, IT has a reputation as a bottomless cost sink run by people who can't explain what they're doing (especially why they cost so much), can't deliver what they promise, seem to feel contempt for their customers, and appear to have no understanding of business concerns. "Necessary evil" is being polite.

Failures of alignment, of projects, and of mission critical systems are far too common and widely reported, both in the popular press and on the golf courses of elite country clubs: IT—can't live with it, can't live without it.

The world is only starting to see the failures of complex system interactions. The Y2K crisis required massive, urgent investment. The atrocities of 9/11 arguably could have been prevented by better information sharing among federal agencies. The 2003 East Coast blackout was caused in part through failures of IT.

In short, the continuous expansion of IT complexity (nowhere near the end of how complex we can make it), is increasing the risk that "unmanaged IT" is imposing on business and on society.

One of the most popular and controversial commentators, former *Harvard Business Review* Editor in Chief Nicholas Carr, has provoked a firestorm of comment and controversy by bluntly proposing the thesis that "IT doesn't matter."[12] One of his key points is that as IT becomes more commoditized, it needs to be managed not for competitive advantage but for risk.[13]

Failures of Alignment and Strategy

IT as a support organization is expected to primarily support the needs of revenue-producing, customer-facing business operations. It's also expected to enable other business support activities: human resources, financial management, legal affairs, facilities, and so forth.

Determining the expectations and tradeoffs of these support responsibilities is often not done systematically; thus, the overall consumption of IT resources is generally poorly governed. Overpromising and underdelivering are common complaints, because the business demand exceeds the IT supply and explicit governance and prioritization mechanisms are lacking—too often the loudest voices win, and if the sum of their demand is 125% of IT capacity, the projects go forward regardless.

When solutions and capabilities are delivered, they are too often "not what we wanted." IT is supposed to automate business processes—but what if the processes are ill conceived or inefficient?

Failures of IT Projects

Success in IT projects occurs after the system has been installed, the process has been changed to take advantage of the system, the old process has been destroyed, and the benefits of the new process have been measured.

—Bennet P. Lientz and Lee Larssen[14]

Spectacular project failures are the norm; the Standish Group's 2004 CHAOS report[15] indicated a 28% success rate for surveyed projects and much less for the largest and most strategic initiatives. (As this book goes to press, serious methodological issues have been raised with regard to this report.) The phenomenon is the subject of numerous books and articles, such as Robert L. Glass's *Software Runaways,*[16] and much coverage in the core software engineering literature.[17] This brief mention does not do justice to the depth of this problem, but this is a well-discussed topic and no more need be said.

"Building software will always be hard. There is inherently no silver bullet."

Fred Brooks

As Fred Brooks and many others have persuasively established, *the core creative activity of defining new automated systems will forever remain risky.* Improvements in IT governance and its supporting systems will assist project management and software development by 1) enabling clearer analysis of the operational enterprise context and 2) clarifying the nonfunctional requirements of well-managed and secure software in a given data center environment. Although both of these are worthy goals (and may provide some incremental benefit in project estimation, scoping, and risk reduction), neither will eliminate the complexity of the software engineering challenge and the fundamental nature of the risk inherent in building *novel* systems.[18]

Project failures cannot be assessed entirely within the framework of project management, either. A "successful" project in the standard sense may still be a real failure if the new capability does not add business value. Furthermore, substantial gains are possible in driving down operational IT costs, and this starts in the project life cycle. While advanced project methodologies may address such concerns in theory, the reality is that victory is too often declared when the system is turned on and insufficient attention is paid to assessing its costs and benefits over time.

Failures of IT Operations

A significant implication of the cash hunger of IT is the fact that the discretionary portion of the IT budget dramatically reduces over time. This financial pressure invariably results in shrinking of development expenditure.

—Dan Remenyi[19]

Operational IT costs can consume 80% or more of the enterprise IT budget.

IT operational failures include system outages, security compromises, and other prominent, pronounced occurrences. However, attention to these (and widely publicized IT project failures) has obscured a more insidious and far more costly failure: that of enterprise IT to effectively control operational costs.

A project by definition is a fixed-time effort. Enterprise IT projects usually result in working operational systems (or enhancements thereto). Such systems require ongoing care and feeding:

- Hardware depreciation or leasing
- Software licensing (typically 15%–20% annually of initial acquisition, required for vendor support)
- Floor space—that is, real estate charges
- Facilities infrastructure: power, heating, ventilating, and air-conditioning (HVAC), raised floor, racks, and so on
- Network connectivity and related infrastructure (e.g., directory services software and security perimeters)
- Operational software infrastructure: monitoring systems, batch schedulers, backup systems, and so on, all with their own associated costs
- Operations and support staff; staffing can come in various flavors:
  - Data center operations monitors
  - Help desk operators
  - Application specialists
  - Senior engineers
  - Senior IT executives and customer relationship managers
  - Business-side "lead users"
  - Vendor relationship owners and contract managers

These costs can consume 80% or more of the enterprise IT budget, resulting in increasing pressure on funding for new innovation. The trend across too many IT organizations is graphically represented in Figure 1.1.

As Mark Lutchen (ex-CIO of PricewaterhouseCoopers) notes in his excellent *Managing IT as a Business,*

IT budgets are too often prepared as if every IT initiative were being developed in a vacuum. This type of budgeting presumes that an IT initiative goes through a development period and then is magically implemented without any extra costs to overall systems maintenance.

In reality, linking any IT initiative into the total existing IT environment involves a cost. The amount of that cost depends not only on the size and complexity of the initiative being undertaken but also on the state of the current environment.[20]

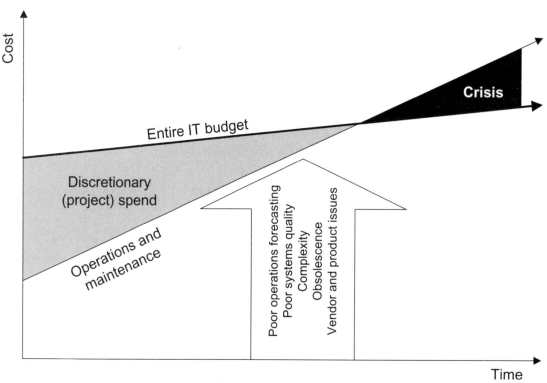

Figure 1.1 The operational IT crisis.

Unfunded Liabilities?

The careless, unexamined assumption of unfunded financial liabilities would be seen as fiscal irresponsibility and might lead to serious concerns as to a company's health and adherence to regulations, such as Sarbanes-Oxley Act of 2002. Why would we not see the assumption of unfunded system liabilities in the same light?

What are the drivers of higher operational and maintenance costs?

▶ Lack of current state visibility and resulting inability to understand impacts and cost drivers and to support IT decision making

▶ Poorly managed IT portfolios—the organization does not know what it has, resulting in duplication of effort and missed opportunities

▶ Too many vendors and technologies, driving expensive staff skill requirements

▶ Ineffective knowledge sharing—crucial information is maintained on paper and in people's heads rather than in an enterprise-class knowledge base

The problem lies not in the core speed and power of computers but in the fragility and brittleness of the applications built on them.

Escalating operational inefficiency is a seeming paradox in light of the well-known Moore's law (processing power[21] doubles every 18 months). If computing is becoming cheaper, why is its maintenance cost not going down? The problem lies not in the core speed and power of computers but in the fragility and brittleness of the applications built on them and the emergence of a peculiar form of nonorganic "rot," resulting in part *from* the perceived abundance of computing.

Because hardware and storage are "cheap," there is little incentive to maximize their efficient use. Applications are never fully sunset, duplicate capabilities are freely built because there is too much perceived overhead in attempting to consolidate them, jobs and reports are run long beyond their operational usefulness, and so the junk piles up in the attic. Teams are reluctant to turn anything off because they don't fully understand all of the impacts. Obsolescence in one area prevents other areas from moving forward, and like rats that breed in filth, operational issues ensue from entropy. The complexity and brittleness of systems is a particular issue; as Robert Handler and Bryan Maizlish aptly state:

Many companies maintain a sequential series of tightly coupled, hardwired systems that dictate business logic and processes. The resulting infrastructure is inflexible and ineffective in data aggregation and synchronization. Costly overruns are commonplace in extending or adding new processes across divergent and distributed environments. The ability to extend, migrate, refurbish, or retire systems or applications is very difficult as key dependencies, support, and constraints with other applications and systems are unknown. Thus, it is not surprising to find multiple and redundant enterprise resource planning, supply chain management, portals, customer relationship management, middleware, and operating systems consisting of ad hoc upgrades and patches analogous to a "spaghetti" architecture.

Technical, business, operating, system, logical, and physical views of the architecture are typically outdated or nonexistent. Misalignment between IT and the strategic intent, inability to establish a common IT architecture, and a highly redundant and undocumented as-is architecture will result in high operations and maintenance costs. Furthermore, this will limit a company's ability to rapidly respond to unforeseen events and prioritize and reprioritize investments. In today's unforgiving economy, the result of not conforming to a disciplined IT portfolio management framework is undisciplined growth and drift of business processes that are typically expressed through lack of innovation, slow market responsiveness, and dissatisfied customers. These shortfalls are exposed swiftly, causing debilitating and adverse effects on valuation and the sustainability of a company as an ongoing entity.[22]

Simplicity is more than a virtue; it is cheaper.

Simplicity is more than a virtue; it is cheaper. A simpler infrastructure is a more agile infrastructure. Fewer vendors are easier to manage than more. Fewer applications, databases, and interfaces are easier to manage than more.

Functionality traceable to active business needs is functionality valued and cared for. An application portfolio consisting entirely of well-maintained, current systems with documented interactions and dependencies is a precious corporate asset, one that should be recognized at the most senior levels of corporate management in the same way that a well-managed portfolio of liquid cash investments would be regarded.

The IT project phase is often optimized at the expense of the entire value chain.

Enforcing such principles is difficult, especially when it comes to aligning projects with the goals of simplicity and operational expense reduction. Because it is the best-understood area of IT activity, the project phase is often optimized at the expense of the other process areas and therefore at the expense of the entire IT capability. The challenges of IT project management are that broader value chain objectives are often deemed "not in scope" for a particular project and projects are not held accountable for their contributions to overall system entropy. This is perhaps indicative of the tension between short-term and long-term views, unavoidable in human affairs, but you should refer back to Figure 1.1 before shrugging it off.

Complex IT systems are liabilities in a sense not well recognized in current financial accounting practices. At least, it seems there's a need for some sort of new approach to long-term discounting or depreciation of IT investments as they start to consume increasingly more operational resources.

Jeffrey Kaplan has an excellent critique of IT exceptionalism:

"For some reason, senior leaders treat the IT department differently from every other department and then complain when it does not perform like the others."

Jeffrey Kaplan

For some reason, senior leaders treat the IT department differently from every other department and then complain when it does not perform like the others. We have to stop treating IT and the IT discipline as if it were a different animal.... IT service development activities parallel those of commercial R&D organizations. IT service delivery and operations activities parallel those of corporate manufacturing and customer service departments. IT governance activities parallel corporate governance activities.... The fundamental management principles of all the disciplines are identical.[23]

A View from the Future

Two historians are discussing the history of IT from the perspective of 2200:

"It's hard to believe some of the mistakes that were made in the early days of information technology development."

"Yes—their technical capabilities far outstripped their ability to manage and control high complexity systems and embed them usefully in the broader organizational contexts.

"There was early recognition of this and a number of efforts to mitigate it, but they were derailed by the fast movement of the technological innovation. Third-generation mainframe computing, for example, figured many things out that needed to be reinvented when distributed systems became the norm.

"Substantial progress did not start until the early 2000s, as operational costs started devouring the entire discretionary spend for projects. The ability to drive down those costs became a strategic differentiator—strategy *through* commoditization. It did matter how effectively companies were able to do this, because the inertia and brittleness of complex information processing environments was a difficult challenge.

"Seeing technology development and operation as one integrated supply chain was critical. Technical professionals could identify the problems with functional silos in other, non-IT departments but seemed strangely reluctant to face the silos in their own value chain that were causing rework and inefficiency. IT is so heavily leveraged that it's critical to have well-crafted management there. I guess it's easier to see the dust speck in your neighbor's eye than it is to see the stick in your own."

1.3 The Proposed Solutions

The first challenge facing managers is to put their IT house in order.

—Nicholas Carr[24]

Piecemeal approaches that are assumed to be *the* answer are as dangerous as no response at all.

—Geary Rummler and Alan Brache[25]

Although new technologies continue evolving at an ever-accelerating pace, the ability of large organizations to sensibly manage their portfolios of hardware and software lags.

The purpose of this section is context. With all of the attention focused on IT over the past decades, it is surprising how poorly managed it is in large organizations. Although new technologies and vendor products for IT continue evolving at an ever-accelerating pace, the ability of large organizations to sensibly manage their portfolios of hardware and software lags. A commonly used metaphor in discussing the IT governance crisis is "the barefoot cobbler's child." That is to say, although IT puts the shoes of automation on the feet of its business partners, it neglects to do so for its own processes.

It is not hard, in looking at these problems, to infer some generally desirable characteristics and capabilities for the large IT organization. Such characteristics include the following:

▶ Responsive, agile support for evolving business needs and strategies
▶ Operational effectiveness: available and high performing systems and infrastructure

- ▶ Cost effectiveness, efficiency, and transparency
- ▶ Capable risk and security management

These major performance factors are easily stated; a plethora of solutions and approaches are proposed to achieve them. Various disciplines, programs, and slogans have emerged as "banners" representing the goal of improving enterprise IT management:

- ▶ "Run IT like a business"
- ▶ "Business–IT alignment"
- ▶ IT governance
- ▶ IT portfolio management
- ▶ Enterprise architecture
- ▶ Outsourcing
- ▶ Demand management
- ▶ Program and project management
- ▶ Software engineering capability maturity
- ▶ IT service management
- ▶ Application management
- ▶ Business process management
- ▶ Information, data, and metadata management
- ▶ Service-oriented architecture
- ▶ Utility computing
- ▶ Software as a Service
- ▶ Enterprise application integration
- ▶ Model-driven architecture
- ▶ Agile methods
- ▶ Enterprise resource planning for IT

I'm starting this analysis from the current state of the industry. These are not precise terms; they have been selected mainly on the basis of their appearance in print, as conference topics, and so forth. They are the Enterprise IT Fashion Show, circa 2006. Think of them as "memes."

Meme

A unit of cultural information, such as a cultural practice or idea, transmitted verbally or by repeated action from one mind to another.[26]

The overlaps and interactions among major IT areas of focus are poorly understood.

Each provides some unique perspective, but the overlaps and interactions among them are poorly understood and increasingly the subject of contention in large enterprises.

Here is a brief definition of each and the story it has to tell in alleviating IT pain. Table 1.1 provides a quick summary of the preceding terms.

"Run IT Like a Business"

A more useful slogan might be "Run IT like a value chain."

This slogan has appeared on the cover of *CIO Magazine*[27] and been echoed in much analyst and vendor literature. The slogan may seem superficial, but when translated into the idea "run IT like a value chain" it has merit. A basis of this book is the long-established thought experiment in which the internal IT capability is seen as an autonomous business—perhaps with only one customer, but autonomous nevertheless.[28] In particular, the slogan can drive a new focus on performance management and customer-focused metrics.

Running IT like a business means identifying the processes that make up IT.

IT is often criticized for its lack of transparency to its business sponsors. Running IT like a business means identifying the processes that make up IT and how to measure them. Even if such processes are indirect business supporters, the simple fact that they are represented as processes and not obscure computing wizardry will help with IT's credibility. Telling a business executive that the TCP/IP stack is corrupted or some such technical information is usually not useful; explaining that this happened because "the change management process has a gap" is more understandable from a business perspective.

However, the slogan also implies that IT has somehow not been "business-like," which is a little unfair. (The first 50 years were spent just trying to make IT work.) It also can prematurely drive thinking about chargeback and even outsourcing.

Table 1.1 IT Enablement Themes and Strategies

The Term	The Problem It Addresses	How It Does So
"Run IT like a business"	The perception exists that IT is not run in a "businesslike" manner.	Promoting a value chain–based, customer-oriented management philosophy.
"Business–IT alignment"	The perception exists that IT is not "aligned with the business."	Promoting the meeting of business needs as the highest goal of IT and the traceability of IT activities to those needs.
IT governance	Overall control of the IT capability is needed.	Defining decision rights and high-level mechanisms for enabling them.
IT portfolio management	Ill-defined IT "stuff" must be managed. There is an inability to make "apples-to-apples" comparisons between things.	Defining major portfolio subjects. Normalizing and where possible quantifying them and their metrics. Enabling a framework for rational evaluation and comparison for invest, maintain, and retire decisions.
Enterprise architecture	Business capabilities are redundant and poorly optimized. IT infrastructures are redundant, unmanageable, heterogeneous, and brittle.	Governing and/or influencing platform selection, product acquisition, and high-level system design; mapping system dependencies and other significant features.
Outsourcing	Management attention has become distracted from the core value chain. There is overreliance on expensive domestic staff for repeatable, noncore business processes.	Using the most economically efficient staffing source for the problem at hand, given various criteria and concerns such as whether the function considered for outsourcing is core to the business value chain or only supporting.
Demand management	Scarce IT assets are misused. IT is treated as an unlimited resource.	Controlling and objectively evaluating or prioritizing requests for IT services through strong customer relationship management and single point of entry. Closely related (if not identical) to project portfolio management.
Program and project management	IT activities are unclear. IT initiatives are not managed to clear objectives or success criteria. Time, cost, and scope expand without control.	Promoting well-established methods (not IT specific) for planning, managing, and controlling projects.
Software engineering capability maturity	Software engineering is a particularly difficult problem domain in which to apply standard project management principles.	Promoting key practices shown to be essential to successful software development, such as requirements management; defined analysis, design, and construction methods; project change management; issue management; and configuration management.

IT service management	Unfavorable business experiences with IT delivery occur. Operational expenses accelerate. IT management is fragmented. There is a lack of a unified, customer-oriented view of IT.	Emphasizing business as "customer" and defining what customers are "purchasing" in business terms. Creating a systematic and standard management framework for operations. Focusing on cross-functional IT business processes: change, incident, configuration, and so on.
Application management	Large-scale production applications are the single greatest IT expense in information-centric organizations.	Focusing on application viability, architectures, road maps, and manageability.
Business process management	Functional and technology-centric views of business suboptimize the value chain and promote negative customer experiences, finger-pointing, and ball-dropping. No overall ownership of value creation.	Focusing on the end-to-end business process as the most important management concept in business today.
Information, data, and metadata management	Terabytes and petabytes of disk space are consumed with little attention to optimal use. Regulated data cannot be identified. Origin of information represented in reports is poorly understood. Reports on the same data generate different results. Systems cannot be easily enhanced because data structures and meaning are opaque.	Treating data as a managed corporate asset, designed, defined, and classified appropriately. Identifying stewards. Managing redundancy and providing incentives for reduction of storage consumption. Making lineage available for all information consumed by business customers.
Service-oriented architecture	Tightly coupled, proprietary architectures are inflexible and cannot adapt to changing business requirements.	Modularizing system functionality into discrete "services" that can be recombined as needed to quickly enable new functionality. Using standard middleware architecture enables superior interoperability, leading to improved manageability and platform cost reductions. Important business process management enabler.
Utility computing	Purpose-built infrastructure is slow to come online and expensive to maintain.	Commoditizing base computing services (CPU cycles, main memory, and storage) and (subject to certain limitations) providing them in a utility mode.

(continued)

Table 1.1 (continued)

The Term	The Problem It Addresses	How It Does So
Software as a Service	Purpose-built applications are slow to come online and expensive to maintain.	Commoditizing functional application services (presentation, business logic, and data management) and (subject to certain limitations) providing them in a utility mode.
Enterprise application integration	System interactions are bewildering in their complexity. Data redundancy abounds. Data feeds are replicated multiple times. Intersystem dependencies are poorly or not understood and disproportionate causes of incidents and problems.	Managing integration as a core function (e.g., through a dedicated center of excellence). Emphasizing and where possible enforcing reuse of data through defining systems of record and publish/subscribe architectures. Focusing on specialized configuration management challenges.
Model-driven architecture and development	A gap exists between business requirements and operational systems. Modeling representations are fragmented.	Defining a standard semantic stack for modeling languages and notations. Defining transformation techniques from high-level models to executable code.
Agile methods	Large-scale projects fail because of mismanaged functional requirements.	Emphasizing the iterative nature of the customer–solution relationship and primacy of customer involvement in solution conception.
Enterprise resource planning for IT	IT itself as a major functional area and value chain has no integrated system of record.	Building a conceptual architecture for an integrated, process-oriented IT system. Driving vendor product suites toward this vision.

"Business–IT Alignment"

Analyzing and documenting the alignment of IT capabilities with a company's business model can be an excellent focus area, for example, for an enterprise architecture organization. If architecture modeling is understood to include nontechnical matters—at a minimum, business processes, capabilities, and functions—and this business model is then linked systematically to the underlying supporting IT services, the organization is far ahead of most. Again, if we accept the premise, the promise is similar to "run IT like a business": stop running IT for the sake of the geeks and start running it for the people who pay the bills.

The notion that IT requires special "alignment" presumes that IT is not part of the business.

However, from another perspective the premise is fundamentally flawed. The notion that IT requires special "alignment" presumes that IT is not part of the business. Would a business ever say, "We need better business–marketing alignment"? On the other hand, there is much in IT that is pure commodity and does not "align" with a business, any more than elevators in a downtown legal firm are "aligned" with the practice of law.

Flawed or not, the term has entered the common vocabulary. The question in achieving "business–IT alignment" is, What aspects of IT are truly reflective of and relevant to specific business objectives? One potential victim of this slogan would be investments in the IT governance-enabling infrastructure this book advocates, such as IT portfolio or service management, because they do not "directly" support business activities—they are merely overhead on the larger overhead of IT.

IT Governance

The question is how to enable IT governance?

IT governance is a contentious concept, with narrower and broader definitions proposed by various parties.[29] Peter Weill and Jeanne W. Ross see the core of IT governance as the allocation of decision rights among IT stakeholders (directors, executive committees, IT organizational leadership, and IT thought leadership). IT governance in this restricted sense is enabled by the other major functions listed. The promise of IT governance is that by carefully structuring decision rights and ensuring transparency better decisions will be made and enacted with greater effectiveness.

While rigorous and precise, the Weill/Ross definition is somewhat limited. This book uses the IT Governance Institute's definition[30]:

The purpose of IT governance is to direct IT endeavors, to ensure that IT's performance meets the following objectives:

► Alignment of IT with the enterprise and realization of the promised benefits

► Use of IT to enable the enterprise by exploiting opportunities and maximizing benefits

▶ Responsible use of IT resources

▶ Appropriate management of IT-related risks

Worthy and high-level goals. The IT Governance Institute goes much farther with the Control Objectives for Information and related Technology (COBIT) standard, which lays out a comprehensive framework for *what* should be done. The question is, *how* should we enable IT governance?

IT Portfolio Management

A board needs to understand the overall architecture of its company's IT applications portfolio.... Physical IT assets...are relatively easy to inventory; intangible assets are not. Despite the fact that intangible assets have largely been ignored by the accounting field, most companies are increasingly reliant on them. Companies have huge investments in applications software, ranging from customer and HR [human resource] databases to integrated supply chains. The board must ensure that management knows what information resources are out there, what condition they are in, and what role they play in generating revenue.

—Richard Nolan and F. Warren McFarlan[31]

IT portfolio management is the application of systematic management to large classes of IT items, typically those with an explicit financial profile. Examples would be planned initiatives, projects, and IT assets in the general sense, such as hardware, software, data, and people. The promise of IT portfolio management is the quantification of previously mysterious IT landscapes, enabling measurement and objective evaluation of investment scenarios. IT portfolio management has an emerging category of useful vendor products supporting it.

Portfolio management started with a project-centric bias[32] but is evolving to include steady-state portfolio entries, such as applications. As the Information Technology Infrastructure Library (ITIL) notes (echoed by dozens of IT commentators), "The majority of IS [information system] budgets are spent on installed applications, but it seems that most of the discussion is around new spending."[33]

IT investments are not liquid like stocks and bonds, and they require both financial and nonfinancial measures for evaluation.

The concept as a whole evokes the concept of financial portfolio management, but there are significant differences between the two. IT investments are not liquid like stocks and bonds, and they require both financial and nonfinancial measures (e.g., a balanced scorecard approach) for evaluation; a purely financial view is not sufficient.

When we consider the obsessive search for information and insight into financial portfolios, and contrast that with the indifferent attention often given IT concerns, the metaphor is most useful. Financial portfolio assets typically have consistent measurement information (enabling accurate and objective comparisons), and this is at the base of the concept's usefulness in application to IT. However, achieving such universality of measurement is going to take considerable effort in the IT industry.

Enterprise Architecture

Architecture is a good metaphor for IT efforts because it implies engineering discipline, as well as aesthetic elegance, simplicity, and creativity.

Enterprise architecture as a concept has been around for some time, at least 15 years. Architecture is a good metaphor for IT efforts because it implies engineering discipline, as well as aesthetic elegance, simplicity, and creativity. Software engineering has made effective use of design patterns (an architectural concept originated by Christopher Alexander in discussing urban planning) as a pedagogical concept.

The rhetorical promise of enterprise architecture is to bring engineering discipline to IT, particularly in large-scale design of systems, promoting reuse and maintainability. The enterprise architecture, according to Weill and Ross, is

the organizing logic for data, applications, and infrastructure, captured in a set of policies, relationships and technical choices to achieve desired business and technical standardization and integration.[34]

Minimally, enterprise architecture groups typically consult on high-level system design strategies, monitor technological trends, and coordinate vendor product evaluations, sometimes serving as a control point for technology acquisitions (an important aspect of enterprise architecture as the federal government defines it[35]). More ambitious groups start to move into formally modeling the enterprise's functions, data, processes, and systems and their interrelationships. Coordination of strategic initiatives and identification of redundancies and dependencies among them is another, often thankless task.

"Boil the ocean" enterprise architecture efforts have failed more than once.

Keeping all such activities realistic and well scoped is a challenge; "boil the ocean" enterprise architecture efforts have failed more than once, and architectural groups often find themselves at cross-purposes with the development teams they are supposed to be supporting.

Another failing is trying to "align the elevators"—a view may arise that enterprise architecture's main function is business–IT alignment. However, if the architecture group has had a bias toward technical matters, they will not be prepared for this role. Such groups can wind up debating questions like the "business alignment" of a particular programming language or application server, which is not a hugely value-add activity. Generally, avoiding the perception that they are "ivory tower" organizations is the top priority for enterprise architecture teams.

There is considerable debate in the enterprise architecture community as to whether it is properly even an IT function, with some thought leaders arguing that enterprise architecture should emphasize "enterprise" and not even report as IT—instead, it should be based, for example, in a corporate strategy group.

Will the Real Architects Please Stand Up?

The use of the word "architecture" in computing circles is not appreciated by professional architects in the building trades, who are subject to lengthy and expensive required professional training, apprenticeship, certification by professional boards composed of senior practitioners, legally binding state licensure, expensive insurance and bonding, and board-enforced continuing education requirements—none of which are formalized for the self-proclaimed IT "architect."

Outsourcing

For something to be outsourced, it must be well understood.

Outsourcing is a specific, well-recognized term representing one aspect of the more general topic of sourcing. Sourcing essentially means who is going to do the work—what is the source of the staffing capability that will perform given activities for the enterprise. It is a subject relevant not only to IT but also to many aspects of business.

It is a response to the perceived distraction of management attention from core business activities and the overreliance on expensive domestic staff for repeatable, noncore business processes. There are several major aspects to determining sourcing strategies:

- ▶ Geographic distance: where the resource physically is located with respect to the client (onshore versus offshore are typical distinctions, with refinements representing the hiring of rural versus metropolitan staff).
- ▶ Organizational distance: whether the resource is external to the client, internal, or some hybrid arrangement. For example, many large companies are hiring staff in India—because they are staff, not contractors, this is not "outsourcing" in the accepted sense, although it is "offshoring."
- ▶ Business process distance: whether the activity to be sourced is critical to the business core value chain or supporting.

One emerging outsourcing lesson is that to succeed any activity to be alternatively sourced must have a certain level of maturity in terms of its definition, repeatability, and dependencies. If a company wishes to "outsource" something, it needs to understand it well, which argues for process improvement. The alternative is misaligned expectations on both sides of the outsourcing deal.

Demand Management

> The promise of demand management is that when IT is positioned as a limited resource, and allocated according to objective criteria, it will be used more efficiently and effectively.

Why…do educated, savvy business professionals, well aware of the laws of economics and fully willing in their private lives to pay for the level of service they desire, expect that these principles do not exist for corporate IT services? For some reason, a myth has grown up in many companies that unlimited funds are available for IT and that people can always ask for "more" and "better" without having to pay for the additional costs.

—Mark Lutchen[36]

Demand management is consumption control for IT products and services. It provides a common front end for business requests for new IT capabilities and a unified means of evaluating, ranking, and authorizing them. The premise is that the relationship between enterprise IT and its business customers is unmanaged, with business customers treating IT like a limitless resource. (Note the contrast of demand management with the "run IT like a business" slogan—the premise of demand management is that it's the business's *consumption* of IT that needs to be "run like a business.") The promise of demand management is that when IT is positioned as a limited resource, and allocated according to objective criteria, it will be used more efficiently and effectively.

Demand management is essentially the same as project portfolio management. However, there are other forms of portfolio management, and managing projects as portfolios is somewhat different from the project and software engineering methodology issues that often preoccupy project management offices.

Program and Project Management

> Project management is a core discipline that will never disappear or be seen as a fad.

Improving program and project management has been a widely held objective in response to IT troubles, and we now have about 50 years of systematized IT project management experience (including some large-scale data sets from military systems engineering) on which to base further efforts. (Project management as a general discipline permeates human history.) The promise of project management is to control what otherwise becomes uncontrollable and to impose predictability on the otherwise unpredictable. It is a core discipline that, although it may have fads come and go within it, will never disappear or be seen as a fad itself.

What happens after the system is built?

Its most important weakness in today's IT environment is its lack of attention to the steady-state consequences of projects—what happens after the system is built? The general pattern is to overoptimize project management at the expense of planning and operations. Underestimation of ongoing costs is a chronic problem, as Dan Remenyi notes: "The costs associated with IT projects appear more tangible in nature because the assumptions and dependencies on which they are based are often *not* fully acknowledged."[37]

A project might define the intended steady-state vision, but once the project comes to an end, it often cannot effectively be held accountable for whether this vision was achieved. Projects do usually have an overall program manager, IT sponsor, or other steady-state executive who can be held accountable after the fact. Unfortunately, this is often not systematically done; the IT portfolio management thought leaders are providing much needed direction here.

Software Engineering Capability Maturity

Increasingly, the software engineering activity is not directly controlled by the IT department.

Closely related but not identical to software project management, software capability maturity's value proposition is in the construction of software, including the analyze, design, and build life cycle, as well as specific enabling practices such as configuration and issue management, and in the rigorous management of project scope changes. The promise of software engineering capability maturity is increasing the success rate of all software projects. With the Capability Maturity Model Integration (CMMI) standard in place, software capability maturity itself is a mature concept and may be seen as necessary *but not sufficient* to solve the problems of enterprise IT, especially in a world of packaged software and outsourcing, where increasingly the software engineering activity is not directly controlled by the IT department.

IT Service Management

The promise of ITSM is a business-focused and systematic approach to managing the IT function.

IT service management (ITSM) and its flagship standard, the United Kingdom's Information Technology Infrastructure Library (ITIL), are increasingly well-known frameworks for best practices in operating IT systems and providing clear business-oriented services meaningful to end users. The promise of ITSM is a business-focused and systematic approach to managing the IT function for drivers such as cost, availability, and performance through the definition of business-intelligible IT services and their support through an interlocking set of core IT processes, including change, release, incident, problem, and configuration management.

ITSM and ITIL (which will be addressed extensively in this book) are the converse of project management and software capability maturity in that they focus on optimizing the steady-state IT capability. The tactical and operational ITIL framework volumes ("Service Delivery" and "Service Support") are well established and the intellectual material backing them is sound, but the ITIL contributions to IT planning, application management, and other areas have been uneven. Other important "universes of discourse" (e.g., enterprise architecture and portfolio management) with their own frameworks for describing IT management have not yet been aligned with the increasingly influential ITSM and ITIL world.

Service

The word "service" in this book generally is used in the ITSM sense. Service in this sense is a higher level concept than a service-oriented architecture concept such as a Web service.

Application Management

Applications are the fulcrum of the IT asset portfolio.

—Bryan Maizlish and Robert Handler[38]

Want to dramatically boost IT productivity? Don't cut 10 percent of the IT budget; cut 10 percent of the IT systems.

—Mark Schrage[39]

If you walk down the halls of any medium- to large-sized IT organization and listen to the hallway conversations, the concept of "application" emerges as paramount. When these day-to-day conversations refer to abstract "services" or "incidents," they are usually with reference to some application system.

The promise of application management is that by focusing on this most important aspect of what the large IT organization actually does, the IT governance effort will reap the greatest rewards.

Applications are an emerging subject of their own portfolio management discipline. They are important structuring elements for the configuration management process; aggressively managing the "application" concept is an emerging strategy in IT governance, one that can contribute great value.[40] The McKinsey

Aggressively managing the "application" concept is an emerging strategy in IT governance.

consulting firm has also noted an inverse correlation between size of application portfolio and IT productivity and value in a detailed survey of Spanish banks (fewer applications = greater effectiveness).[41]

Business-facing applications are generally less commoditized than infrastructure, and stories of technically archaic yet functionally indispensable systems embedding a company's core business model abound.

The issue of "shadow" or "rogue" IT surfaces here, in which workgroup-sized solutions are implemented (e.g., in tools such as Microsoft Access or FileMaker Pro) because the central systems of record are not agile enough to meet specific workgroup needs.

Application management will be a recurring theme throughout this book. Application life cycle management is a development-centric variation on this theme, focusing on the interoperation of development activities within the overall construction of a solution.

Business Process Management

BPM insists on the primacy of the end-to-end business process.

Business process management (BPM) emerged from management theory gaining traction in the late 1980s, most notably from Michael Hammer,[42] and more rigorously from Geary Rummler and Alan Brache.[43] Six Sigma has emerged as a valuable overall methodology for measuring and optimizing processes, although it has less to offer on the key issue of defining the processes.

BPM insists on the primacy of the end-to-end business process, a value adding, repeatable sequence of activities typically spanning an organization's functional structures. BPM is critical to this book in two respects:

First, business processes are key elements of understanding just what IT does for a business in terms of the business's real activities. A BPM orientation will strengthen an IT organization's alignment with their business clients, especially if business processes are, in turn, mapped to the enabling IT services.

A BPM orientation will strengthen an IT organization's alignment with their business clients, especially if business processes are mapped to the enabling IT services.

Second, BPM is a valuable tool for understanding IT processes themselves. Although IT processes in an overall business context might be seen as supporting, when examined through a BPM lens it's clear they have end-to-end, cross-functional characteristics and need to be designed and managed with the same techniques used for an enterprise's primary business processes. In the context of "running IT like a business," IT's processes are essential to realizing ITSM. BPM will therefore be an instrument of analysis in this book.

Information, Data, and Metadata Management

Data and metadata management are concepts that in one form or another have been around for decades. Their promise is somewhat the converse of BPM, that in the end, "it's all about the data." Process and data are yin and yang, and it does seem that people inherently have a bias toward one or the other (remediation toward a personal balance is possible but takes discipline).

Metadata (data about data) as a discipline and specialized function had its 15 minutes of fame in the mid-1990s (corresponding to first-generation computer-assisted software engineering, or CASE); the interesting thing with metadata is that it overlaps with the ITSM process area of configuration management. What is the difference between a metadata repository—especially one that has branched out from the mere data dictionary into tracking application or data dependencies—and a configuration management database? No industry consensus has emerged, and vendor products are converging.

Data management is having a bit of a renaissance in that it is an enabler of IT governance requirements, for example, customer privacy. The concept of "data stewardship" has emerged as a theme both for such regulatory drivers and for more general issues of data quality; data stewardship also can represent a desirable goal of increasing business–IT alignment in this specific domain. On the capacity front, the consumption of raw disk storage is skyrocketing, and redundancy caused by lack of data management shares some of the blame.

Service-Oriented Architecture

SOA promises greater flexibility and agility of designing and enhancing systems.

Service-oriented architecture (SOA) is one of the latest trends in the pure software development and architecture space. SOA promises greater flexibility and agility of designing and enhancing systems to meet ever-evolving business requirements and is an enabler of automated BPM; "services" are unitary, granular blocks of functionality that (in theory) are reusable and can be recast into a variety of value-adding end-to-end processes.

The use of the word "service" in SOA often provokes confusion with ITSM, and there are interesting controversies as of this writing. In some views, an SOA "service" is just a specialized, small-grain application or component, and a "service" in the ITSM sense is something visible in the business, which most SOA services would not be.

Another point of view is that SOA is a larger-grained architectural view on the IT capabilities and that the SOA "service" is identical to the ITSM "service." Web services should not be confused with SOA in this view.

As an integration enabler, SOA is of interest to this book because of its potential as a complexity reducer, complexity being a major driver of IT expenditure.

Utility Computing

Fundamental computing infrastructure continues to advance. While purpose-built infrastructure is slow to come online and expensive to maintain, base computing services (CPU cycles, main memory, and storage) can be commoditized and (subject to certain limitations) provided in a utility mode.

Current trends include systems that are more dynamic in the establishment, allocation, and reallocation of computing capacity, in response to fast-changing business demands in terms of new capabilities, or simply increased capacity for accelerating transactional volume. Similarly, there is increased interest in more self-managed computing infrastructures to reduce the need for manual systems administration and (in theory) increase the usability of computers through such approaches as "self-healing" architectures.

Software as a Service

Purpose-built
applications are
slow to come
online and
expensive to
maintain.

Purpose-built applications also are slow to come online and expensive to maintain. Functional application services (presentation, business rules, and data management) can be commoditized and (subject to certain limitations) provided in a utility mode.

Software as a Service (SaaS) is a model of software delivery in which centrally hosted applications are provided on demand to customers, typically (but not always) over the Internet. It is an evolution of the application service provider concept, with an implication of more domain and application expertise on the provider's part and single, large instances of applications designed to support multiple customers (multitenancy). SaaS is important for its promise of reducing complexity through outsourcing provisioning and hosting activities in a more granular model easier to manage than outsourcing the full complexity of a built-up data center. It also is a better model for leveraging utility computing.

SaaS will provide challenges for, but not eliminate, the problem of enterprise application integration.

Enterprise Application Integration

The hairball is the result of years of incrementally building interfaces between applications by project teams operating in silos.... Over time, the inconsistencies between interfaces and imperfect understanding of dependencies between applications result in unstable operations, production "surprises," high cost to maintain systems, and delays in implementing new business solutions.

—John Schmidt and David Lyle[44]

Enterprise application integration (EAI) as a concept is a little older than SOA in the software development world. The promise of EAI, like SOA, is greater agility and flexibility in building new application functionality. EAI also implies achieving greater conceptual simplicity and decoupling of data through message-oriented middleware.

Both EAI and SOA have relevance for IT governance enablement in that the configuration management challenge around systems integration is difficult, probably the most challenging in all of enterprise IT. The term "hairball" is often used—not affectionately—to refer to the integration architecture in a typical large IT organization.

The Hairball

Each organization usually feels uniquely bad when confronted with the Rube Goldberg nature of their systems interconnections. Cheer up, folks; the grass is no greener anywhere else in my experience.

Beyond understanding them for troubleshooting, assessing the number and nature of system interconnections is important for assessing an overall application portfolio and developing future-state architectures.

Enterprise information integration is another term emerging in this area, covering both general conceptual issues and specific technologies for federated database queries.

Model-Driven Architecture and Development

Model-driven architecture (MDA) is a methodology and set of technology standards developed by the Object Management Group (OMG), an important standards organization. The promise of MDA is the representation and manipulation of difficult computing analysis and design in graphical formats from which operational systems can be derived. The MDA technologies are based on a precise interlocking set of semantics that enable conceptual interoperability among various types of models at different levels of abstraction.

(Microsoft is pursuing similar goals that are explicitly not aligned with the OMG standards stack.[45])

This is similar to first-generation CASE, and some of the intellectual lineage behind the OMG's standards can be traced to the problems of first-generation CASE.[46] Other drivers include distributed systems integration and finding a way to specify abstractly how integration occurs while ignoring the underlying distributed integration technology.

Skepticism from those who saw the challenges faced by first-generation CASE will be only one of various challenges the OMG will face in this effort, but hopefully the hype cycle will be subdued and MDA will take its place as a useful tool while dodging the "silver bullet" overselling that damages so many promising technologies.

Agile Methods

The continued failures of large-scale software projects have provoked various responses. One extreme is heavyweight, detailed (prescriptive) methodologies describing a broad array of required and recommended deliverables. Such approaches are often used by large consulting firms and often call for linear sequencing of requirements, analysis, design, and build, with strict, signoff-enforced "stage containment" between them—once exited, a stage can never be reentered.

This approach has been given the term "waterfall" because it appears similar to a 1970 method proposed by software engineering theorist Winston Royce.[47] However, Royce did not propose strict stage containment—quite the opposite, he called for feedback loops between the stages. The more dysfunctional forms of waterfall probably can be traced with greater accuracy to the methods of the large consulting firms, amplified by misguided attempts to apply linear non-IT project management theory to the technical activities of IT projects.

For systems with unclear, user-facing functional requirements, agile methods are the least risky approach to ensuring value delivery.

The essential problem with solutions development is that developers often do not know what they are trying to build until they are 80% done building it, at which time it is often too late to deliver the optimal product. Agile theory attempts to incorporate this core insight into a coherent approach to software development. There seems to be little doubt that, especially for systems with unclear, user-facing functional requirements, agile methods are the least risky approach to ensuring value delivery.

Agile methods' key contribution can be summarized as reducing feedback loop cycle time for IT projects.

However, agile methods' relationship to nonfunctional requirements (scalability, security, interoperability, supportability, reusability, and vendor suitability) is more problematic, given their strong emphasis on customer interactions and "working software" over process. Sometimes, a more heavyweight, prescriptive development and product acquisition process is the only way to ensure that nonfunctional requirements are met.

IT Resource Planning, or Enterprise Resource Planning for IT

An ERP system is an automated solution supporting a major business process or value chain.

The rise of packaged software culminated in the 1990s with the introduction of enterprise resource planning systems. Pioneered by the German firm SAP, ERP packages promised to solve, and sometimes did solve, one of the most daunting and expensive problems facing modern companies: the proliferation of narrow, discrete software applications.

—Nicholas Carr[48]

IT has enabled a high level of business process integration with ERP solutions, yet there are no ERP solutions for IT itself.

—ITIL[49]

Finally, the concept of enterprise resource planning (ERP) for IT, or more concisely IT resource planning (from AMR Research), is a recurring theme throughout this book. Other emerging terms are integrated IT management (Forrester Research), IT business management (Gartner Research), IT life cycle management (IBM) and systematic technology management (DiamondCluster).

An ERP system is an automated solution supporting a major business process or functional area. Most of the concepts discussed in this section have some corresponding attempts at automation. Currently, such systems are badly fragmented. Just as accounts payable, general ledger, and accounts receivable systems converged into financial ERP systems, these enablement systems for enterprise IT will eventually converge into a centralized capability that might be called ERP for IT.

Not all automated functions of each IT area will be centralized.

This does not mean that all automated functions of each IT area will be centralized—rather, it means that their touch points of shared process and data must be formalized and managed to maximize alignment and minimize redundancy and non-value-added work.

ERP as a concept has a lot of baggage, and others might propose the phrase SOA for IT; however, large-scale ERP implementations have been shown to work, and the jury is still out on SOA in crucial respects such as scalability and manageability.

This buzzword was left to last because it implies a technical solution, which cannot succeed until the IT process and data architectures are solidified for the purposes of requirements definition.

ERP Blues?

If the ERP connotation doesn't work for you, try IT enablement. Or IT governance infrastructure. The history and implications of the ERP term are discussed in the introduction to Part II.

1.4 The Business Case

As the strategic value of the technology fades, the skill with which it is used on a day-to-day basis may well become even more important to a company's success.

—Nicholas Carr[50]

It's long been recognized that the IT business case is often difficult to make. Infrastructure does not directly pay for itself, yet without it the business can't run; companies that held off too long on implementing email or a Web presence (asking, instead, "Where's the return on investment?") were perceived as dinosaurs and suffered competitive disadvantage in negative customer perceptions after the Internet became an expected communication channel.

Viewed uncharitably, IT enablement is "overhead on the overhead."

Because IT is a supporting process, investments in enabling it are supporting the support; viewed uncharitably, IT enablement is "overhead on the overhead." This argument can be turned upside down however. If IT enables business efficiency, then further enabling IT should be seen as leveraging the leverage. The truth probably lies somewhere between the two views.

The systems described in this book are not cheap to implement or run, and they will be subjected to the same scrutiny that customer-facing IT services are for business case. Refer to Jeffrey Kaplan's *Strategic IT Portfolio Management*,[51] especially the chapter titled "Articulating—and Achieving—the Benefits of IT Portfolio

Management," which has an excellent discussion of how to make the business case in terms of the following:

▶ Increasing throughput
▶ Optimizing resources
▶ Increasing efficiency, capacity, and value
▶ Giving IT enablement tooling its own portfolio—that of continuous improvement

The bottom line for those advocating improved IT management infrastructure: if human resources and finance departments (both supporting activities) can have their ERP systems, so can you.

1.5 Making It Real

There is an endless IT fashion show, continually recycling well-understood, recurring themes in IT management into next year's model. The previous section provided an overview of some of the more prominent themes and rallying cries in the IT world today.

Making it real here means remembering some basics:

▶ The problems your IT organization is facing are neither unique nor unprecedented. There is nothing new under the sun.
▶ Everything worth doing in IT management is difficult and risky; otherwise, it would already have been done. There are no free lunches or silver bullets.
▶ And most importantly: what are *your* requirements?

Implementing IT enablement automation can be approached from several directions, depending on the drivers for an IT organization. An organization suffering from uncontrolled incidents and outages should prioritize differently than an organization whose main IT challenge is escalating maintenance costs.

The overall problem of IT enablement can seem overwhelming. It's essential to assess where the organization is feeling the greatest pain. Some common yet distinct areas include the following:

▶ Service management: IT's face to the customer
▶ Incident and problem management: restoration of service and prevention of outages
▶ Financial transparency, efficiency, and effectiveness

▶ Change impact analysis

▶ Change and configuration management

▶ Capacity and provisioning management

▶ Identity and authorization management specifically and security and risk management more broadly

Any one of these areas can serve as a springboard for improving IT governance and making a business case for IT enablement systems investment.

1.6 Chapter Conclusion

In this chapter, we reviewed the endemic problems of large-scale enterprise IT and some proposed industry solutions at a thematic level. All of the solutions have something relevant to contribute; this book will draw on insights across their spectrum in developing more concrete patterns and architectures for addressing the IT challenge. However, a unifying framework is needed, the subject of the next chapter.

1.7 Further Reading

For IT governance, see IT Governance Institute (2003), Lutchen (2004), and Weill and Ross (2004); also see Office of Government Commerce (2004). For the "run IT like a business" concept, see *CIO Magazine* (2004) and Lutchen (2004).

There are several visions of IT portfolio management that are not completely aligned with one another. It was first called for by McFarlan (1981) in a project-centric sense. Bryan Maizlish and Robert Handler in *IT Portfolio Management Step-by-Step* (2005) have a comprehensive yet practical vision that covers the entire IT life cycle. Jeffrey Kaplan's *Strategic IT Portfolio Management* (2005) focuses more on project and funding questions. Also see Benson, Bugnitz, et al. (2004); Office of Government Commerce (2002a); Schrage (2005); and ASL Foundation (2005a). McKinsey (Bahadur, Desment, et al. 2006) correlates the effectiveness of application portfolio management with IT performance at large Spanish banks. Nolan and McFarlan (2005) also call for application portfolio management in the *Harvard Business Review*.

Forrester Research has published research on the subject of application portfolio management, but the firm's view of this topic is more technical than financial.

Finally, academic Christopher Verhoef (2002) has made significant contributions in defining an IT portfolio management theory, discovering in the process that IT portfolios behave more like biological populations than financial instruments.

For enterprise architecture, see Spewak and Hill (1993), Cook (1996), The Open Group (2002), Carbone (2004), and Fowler (2003); also see Clements (2003). Demand management is referenced briefly by Hertroys and van Rooijen (2002); little other published material on this important topic is evident outside the proprietary material of the major IT consulting firms and the vendors specializing in demand management and IT portfolio products. For IT resource planning, see Dennis Gaughan's work for AMR Research (fee-based).

There is a wealth of material on project and program management; start with the Project Management Institute (2004) and the Office of Government Commerce's Prince2 (Hedeman, Frederiksz, et al. 2005).

Software capability maturity is the focus of the CMMI Product Team (2001). For MDA, see Frankel (2003) and the OMG standards available at *www.omg.org* and *www.omg.org/mda*. For software engineering generally, see the Institute of Electrical and Electronics Engineers (IEEE 2005). For the much-caricatured original "waterfall" method, see Royce (1970). For agile methods, see Agile Alliance (2001) and Beck (1999). Heffner (2005) covers SOA versus application portfolio management. For autonomic computing, see IBM (2005).

For ITSM, see van Bon, Kemmerling, et al. (2002); van Bon (2002); and the Office of Government Commerce (2000 and 2001). For BPM, see Rummler and Brache (1995), Hertroys and van Rooijen (2002), and Harmon (2003). For EAI, *Integration Competency Center* by John Schmidt and David Lyle is an excellent reference (2005); see also Hohpe and Woolf (2003) and Linthicum (2004). For data and metadata management, see Tannenbaum (1994), Marco (2000), Tannenbaum (2002), Marco and Jennings (2004), English (1999), and Dama International (2000).

2

The IT Value Chain: A Process Foundation

Is a firm a collection of activities or a set of resources and capabilities? Clearly, a firm is both. But activities are what firms do, and they define the resources and capabilities that are relevant.

—Michael Porter[52]

THIS CHAPTER ESTABLISHES the analysis framework for this book. If we are going to run IT like a business, we must understand how businesses run. Some of IT's problems can be traced to overly functional approaches, leading to silos and finger-pointing. Business theorists have been addressing this issue since the 1980s, and the most compelling framework has been the value chain, developed by Michael Porter in his landmark book *Competitive Advantage*.

> If we are going to run IT like a business, we must understand how businesses run.

Michael Hammer is another important figure for his promotion of the concept of business process reengineering; although the concept did not succeed in its more radical objectives, it did accelerate a focus on process management and cross-functional process design now pervasive throughout business.

With all the frameworks created for enterprise IT, it seems redundant to create yet another, but there are limitations to existing frameworks. Rather than a laundry list of IT process areas and functional capabilities, the value chain framework adopted here distinguishes between the primary and the secondary IT processes and maintains focus on the value-adding activities.

Process Flakes

I suspect you techies will want to get to the fun stuff of the data model and patterns architectures, but that kind of thinking is how we got into this mess in the first place. Eat your Process Flakes™.

2.1 Frameworks, Frameworks Everywhere

Vendors, consulting firms, and academics have been applying analyses of various types to IT for years. Many frameworks have emerged to help understand the overall problem. (See the "Food for Thought" section "What Is a Process Framework?") The three major frameworks with the most effect on enterprise IT in the United States at this writing are COBIT, CMMI, and ITIL. (There are other public frameworks such as the Application Services Library, Business Information Services Library, and Information Systems Procurement Library, as well as proprietary frameworks owned by the major consultancies, service providers, and research firms.)

COBIT

> COBIT may have been created for audit and control purposes, but it provides a complete view of the large IT organization useful for a variety of purposes.

Control Objectives for Information and Related Technology (COBIT)[53] is a risk management framework published by the Information Systems Audit and Control Association (ISACA). It is of interest because the risk management framework is essentially a comprehensive IT process framework identifying all major activities of a typical IT organization in a representation that supports process measurement and management control.

COBIT divides IT into four areas:

▶ Planning and organization
▶ Acquisition and implementation
▶ Delivery and support
▶ Monitoring

Each of these areas has a number of processes, ranging from "define a strategic IT plan" to "provide for independent audit." A maturity model for each process is proposed, and matrix-based analysis maps processes to IT resources and what are termed "information criteria": effectiveness, efficiency, availability, and so forth.

COBIT may have been created for audit and control purposes, but it provides a complete view of the large IT organization useful for a variety of purposes. In particular, each process description includes metric definitions and a concise maturity model (see the next section).

CMMI

A widely noted characteristic of CMMI is the concept of maturity "levels" through which organizations pass.

The Capability Maturity Model Integration (CMMI) is a framework for developing and assessing the software development maturity of an organization. It is based on long-term research performed by the Software Engineering Institute (SEI) at Carnegie-Mellon University. A widely noted characteristic of CMMI is the concept of maturity "levels" through which organizations pass.

As a framework, it includes specific guidance on software engineering best practices, as well as some generic characteristics that enable its translation to domains other than software engineering; there are CMMI-based SEI frameworks for systems engineering, software engineering, integrated product and process development, and supplier sourcing.

CMMI for software engineering defines four major process area categories:

▶ Process management
▶ Project management
▶ Engineering
▶ Support

Each of these breaks down into further process areas. A sophisticated model including generic goals, generic practices, and common features is used to elaborate these and define various standards of maturity. The previous "staged" representation with its levels has been supplemented (after industry criticism) by a "continuous" representation that is somewhat more flexible. The well-known five "maturity" levels used by the staged representation have a corresponding six-level "capability" framework used for the continuous representation.

Efforts independent of the SEI have started to apply CMMI-like principles to data management and ITSM, and (as noted previously) COBIT stipulates maturity models for its representation of IT processes.

CMMI does not recognize ITSM as a potentially important source of feedback for project quality.

The focus of CMMI is unclear: is it primarily about software engineering, or is it a general staged process improvement model gradually being extended to many IT-related activities? The CMMI Web site states that "Capability Maturity Model® Integration (CMMI) is a process improvement approach that provides organizations with the essential elements of effective processes."[54]

Certainly the staged maturity model can be applied to virtually any type of skilled, collaborative, process-based human endeavor. However, this book assumes the former: CMMI as discussed here is about software engineering and closely related fields.

CMMI has been criticized from a variety of perspectives. First, it is highly abstract and academic. Process centricity to the exclusion of human factors is one critique;[55] another is that it is project centric and disregards operational challenges of day-to-day service management and even software maintenance. The CMMI work does not well account for the possibility of ITSM-based processes (e.g., incident management) being an important source of feedback for project quality. This is because CMMI needs to address many types of projects, including those creating packaged software, embedded systems, and products.

Nevertheless, it remains the most influential software engineering framework in the world; the Agile movement and the proprietary Rational Unified Process™ are also significant players.[56]

ITIL and ITSM

The Information Technology Infrastructure Library (ITIL) is a best-practice framework originating in the United Kingdom (it is published by their Office of Government Communications). ITIL is gaining great momentum worldwide, with increasing (if belated) adoption in the United States.

ITIL at this writing consists of nine volumes:[57]

▶ *The Business Perspective: IS View*
▶ *The Business Perspective: Business View*
▶ *Application Management*
▶ *Service Delivery*
▶ *Service Support*
▶ *Software Asset Management*
▶ *ICT Infrastructure Management*
▶ *Security Management*
▶ *Planning to Implement IT Service Management*

"[ITSM is] a set of processes that cooperate to ensure the quality of live IT services, according to the levels of service agreed with the customer."

Jan van Bon

ITIL is a concrete expression of the larger concept termed "IT service management," with roots in IBM research and European industry practice.[58] Among the most important precursor works were the IBM "Yellow Books," *A Management System for the Information Business.*[59] This seminal work reportedly was a direct antecedent and input to the first ITIL drafts.

ITSM, according to Van Bon, is "a set of processes that cooperate to ensure the quality of live IT services, according to the levels of service agreed with the customer."[60] The focus in ITSM and ITIL is the concept of "service," a business-intelligible manifestation of the IT capability that represents value-adding functionality, from the business perspective.

ITIL is an important and influential center of gravity in IT management. It is helping to standardize language and provide a common reference model for IT operations in particular. It is often seen as synonymous with the *Service Delivery* and *Service Support* volumes, which cover the following process areas:

- ▶ Service support
- ▶ Service desk
- ▶ Incident and problem management
- ▶ Configuration management
- ▶ Change management
- ▶ Release management
- ▶ Service delivery
- ▶ Service-level management
- ▶ Financial management for IT
- ▶ Capacity management
- ▶ Continuity management
- ▶ Availability management

The *Service Support* volume in particular has a compelling, integrated vision of its processes with a unified service desk. The processes in this volume are what many organizations mean when they say they are "doing ITIL."

Note that ITIL considers the *Service Delivery* and *Service Support* volumes to be the Service Management volumes; this is not necessarily aligned with other industry uses of the term "IT Service Management."

As with CMMI, there are many critiques of ITSM and ITIL. The ITIL volumes are not uniform in quality; the *Application Management* and *Security Management* volumes in particular have not been well received. Overlapping frameworks (e.g., the Application Services Library) exist. While claiming to be based on process, ITIL does not address process improvement (e.g., see COBIT's process of "develop and maintain procedures" or the CMMI "process management" process area).

ITIL does not include the activity of IT portfolio management.

ITIL does not effectively address the activity of IT portfolio management or the function of enterprise architecture and thus is weak in higher-level planning and control concepts. As Hans van Herwaarden and Frank Grift note, "the consistency that characterized the service support processes…is largely missing in the service delivery books,"[61] meaning that although the material on incident, problem, change, release, and configuration management is strong, the material on capacity, availability, continuity, finance, and service-level management is less so.

Another significant issue is that the entire software development life cycle is encapsulated in the release management function, which does not provide enough detail to make ITIL seem relevant to those activities.[62]

Jan van Bon says it well:

There is a lot of confusion about ITIL, stemming from all kinds of misunderstandings about its nature. ITIL is, as the Office of Government Commerce (OGC) states, a set of best practices. The OGC doesn't claim that ITIL's best practices describe pure processes. The OGC also doesn't claim that ITIL is a framework, designed as one coherent model. That is what most of its users make of it, probably because they have such a great need for such a model.[63]

Because ITIL is not a holistic framework, the framework presented in this book has no choice but to redefine certain ITIL areas when they imply a breadth of coverage that overlaps with other areas; for example, the broad ITIL request for change (RFC) concept is scoped down considerably in this framework in favor of a more specific discussion of service entry points.

However, like CMMI, ITIL seems to have a critical mass of acceptance and will be an important part of the landscape.

> "The OGC... doesn't claim that ITIL is a framework, designed as one coherent model."
>
> Jan van Bon

FOOD FOR THOUGHT

What Is a Process Framework?

From *www.erp4it.com*

A business process is not just a random collection of activities—it meets certain precise criteria.... A business process is a collection of interrelated work tasks, initiated in response to an event, that achieves a specific result for the customer of the process.

—Alec Sharp[64]

The term "process framework" is generally used to characterize comprehensive and systematic representations of a major business area by focusing on its activities. There is typically an attempt made to distinguish between what the organization is doing and who is doing it. This desire to avoid entanglement in the politics of organization structure leads to the term "process framework."

However, in the BPM movement, there is also a distinction between process and function. Function is a *steady-state set of responsibilities,* and process is a *repeatable, event-driven chain of events.* Functions also may be independent of organization structure: a federated corporation may have several human resource management organizations, but there is still just one logical human resource function.

The thing to understand in examining the "process" frameworks is that they include both functions and processes.

For example, in ITIL, change, release, incident, and problem management all are true business processes: they are repeatable, measurable, start with a defined event, and have a clear value-added end state.

On the other hand, availability, capacity, and financial management are functions, not processes. They may contain multiple true-event or calendar-driven processes, but as a whole these are steady-state capabilities with no defined beginning or end. They are also often owned by organizations tending toward silos, which change, release, incident, and problem cross. Their staffing is specialized, as are their tools, which are not generally shared with other areas (unlike change, release, incident, and problem, whose tools have cross-functional user bases).

If this seems radical, ask these questions: What is an Incident? Do I know when one is identified, how its life cycle progresses, and when it ends? Are the activities measurable and repeatable? Then it is a true business process. Now ask yourself, What is an Availability? What is a Capacity? And so forth.

Configuration management is a bit of a special case. Even though it fundamentally supports many areas, that contact generally is initiated as a result of one of the true processes and it requires an organizational model with a deep center of excellence to do right.

One thing that would help is adopting the principle that (at least in the English language) processes start with active verbs and functions are passive verb–based nouns: for example, "resolve incidents" or "execute changes" versus "capacity management" and "availability management." BPM author Alec Sharp frowns on using vague verbs like "manage," "coordinate," and "analyze," favoring concrete verbs such as "resolve," "execute," and "complete."

The following scenario from Sharp illustrates the dangers of calling something like "Capacity Management" a process:

A project team attempted to model the workflow for a major area they had improperly described as a single process—Supply Chain Management…. Because their scope actually included some five processes, it was impossible to express in a single diagram. There was no clear beginning point—there were many—and there was no clear ending point—there were many. It was impossible to trace a path (a workflow) through all of the included activities, especially because of timing issues. Some tasks were part of transaction-oriented processes that happened hundreds of times per day, others were part of ad hoc processes that occurred several times a month, and others still were monthly or quarterly…. Moral: Too many Processes spoil the broth.[65]

An issue the BPM community is still debating is the concept of *process area,* which is a grouping of cross-functional processes. The classic example of this is Customer Relationship Management.

Why does this matter? It matters because functions can lead to silos and need to be recognized as potential danger zones. It also matters because strictly defined business processes can be modeled and automated with increasing ease. A business process "Resolve Production Incident" could be modeled, simulated, and made operational through today's BPM tools. However, this would not be possible for a function such as "Manage Capacity" because it is not precise enough.

2.2 A Value Chain Framework

Through the application of Process Management, we have learned that managers…should concentrate as much or more on the flow of products, paper, and information between departments as on the activities within departments. Process Management provides a methodology for managing this white space between the boxes on the organization chart.

—Geary Rummler and Alan Brache[66]

Much mischief has occurred in enterprise IT in the name of "build the thing and deploy it."

With such breadth and depth available in COBIT, CMMI, and ITIL, why spend any time developing a new framework? As Jeff Kaplan notes,

The last thing the IT industry needs is another proprietary framework. The best thing that could happen would be if all the disparate IT associations (ITIL, SEI, COBIT, etc.), as well as academics who study and teach IT management, were to consolidate their frameworks into one definitive, comprehensive, public-domain reference model that would align industry terminology and create a single blueprint for IT managers.[67]

Enterprise architecture, project management office, and other such teams are perpetually at risk in many IT organizations, where they are viewed as bureaucratic distractions.

Well stated. However, the primary reason for YAFW (yet another framework) is that, even though all these frameworks are (to varying degrees) seen as process oriented, none have a true value chain orientation. They do not define what the core value-adding process is for the IT organization, and it is easy in reading them in all their detail to lose perspective as to what is primary and what is supporting in enterprise IT.

This is partly because IT has been weak in understanding and leveraging supporting processes. Enterprise architecture, project management office, capacity planning, data administration, quality assurance, and other such teams are perpetually at risk in many organizations, where they are viewed as bureaucratic distractions. The core imperative is…

Build the thing and deploy it!

The major frameworks overcompensate through exhaustive coverage of secondary processes.

The COBIT, CMMI, and ITIL frameworks recognize this mentality as a problem but overcompensate through exhaustive coverage of secondary processes to the point that we start to wonder, "Where's the beef?" For example, in CMMI, engineering is only one of four process area categories, and within engineering, the technical solution process area ("design, develop, and implement solutions to requirements") is only one of six process areas.

This deemphasis of the basic construction activity is deliberate, as much mischief has occurred in enterprise IT in the name of "build the thing and deploy it." However, there is a reason the software construction activity (or package implementation and configuration) is seen as "real" work by many practitioners: *it is a primary value chain activity.* Without actually constructing software, activities such as configuration management, verification and validation, and process and product quality assurance have no meaning. The core activity has become deemphasized until bureaucracy swamps it:

Secondary process	Secondary process
Secondary process	Secondary process
Build the thing and deploy it!	Secondary process
Secondary process	Secondary process

Working software is the primary measure of progress.

Agile Alliance

Newcomers to CMMI thus examine the framework and are baffled at how actually writing code appears to be marginalized, seemingly no more important on a process level than secondary activities such as risk management or decision analysis and resolution. The Agile movement is in some senses a response: "Working software is the primary measure of progress."

The same is true of both COBIT and ITIL. Each is comprehensive in its way (if you consider *all* ITIL volumes), but both mix primary and secondary IT activities into what might be called laundry-list frameworks. Capacity management is a high-profile activity in ITIL but would probably not be identified by an IT customer as adding value; however, incident management probably would be. The entire system design and build activity is seen as one small part of the release process area. COBIT (the most holistic framework) similarly has "develop and maintain procedures" (clearly a supporting process) as a peer process to "install and accredit systems" (clearly core value chain).

The solution is not "either-or," but "both-and":

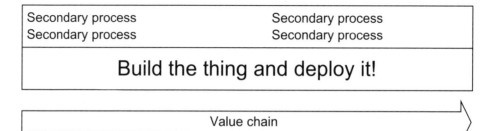

The supporting processes take their rightful place as enablers, but the central priority of *delivery* remains.

ERP systems enable value chains.

This is why an enhanced framework is called for. The concept of ERP for IT is a driver for this book, and the salient characteristic of ERP systems is that they enable value chains. Without a value chain perspective on IT, there is no basis for using ERP as an architectural concept.

However, because the purpose of this book is to write about IT enablement, the value chain discussion is restricted to this chapter. Much more could be written on this topic alone. The existing process frameworks do well in their scoping and descriptions of particular activities, and it is not the purpose of this book to reinvent such wheels. I'll reference relevant material from the existing process frameworks wherever appropriate, also noting overlaps and gaps. This is where access to ITIL and COBIT (especially) and/or CMMI will be of assistance in reading this book.

Value Chain Illustrated

Functional optimization often leads to the suboptimization of the organization as a whole.

—Geary Rummler and Alan Brache[68]

The modern business is often represented in context (an approach deriving from systems theory) something like Figure 2.1 adapted from Geary Rummler and Alan Brache.

Current management theory has the central concept of "the business" identified with the concept of a value chain.[69] The value chain is a concept in which

each activity in the chain or sequence adds some value to the final product. It's assumed that if you asked the customer about each of the steps, the customer would agree that the step added something to the value of the product…. Human resources, senior management functions, and IT processes are all considered supplementary or secondary processes…. They don't produce outputs that are consumed by customers and generate income.[70]

This is not to say that they are dispensable! Neglect of supporting processes can wreck the value chain; when cared for, they *enable* it.

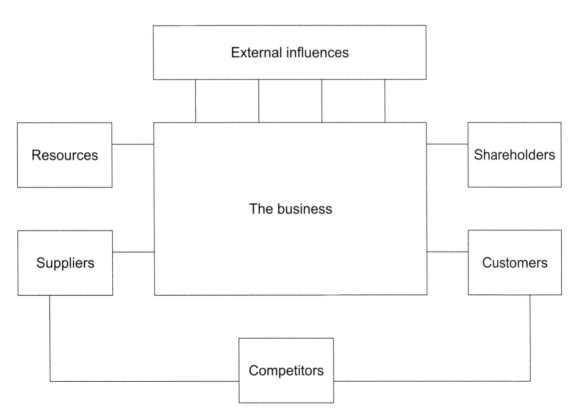

Figure 2.1 System in context.[71]

Michael Porter's generic value chain representing a manufacturing firm appeared as shown in Figure 2.2.

One company's supporting activity is another company's primary activity.

Information technology is clearly an enabler, concentrated in the firm infrastructure and technology development secondary processes (but supporting all other areas, primary and secondary).

However, one company's supporting activity is another company's primary activity. A common thought experiment is, What if the entire IT capability (planning, building, and running) were spun off into an organization with its own profit and loss statement, selling services back to its parent? Such a spin-off would have its own system context (Figure 2.3).

And its value chain might look similar to the one shown in Figure 2.4.

In the primary IT value chain, a demand request is the initial event and an entry in the application portfolio, service catalog, or both is the result.

The five activities in the value chain are consolidated to three that correspond to classic functional distinctions in enterprise IT, but the value chain adds needed emphasis to the end result and (hopefully) the need for overall optimization is clearer.

In BPM terms, the core value chain is quite clear and measurable; the overall process could be termed "deliver services" and is event driven and countable—a demand request is the initial event and an entry in the application portfolio, service catalog, or both is the value-added result. The complete process includes the *retirement* of that service, not an objective well supported in today's IT management approaches.

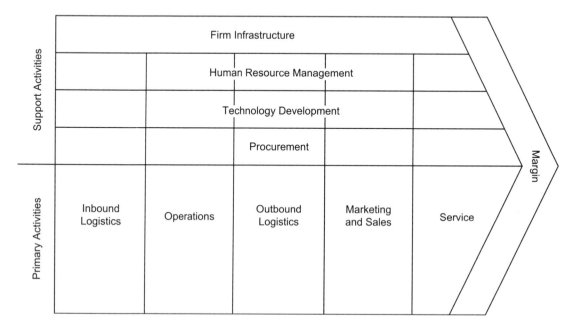

Figure 2.2 Classic value chain.[72]

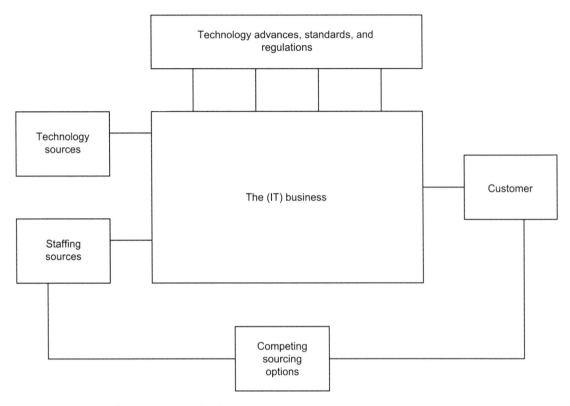

Figure 2.3 IT as a business: system context.

Value chains and large processes often have pithy names, such as hire to retire, order to cash, or procure to pay. The proposed shorthand name for the IT value chain is "inspire to retire."[73]

The proposed shorthand name for this value chain is "inspire to retire."

Regardless of whether the IT value chain is financially internal or external to a company, the "run IT as a business" perspective is the foundation of this book.[74] Note that IT as a value chain *requires its own IT infrastructure* (IT enablement)— a core concern of this book.

There are several principles that emerge from using a value chain as the primary framework:

▶ No one activity can be completely optimized. To do so suboptimizes the entire value chain.
▶ The primary value creation process must be recognized as such.
▶ Classifying an activity as supporting does not mean it is dispensable.

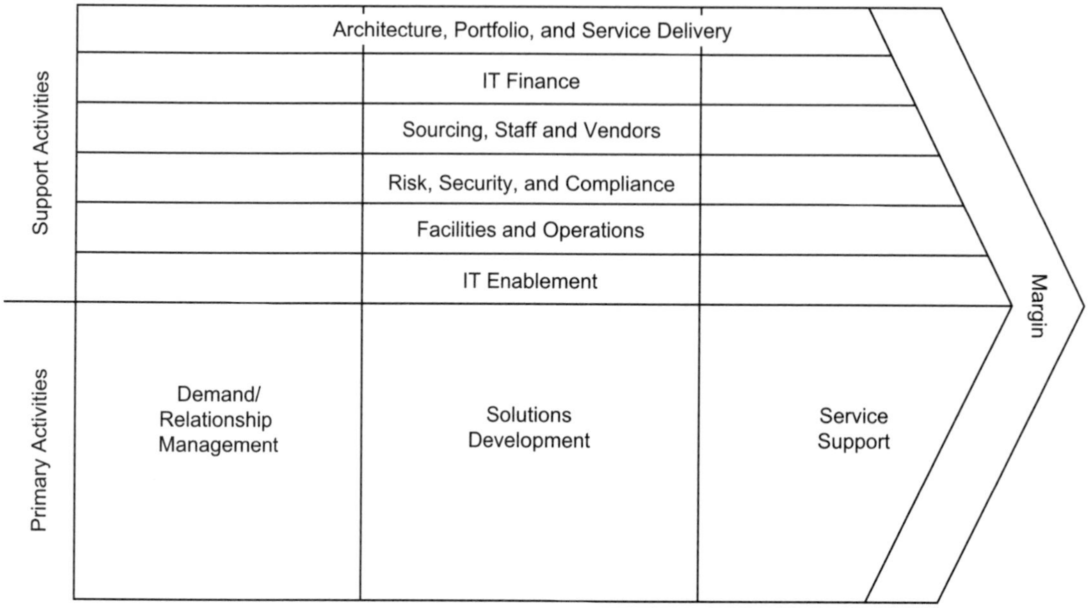

Figure 2.4 IT value chain.

The primary and support activities will form the process outline for this chapter:

▶ Primary IT activities
  • Manage customer relationship and demand
    - Manage customer relationship
    - Fulfill demand requests
  • Develop solutions
    - Manage project
    - Manage requirements
    - Design and build solution
    - Ensure solution quality
  • Manage services
    - Manage release
    - Manage production change
    - Manage production configuration
    - Fulfill service requests

- Sustain services
- Resolve incidents and problems
▶ Supporting IT activities
  - • Manage architecture, portfolio, and service delivery
    - Develop IT strategy
    - Manage IT portfolio
    - Manage capacity
    - Manage availability
    - Manage service levels
    - Manage process
    - Manage data
  - • Manage IT finance
  - • Manage sourcing, staff, and vendors
  - • Manage risk, security, and compliance
  - • Manage facilities and operations
  - • Enable IT

It's important to recognize that even the core value chain activities (which can casually be called plan, build, and run) may not be recognizable to the customer. At the highest level, the customer is seeking services delivered by the IT organization with the following quality attributes identified previously:

▶ Responsiveness to changing customer needs and strategies
▶ Cost effectiveness, efficiency, and transparency
▶ Effective risk management (e.g., assurance of confidentiality)
▶ Operational effectiveness (e.g., availability and performance)

Again, the key to understanding the value chain concept is the mental experiment: what would the customer see as value adding if the customer could see inside the factory?

Value Chain Notes

Every use of language and terminology has consequences.

There are always compromises and clarifications required in developing a high-level framework. Every use of language and terminology has consequences when dealing in such generality, and some decisions are essentially political in nature.

First, a detailed consideration of the concepts of process, process area, function, and organization is necessary. The major frameworks are built on process areas, which are large in scope; to comprehensively decompose a process area into specific event-driven processes is time consuming. This analysis focuses primarily on process areas, delving into individual processes only when they are well established in the industry and of key importance to the IT value chain.

These methodology questions are further covered in the preceding "Food for Thought" section "What Is a Process Framework?" and Appendix A.

Under "manage services" is the process "manage production change." Notice that this process is limited to deployment concerns, for example, the turnover from the development phase to the service management phase. This is in contrast to the ITIL representation of the change management process, which is seen as pervading the entire IT value chain. This ITIL interpretation is inconsistent with much industry practice; see the detailed discussion in the section on service entry points later in this chapter.

One major area in the supporting processes is "architecture, portfolio, and service delivery." This area contains the detailed, deep-practitioner subject areas of expertise to which many IT professionals might aspire as a career goal. The category derives conceptually from the ITIL *Service Delivery* volume, which has the avowed scope of focusing on proactive, tactical concerns (as opposed to the reactive, operational *Service Support* volume). This section includes other architectural activities, as well as process and data management. The combination of portfolio management with aspects of capacity, availability, data, and process management well describes the scope of many enterprise architecture organizations.

Each process area in the framework includes an overview of its purpose, metrics where relevant, and a statement of requirements for automation (IT enablement).

Mapping the Frameworks to the Value Chain

The industry frameworks can be mapped to the value chain as shown in Figure 2.5. In addition to addressing the Risk, Security, and Compliance domain specifically, note that COBIT includes a broad overview of all process areas and all frameworks are potentially relevant to IT Enablement as statements of requirements.

CMMI applies generally to solutions construction, but note that many of its process areas would be managed in supporting activities, such as those concerned with risk management, vendor management, or the concept of process management itself.

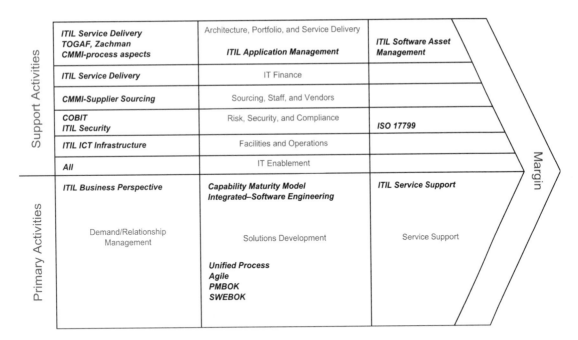

ITIL Service Delivery **TOGAF, Zachman** **CMMI-process aspects**	Architecture, Portfolio, and Service Delivery **ITIL Application Management**	**ITIL Software Asset Management**
ITIL Service Delivery	IT Finance	
CMMI-Supplier Sourcing	Sourcing, Staff, and Vendors	
COBIT **ITIL Security**	Risk, Security, and Compliance	**ISO 17799**
ITIL ICT Infrastructure	Facilities and Operations	
All	IT Enablement	
ITIL Business Perspective	**Capability Maturity Model Integrated–Software Engineering**	**ITIL Service Support**
Demand/Relationship Management	Solutions Development	Service Support
	Unified Process **Agile** **PMBOK** **SWEBOK**	

Support Activities / *Primary Activities* (left axis labels); *Margin* (right label)

Figure 2.5 Industry frameworks applied to value chain.

2.3 Primary IT Activities

Primary activities…are the activities involved in the physical creation of the product and its sale and transfer to the buyer as well as after-sale assistance.

—Michael Porter[75]

A value chain perspective encounters challenges with pervasive frictions among the planning, construction, and operations functions in IT.

The primary activity of the IT value chain is the overall process by which technological needs are identified and solutions are authorized, built, deployed, supported for an indeterminate time, and retired. In an overall industry context, it is akin to product development, with the end products being IT services. Arguably, the IT industry started as supply centric but is increasingly demand driven as the technology becomes more and more commoditized.

A value chain perspective may seem obvious, but it encounters considerable challenges in reality, with pervasive frictions among the planning, construction, and operations functions in IT.

Manage Demand

> Some organizations consider the capture of an idea or potential development…as the first stage of the change life cycle.
>
> —ITIL[76]

The request (or demand) for IT services is managed through an intake function known appropriately as "demand management," a non-ITIL term being used by large IT solutions delivery providers, IT portfolio management solutions vendors, and research firms.

Manage Customer Relationship

Manage demand (in this book's framework) includes high-level customer relationship management (that is, between the IT capability and the sponsoring executive). This activity is closely related to the "develop IT strategy" process area.

Manage Customer Relationship: Requirements

Customer relationship management in the IT demand management sense is typically not automated, except using simple office productivity tools. It is possible that a truly independent, large IT service provider might have sufficient customer relationships to automate; in this case the service provider might look to customer relationship management software.

Fulfill Demand Requests

Demand management is the initial intake of requests for larger-scale IT services.

Demand management is the initial intake of requests for larger-scale IT services. "Large scale" typically implies a project-based request.

The demand process captures requests for new or changed systems, consultations, and even brainstorming. (The term "ideation" is used by some.) These requests are assessed, their preliminary scope is established, and then they are prioritized against strategic objectives (coming from the portfolio management process and other forms of strategic planning). The proposed work may be assessed in several dimensions, such as projected benefit, complexity, and cost. Projected return on investment is established, and some form of ranking algorithm is applied (subject to close human review).

Prioritized and authorized demand requests typically become projects.

Demand management implies a balance between supply and demand.

Demand management implies a balance between supply and demand. Therefore, demand management, portfolio management, service request management, and the staffing process should be aligned so that required increases in support staff for new IT capabilities are correctly anticipated. More mature organizations would also integrate capacity management at the technical level.

Demand management in some organizations is simply identical to the annual IT planning process; however, many organizations do not wish to limit opportunities for new IT capabilities to a once-a-year cycle, which is *why this framework sees demand management as event driven and separate from the IT strategy process area.*

IT-Driven Demand

Demand requests are usually seen as originating from the customer; however, they also can originate from the IT organization. Typical examples include the following:

IT-driven demand is a sensitive issue, as it competes for the same resources as business-driven demand.

▶ Technology refresh
▶ Proactive technology implementation
▶ IT enablement and continuous improvement

Technology refresh includes things like replacing core technologies in the environment, for example, because a vendor stopped providing support. Proactive technology implementation is a polite term for what many IT organizations did in the late 1990s: rushing to bring in new technologies in a sometimes misguided attempt to position themselves for the anticipated business requirements in e-commerce.

A classic statement of this view comes from Lientz: "By waiting for user requests, IT is placed in a reactive mode…. IT is not like a village fire department…. [It should] seek out opportunities."[77] It can be a valid approach, but the failures here are sobering.

IT enablement and continuous improvement is the major topic of this book; the enablement systems described herein are IT driven and of little concern to business customers.

IT-driven demand is a sensitive issue because it competes for the same resources as business-driven demand and can easily degenerate into "IT for IT's sake." Nevertheless, it will always be a part of running any significant IT capability.[78]

Fulfill Demand Requests: Requirements

A demand management system is the first automated solution encountered in the value chain. This system needs to support the IT supplier–customer relationship as it moves into the details of just what services the customer requires from its provider. This would include tracking the customer's requests for new and enhanced functionality from small to large scale (hours to years of effort). These requests progress from an initial brainstorming or ideation phase and through greater elaboration until their general scope is understood well enough to support funding either the entire effort or a dedicated estimation project. Note that this implies early-stage estimation techniques and potentially supporting systems.

This life cycle includes various "gates" at which the proposal is competitively evaluated against others and assessed with respect to available resources (project funding, base funding, facilities, and staff). Data must be collected and managed along several axes, such as strategic alignment, benefit, complexity, and risk, and scoring algorithms must be supported.

Scoring algorithms can become complex, for example, with governing criteria to ensure consistency across subjective assessments (preventing people from "gaming" the system to some extent).

Visual means for comparing an individual demand request to others are needed, such as bubble charts.

Generally, the solution should track the ordered and delivered IT capability through what can be called the "inspire to retire" life cycle of IT solutions and services. Currently, there are silos between 1) architecture, planning, and authorization; 2) systems development and integration; and 3) systems operation functions.

In particular, the IT operations area in too many organizations does not have visibility into "what's coming," and the result is suboptimized from an operations point of view. An integrated system providing transparency into all systems at all points of their life cycle would be helpful in many organizations.

DIALOG

Advance Notice

Pat: Why would you need this?

Kelly: Have you ever heard of "over the wall"?

Pat: Yes, our data center and applications support people are always mumbling this.

Kelly: Right—because they don't have enough warning that a new system is coming and aren't able to influence its development sufficiently to meet their needs: application architectures that are compatible with data center operations, reuse of existing platforms and skills, instrumentation for availability, support documentation and procedures, and all the rest.

Most of this gets sorted out sooner or later, but it seems like we're always painfully reinventing the wheel here, and when you dig into the root cause, the fundamental issue always seems to be one of visibility.

An important
distinction
is between
demand for
new or changed
functionality
and demand for
defined services.

Demand requests can be integrated with the concept of a service desk if a "single pane of glass" is sought for all business–IT interactions; however, the workflow behind a system initiation or enhancement request requiring significant budgeting is quite different from a routine service request for a new PC, and it's not clear that a single pane of glass to be used by both customers and senior vice presidents adds much value.

It is true that understanding current resource consumption is essential for demand planning, so at least summary metrics from the service request, incident management, and project management systems are essential for the demand management system.

Metrics for demand management include new requests, status of requests in the pipeline, approved requests, requests in progress, and completed requests (integration with project management system required). This may or may not be integrated with service request fulfillment; an important distinction is between *demand for new or changed functionality* and *demand for defined services*. The latter is "fulfill service requests" in this framework, part of service support.

Develop Solutions

Judging by available research and literature, the process area of building and integrating software solutions is somewhat better understood compared with most other aspects of IT management. (This is not to say it is mature; large-scale software project failures pervade enterprise IT.) Winston Royce's classic "waterfall" software development life cycle established the core activities of requirements capture, analysis, design, and construction.[79] Although there has been much research and discussion regarding software development life cycles, it is still possible to usefully distinguish the major development activities along these lines. This is not to say they are performed sequentially; it's just that most projects perform all of them at some point, sometimes repeatedly (iteratively, incrementally, or both).

Many of the
supporting
CMMI processes
have correspond-
ing activities for
the operational
side.

"Manage project" and "ensure solution quality" are also included as process areas.

Infrastructure platforms must be designed and built, as well as application functionality; see the section on "Applications, Infrastructure, and the Hosting Zone of Contention."

CMMI Mapping

For those familiar with CMM and CMMI, here are some notes on reconciling that framework with this book.

First, this book does *not* see all of CMMI as part of the primary IT value chain. Much (most?) is supporting activity.

Many of the supporting CMMI processes have corresponding activities for the operational side. For example, CMMI activities concerned with process design or quality assurance are considered covered under "manage architecture, portfolio, and service delivery," where they would be undertaken with the same approach used for defining operational processes. Supplier management is likewise handled for the entire supply chain under "manage sourcing, staff, and vendors," and risk management is run through the "manage risk, security, and compliance" area.

Project management and related activities, along with core software construction and quality control, remain in the "develop solutions" process area and are considered primary IT activities.

Manage Project

This is the core of the software development life cycle. Once a solution is authorized through the demand management process, the well-understood disciplines of project management and the software development life cycle come into play. Subdisciplines include project change control, estimation, and software configuration management.

There is a wealth of research and theory in this field (see the "Further Reading"); the brief treatment is possible here because it is so well covered elsewhere.

Manage Project: Requirements

Project management is the applied discipline of defining and controlling scope, resources, timelines, and deliverables in support of a specific and time-bound objective.

The core build activity is controlled by project management, which is the applied discipline of defining and controlling scope, resources, timelines, and deliverables in support of a specific and time-bound objective. Project management requires the ability to track expenditures on staff and other resources, manage and report on progress to goals, and analyze dependencies so that efforts are executed in the correct order. Issue management is also required, and often some degree of formalized, tool-supported estimation is necessary.

Support for individual time tracking against chargeable accounts (buckets) is a typical feature, which poses the question of integration with human resource and financial systems.

There are a number of mature metrics commonly used for managing large projects, such as Net Present Value (NPV) and Economic Value Add (EVA). Project portfolio management tools support many variations on such metrics, often providing digital dashboard type functionality so that senior executives can see overall status across programs at a glance.

This is a well-understood area of IT management, and a project management tool might be one of the first IT enablement products purchased by a growing IT organization.

Manage Requirements

After demand initiation and the establishment of the business case, the next need is well-documented requirements: the functionality, as experienced by the consumer, envisioned for the new or changed software system. Requirements management has repeatedly proved one of the most critical success factors for any development project, in particular the *control* of new requirements through a defined process.

However, there is a problem with this philosophy: what if the requirements cannot be understood before some exploratory development? This basic issue has given rise to the Agile movement in software development, an important development approach that any overall IT governance enablement framework must support. (This is not to say that Agile methods are unconcerned with requirements, simply that they have a somewhat different approach to them compared with more traditional methods.)

Manage Requirements: Requirements[80]

Requirements management has two major aspects: traceability and change management. Traceability is the ability to navigate from more abstract requirements to more concrete ones and from any requirement to actual project artifacts (configuration items). Change management means that at some point the requirements are "baselined" and further changes are managed, perhaps by a project change control board. Managing such changes at scale may require workflow capabilities in automated tooling—and a requirement for improved workflow would be a good reason to automate this area. Again, agile techniques may require new interpretations of these principles.

Design and Build Solution

Systems analysis and design includes the application of architectural techniques (similar to those displayed in this book) to the large-grained structure of application systems. Professionals can spend their entire career in such endeavors. Current debates revolve around concepts such as agile programming and model-driven architecture.

Too few enterprise IT software developers understand their craft in context, leading to frustration with "bureaucratic" processes.

Go into any major bookstore's computer section, and you will find this single aspect of the overall value chain lavishly supported by hundreds of volumes. Although enterprise IT professionals can dedicate a lifetime to learning the craft of software development, too few understand it in a broader value chain context, which manifests sometimes in frustrations expressed toward "bureaucratic" processes, "ivory tower" architects, and "rigid" infrastructure engineers.

However, as noted previously, the act of construction (or implementation and integration, in the case of packaged software) is part of the *primary value chain activity* and needs to be respected as such. Maintaining the balance between primary and supporting activities of IT in the overall value chain context is a central problem of IT governance.

At one point in the history of IT, it was thought possible (although widely debated) to make meaningful distinctions among major stages of the solutions development life cycle, and "requirements," "analyze," "design," and "construct" were arguably the most widely used. However, the emergence of computer-assisted software engineering (CASE) started to blur the boundaries between design and construction, seeking to reduce construction to the automated generation of code from well-specified, often graphically based designs.[81]

The Agile movement, although in some senses opposed to the methods of CASE (especially the tight coupling of early CASE systems to specific methodologies, as well as the naïveté of complete code generation from graphically specified models), has blurred the boundaries between the major phases as well. Generally, it is still recognized that these phases (or something like them) may exist as logical functions, but developers actually performing systems construction may move through any and all stages as needed.

The analysis–design boundary remains conceptually important because it's generally recognized that a logical representation of a system's function, independent of technology, assists in system flexibility.[82] Maintaining this representation has proved challenging.

Design and Build Solution: Requirements

The concept of production is paradoxical because the development of new software solutions is a production business process undertaken by the IT organization.

The development activity requires supporting both graphical and computing language–based representations of processing (with translations between the two paradigms) and tools that can manage the artifacts produced in the development life cycle *with little or no coupling to any concept of software life cycle or method.*

Development also requires the provisioning of "nonproduction" platforms for the development and testing of new functionality. The concept of production is paradoxical because the development of new software solutions is a production business process undertaken by the IT organization. The establishment of defined platform "stacks" supported by the infrastructure organization makes the recognition of development machines as a form of production even more imperative—for too long, such machines have not been well managed in terms of their configuration—yet developers need more flexibility to meet the requirements of their particular business process without needless, non-value-adding bureaucracy.

Enabling reuse is a key concern with component architectures and architectures based on service orientation. Developers must be able to easily find potential solutions or they will simply reinvent them. Consistency of delivered code is another perpetually sought quality, increasingly important with globally dispersed development, support, and operations teams.

Infrastructure development requires attention to how computing and network services are provisioning to the solutions providers requiring them. Concepts such as capacity on demand and standard technology stacks come into play here.

Finally, software development requires a host of specialized scaffolding services: build management, debugging, code analysis, and so forth. While a comprehensive CASE approach remains elusive,[83] the continued use of such tools is CASE in a smaller, more focused sense, and critical to today's development practices.

Ensure Solution Quality

This would include testing, verification, and validation for specific solutions moving through the value chain but not software process quality assurance, which is incorporated into the overall process quality assurance activities for the entire IT value chain.

Ensure Solution Quality: Requirements

Quality assurance in the context of solutions development consists of validating that "the thing was built right" and in particular meets functional and nonfunctional requirements; that is, it has correct behavior and meets operational standards for performance, availability, and manageability. Quality assurance requires test management and often quite sophisticated scaffolding to validate the nonfunctional requirements (e.g., load testing).

Manage Services

Service management represents the "exploitation" phase of solutions development: having built something, return on the investment is now sought. Receiving value means that the service is available, performs acceptably, and can be changed within reason in response to new business requirements; it implies the control, measurement, and monitoring of operational services.

Judging by available research and literature, service management ("service support" in ITIL terms) is not as well understood as project management or software development. Actually running the software as a useful, value-adding business service receives scant attention in the mainstream computing press. This vacuum is being rapidly filled by the discipline of ITSM and the ITIL framework, driven in part by regulatory and compliance perspectives described by the COBIT framework.

Manage Release

Actually running
software as a
useful, value-
adding business
service receives
scant attention
in the main-
stream comput-
ing press.

Release management is the transition of delivered solutions (or subsets thereof) into a stable production status. It is closely tied to change management, dealing more with the operational issues, packaging, and so forth. Release management may also require functionality similar to project management: coordination of timelines, monitoring of rollout milestones, and the like. It is also a key gateway process between the development and the operations worlds, often charged with ensuring sufficient documentation and full budgets for the staffing effects of new solutions. Human change management concerns, including communications and training plans, are covered here.

This definition is deliberately more restricted than that found in ITIL, which equates release generally with the entire demand and solutions development life cycle.[84] Again, this is because this framework covers the entire IT value chain, which ITIL does not. In ITIL terms, an RFC initiates the release process;[85] in this framework, a demand request initiates the deliver solution process. See Figures 3.5 and 3.6 and the accompanying discussion.

Manage Release: Requirements

Release management is the gateway from the project life cycle to operational service management. It requires a foot in both worlds, with the ability to manage specific solutions artifacts (e.g., software components) through a defined change control process into the production environment. Automated software distribution (a.k.a. provisioning) is part of the required functionality. It is an important gatekeeper for the accuracy of IT portfolios. "Application lifecycle management," or ALM, is an emerging term here.

Manage Production Change

Change Management is a broad concept in ITIL. ITIL sees Change Management as essentially equivalent to the entire IT value chain outlined here.[86]

In this book, Change Management centers around the well-understood task of managing changes to production or preproduction infrastructure that may have an immediate effect on operational services. (See the discussion of service entry points later in this chapter.) The ITIL concept that an authorized RFC *precedes* software construction[87] is not supported here; this is a confusion of the change process with demand and portfolio management.[88]

Managing change is critical for IT operational stability and the effective exploitation of new services. Change drivers, types, success rates, and aggregate trends should all be available for analysis.

One distinction heard in the industry is that between change control and change management. This framework emphasizes change control; change management might be essentially the same as demand management.

Regardless of the linguistic representation chosen, the need to systematically assess all proposed system initiatives for impacts and gain buy-in from all stakeholders remains; this is arguably the intent of the broad ITIL RFC concept. The point is that the higher-order impact analysis sought by the ITIL change management concept is best performed by enterprise architects and not enterprise change managers, who are typically focused on operational stability.

DIALOG

What's a Change Manager to Think?

Bob is the Enterprise Change Manager for a large Midwestern insurance firm. His team's role consisted primarily of running the change management process, which controlled the deployment of new functionality into the quality assurance, preproduction, and production environments on the mainframe and the enterprise servers. This process was well-understood in the enterprise; it typically had a 2-week lead time, with various exceptions available for low-risk and urgent changes. The success of the development teams' changes was reviewed every week, and figures relating outages to unsuccessful changes were compiled. All in all, it was a reasonably well-run enterprise process.

Then ITIL came, and Bob's staff started going to training. They were returning with some strange ideas, so Bob called Gary, the lead ITIL consultant doing the training.

Gary: You've got to understand that ITIL sees a request for change very broadly. It can even be a business-driven request for altering the functionality of some system.

Bob: So let me get this straight. We've had a change process in place for 5 years— even benchmarked it against a couple other Fortune 100 corporations in the region—and now you tell me its scope is incorrect?

Gary: What you've been doing is change control. You need to move into true change management.

(continued)

Bob: We have a project initiation process. Are you saying that I am now somehow involved in that?

Gary: Well, maybe not you—but all new requests for change to IT should be reviewed by the change advisory board.

Bob: We have one of those. Its mission is tightly defined, just focusing on operational concerns about changing production or preproduction environments, typically on a 2-week lead time (sometimes longer).

Gary: That's not good enough; changes need to be assessed much further in advance.

Bob: That's what we use the portfolio and demand management capability for. That's where the longer-horizon changes are discussed, by the project advisory board. The enterprise architecture group is responsible for detailed impact analysis. Sounds like you are saying the change advisory board should be doing the same thing. But the folks we have on that group are not currently suited for the longer-horizon assessments; it's just not their job. Their main focus is availability.

Gary: Maybe you should have a change advisory board whose membership composition can vary.

Bob: What value would that add? It's already confusing enough for people as to which committees they are on. Everybody would be on the change advisory board at one time or another. Why not leave things as they are?

Gary: Because it's not what ITIL says…

Bob: I'm sorry, but I have a business to run. You'll have to do better than that.

Manage Production Change: Requirements

Change requires a tracking capability, centered on the concept of RFC. The tracking capability in turn leads to (or integrates with) activities of quality assurance, risk assessment, work assignment, configuration management, and release management. A workflow capability is needed, including the ability to track approvals. Whether and how the change approval process should interact with the service request management necessary to enact the change is a process and system question needing consideration by the IT enablement team.

Manage Production Configuration

Many companies simply do not know in any sort of detail or with any accuracy what IT assets they own, where those assets reside, and how much it costs to run them on an ongoing basis.

—Mark Lutchen[89]

Configuration management is the tracking of and accounting for IT elements of concern to the IT organization and their dependencies. Classic configuration management includes smaller-grained processes of configuration audit and configuration status accounting. This critical area will be discussed in further detail in subsequent sections.

Configuration management is one of the most troubling areas in the IT value chain, yet without the compilation of data that it implies, accurate and informed decision making is handicapped. It's even questionable whether it belongs in the core value chain, as the IT customer might not see it as adding value—yet the information maintained through configuration management processes is so critical for so many aspects of value delivery that relegating it to a supporting process seems inadvisable.

Configuration management will be a recurring theme throughout this book. This section examines it from a process perspective.

IS CONFIGURATION MANAGEMENT A PROCESS? OR IS IT A FUNCTION? Although many frameworks present configuration management as a process, this is problematic. Configuration management is primarily a function that supports true event-driven processes such as incident, release, and change management, which should be primarily responsible for updating the configuration data. The only true process owned by configuration management is the configuration audit process, usually a calendar-based cyclical reconfirmation or confirmation of the configuration data with current reality. (For discussion on true process versus function, see Appendix A.)

CONFIGURATION MANAGEMENT AND ASSET MANAGEMENT A difficult distinction to practically make is that between configuration and asset management. This book sees asset as primarily a portfolio and IT finance concern; however, the two process areas will likely use some of the same tooling.

TWO FLAVORS OF CONFIGURATION MANAGEMENT Configuration management (in ITSM) has two distinctly different interpretations. The first is the hard-nosed, bits and bytes, *change detection* aspect:

"Why is the SVR001 server broken?"

"Something changed in httpd.conf."

"Well, who changed it and why?"

Integrity and security are high priorities from this viewpoint. Knowing that something has changed may be essential to staving off an incident or recognizing a security exploit in progress. This is also where unique configurations are managed—an important complexity reduction objective. Another name for this general area is "drift control."

Then there is the *portfolio, dependency, and asset* aspect of configuration management:

▶ What applications are on this server?
▶ What business processes do they support?
▶ Which databases do they interact with?

These questions are important for activities such as risk, incident, and problem impact analysis, as well as longer-horizon portfolio analysis and planning.

Dependency Management, the Foundation of IT Governance

From *www.erp4it.com*

A foundation of IT governance is the simple dependency: business process depends on IT service, functional capability depends on application, application depends on database, database depends on server, server depends on switch, application depends on application, and so forth. IT organizations deal with this critical data daily and treat it shamefully: essentially as a disposable commodity. Dependency information is expensive. It is typically gathered by assembling two or more highly compensated individuals to (repeatedly) go over what is installed where, what it talks to, and what it needs to run. Dependencies are captured in transient Visio diagrams, Excel spreadsheets, and PowerPoint graphics; rarely if ever updated in synch with any enterprise process; and not made available for the variety of purposes that need them.

Consider some of the producers and consumers of dependencies in your IT organization:

▶ Enterprise architecture/portfolio management
▶ Software development (especially when enhancing existing systems)
▶ Information management, business intelligence, and data warehousing
▶ Service support (production turnover, change management, business service mapping, impact analysis, and break/fix support)
▶ Capacity planning
▶ Compliance initiatives

▶ Continuity planning
▶ Security management
▶ IT finance (dependencies are used in establishing cost models)

I have seen all of these areas diligently redrawing and recapturing various views on much the same core essential data set, with complete disregard for the work of others, and I have seen (especially) application support teams suffer for it; they tend to be the ones continually called in for interview after interview. What server is your application on? What databases does it use? What programming language was it written in? Does it handle sensitive customer data? What interfaces does it have with other applications? Data feeds? Direct network dependencies (e.g., load balancers and firewall punchthroughs)? Again and again.

Try a small thought experiment. Assume you have a portfolio of 300 applications (a medium-sized shop in this day and age). Suppose that your unmanaged dependency data requires 40 staff hours (on average) per application in rediscovery each year (this is probably conservative). That's the equivalent of six full-time staff members, fully burdened at $125,000 a head. That's $750,000 each year going down the drain of poor dependency management.

This does not include the costs of outages due to incidents caused by changes where the IT dependencies were not understood or prolonged because the system wasn't understood well enough to quickly restore service. I have seen an expensive customer-facing system outage prolonged for 8 preventable, painful hours simply because a key individual and his dependency knowledge couldn't be reached.

Dependencies are the most precious information an IT shop deals in, yet we treat them like junk or, worse, people's private kingdoms. Some individuals see their expertise in a given system's dependencies as job security. Contractors love to take charge of dependencies and, in my experience, are loath to surrender control over key dependency information once they have it.

Note that I'm skeptical toward the tools that claim to provide automatic mapping of dependencies; they have challenges in the higher, more subjective levels of the IT world with concepts like application, process, and IT service and their tricky interrelationships. Mapping these requires both manual and automated activities coordinated in a clear process framework.

Whether automated or manual, without a central repository and maintenance process your captured dependencies are going up in smoke every week. So, the next time you encounter yet another project gearing up a bunch of contractors to go out and survey your IT environment into throwaway spreadsheets for some compliance initiative, ask yourself, "Isn't there a better way?"

Dependencies are the most precious information an IT shop deals in, yet we treat them like junk.

A CONFIGURATION MANAGEMENT MATURITY MODEL   Integrating the two types of configuration management might be represented through a configuration management maturity model (Table 2.1).

Table 2.1   A Configuration Management Maturity Model

Level	Hardware	Software
Level 1	Hardware (computing and network) inventory, manually maintained through periodic inventory.	Software licenses manually maintained through periodic inventory.
Level 2	Hardware inventory maintained through procurement and change management processes, supported by basic automated scanning.	Software licenses maintained through procurement and change management processes.
Level 3	Hardware characteristics and dependencies (e.g., network topology) discovered by automated scanning. Configuration scanning to enforce change control.	Enterprise application portfolio, including ownership or responsibility baselined and maintained through change management processes. Application-to-server dependencies maintained and used as a basis for change impact notification. Change detection scanning. Detected changes reconciled with change management and corrective action taken on unauthorized or unplanned changes.
Level 4	Hardware-to-software dependencies compiled and maintained through fingerprint-based scanning.	IT service-to-software system dependencies maintained through fingerprints defined in the solutions development life cycle. Database catalogs maintained as first-class configuration items. Application-to-application dependencies captured and maintained. Synchronous and asynchronous dependencies distinguished. Application-to-software product dependencies compiled and maintained. Change risk assessment based (at least partly) on automated exploration of system dependencies. Configuration management database (CMDB) accuracy enforced by security processes: "If it's not in the CMDB, you can't have access to it."

Table 2.1 *(continued)*

Level	Hardware	Software
Level 5	Change control scanning integrated with asset-oriented configuration management.	Provisioning manifests used as input for CMDB. Middleware dependencies fully mapped out at the component level. Component-level management possible for other areas if return on investment is there. Configuration management data used by enterprise architecture and portfolio management for what-if modeling. CMDB accuracy enforced by service management processes: "If it's not in the CMDB, we don't support service-level agreements, availability, or capacity modeling." Data dictionary integrated with CMDB to support regulatory compliance.

The problem of configuration management only promises to become more difficult with the emergence of grid computing and dynamic middleware; both add further levels of indirection to already difficult dependency mapping problems.[90]

CONFIGURATION MANAGEMENT AND PACKAGED SOFTWARE
The configuration management problem takes on somewhat different dimensions for packaged software. In particular, detailed software dependencies typically become opaque, and the logical application or service is the primary unit of control. Its coupling to infrastructure through defined deploy points or root directories is the pivotal configuration information to manage.

MANAGE PRODUCTION CONFIGURATION: REQUIREMENTS
Configuration management in this analysis also is somewhat more restricted than ITIL, with (again) special focus on those configuration items relevant to core operational processes. Configuration management as a function is critical to many operational IT processes but as a process may be somewhat light, depending on how it is viewed. Minimally, configuration management requires advanced data management, encountering particular challenges in the dependencies inherent in a large IT organization.

The data under management must be accurate and up-to-date. Ensuring this accuracy can be achieved through several means:

▶ Requiring configuration data correctness for a given process (e.g., a change or service request) to proceed

▶ Automated and/or manual validation against actual resources

▶ Defined exception reporting indicating poor data quality or staleness (length of time a configuration item record has not been updated).

Many issues related to configuration management are covered in detail in upcoming chapters.

Fulfill Service Requests

Service request management provides defined "orderable" services to users, such as new workstation, security access, and email and network services. It also may include the provision of defined orderable infrastructure services to projects, an important maturity step in eliminating delivery risk and increasing estimation accuracy.

These service offerings may be contained in what ITIL terms a "service catalog." (The definition of service may also include *nonorderable services,* typically operational applications.) There is a blurry line between help desk–managed requests and demand management, which is targeted at higher-level requests for IT resources and changes to IT services themselves. See the "Clarify Service Entry Points" Pattern.

Although ITIL also emphasizes that "it is important to know the difference between a Service Request and a Change Request,"[91] it then provides many examples of changes that would appear to be mere service requests, such as "an upgrade of a PC in order to make use of specific software."[92]

ITIL emphasizes that the service desk is a function, not a process, which is debatable. Service request management is repeatable and measurable, which qualifies it as a first-class *process* (although it will need to be supported by a service desk *function* as well). See the methodology notes in the appendix if this is not clear.

As a function, the service desk may also support incident management; this is a recommended best practice because it is sometimes not possible to distinguish between an incident and a request for service.

Service request management is repeatable and measurable, which qualifies it as a first-class process.

Is It an Incident or a Service Request?

A new user joins a team of financial analysts. As is often the case, she's given basic support in getting started but some of the fine points of her setup are overlooked. The user discovers one day that she cannot run some advanced analytics in Excel that others on her team can. Her manager being out that day, she assumes that something is "broken" in her system and calls the service desk to report what she thinks is an incident.

The service desk determines that her computer was not set up with certain third-party Excel plug-ins—nothing is broken, she just needs to have some additional software installed at cost. It's not an incident but a service request. A more integrated system would handle either case seamlessly; separate incident and service request systems might require the user to initiate a different process to acquire the software, which might be cumbersome and create a perception of IT inefficiency.

To summarize:

▶ Service request—Install something on my PC.
▶ Incident—The software configuration on my PC is corrupted.

Fulfill Service Requests: Requirements

Service request management most importantly requires a user interface (online, phone, fax, walk-up, etc.), and workflow, so that requests are tracked and routed for correct fulfillment. It requires a defined process for establishing new orderable services and assessing the performance of those currently offered (perhaps through the "portfolio management" process area).

It requires a robust workflow capability with complex conditional routing of tasks and the ability to monitor and manage request queues for performance.

It also requires knowledge management, in the sense of managing unstructured data, for the frequent use of "scripts" or documented interactions or activity sequences undertaken by the service desk staff.

One requirement for this area is to support self-service, automated interactions as much as possible.

User support metrics are process based, measuring the responsiveness of various request-driven activities such as resolving reported incidents, fulfilling user requests for new software and hardware, and providing access to central services (e.g., security provisioning). To measure the responsiveness of the IT organization to these requests, some sort of workflow or process management capability is required.

Sustain Services

These are defined as base support activities intended by design. Not all service management is incident or request driven: databases need tuning, application logs need occasional inspection, and other such activities take place in a modern IT organization that do not easily fit into the strict ITSM definitions. It is true, however, that all such activities should be carefully scrutinized; automated IT systems by definition should not require much human oversight.

Sustain Services: Requirements

The primary requirement for service sustenance is to measure it. The base service activities must be tracked through some sort of time reporting correlated with the service or application portfolio. This implies the alignment of the time tracking system with reference data from the portfolio management capability, especially the service or application—not project—portfolio. (These are the activities that take place after the project is over.)

Resolve Incidents and Problems

The core of service management is "keep it running." The most functional software in the world is not useful unless it is available and performing well, and stories of great software concepts coming to operational grief abound.

The overall process of incident and problem starts with the identification of an interruption to established production services. This can be through a user contact or through operational monitoring. The service is first restored to operational status (incident management) and, if warranted, forwarded to problem management. This provides proactive root cause analysis and recommended resolutions, which may involve software or hardware changes, process changes, training changes, and so forth.

As extensively covered in ITIL and other sources, one of the main reasons for keeping incident and problem separate is so that staff members focused on proactive problem solving are not pulled into reactive service restoration activities.[93]

Resolve Incidents and Problems: Requirements

Incident and problem management is considered in this framework to be identical to the ITIL definitions: incident is the restoration of service, and problem is the root cause analysis and prevention of future outages, including proactive initiatives. Incident and problem management require a user interface akin to that for service request management; in fact, they may be integrated. Workflow and tracking (e.g., the incremental addition of working notes) are also required, as well as visibility into configuration and change management and operations. Problem management should be driven from incident and/or other internal IT processes (e.g., capacity). Problems when established then need to be worked, which presents a similar set of tracking and workflow requirements to incident.

A knowledge management capability (e.g., a searchable knowledge base of incidents) is essential for this process area.

Maximizing the automation (e.g., through self-service systems) of incident reporting and resolution (as with service requests discussed earlier) is an important objective, given that this is one of the highest-volume processes in IT.

2.4 Supporting IT Activities

An army marches on its stomach.

—Napoleon Bonaparte[94]

We now turn from the primary value chain to the supporting processes essential to its proper functioning.

The preceding section was about the primary activity of the IT value chain: identifying, prioritizing, constructing, deploying, and supporting new functionality. We now turn from this primary activity to the supporting processes essential to the proper functioning of the value chain.

Consider an assembly line metaphor for the value chain: A car moving down the line may be the primary value-adding activity of interest to the customer. However, someone designed and built the assembly line. It is maintained, monitored, and tuned regularly. None of these activities directly adds value for the customer, but they are nevertheless essential to the production process. If the line is not lubricated, it will stop. If its performance is not measured and monitored, improvement will be difficult, and if the line is not improved, the enterprise will find itself at a competitive disadvantage. Risks must be monitored, regulations followed, safety assured, and so forth. The secondary activities are akin to seed corn, which the enterprise consumes at long-term peril.

Balancing the primary and the supporting activities thus becomes an important IT leadership challenge. The primary value chain must be optimized end to end, supported but not overshadowed by the secondary processes.

Achieving such balance is one of the most troubling and contentious areas of IT governance. The pattern is too often a pendulum: some failure of IT execution impels leadership to institute or strengthen one of the supporting processes as a control mechanism (e.g., enterprise architecture). The supporting process is too often cast into the role of a "silver bullet" at this point.

The institution of such control inevitably adds overhead to the value chain, slowing delivery and impeding agility to some degree (that is the fundamental nature of a control process). After a period of political tension, support for the control process wanes and it is either rendered optional or fully abandoned—until the next catastrophe. This pattern has been observed for enterprise architecture, security, data administration, software quality assurance, and many other supporting processes.

A solution to this pendulum is a continuous process improvement approach. The supporting process must be measured and its effect on the primary value chain process must be quantified. Once such metrics are established and accepted, a continuous improvement cycle can be instituted so that the control process's consequences are fully understood and can be mitigated without its complete abandonment in favor of the next big thing.

Rotation of staff between the primary and the supporting processes is another critical practice. Rotation of staff between the primary and the supporting processes is another critical practice. Supporting processes must not become "dumping grounds" for less qualified staff or cliques of groupthink who have lost sight of the IT value chain in their quest for purity.

Manage Architecture, Portfolio, and Service Delivery

This overall section is a major aspect of the supporting processes. The title "service delivery" was inspired by the ITIL volume of the same name, which details the capacity and availability process areas, two of the more architecturally related aspects of ITIL. It therefore seemed appropriate to expand this general concept with other major architectural activities.

After working on the assembly line, someone might graduate to maintaining, evaluating, optimizing, and even redesigning it—the IT equivalents are the primary purpose of this overall area. It contains some of the most stimulating professional opportunities for those whose career paths don't include managing large numbers of people. In a line/staff organization model, this would clearly be a staff function, with significant advisory capability when well positioned and mature.

Note that enterprise architecture is not called out as its own process area; this is because (depending on the organization) it can cover various aspects of portfolio management, capacity management, availability management, process management, and data management. Enterprise architecture as a functional team definitely has a role, however; covering all of those various process areas requires related, highly professionalized skill sets and great depth of experience.

Enterprise architecture occasionally surfaces as a desire to boil the ocean and map the entire IT operation. This typically fails when undertaken only for enterprise architecture purposes. The key here is to align the data required and produced by this area with the primary IT value chain and other supporting processes, such as security and financial management, that have other reasons for requiring the same data set.

Enterprise architecture occasionally surfaces as a desire to boil the ocean and map the entire IT operation.

This general area has diverse tooling requirements. There is much overlap and ambiguity in the product offerings. It requires first an integrated view (e.g., based on configuration management) of the entire IT operation, from high-level supported business process down through application to base machinery and from initial ideation through service retirement.

Architects require graphical modeling tools, which have a complex and evolving relationship with dataset-based IT management tools (e.g., portfolio, asset, and ITSM systems). If the architecture team is to be effective in systematically reviewing and controlling initiatives, some sort of workflow system integrated with the demand and/or project management systems is required.

Develop IT Strategy

This is the highest-level, longest-range work to establish the foundation principles and long-horizon objectives of the IT organization in its service to its customers. This work must look first to the defined business strategy and business models as primary input and consider feedback metrics from current IT activities.

An interesting current debate in enterprise architecture circles is whether business modeling should even be considered an IT activity. IT might support it, but the modeling of business strategies, capabilities, functions, and processes should arguably be seen more as a pure business function—business transformation would be a business-driven capability, using IT support for modeling techniques and tools. It would be a primary input into IT strategy, process management, data management, and customer relationship management.

Developing IT strategy is seen by some as the start of the IT value chain,[95] a view not supported in this book. Instead, the planning process here is seen as akin to city planning—*an important but non-value-adding activity* intended to support and structure the true value chain, which in a city is economic development as represented by new construction, commerce, and the like. Similarly, the IT value chain is event driven, not cyclical.

"Strategic alignment" is often a gating factor for IT demand request assessments.

Develop IT Strategy: Requirements

High-level strategies often require no more than basic office automation tools, being captured in spreadsheets, presentations, or word-processing documents. However, if strategies are to be called on as justification for portfolio investments, they may need to be captured (at least as references) in the portfolio management or enterprise architecture tool.

There are more formal strategy development methods such as Hoshin Kanri, and strategy development can overlap with higher-level business modeling, focusing on concepts such as strategy, goal, objective, external influence, and risk. Such modeling is by nature abstract and somewhat subjective, but a formal conceptual model or ontology supported by a structured tool can assist.

IT strategy must also integrate with demand management so that demand requests can be assessed with reference to established strategies.

Manage IT Portfolio

Managing IT as a portfolio was first proposed by F. Warren McFarlan;[96] a number of more recent authors have contributed substantial work here.[97] IT assets can be well managed through a portfolio paradigm in which "things" of a given type are grouped and comparatively assessed. The major portfolio classes Robert Handler and Bryan Maizlish identify are planning, project, and asset; the asset portfolio subdivides further into services, applications, technologies, data, hardware, and people.

If this seems too generic, consider the Wikipedia definitions of "account" and "portfolio":

In accountancy, an account is a label for recording *a quantity of almost anything.* Most often it is a record of an amount of money owned or owed by or to a particular person or entity, or allocated to a particular purpose. It may represent amounts of money that have actually changed hands, or it may represent an estimate of the values of assets, or it may be a combination of these.[98]

In finance, a portfolio is a collection of investments held by an institution or a private individual. Holding a portfolio is part of an investment and risk-limiting strategy called diversification. By owning several assets, certain types of risk (in particular specific risk) can be reduced. The assets in the portfolio could include stocks, bonds, options, warrants, gold certificates, real estate, futures contracts, production facilities, or *any other item that is expected to retain its value.*[99]

Portfolio management's primary goal is the proper balancing of strategic priorities. Different resource pools are defined in terms of dollars or headcount, and within each of those pools the same assessment techniques are applied.

Because the portfolios are essentially statements of strategy, their definition becomes one of the most critical questions; some may divide them in terms of development life cycle (build, enhance, maintain) while others may divide them by line of business or value chain objective (Figure 2.6). Large or complex organizations might do both: each line of business would have its own set of portfolio pools.

A "continuous improvement" portfolio may be the source for the portfolio management capability itself.[100]

The highest-level concerns of ITSM should be seen as identical to IT portfolio management. Both concepts, while emerging from different professional contexts, essentially address the fundamental question of business–IT alignment. Services should be managed as a portfolio, and whether this is called an "application portfolio" or a "service catalog" is secondary.

IT portfolio management is an enabling process area for the primary value chain activity of demand management. The two are closely aligned, but portfolio management takes an enterprise perspective and a demand request is a specific,

Margin notes:

IT services should be managed as a portfolio, and whether this is called an "application portfolio" or a "service catalog" is secondary.

ITSM and portfolio management both address the question of business–IT alignment but from different perspectives.

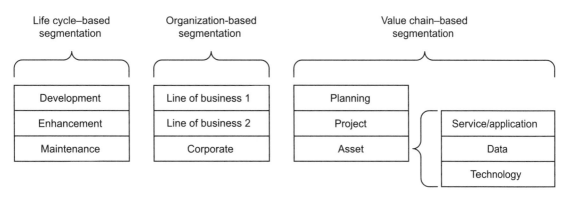

Figure 2.6 Portfolio segmentation examples.[101]

customer-focused interaction driving the primary value chain. Portfolio management supports demand requests through analytics and a prioritization framework.

Portfolio management generally should be the first line of defense for the following types of expense drivers:

▶ Throwing money down a hole—is the (proposed or in-flight) project a good idea? Will it add value? In light of changing business conditions?

▶ Expensive and unanticipated sourcing requirements. Does the IT organization have the staff to execute the project portfolio? Will local contractors need to be brought on at the last minute, at a negotiation disadvantage?

▶ No project plan for steady state. Was total cost of ownership (TCO) analyzed and defined? Were the resulting staff increases for operations and maintenance agreed to as additional to the current base budget?

▶ Poor systems quality—even when the project is deemed a "success." What is the incident rate? Unplanned maintenance releases?

▶ Lack of reuse and reusability. Were expensive investments made in functionality that cannot easily be integrated into new business models? Is there redundancy in the infrastructure or applications?

▶ Were new technologies acquired that require new systems engineering skills?

▶ Complexity—even when the system "works." Does it take 8 hours of staff time on average every week (or night) to complete the overnight batch? Did the last team working on a maintenance release spend half its time reanalyzing the system's current state?

▶ Obsolescence. Are knowledgeable staff members increasingly more expensive? Is the hardware beyond a TCO "sweet spot"?

▶ Vendor or product issues. Did your database vendor force you into a new version, imposing new maintenance releases across 25% of the applications in your portfolio? Did you understand the effect of this sufficiently in advance?

▶ Service nonuse. Has this capability simply outlived its usefulness?

There are various representations of portfolio management—Jeffrey Kaplan[102] focuses more on the project portfolio concept, and research firm Forrester Research has covered the more technical aspects of application portfolio management in some depth. The Forrester perspective brings in software engineering concerns such as internal analysis of application dependencies and complexity. In a packaged software world such analyses may seem less useful, but the same techniques can be applied to the overall complexity of application interfaces across the entire portfolio.

The term "portfolio management" might start to encompass enterprise architecture–related functions, especially in an organization skeptical of the term "architecture."

What are the system implications for a two-point increase in interest rates?

A highly mature portfolio management capability would start to integrate seamlessly with business architecture. What are the system implications for a two-point increase in interest rates? What are the implications for IT services if the cost of gasoline increases 25%? If transportation costs decrease by 10%? If disposable consumer income goes up? Down?

Along similar lines, the ability to measure the business benefits of a system is essential, although notoriously difficult. As Robert Benson notes, "From the beginning of IT in business, we have experienced a dichotomy between the immediate cost and revenue aspects of IT justification…and the 'strategic' or 'infrastructure' aspects of IT justification."[103] There are a number of approaches, often involving indirect or subjective means.[104]

Asset Management

Note that asset management–related processes would be included here, and ties to financial processes would be expected in this process area. This is where the aspects of configuration and asset management as control processes (not primary value chain) come into play.

Manage IT Portfolio: Requirements

The ability to model and compare different investment scenarios is a core requirement for project portfolio management.

This specialized analytical activity requires the ability to establish "apples-to-apples" comparisons between objects of a defined portfolio class, typically for planning and investment purposes. The comparison metrics may be quite varied and based on complex calculations; the base data may be objective, subjective, or both. The ability to model and compare different investment scenarios is a core requirement for project portfolio management.

Because there are a variety of portfolio categories, the determining relevant metrics backed by available high-quality data must be distinguished for each major portfolio category—obviously, project management metrics are of limited use in assessing a technology portfolio.

Portfolio management implies the assignment of prescriptive guidance on portfolio items or classes of items, and governance ensuring this guidance is followed (or exceptions noted).

Portfolio management is often based on subjective assessments.

Portfolio management is often based on subjective assessments: a portfolio of items is compiled, and then interviews are undertaken to determine the quality, business alignment, efficiency, and other attributes of the portfolio elements. The assessments are often captured as a numeric range, for example, "Rank this application on a scale of 1–10 for its usability."

The disadvantage to this is that it is subjective. It can still be effective, if sustained over time; survey research is based on such techniques. Qualities such as "business alignment" would be difficult to assess any other way.

However, there is also the opportunity—unrealized in many portfolio tools today—to base portfolio assessment on objective data: service levels, changes, incidents, complexity, and so forth. Therefore, portfolio management should be aligned with configuration management and ITSM generally. The service-level metrics for an application's availability would be key information to have at hand for portfolio decision making and often more valuable than subjective information of the "rank this on a scale of 1–10" variety.

Under the general category of objective portfolio assessment, the use of dependency data (i.e., system topologies) in portfolio management is predicted as a next maturity step because complex system topologies (inter- and intra-) are associated with higher system operational costs. This in turn requires access to algorithms such as cyclomatic complexity.

(Note that the preceding discussion applies more to application or service portfolio management; project portfolio management will inevitably have more reliance on subjective assessments because the system is not operational yet.)

Portfolio planning should draw on enterprise architecture activities of mapping real-world portfolio entries to reference categories to assist in rationalization and elimination of duplicates. It also includes designing target systems architectures that reduce complexity and creating transitional road maps to reach these desired states. Such activities often require graphical artifacts for effective analysis, which drives a requirement for traditional diagram-based architecture tools to integrate systematically with repository-based data. Portfolio management also requires hooks into IT financial management and should inform the other architecture, portfolio, and service delivery process areas. Characteristic displays (e.g., bubble charts and heat maps) are expected from supporting systems.

This book sees portfolio management as also encompassing the enterprise architecture responsibility of monitoring technology trends, managing technology platforms, and minimizing their complexity and redundancy. To do so it must interface with vendor management and procurement systems.

See the rationalization patterns in Chapter 5 for specific guidance on portfolio management.

Manage Capacity

The purpose of this process area is to ensure that the IT organization has sufficient operational capacity to meet future business needs. In ITIL, it is focused on technical capacity; human capacity should also be considered as part of this. (Do we have the staff we need to operate X system at 200% of where it is today? Do we have enough staff for $10 million program Y next year?)

Capacity management in ITIL terms also includes core enterprise architecture functions such as monitoring technical trends. This framework views that activity as properly the domain of portfolio management, which is where high-level strategic technology acquisition decisions should be made.[105]

ITIL's capacity management representation includes a subsidiary concept of "demand management" that is purely technical. This is one of the divergences this book has with ITIL; this book adheres to the (perhaps more U.S.-based) interpretation of demand management as the service entry point for IT service addition and change requests.

Capacity management at this writing is a driver for infrastructure initiatives in many IT organizations, as the realization is dawning that utilization metrics are abysmally low (10% aggregate use of distributed servers is often encountered in large IT organizations). Initiatives to consolidate servers for more efficient capacity use are increasingly common. Improving capacity provisioning is a key challenge in this area, as the primary reason for underused capacity is the "one server, one application" default acquisition model. Challenging this model, in turn, will require a reframing of the relationship between applications development and infrastructure engineering.

ITIL sees "understanding new technology" as a capacity management activity.[106] This activity is undertaken under portfolio management, typically by an enterprise architecture organization, in this framework.

> Capacity management at this writing is a driver for infrastructure initiatives in many IT organizations to increase utilization rates.

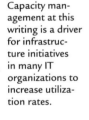

Capacity Challenges

From *www.erp4it.com*

The aggregate supply of computing resources far outstrips the valid demand in many businesses; "considerably less than half of [installed] IT capacity is actually used," according to the *Financial Times*,[107] and rates as low as 5–10% are reported. Why is this?

In shared mainframe environments, the engineering of the hardware and the management of its computing capacity is the concern of a capacity team often aligned with the operations group. However, this model was not followed when distributed

(continued)

infrastructures became prevalent. A large distributed application project might have server engineers assigned, but these engineers are typically only held accountable for the runtime success of the project's delivered application, not the overall enterprise use of computing resources. There is also a strong assumption that the servers are "owned" by the application; sharing capacity, while it does occur, is not a prime consideration and often entails political wrangling that the mainframe model did not encounter.

Furthermore, the variety of server and middleware architectures available to the application teams is so wide that sharing becomes difficult; the server configurations are simply not consistent enough.

All of this is well known; however, the excess capacity problem has been picked up by Nicholas Carr in his critique of the corporate IT capability—to him, it is evidence of "wasteful IT spending."[108]

This is ironic, as Carr (echoed by some research firms) has also been calling for the further decentralization of the IT capability.[109] It is precisely this decentralization that has led to projects acquiring and treating overpowered infrastructure as "theirs" and not to be shared. If the goal is truly to reduce "waste," then a strong centralized model with enforcement of consistent architectural standards is a must.

Each degree of freedom comes with a cost of management.

This does not necessarily mean a complete throwback to the mainframe days. The most interesting developments in this area are the emergence of dynamic provisioning architectures, in which standard technology stacks can be quickly created in response to new project demands or even fast-changing transactional loads. However, even this model will require stronger architectural governance. A standard stack means, for example, a single preferred Java application server, middleware, and many other elements that have been far too diversified. Some variability can be supported—certainly more than the monolithic mainframe—but each degree of freedom comes with a cost of management.

The usual arguments over governance will ensue; "we need XX infrastructure because our business needs are different," but if hard dollars are to be saved through addressing capacity underutilization, hard decisions will have to be made.

Manage Capacity: Requirements

Capacity management is the forecasting of, and planning for, future demand on the IT technical resource. It requires access to both configuration data and potentially voluminous monitoring data, with all that large-scale data management implies. The base performance data may be captured by the availability management process area (described later). A more comprehensive view of capacity management would also include human capacity; this starts to overlap with IT human resource planning and is in scope for demand management as represented in this book.

Capacity-driven initiatives for server rationalization require strong configuration management capabilities. Understanding which applications are running on what servers, and their interactions with other applications and resources, is essential to replatforming these applications onto shared hardware. Maintaining accurate usage records is even more important for shared servers, which may support multiple business processes and have no single application "owner." Allocating costs across applications for shared servers affects both capacity and IT financial management.

Manage Availability

Availability management is concerned with ensuring that systems are available for their intended purpose (e.g., user access), in keeping with any service-level agreements. Project by project, availability management should be built into operational services as part of the systems development life cycle. "Manage availability" as a capability focuses more on ensuring that this happens and planning for the architectural approaches and core infrastructures needed.

Availability management is concerned with ensuring that systems are available for their intended purpose.

Manage Availability: Requirements

Availability management implies first the existence of a robust monitoring and event management architecture, typically one of the earlier internal tool acquisitions for most IT organizations. It also requires that the project management activity in the core value chain ensure that the solutions under development are manageable for availability. The ITIL *Application Management* volume[110] is useful in this regard.

As its sophistication increases, business service mapping of topological dependencies emerges, tied to the core monitoring capabilities (related to the concept of end-to-end transaction management), and more specialized monitoring such as synthetic transaction response monitoring is implemented. All of these operational functions should feed data to both operational dashboards and historical trending repositories used for capacity management (described earlier). The business service topology mappings built for availability purposes should be aligned with the central configuration management information store to prevent redundant dependency management.

Manage Service Levels

Service-level management is "the name given to the processes of planning, coordinating, drafting, agreeing, monitoring, and reporting on SLAs [service-level agreements]."[111]

It is the measurement of anything that is a defined service with agreed to levels of quality and performance. Virtually any measurable aspect of the IT organization might be part of a modern service contract:

▶ Operational measurements
  • Online availability and response times
  • Batch completion times
▶ User service request turnaround times
▶ Project performance
  • Time
  • Cost
  • Objectives
  • Quality (e.g., rework rates)

Service-level management is akin to the demand management area insofar as it implies customer relationship management. Because that customer management is part of the core value chain, this is not a pure ITIL reading of the process area; the activity in this framework would be more concerned with providing the frameworks and processes to the service and relationship owners, informing their interactions with their business customers.

Some might question why this is not in the core value chain. The core chain includes change, release, and incident management, which are the processes that 1) make the new service available operationally and 2) keep it running. Service management beyond those two value chain activities is more about longer-term aspects of supporting customer relationships and managing measurement and reporting functions, and it would not be seen by the hypothetical customer as a value-adding process.

Service management has an unclear and contradictory relationship with application management. ITIL sees applications as more technical than services, but this is as much a terminology issue as anything.

Manage Service Levels: Requirements

Service-level management requires close coordination with demand, portfolio, incident, request, and availability management, as these may all be sources for service-level measurements. Service-level management requires metrics and business intelligence capabilities (e.g., rollup or aggregation and advanced data analytics). Data lineage and integrity is a key concern, as in all business intelligence–based capabilities.

Manage Process

BPM is the "process of managing process."

Business process management (BPM) is a *reflexive* concept; it is the "process of managing process." Such a team would be responsible for establishing the principles by which IT process is defined and ensuring that they are followed. (Members of such groups should be particularly interested in this entire chapter; it is essentially written for them.)

The process group might support process modeling tools, analytic frameworks, and overall guidance such as Lean Six Sigma. It would be primary liaison with the corporate process group, if such a group exists. It should be the champion for breaking down functional boundaries and ensuring the optimization of the entire value chain.

One of the more controversial questions in current enterprise architecture practice is the role of enterprise architecture organizations in business process modeling. The general assumption (evident in enterprise architecture frameworks such as Zachman and The Open Group Architecture Framework) is that business modeling is in scope; however, if enterprise architecture is seen as an overly technical capability or bringing an overly technical bias to such modeling, the business organization may establish its own modeling capabilities.

The process development and quality assurance role of many project management office organizations would fall here—*not* in the primary value chain.

Manage Process: Requirements

This process area requires at least a modeling capability, maturing into analysis and simulation, automated process and workflow management, and ultimately business activity monitoring and business performance management. Processes should be managed as configuration items and therefore hooks into configuration management are needed. Process management in context requires integration with portfolio management (especially data and applications so that support dependencies can be maintained, for example, "application A supports process B" and "process C maintains data topic D").

As noted previously, if business modeling is in scope for enterprise architecture, the supporting tools must support notations and analytic approaches that are acceptable to business users and not too technically biased. Subtle differences in notations can lead to dramatically different responses among potential users; great care in initial presentation of a proposed modeling capability is called for. Support for industry standards (Business Process Modeling Notation, XML Processing Description Language, Business Process Execution Language) is another functional requirement.

Manage Data

Data management is a long-established practice area that seems forever on the periphery of many IT organizations. It is concerned (akin to the process team) with the crosscutting issue of managing IT data assets for efficiency and integrity, manifested in such concerns as controlling data redundancy, ensuring sound data warehouse architecture, defining systems of record for data topics, establishing consistent "dimensions" for rolling up enterprise reports, and evaluating data integrations between systems. The goals of establishing business data stewardship also fit here.[112]

> It is bewildering why capacity management practices do not pay more attention to the importance of data management, as data redundancy drives much costly disk consumption.

This is a difficult area to manage, and optimizing it can have detrimental effects on other processes if it is not managed carefully; however, doing without it can be catastrophic (e.g., regulatory compliance often translates to data management practices). Although ITIL does not recognize it, COBIT does and gives it considerable coverage—the second "plan and organize" control objective is "define the information architecture."[113]

It is bewildering why capacity management practices do not pay more attention to the importance of data management, as data redundancy drives much costly disk consumption. The term "information lifecycle management" has emerged as a more technical response to the problems of large-scale data management, but to date much of the discussion around information lifecycle management has been driven by the agendas of the storage vendors with little or no crossover into the domain of logical data management.

The Capacity Consequences of Unmanaged Data Redundancy

A large U.S. retailer required a powerful database server in each store. These servers were configured identically for ease of management, and many were purchased when disk storage was more expensive than today. The development teams using these servers were able to avoid the enterprise data architecture team's concern for data reuse, and as a result multiple copies of the largest data table were created by developers—each project argued that it had a compelling need to re-create this table with slight modifications; arguments in hindsight seen to be dubious. (In reality, the projects were simply trying to shave a little time off their schedules because reusing shared data does take more analysis.)

As the retailer grew, the redundant tables expanded until they began to bump against the disk capacity on the servers. The IT department then had to explain to the business sponsor why the in-store servers were in urgent need of capacity upgrades that were something of a surprise and unbudgeted. (Because of the engineering particulars and age of the servers in question, the upgrade turned out to be not just cheap hard disks but entire servers.) Total cost was in excess of $2 million.

The business sponsor was unimpressed to learn of the massively redundant data that was driving the upgrade request; the servers, though old, could have lasted somewhat longer otherwise.

Manage Data: Requirements

Data management requires data modeling tools ideally with some centralized administration and workflow capabilities; such models require quality assurance that can be quite involved, such as checking data structure names against lists of standard abbreviations and evaluating (as much as possible) for correct data normalization. Also needed is a means to publish the data inventory (i.e., metadata or data dictionary capability) to help drive data reuse and support research initiatives, for example, for regulatory compliance. Documenting stewards for given data topics and maintaining that metadata also require some sort of system.

Data quality usually connotes data profiling and quality assurance capabilities.

Data management in context requires integration with process and portfolio management (especially applications so that defined systems of record for data topics may be maintained). Integration with configuration management is also highly desirable, and the relationship between metadata repositories and configuration management databases is discussed in depth elsewhere in this book.

Manage IT Finance

Getting a handle on IT for the purpose of impact-based resource allocation is difficult because of its dispersion throughout the enterprise, a complex mixture of people, space, hardware, and software, and management practices in managing support, operations, and infrastructure. Development projects, of course, are not difficult. It is the rest of the IT spend that is hard.

—Robert Benson, Tom Bugnitz, and Bill Walton[114]

This area is the interface between the corporate finance and the IT worlds, handling the proper accounting and cost allocation function in the IT organization. As Jenny Dugmore states, "As a minimum, it is a process that allows a judgment to be made on whether or not the service is good value for the money."[115] Simplicity, fairness, predictability, and controllability are the major objectives for this area. There are two key areas to managing IT finances:

▶ A knowledge of financing and cash flow
▶ An understanding of fixed versus discretionary costs

Understanding the latter bullet is where many of the other IT disciplines enter; understanding fixed costs in particular is difficult to manage without a portfolio or configuration management capability of some sort. The easy way out is to focus on projects, but the bulk of the IT expenditure is typically in operations.

Maintenance and operational spending is the "dark matter" of IT finance.

The total IT cost includes project spending and ongoing maintenance and operations. Project financials are well understood and, because of this, tend to take undeserved center stage in too many IT financial discussions. Maintenance and operational spending consumes up to 90% of total IT budgets yet (to borrow a term from astrophysics) is the "dark matter" of IT finance: poorly understood and the majority of the problem.

The application portfolio can serve as a base model for activity-based budgeting.

Allocation of costs across complex IT operational dependencies is an accounting and technical challenge,[116] calling for links with the IT portfolio management and configuration management capabilities. The models for tracing business activities to deployed IT assets are imprecise and subject to much debate. The application portfolio, service catalog, or both may emerge as a basic structure for an IT activity-based costing initiative, playing a role analogous to a chart of accounts for IT. The suitability of proposed service catalog entries for this purpose may be a useful filter for determining their appropriateness.

Whether and how to implement chargeback (a.k.a. transfer charging) is a critical debate and decision point for the organization.[117]

Manage IT Finance: Requirements

IT financial management ties across all primary and supporting process areas, in particular demand, portfolio, project, and configuration management. It depends on core enterprise accounting capabilities, as do most other corporate functions; it also faces challenges in balancing the goals of transparency and simplicity. Comprehensive visibility into IT finances often implies significant overhead in data capture, but simplistic approaches can conceal material issues from decision makers' scrutiny.

The IT finance process area would support demand management especially in terms of establishing return on investment for proposed initiatives and determining their financial feasibility.

Asset information, as it represents capital and expense expenditures, is required by this process area. The correct management of software licenses presents an opportunity for financial savings, and automated capabilities supporting this are required.

IT financial management requires the ability to build cost models that represent dependencies also present in operational views of IT infrastructure.

IT services should be traceable to revenue streams wherever possible, which is why transaction-based metering is preferable to technology-based metering. Even if it is not a true revenue stream (e.g., corporate systems or IT support for regulatory compliance), the IT resource allocation should be traceable to some representation of business activity, such as business process, capability, or function.

Manage Sourcing, Staff, and Vendors

This area contains the activities of establishing binding financial relationships with vendors of hardware, software, consulting, and staff augmentation services. This process area should be joined at the hip with portfolio management to ensure that the portfolio strategies established are in fact followed. For example, if a given technology is deemed too complex to administer and therefore classified as "to be retired," the procurement process should provide information to the portfolio process supporting such objectives (was the technology purchased anyway?). Contract management generally is known to present substantial opportunities for cost savings, for example, through double-checking and ensuring that all negotiated discounts are applied.

This area's importance is growing with the increasing diversity in sourcing arrangements; managing "underpinning contracts" (in the ITIL sense) is one important responsibility. This area typically has a strong dotted line into the organization's legal department.

IT human resource management is included here, in view of the management philosophy that employees are essentially vendors selling their own labor. Human resource management implies contractor management, which implies vendor relationships with companies that may also sell solutions, so the entire process family seems to have a natural affinity. Some interpretations of portfolio management include human resources under that area, and although this makes some sense conceptually, managing the human resource "portfolio" is a specialized skill and probably should remain aligned with its historic functional home. Training would also be covered here, as well as general organizational change management capabilities.

There are numerous standard human resource metrics, including staff retention, training, and compensation benchmarks by skills. Opportunities may exist to refine and align such metrics with technology portfolios—for example, if an organization is retiring an obsolete technology, what are the human capital management implications? Are the staff members being retrained?

Manage Sourcing, Staff, and Vendors: Requirements

Managing sourcing and vendors requires similar functionality to non-IT capabilities also doing this; vendor management is becoming a mature area in many corporations. IT, however, requires the core activities to be expanded with hooks into portfolio management (to ensure that portfolio guidance is followed in acquisitions) and the project life cycle (to enforce enterprise policies).

This process area also requires core human resource management (including training) systems and generally will leverage those provided by the enterprise. The overall requirement is supporting the "hire to retire" employee life cycle, including hiring, compensation, career progression, performance evaluation, and training. There are interactions with many other process areas, for example, project and security management.

To support demand management, aggregate staff resource management capabilities are required; these are not part of the primary value chain per se (although they were previously mentioned in the "Manage Demand" section).

The impending retirement of workers born between 1945 and 1962 (the "postwar baby boom") will present many challenges and opportunities. Just as these individuals will eventually bequeath trillions of dollars in assets to their familial heirs, their professional heirs will (somewhat sooner) inherit complexity of knowledge comparable in scope.[118] This mass migration of knowledge will require infrastructure, and the IT enablement systems (with the knowledge-centric systems such as configuration and metadata management in the lead) will play an important role here.

> The impending retirement of workers born between 1945 and 1962 will present many challenges.

Manage Risk, Security, and Compliance

This area is concerned with the physical and virtual access controls and defenses of the IT infrastructure, and the ongoing certification of same, with respect to audit standards and legal regulations. It would be the primary IT contact area for internal audit and would also have ties to the legal department. Note that defense of IT infrastructure also includes disaster planning. It is also concerned with risk management in the more generic sense of identifying negative scenarios, their likelihood, and potential costs of impact.

Disaster preparedness (or business continuity planning) comes with its own specialized set of terms and metrics. At the highest level, understanding the degree of continuity preparedness is key: Have continuity plans been executed for all major processes and their underpinning services and applications? Have these plans been refreshed to reflect changes to these systems? Initiating a change to a process or system is a definable event and should result in continuity plans being updated.

The establishment of security credentials should be used as a leverage point for ensuring that configuration management as a documentation process is adhered to: "If it's not in the configuration management database, you can't have access."

Note that multiple functional teams are required to cover this process area because of the need for segregation of duties.

Manage Risk, Security, and Compliance: Requirements

Security, risk, and compliance require, first, the infrastructure systems that manage identity, authentication, and authorization in the IT infrastructure, as well as proactive and reactive security defenses.

Beyond this core activity, they require a means for the identification of risk in a structured format, preferably aligned with configuration management. Analyzing security policy for IT systems requires understanding dependencies. The activity of disaster recovery (business continuity) requires in-depth process analysis tied to configuration management so that all dependencies for a given business process are understood and can be restored within a given recovery time objective. Managing recovery steps may require a documentation or knowledge management capability tied to both workflow and configuration management. Compliance requires systemic tracking of external regulatory drivers in particular, and ensuring those regulations are addressed requires workflow similar to other forms of risk management.

This general process area is the source of much reanalysis in the modern enterprise. Teams of contractors are often brought in to resurvey IT infrastructure (e.g., for compliance initiatives) because there is little confidence in existing portfolio and configuration data. Proper risk analysis and avoidance requires comprehensive understanding of the entire IT stack: business process to business application service to software components to databases, servers, and other infrastructure. The wasteful continued reanalysis of such dependencies, into throwaway data sets, presents an opportunity for cost avoidance in modern IT management.

This process area also requires the services and collaboration of configuration management capabilities to determine (for example) that all changes to infrastructure

---

Marginal notes:

If it's not in the configuration management database, you can't have access.

Proper risk analysis and avoidance requires comprehensive understanding of the entire IT stack. Expensive resurveying of IT infrastructure is an opportunity for cost avoidance.

are authorized—unauthorized changes may be evidence of security exploits and at the least are process risks.

Manage Facilities and Operations

This area is focused on the planning and control aspects of facilities and operations; the core value chain covers the daily provision and management of services. It includes oversight of physical facilities, including the complex engineering involved in data center construction and management. It also includes the staffing of those data centers and related issues of operations management.[119]

Manage Facilities and Operations: Requirements

This capability requires the ability to manage physical property, including real estate transactions, valuations, taxes, leasing, and zoning. It also includes the operational staffing of 24/7 data centers and call centers (which may require shift management software).

Because incremental project work often results in demand for staff space, this process area should be tied to demand management in some form.

Support for standard facilities blueprinting is required: floor layouts, plans, and mechanical perspectives.

Data center facilities management has interesting overlaps with configuration management. Often, the physical computing device is seen as the base unit of concern, but there are racks, cabinets, HVAC, and power distribution architectures in play. What business services will be affected if a given AC circuit must be shut down for maintenance? If a rack location needs physical upgrading? If the cooling system is degraded in part of the facility?

An interesting new trend in power and cooling management (given recent trends in computer hardware evolution) is to charge back these services by consumption (they have historically been treated as overhead); this will require new forms of configuration management and monitoring capabilities.

Enable IT

If IT is an enablement function when viewed from the business perspective, how is IT itself enabled? A variety of tools may be required, including the following:

▶ Portfolio management system
▶ Enterprise architecture system

► Demand management system
► Project management system
► Requirements management system
► Software modeling system
► Nonproduction environments (dev, QA, test, etc.)
► Source code control system
► Release and deployment system
► Configuration management system
► Change management system
► Capacity management system
► Incident or problem management system
► Service management system

(The details of these and other tools are covered in the reference architecture in Chapter 4.)

If IT is an enablement function when viewed from the business perspective, how is IT itself enabled?

These tools are not simple to implement or run. They should be designed with the same architectural discipline as other business systems. They require production infrastructure and ongoing base staff support. Their data structures are complex and challenging to connect together. Qualified software engineering and project management staff should be used appropriately in their design and implementation. This general area is where "the barefoot cobbler's child" problem becomes most apparent.

The same engineering capability should ideally own most of these tools to ensure maximum interoperability and build a value chain–oriented nucleus of engineering sophistication. As you will see later in this chapter, all are involved with a common, tightly coupled conceptual data set and opportunities for integration will be more easily identified if the same engineering team owns the majority of them.

This "enable IT delivery" secondary process area is perhaps the preeminent concern of this book, and Part II will cover it in great detail.

Enable IT: Requirements

This process area has the same requirements as IT as a whole: it has the same value chain on a smaller scale and all the same supporting processes. The specific systems it manages are the systems required by the other process areas, as described in this section and in the systems architecture section. This idea is discussed in more depth in Chapter 5.

As a function, it might be collocated with other corporate systems development and support groups, such as those for finance and human resources.

2.5 Relationship between Primary and Supporting Processes

One approach, shown in Table 2.2, for elaborating the relationship between supporting and primary processes is to matrix them and analyze each matrix intersection.[120]

Each cell becomes a governance touchpoint, and activities undertaken therein should be measured for both effectiveness and efficiency.

Table 2.2 Supporting Processes by Value Chain

	Manage Customer Relationship and Demand	Develop Solutions	Manage Services
Architecture and portfolio	Overall, helps establish strategies, parameters, and bounded expectations so that demand requests can be effectively evaluated.	Sets a high-level architecture approach.	Architecture consumes service measurement results as key inputs to the next cycle of portfolio planning.
IT finance	Sets boundaries and authorization approach. Controls overall funding of portfolios.	Authorizes and tracks incremental (project-based) spending.	Manages cost reporting and/or recovery for runtime services.
Sourcing, staff, and vendors	Provides resource forecasts and proactive management of sourcing relationships and human capital.	Supplies contract management, tactical sourcing, and staff hiring.	Provides ongoing vendor and workforce management.
Risk, security, and compliance	Reviews demand requests for potential regulatory and compliance issues.	Supplies detailed project reviews when warranted.	Provides ongoing monitoring of IT operations for compliance and regulatory concerns.
Facilities and operations	Reviews demand requests for facilities and operations effects.	Reviews solutions for operability, turnover quality, and completeness.	Provides ongoing and continuous operational improvement.
Enable IT	Supports IT customer relationship management and demand management capabilities.	Supports solutions development infrastructure.	Supports service-level management tooling and metrics.

2.6 Major Framework Issues

Having completed the overall process framework, turn to some of its more troublesome issues: service entry points, configuration management, and the hosting "zone of contention."

Service Entry Points

A challenging aspect of ITSM is the service entry point, or SEP. The SEP is an interface or avenue of contact between IT and its customers, users, or both. The classic representation is something like the one shown in Figure 2.7.

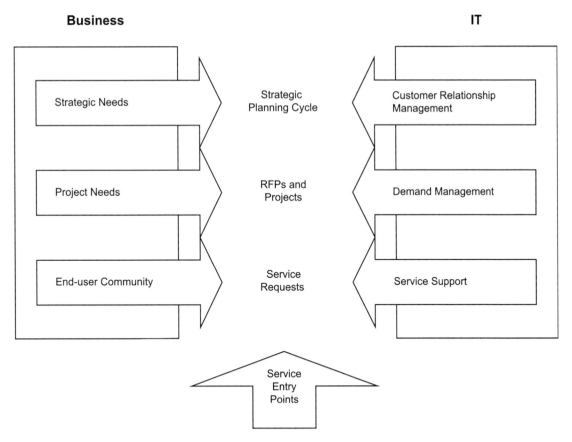

Figure 2.7 Service entry points.[121]

At the top is the highest-level strategic IT planning, characterized here by requests for information, or RFIs. (Not all high-level business—IT planning is carried out using these means, of course.) The IT value chain as represented in this book initiates in the customer demand and relationship management process area, characterized here by the request for proposal (RFP) and response. This is the gateway for the creation and modification of larger-grained services.

For project initiation, ITIL offers the concept of change management extended upstream to initial solution request. However, ITIL has not yet presented a solid conceptual framework effectively differentiating the various types of customer–IT interactions (see the discussion at the end of this chapter and the section on clarifying SEPs in Chapter 5).

Routine requests, as defined through the service catalog and incident management, are considered part of the service support function.

Is There, or Ought There Be, a Boundary between the Service Catalog and Demand Management?

Some interpretations of the service desk idealize it to including everything that an IT service provider might offer to potential customers. Its interface would be a "single pane of glass" (i.e., integrated application) presentation to be used by everyone from a customer requiring a password reset to a vice president seeking a major new suite of application functionality.[122]

However, it's not clear that this level of integration adds much value, given the considerable differences between requesting time- and materials-type services and defined, fixed cost services. Demand management activities (at least at the high level) are often cyclical, intense, and relationship-driven characteristics that make an impersonal service request management tool inappropriate.

It is true that time- and materials-based project costing may become increasingly commoditized with the definition of standardized hosting services based on defined technology stacks and may start to move ever further into fixed price costing (application development will never be completely fixed price costing because of the inherent nature of software development). It's also important that strategic forecasting and demand management have visibility into the volume and nature of current work, including service requests, to accurately predict whether the resources are available for a given initiative. However, short-term service request traffic has a different time horizon than large-scale demand requests. Determining the future staff availability for a large-scale project requires summarizations and trending of the work request traffic, not visibility into specific requests.

While this book advocates clear differentiation of the SEPs, their management via a common metrics structure would be highly desirable. For further information see the section on clarifying SEPs in Chapter 5.

Applications, Infrastructure, and the Hosting Zone of Contention

Designing and building solutions is often equated with software development and integration or configuration. However, any solution requires a platform, and in larger organizations the engineering of computing and network platforms capable of supporting the desired software solutions becomes a significant activity in its own right, albeit one less well covered in the popular computing press. The value chain can be seen as having both application and infrastructure tracks, with a hosting zone of contention between them (Figure 2.8).

There is a tendency to see applications as being about development and infrastructure as being about support. This is because production support teams are

Demand, development, and support all cross the application–infrastructure distinction.

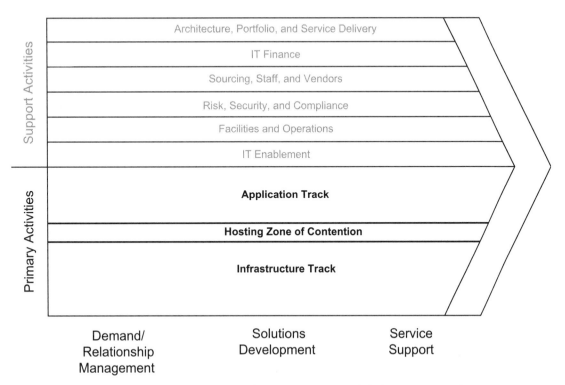

Figure 2.8 Application and infrastructure tracks and the hosting "zone of contention."

often aligned with infrastructure organizations and application support teams are aligned with development organizations. A more accurate picture is to see application and infrastructure as separate "tracks" in the value chain, with both crossing all major value chain activities.

The hosting zone of contention is the continuing debate between application teams focused on functional requirements (what the application or service does) and infrastructure teams focused on nonfunctional requirements (how it runs). There are many variations on organizational approaches to the zone of contention; in some models the hosting team controls the technical stack up through middleware, and in other models the hosting or infrastructure team may only be responsible for the data center facility and physical access to servers and application teams may do their own operating system and middleware support. Industry trends seem to be toward recentralization of the hosting function, as economies of scale can be had here, for example, through the establishment of standard technology stacks as service offerings (a subject of recurring coverage in this book).

Figure 2.9 shows a typical progression of the application–hosting relationship. Although mainframe systems usually are all the way to the right, organizations with a bias toward distributed systems may be anywhere along the spectrum. It is usually a progressive model; for example, the hosting team will not typically manage middleware unless it also controls the operating system (OS).

Table 2.3 provides an overview of how the application–infrastructure tracks interrelate through the value chain and common issues encountered in the zone of contention.

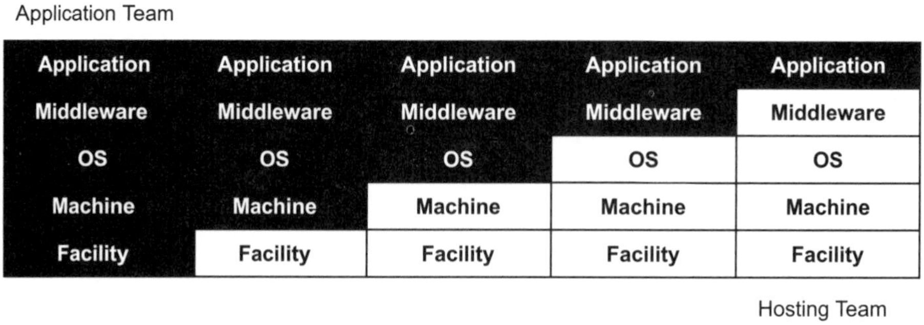

Application Team

Application	Application	Application	Application	Application
Middleware	Middleware	Middleware	Middleware	Middleware
OS	OS	OS	OS	OS
Machine	Machine	Machine	Machine	Machine
Facility	Facility	Facility	Facility	Facility

Hosting Team

Figure 2.9 Hosting progression.

Table 2.3 Application versus Infrastructure Tracks and the Zone of Contention

	Demand Management	Solutions Development	Service Support
Application track	This is where demand for new functionality and software engineering or solutions development resources is identified. This area should include discussions regarding the ongoing headcount required to support the new functionality (lead users, etc.).	Analysis, design, and construction of new functional solutions are performed here. In less mature hosting environments, the application team may also concern itself with middleware, operating system, and even hardware.	Ongoing application-level support is performed here: user support (including training), data integrity, and the like. The application team often takes on business-facing service management, dependent on the hosting service through an internal operational-level agreement.
Zone of contention	The infrastructure track is often poorly considered and served in the demand management phase. Infrastructure teams often feel that they are invited too late to the table when major new functionality with significant infrastructure implications is under consideration.	Debates over the level of hosting service to be provided and the standard technology stack often emerge here. For example, "the hosting team is pushing back on product X because it only runs on application server Z." Access rights to the environments may also be a source of contention. Turnover to the support organization is typically contentious because of both application and infrastructure issues.	Pressure is often brought to bear upon the service support organization to accept turnover of the delivered system, regardless of its stability or architectural soundness. Infrastructure-driven service outages are a common complaint in hosting environments. ("They patched my server and rebooted it without telling me.")
Infrastructure or hosting track	From the infrastructure perspective, an application is an instance of a hosting service. Discussion about capacity and platform options need to be initiated here as part of the demand request value chain.	Technical design and build for the infrastructure takes place. Standard technology stacks can reduce complexity and enhance estimation confidence if they are acceptable offerings for the application teams.	The hosting service is the end result of the value chain from the perspective of the infrastructure track. Concerns here include TCO, efficient capacity utilization, and the like.

2.7 The Functional Viewpoints

> Institutionalization of Process Management requires the peaceful coexistence of the vertical and horizontal dimensions of an organization. In most cases, organizing around processes is not practical. While a process organization structure…eliminates the tension between the vertical and horizontal, it merely creates a different kind of white space… between processes. Furthermore, it may require additional people, obstruct sharing of learning and resources, and erect career path barriers. In most process-based organizations, functions remain as "centers of excellence."
>
> —Geary Rummler and Alan Brache[123]

This discussion has primarily been framed in terms of the overall IT value chain, which is a true process ("inspire to retire"). The IT organization historically has segregated into three logical functional areas, often at cross-purposes with one another: planning, building, and running.

A functional view of large-scale IT might be as shown in Figure 2.10.

Governance is the planning and control function (plan, direct, control, and organize). Portfolio management, demand management, and enterprise architecture all fit here.

Development is project management and the software development life cycle.

Operations is the steady-state IT function—data center operations, help desk, and so on.

The decision to partition into three rather than two, four, or five is significant and was not made lightly. Mark Lutchen and Rick Sturm take this approach, as well as others.[124]

The problem with this framework is the functional bias; the large- and small-scale value chains often cross the functional boundaries. This is a widely understood problem with functional modeling; nevertheless, the functional view is still valuable in identifying exactly where difficult interfaces will arise. The core insight from this figure is that the worst problems of enterprise IT management center on the arrows in Figure 2.10.

IT internally is too often a squabbling family; Jan van Bon aptly notes the existence of the "drama triangle: the troublesome communication between customer, application management and … Production/Operations. This leads to the 'throwing over the wall' syndrome, responsible for lots of trouble in IT for decades now."[125] The functional plan or control areas (e.g., project management offices and enterprise architecture teams) also have issues with the other areas.

The worst problems in enterprise IT center on the arrows in Figure 2.10.

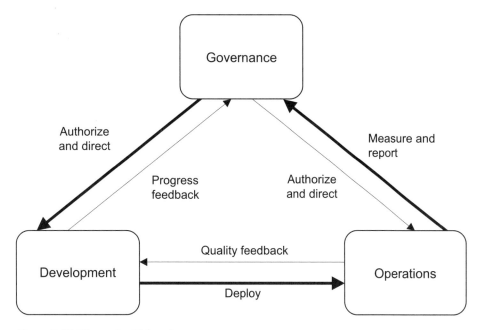

Figure 2.10 The major IT functions.

The functional boundaries become especially apparent when analyzing the supporting application system architectures; with few exceptions, vendor products clearly fragment along these lines. Their viewpoints are important requirements drivers from a timing perspective; most IT information has planned, in flight, current, and historical states—the need to support these drives complexity in the data and systems architecture for IT enablement.

Each perspective has a set of characteristic questions:

Plan or Control Perspective

▶ What are the most promising future investments in my IT portfolio?
▶ What does it cost us to support the order to cash process every year?
▶ What current investments are good? Questionable? Bad?
▶ For an application or service, what are the total costs (with drilldowns linked to supporting detail) of acquisition and operations? Include shared or amortized costs.
▶ What are the steady-state drivers of my operational costs?
▶ What cyclic events (lease, capacity, technology refresh) do I need to plan for?
▶ What are the effects or dependencies?

Build Perspective

▶ I need to upgrade service or system X.
  • What is its complete bill of materials?
  • What are the top to bottom interdependencies and their nature?
▶ What systems use data element Y?
  • What does it mean?
  • What is its lineage?
  • What security or privacy policies apply to it?
▶ What is the current status of the software development life cycle across and within projects?
▶ What major changes are upcoming?
▶ What is the current overall degree of change in my systems?

Run Perspective

▶ How am I spending my IT dollars?
  • Development
  • Support/operations
▶ What is the operational status and trending of my systems?
  • Incident and problem
  • Support and maintenance
  • Change
▶ How do my incident and problem metrics relate to my change activities?
▶ What are the business effects of technical issues?

These requirements may be more critical than process-focused requirements in many organizations that have a primarily functional orientation toward their operation. (Many of these requirements could be tied directly to processes as well.)

2.8 Nonfunctional Requirements

The process framework presented in this chapter is the essential statement of *functional* requirements for the IT enablement systems. The first requirement for the system or systems is to support the primary and secondary value chains' business activities: the "inspire to retire" service life cycle, as well as its support activities with respect to staff; facilities and operations; finances; sourcing and vendors; security, compliance, and risk; and architecture.

Beyond the specific functional requirements of each process area and activity, there are a number of further requirements that are critical to the efficient and effective system we are seeking. This section transitions from the business analysis of Part I into the detailed architectural discussions of Part II.

Directly Support the Major IT Quality Objectives

Again, consider the highest-level drivers for the well-managed IT organization:

▶ Responsiveness to changing customer needs and strategies
▶ Cost effectiveness, efficiency, and transparency
▶ Effective risk management
▶ Operational effectiveness (e.g., availability and performance)

These objectives have been implicit in much of this discussion of the process framework. However, it is a good practice to keep them in view throughout systems analysis, as these drivers may also inform nonfunctional requirements and specific points in the data, systems, and patterns analyses.

Support Diverse Enterprise Strategies

One requirement not easily reduced to a given process area is that a robust, integrated IT value chain must support any combination of firm strategies, performance measures, and IT governance arrangements. It should be agile enough to underpin enterprise strategies based on various mixes of cost leadership, customer intimacy, and product differentiation and to provide accurate feedback to the enterprise leadership on the cost tradeoffs for IT in supporting a given strategy.

An IT governance function should not blindly oppose architectural exceptions but rather should focus on cost transparency so that the consequences of such exceptions can be assessed.

For example, an enterprise basing its strategy on customer intimacy might be prepared to accept architecture variances in its customer relationship management systems—such variances often emerge if there is intense time-to-deliver pressure on the solutions development process area. It is not the role of an IT governance or enterprise architecture function to blindly oppose all such innovation, but seeking cost transparency is essential. Did the architectural variance lead to 50% higher TCO than a less functional but more compliant alternative? Was that TCO offset by the revenues gained through fast time to market?

Similarly, a company seeking to grow organically may have different IT objectives (a rigorous operating model, for example) compared with those of a company growing by acquisition (which may prioritize a strong integration capability, for example). The IT capability should recognize the tradeoffs in supporting such diverse strategies and be prepared to adapt to a change in strategic direction.[126]

The strategic alignment model of Henderson and Venkatraman[127] is another useful framework, which postulates that the enterprise IT organization serves as one of the following:

▶ Investment center
▶ Profit center
▶ Service center
▶ Cost center

These are the IT organization's business models, and understanding which applies is critical. Again, if IT is an investment center, there may be more tolerance for fast time to market and corresponding higher system TCO; if IT is a cost center, then architectural rigor and common platforms may have higher priority.

Capture Data Early and Once

The most effective portfolio management processes tightly integrate with adjacent processes…. Information is entered only once…. For example, the information entered into a service request feeds the project charter documentation. Project charter documentation feeds the business case. The business case feeds portfolio analysis and technology planning. Portfolio analysis feeds and is fed by resource management. Technology, portfolio, and resource management feed budgeting. Budgeting feeds IT financial management project and service accounting. Accounting feeds the project phase reviews and status reviews.

—Jeff Kaplan[128]

Another nonfunctional requirement is the basic process improvement principle of capturing the data early and once. This is an objective that IT is currently poor at, with much rekeying of data (especially reference or portfolio data) across isolated functions. Striving for this objective will have clear effects on systems architecture.

Dependency capture in particular is expensive and poorly managed. Dependency analysis is the core of understanding change risk impact, yet many large IT organizations do not track even the basic dependency of application on server. Instead, dependencies are reanalyzed based on word of mouth and whoever may be available for a quick meeting to determine possible change impact. The same essential topologies are redrawn repeatedly in a variety of graphics tools and spreadsheets and then lost or mistrusted for subsequent work.

Considering that most people involved in such dependency capture are highly compensated professionals, this seems to be a clear financial opportunity for the IT capability.

It even appears that some large outsourcers and contract vendors may be resistant to establishing a system of record for IT dependencies, as some of their revenue stream derives from continually reanalyzing dependencies or monopolizing their knowledge of them. Being the sole source of understanding for complex system dependencies gives any outsourcing partner a measure of power over an organization's operations that should be construed as significant risk. As ITIL states, "Insist that you have complete access/ownership to management information at its source."[129]

On the other hand, some outsourcers may be starting to realize that a robust shared CMDB may be a critical success factor for outsourcing success because it helps clarify the exact scope of what is being outsourced, minimizing the potential for misunderstandings and finger-pointing.

A corollary principle to this is to capture data as part of primary value chain activities. Supporting activities should not be the primary generators of key IT governance data; they do not have the leverage.

> An externally held monopoly on an organization's IT dependency information should be construed as significant risk.

Information Is Power

In my experience, metadata and configuration data, when collected and managed well, goes quickly from an obscure and tenuous exercise to becoming a rather politicized topic. When it's clean and accurate, imaginative IT leaders immediately recognize it as a significant lever of control.

Flexibility and Interoperability

Just as ERP systems in other value chains and functional domains require substantial integration with more specialized systems, so will the suites emerging as comprehensive IT resource planning or ERP for IT solutions. Such solutions will need to interoperate with many sources of highly complex data, some of it generated by systems and presenting technical challenges more akin to hard engineering problems than to automation of traditional business processes. Industry standards are emerging but are currently in their infancy.

Because the IT value chain requirements are still emerging, any systems intended to manage it will require flexibility, just as current ERP systems provide frameworks for adapting them. Such adaptations, however, limit the forward compatibility of the systems with subsequent vendor releases; techniques for managing this problem must be part of the automation strategy.

Provide Business Intelligence on IT Processes through Metrics

Many of the process discussions in this chapter covered metrics—how the processes are measured. The complex, interconnected information processing environment has tangible, measurable characteristics crucial to management control; however, such measurements require a level of discipline in IT operations so that they are consistent. Ensuring apples-to-apples metrics is a challenge.

A "business intelligence" capability blurs the boundary between functional and nonfunctional requirements. Functionally, various metrics may be required, in the case of IT including such measures as the following:

▶ Overall IT financial profile
▶ IT demand
▶ Project management
▶ Availability
▶ User support
▶ Service-level management
▶ Total IT cost and return on investment
▶ Change management
▶ Disaster recovery
▶ Training

Not all metrics can or should be financial; the Norton/Kaplan Balanced Score-card concept applies here as well as any other part of the business. Metrics quantifying complexity date back to the earliest large-scale software engineering efforts and may be increasingly useful in many IT activities (see the proposed pattern on application points costing in Chapter 5).

Nonfunctionally, the existence of requirements for a set of metrics such as this drives technical need for an important class of system, the business intelligence system, supported by data warehouse/mart infrastructure. As Jeff Kaplan notes, "to aggregate the information, the organization needs common taxonomies."[130] This is a recurring issue in any large-scale automated system, known in the data warehousing world as "dimensions." Further specifics of these requirements will be discussed in the data and systems architecture sections.

The cutting edge of metrics-based process management is to be found in the emerging fields of business activity monitoring and business performance (not process) management.

2.9 Process Maturity

Process maturity in general is often assessed with a staged framework such as the Capability Maturity Model. Maturity implies definition, adherence, repeatability, measurability, and continuous improvement; it does not imply sophistication of technical platforms or depth of staff expertise.

This book extensively discusses the automation requirements of IT processes, so it is important to note that processes also can be manual. For many organizations, the old standby of Microsoft Office, with printed documents in file cabinets or 3-ring binders, can work quite well. Even for the largest organizations, some processes may not merit full automation, vendor claims notwithstanding. The advantage to automated, integrated systems is that process "gates" can often be easier to achieve, requiring that process A be completed before process B can start. Manual processes require somewhat more diligence and executive attention; in an IT organization in particular, they are easily ignored if they are not enforced.

2.10 The Business Case

The business case for a process framework approach has been well stated by management theorists for years. Businesses are about activities, and optimizing these activities is a primary challenge. The creation and use of process frameworks to understand a large and complex set of activities is by now standard industry practice.

The overall concepts of process improvement will resonate more successfully than any technical jargon with business partners.

Framing IT activities in terms of business process leads to increased credibility with business stakeholders. Metrics-based process management means the use of management concepts familiar to business partners: leading and lagging indicators such as critical success factors and key performance indicators and so forth. Even if the business customer is unfamiliar with the particulars of IT process, the overall concepts of process improvement will resonate more successfully than any technical jargon.

IT is more than a collection of related components. The processes represent a fundamental value chain and therefore require systems support as much as any other business process. IT should be architected, implemented, and operated as a cohesive set of related systems, as an ERP and execution system.

2.11 Making It Real

Most IT organizations of any size start to partition themselves naturally into at least construction and operations silos, with the senior leadership also fulfilling a planning function, which becomes more formalized over time. As your organization goes through this natural evolution, it's critical to maintain the value chain perspective, and the way to make this real is to focus on the handoffs:

▶ Get your architects, development managers, and operations staff together and discuss the end-to-end IT value chain. Where are you having the most problems?

▶ Is planning guidance being reflected in solutions development and technology acquisitions? Are your control processes for this optimized to minimize bureaucracy?

▶ Is the release transition from development to operations seamless, and are both functional areas partnering effectively and seeking continuous improvement? Are systems being built for operability, as well as functionality? Or are new systems tossed "over the wall" with finger-pointing on all sides?

▶ Are projects, programs, and portfolios being held accountable for system quality and TCO, as well as the usual drivers of functionality, cost, and schedule? Are metrics on all these matters used for further IT planning?

▶ Is the IT value chain generating its own high-quality, managed data as an inherent result of its operation? Or is data an afterthought?

▶ Do your support processes intersect with the primary value chain appropriately and in a balanced way?

▶ Are people rotating between support and primary processes? Or are the support processes being used as a dumping ground for less qualified staff?

2.12 Chapter Conclusion

This chapter took the ambitious goal of creating yet another IT process framework, this one based on value chain theory. This is a critical step in understanding enterprise IT, which remains functionally blinkered.

While I did not dive into the value chain in tremendous detail, it provided the central insight into what is primary and supporting in IT delivery, a distinction not clearly drawn in current influential frameworks (or any literature I am aware of).

The central plan, build, and run value chain is an event-driven flow, which can be casually referred to as "inspire to retire." It is measurable and has defined stakeholders, and to that extent it meets the demands of current BPM thinking. Further work could be done on elaborating the IT value chain concept, but that is not the purpose of this book.

> The central plan, build, and run value chain is an event-driven flow, which can be casually referred to as "inspire to retire."

The framework was required as essential statement of business requirements for the analysis in Part II—without requirements, how can we know what we need to enable through data and systems architectures?

2.13 Further Reading

The IT value chain by definition is a broad concept, and a complete bibliography could fill a book. Here are some sources.

For the source material on value chain, see Porter (1998). I am not by any means the first to apply the concept of value chain to IT; please see Gibert (2006) for a different, more detailed approach—work predating this book by some years. Gibert's work in turn has influenced the ITIL *Business Perspective* volume (Office of Government Commerce 2004). Benson, Bugnitz et al. (2004) also use an IT value chain metaphor. For a contrasting, similarly comprehensive framework (not based on a value chain), see Kaplan (2005), p. 53. The major research and IT services firms also have deep intellectual property in this area.

For BPM, see Rummler and Brache (1995). For a concise overview of the rise and fall of the business process reengineering fad, see Harmon (2003), pp. 25–27.

For IT governance and portfolio management, see Weill and Ross (2004), Maizlish and Handler (2005), and Lutchen (2004). Aitken (2003) and Remenyi (1999) are also essentially statements of IT portfolio management. For the software development lifecycle, see Royce (1970)—the first introduction of iterative principles, unfortunately and inaccurately termed the "waterfall" method. See also McConnell (1999) and anything else by him. See also Humphrey (1989); the extensive works of DeMarco, Yourdon, Finkelstein, and Fowler; and the journals *IEEE Software* and the Association for Computing Machinery's *Transactions on Software Engineering and Methodology*. The IEEE Computer Society has established the Software Engineering Body of Knowledge, or SWEBOK, (IEEE 2005). Don't overlook the Agile movement (Agile Alliance 2001). Project management generally is covered in the project management body of knowledge (Project Management Institute 2004). CMMI (CMMI Product Team 2001) is an important if controversial standard.

For IT finance (overlapping into performance management and metrics in many cases), see Aitken (2003); Remenyi, Money et al. (2000); Remenyi (1999); Curley (2004); and the Office of Government Commerce (2001).

For data management as a process area, see Dama International (2000) and English (1999); the latter is also a good source on data quality. The ITIL back-catalog volume on Data Management (CCTA 1994) is also good; it is unfortunate that the Office of Government Commerce chose to discontinue it.

The first use of a staged maturity model (predating CMMI) was Nolan (1973). The classic statement on the inherent difficulty of novel system creation is "No Silver Bullet: Essence and Accidents of Software Engineering" in Brooks (1995). For service management, support, and delivery and IT operations in general, see van Bon (2002); van Bon, Kemmerling et al. (2002); and the ITIL library (all Office of Government Commerce citations). For discussion of software maintenance in an ITSM context, see Ruiz, Piattini et al. (2002).

The ITIL *Application Management* volume (Office of Government Commerce 2002a) has material addressing the build–run gap, especially Section 5.1.1, "Aligning Application Development and Service Management." Compelling arguments regarding the insufficiency of ITIL and CMMI to describe application management are raised in ASL Foundation (2005a and 2005b).

For IT service support and operations, see Office of Government Commerce (2000 and 2002b); Sturm, Morris et al. (2000); Kern, Schiesser et al. (2004); and Walker and Harris Kern's Enterprise Computing Institute (2001).

PART II

SUPPORTING THE IT VALUE CHAIN

The customer and partner community is communicating quite clearly…
that what they're looking for is an *integrated family of applications* that
minimize their cost structures going forward.

—Tom Siebel
CEO, Siebel Systems[131]

H AVING COMPLETED AN EXAMINATION of the enterprise IT value chain, let's turn to the question of how to support it in an integrated and comprehensive manner. Currently, IT as a value chain is supported by fragmented data and processes, contained within functional silos, suffering from much redundancy and lack of integrity.

As Roger Burlton notes,

It's one thing to have enterprise information available whenever you want it. It's something else for that information to have integrity. *Integrity* for data management purposes means that, if the information is redundant, it must be consistent…. [This is] key if you want to avoid different people making decisions based on information that varies but that should be the same.[132]

Because of this requirement for data consistency, the architectural analysis then moves to a data model. Enterprise IT can be represented by a comprehensible set of information concepts, which I will detail and then cross-reference to the process model.

The cross-referencing among process, data, and system will be further explored in terms of pattern analysis. If you don't know what a pattern is, read on!

Discussing the large-scale technical enablement of IT immediately brings up the question of other large-scale applications, such as those used by human resources, finance, customer relationship management, and supply chain organizations. The overall term for such applications is "enterprise resource planning," a concept now relevant to IT itself.

Enterprise Resource Planning?

Companies that attempted to install ERP encountered grave difficulties, for they were unprepared for the shifts in jobs and power that focusing on end-to-end processes entailed. Companies that managed their installation in terms of process change rather than software were far more successful.

—Michael Hammer[133]

There are differing representations of what the major enterprise "resources" are, but one reasonable version is the following:

▶ Liquid capital
▶ Fixed (productive) capital
▶ Stock of goods
▶ People

However, as Peter Drucker noted, a distinguishing feature of the 20th century was the emergence of knowledge (information) as a resource to be exploited in and of itself, with emergent properties at scale requiring significant experience, specialization, and infrastructure for support.[134] Hence the emergence of information as a first-class enterprise resource.[135] Treating information in this respect parallels the evolution of other enterprise resources; a small company may not need a dedicated human resources or supply chain system, but as the company grows, the pressures for increasing professionalization of their management grow.

When the $100 million company becomes a $30 billion enterprise with hundreds of distinct systems and thousands of servers, informal understanding becomes impossible.

The same is true of information, albeit at a larger scale: a $100 million company might have an IT organization of a couple dozen staff members, who understand the system architectures through experience. However, when that $100 million company becomes a $500 million or $30 billion firm with hundreds of distinct systems and thousands of servers, informal understanding becomes impossible and the IT capability requires its own management infrastructure, with capabilities analogous to the ERP systems found for other major value chains and functional areas.

The original manufacturing resource planning (MRP) systems focused on core manufacturing functions such as materials management and work planning. Their comprehensive approach expanded and evolved through MRP II and the first-generation ERP systems; ERP, circa 2006, generally means large-scale systems that support multiple large, complex business processes for entire enterprises, processes such as human resource management, manufacturing logistics and supply chain, and financial management, as well as next-generation resource management for customer relationships, intellectual property, and information and its technological infrastructure.

Enterprise Resource Planning for IT?

As I was starting to make sense of what metadata management might mean for an integration competency center, an enterprise architect approached me and asked, "What's the difference between an ITIL configuration management database and a metadata repository"? I pondered this for some time, and then saw (General Motors CIO) Ralph Szygenda's call for "ERP for IT." That gave me the answer—there is no essential difference. They are two attempts at answering the same problems of enterprise IT.

IT as a general organization capability, just like its counterparts in Finance or Human Resources or Manufacturing, has processes and data elements it needs to manage. It manages the definition of process, data, and system architectures; the creation and operation of physical data and software artifacts implementing them; hardware computing platforms supporting those artifacts; and process concepts: change and incident tickets, work orders, services and systems as cooperatively defined with the client, and more. It also manages the human and financial resources necessary to support the IT capability.

If this seems misguided, consider some questions.

The definition of an "entity" would generally be accepted as "metadata." Is the name of the analyst who defined that entity metadata? Many tools can and do store it. What about the project in which the model was created? What about the financials underlying that project? The software quality practices? Were inspections carried out on the data model?

A logical evolutionary step for metadata repositories was to extend their data dictionaries to include the programs that accessed the various data elements. But are the change tickets that put those programs into production metadata? Are incident tickets related to those programs metadata? Is the headcount and budget required to maintain the system in production ongoing?

(continued)

Hence my argument that it's all really just "ERP for IT" (a.k.a. IT resource planning, IT business management, or integrated IT management). The acronym ITRP, for IT resource planning, will be used.

The history of ERP systems is not distinguished.

ERP is used evocatively and provocatively in this book. Reality check: the reputation of real-world ERP systems is not distinguished. There have been widely publicized failures of implementation and acceptance.

Secondarily, ERP systems have a poor technical reputation; earlier versions traced their lineage back to mainframe, flat file–based systems with intricate, proprietary, and obscure architectures. Their monolithic architectures have proved inflexible and costly to upgrade. Such a platform would have serious challenges in supporting internal IT business processes, which depend on complex data structures requiring state-of-the-art infrastructure and are quite varied in their interactions.

However, it clearly has been an advance to have one system covering accounts payable, accounts receivable, payroll, and general ledger, where previously those systems might have been separate and joined by inefficient interfaces.

The major IT process areas produce and consume common data and suffer greatly when no system of record exists.

IT governance presents similar challenges: even thought the track record of ERP systems has not been stellar, there seems little alternative. As will be detailed in the following analysis, the major IT process areas produce and consume common data and suffer greatly when no system of record exists. Unification is the challenge of the day.

Component-based architectures (most recently SOA) are an alternative paradigm, holding the promise of loose coupling and easier interoperability among systems; however, this paradigm is still emerging. Standards-based integration of loosely coupled ITRP systems would be ideal but may be difficult to achieve given the momentum of more traditional enterprise application software approaches and the immaturity of SOA.

DIALOG

Tail Chasing

Chris: I was just talking to one of your consultants and he was recommending we put in place a portfolio management tool. It seems to me that such a tool is an application that will manage applications.

Kelly: Right. It's kind of like metadata, which is data about your data.

Chris: My head is hurting.

Kelly: And one of the services in your service catalog is "service creation and management." It's the service of managing services!

Chris: I guess I shouldn't get too bent out of shape; after all, the Human Resources people have to manage their own staff, and Finance gets a budget for its own operations. But it still seems like a hall of mirrors.

Kelly: Welcome to IT. We're going to talk about the requirements of requirements management, by the way. And don't forget your new Six Sigma initiative. You realize, of course, that the essence of Six Sigma is a process that manages processes?

3

A Supporting Data Architecture

I would not give a fig for the simplicity this side of complexity, but
I would give my life for the simplicity on the other side of complexity.

—Oliver Wendell Holmes[136]

3.1 Metrics: Gateway from Process to Data

AS YOU HAVE SEEN, PROCESS-CENTRIC THINKING is a hallmark of modern business practices.

COBIT, CMM, and ITIL, at their base, are process frameworks. They focus on overall functional capabilities and the sequences of activities (business processes) that *add value for the customer* (internal or external).

The metrics-based management control of processes requires carefully and clearly structured data.

Business processes require optimization, and to optimize them they must be measured. The concept of metrics management is essential to process improvement frameworks such as Six Sigma. Processes are controlled by metrics.

But what is a metric? A metric is a measurement. It is information, not activity—information that *drives* activity.

What is information? Information is actionable, context-relevant data. So, metrics at their base are data.

This brings us nicely to the next major architectural view: data. When architecting systems (defined as combinations of people, process, and technology) the concept of "data" is critical. The frameworks *imply* shared data, but they do not go far in discussing its implications, which are significant.

Processes are controlled by metrics, and metrics are based on data.

In reading the major frameworks as requirements specifications, the need for a consistent data architecture emerges; however, to date the major frameworks have been circumspect about this reality, consigning it to some unspecified other forum (which defaults to the intellectual property of consulting firms or vendor application products).

Trends are always carried to the extreme, and BPM is no exception. One of the unfortunate extremes of BPM thinking (an extreme not represented by its careful thought leaders but evident among some practitioners) is the idea that process is everything and data is nothing, or is some mere technicality whose consideration can be deferred to the developers.

Data has been either absent or, at best, a second-class citizen in much of the IT governance literature and frameworks.

The consequences of this are clear from an enterprise architecture perspective: processes can't be fully optimized, because the "things" that the processes are managing are still unclear to the process stakeholders. In many cases redundancy is the result: two processes may be managing the same thing but calling it by two different names. Or—for example, with the broad ITIL concepts of Configuration Item and Change—different things may be lumped inappropriately together in a given process context.

Without a product-independent data perspective, ITRP and its implementers will be hostage to product vendors.

This is compounded by the current vendor landscape, in which many vendors are selling overlapping products that refer to the same logical concepts with different terminology—sometimes, this appears to be a deliberate strategy to create the illusion of product differentiation where none exists. Without a sound, product-independent data perspective, ITRP and its implementers will be hostage to product vendors.

Of the views this book takes—process and function, data, and system—data is the most precise. Even at the verbal, conceptual level, it provides the basis for system interoperability, business rules, and application design. The data necessary to the domain of IT management is a fascinating topic. It's not impossible, as some seem to feel—the data structures needed to run IT, although tricky in some ways, are comparable in number and complexity to other functional areas.

IT Metrics

Business processes require metrics, and at the most general and abstract the use of metrics to assess and guide process is called "performance management" or "business performance management" (sometimes abbreviated BPM and confused with business process management).

There is no established suite of IT metrics comparable to standard financial measures of corporate performance.

A hierarchical metrics structure is characteristic of performance management and the business intelligence methods supporting it. The hierarchy of metrics may progress from simple operational reporting to complex, derived leading indicators. Such approaches have become well established in many types of business activities, and attention is now turning to measuring IT similarly. Unfortunately, there is no established suite of IT metrics comparable to standard financial measures of corporate performance. This is an area of activity for a number of standards bodies, academics, and other players.[137]

Business intelligence software at its most sophisticated provides robust support for building expressions based on metrics. Before investing in a limited-function service-level management tool, it may be worthwhile considering this as a special case of a business intelligence problem and handle it through standard business intelligence or data warehousing techniques.

Both ITIL and COBIT have extensive coverage of metrics, which this book will not replicate. However, consider a couple of examples from those frameworks.

Example 1: Change Management. ITIL, in the "Change Management" section, calls for tracking the number of Incidents traced to Changes. This implies the existence of separate Incident and Change data entities, which can be joined together and summarized to derive the counts. This is a clear statement of data requirements.

Example 2: Technology Obsolescence. COBIT, in the Acquire and Maintain Technology Infrastructure Control Objective, calls for the metric "# of critical business processes supported by obsolete (or soon to be) infrastructure."[138] This implies the existence of business process and technology entities. The technology entity would require a life cycle state or obsolescence attribute of some kind (implying, in turn, a process for maintaining this information). A good data architect will also question whether business processes should be tied directly to technology platforms or tied first to IT services, which are then dependent on technologies.

This book's data model was derived through just such systematic consideration of ITIL, COBIT, and other industry literature serving as requirements statements.

IT performance measurement is a nontrivial and evolving field; refer to the references and footnotes for discussion of specific IT metrics. The discussion here is focused on the architectural requirements of metrics management generally, including their basis on clean, normalized, well-architected data (an aspect overlooked in most discussions).

Rollups and Dimensions

Most reporting is characterized by a requirement to summarize detailed data along standard hierarchies. In data warehousing, such standard hierarchies are known as "dimensions." In the ITSM and IT governance space, these common dimensions include the following:

- ▶ Organizational hierarchy
- ▶ Organizational and IT strategic goals
- ▶ Application portfolio (rolling up into both the organizational hierarchy and the service-level agreements, or SLAs)
- ▶ Service (in the ITSM sense, if separate from application)
- ▶ Program or project portfolio
- ▶ Data subject areas (hierarchical, not relational)
- ▶ SLAs
- ▶ Enterprise calendar
- ▶ Enterprise operational locations and hierarchy (e.g., District and Region)

Intractable process and political difficulties may emerge in the search for standardized reference data.

Some of these will be well understood by the enterprise's data warehousing group (e.g., calendar and location); others will be new ground. A well-known challenge in data warehousing is "nonconformed dimensions," that is, dimensions that are not in synch across different systems—for example, different calendars in use by different lines of business. Intractable process and political difficulties may emerge in the search for conformance. Generally, the dimensions should be managed by the IT portfolio and architecture processes (preferably with Data Management guidance), and the facts should be managed by the operational processes.

The application portfolio is perhaps the most important and difficult. Organizations may have 10 or more different lists of applications, causing no end of confusion around what IT is doing and who owns it.

The project portfolio can also be a source of pain. As with systems, people tend to refer to projects by myriad imprecise names. What is the system of record for projects? Does every system that references a project do so using an unambiguous project identifier or picklist derived from the system of record? Or is just the project name casually typed in with no check for accuracy?

Another problem is the challenging topic of "slowly changing dimensions." Suppose incidents are rolling up by application portfolio and organizational hierarchy, with trending reports over the years. Then reorganization happens. How should this be handled? There are three approaches, all with pros and cons that need to be understood in depth.[139]

A related matter is the establishment of common IT reference data (generally termed "master data management," or MDM in the industry). Dimension conformance is an issue of MDM, but MDM is somewhat broader in implication (e.g., Server might not be a true dimension, but ensuring that there is an accurate single list is an MDM problem). See Figure 4.26 and the related discussion.

The metrics-based management control of processes requires carefully and clearly structured data.

Generally, the metrics-based management control of processes requires carefully and clearly structured data. This chapter thus turns to a detailed examination of the conceptual data structures involved in IT management.

3.2 A Conceptual Data Model

Data modeling is arguably the most widely used technique in modern systems analysis and design, but it isn't always used well. Too often, technically oriented "modelers" jump straight into excruciating detail, dense jargon, and complex graphics, incomprehensible to process-oriented participants and other mere mortals.

The root problem is a misconception—data modeling has been equated with database design. That's like equating architecture with the drafting of construction blueprints. Of course, the architect's work will eventually lead to precise, detailed blueprints, just as the data modeler's work will eventually lead to precise, detailed database designs, but…it can't start there, or the subject-matter experts will soon mentally "check out." Without their participation, the data model won't be a useful and accurate description of their business. And that's exactly how a data model should be regarded—*not as a database design, but as a description of a business.*

—Alec Sharp[140]

Data Model Discussion

Chris: One thing that has us all puzzled is exactly how the ITRP concepts fit together and work with other non-ITSM concepts. There's a lot of terminology, and it seems like things overlap sometimes. For example, what is the relationship

(continued)

between a Configuration Item and an Asset? Also, some of what ITIL calls for is not exactly how we do business. Do *all* Configuration Items go through our data center change control process? What is the relationship between a Service Request and an Incident? Is a Service a Configuration Item? Is a Service Offering? Are Applications Services?

Kelly: That's why we're going to turn to one of the most important aspects of enterprise architecture: the creation of a conceptual data model.

Chris: A conceptual data model? What good is that? We're probably not going to build anything—we're going to purchase products. Sounds pretty technical.

Kelly: That's why I call it a *conceptual* data model, and yes, it's relevant even if you are purchasing products. There are a lot of vendors out there selling various flavors of IT enablement and IT governance tools, and they have a lot of overlap between their products, often with slightly different terminology.

A conceptual data model is not technical—it's about *clarifying the language* describing our problem domain so that we understand exactly what we mean by a Configuration Item and how it might relate to a Service. And this is something you need to put together independent of the products—because it's going to be your road map that helps you determine *what* products you need.

Chris: Will it help me translate the vendor-speak?

Kelly: Absolutely. One vendor may have a "service catalog entry" and an "order," and another vendor may call the same two things a "template" and a "service instance" In the conceptual data model (also called a "reference model"), they are Service Offering and Service. It doesn't matter what the vendors call them, but you need to understand that any service request management solution should have both concepts. Doing the data model helps us understand our requirements better and communicate them to the vendor.

How do we gain more precision around hard-to-define concepts like Change or Configuration Item.

How do we gain more precision around hard-to-define concepts like Change or Configuration Item? One technique used for many years is an "entity relationship model." Other (not necessarily synonymous) terms used in this general area are "conceptual model," "logical model," "domain model," "ontology," and "class model."

An entity relationship model helps clarify language by relating concepts together in certain ways:

▶ A Configuration Item may have many Changes applied to it, and a Change may be applied to multiple Configuration Items (many to many).

▶ A Machine may be related to one and only one Asset, and an Asset may be related to one and only one Machine (one to one).

▶ A Configuration Item may be a Service, Process, or Application (subtyping).

These relationships are visually represented as shown in Figure 3.1.[141]

Some data modeling methodologists emphasize naming the relationships (typically with a verb phrase such as "is a part of"), but others do not see this as critical, and this book does not systematically do this.[142]

Using these tools, we can start to carefully structure the relationships between the various loosely used terms of IT governance (Figure 3.2).

KEY POINT

Vive La Difference

Your Organization's concepts and terminology will be different. Count on it. This does not make either your Organization or this model right or wrong. The point is to start asking the questions: Why does the model call for two concepts when we use one? One concept where we use two? Do we have any ability to relate concept A to B as the model calls for? Do we need it? Why do we relate X to Y when the model doesn't?

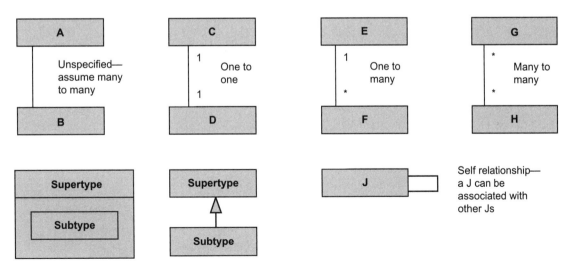

Figure 3.1 Data modeling key.

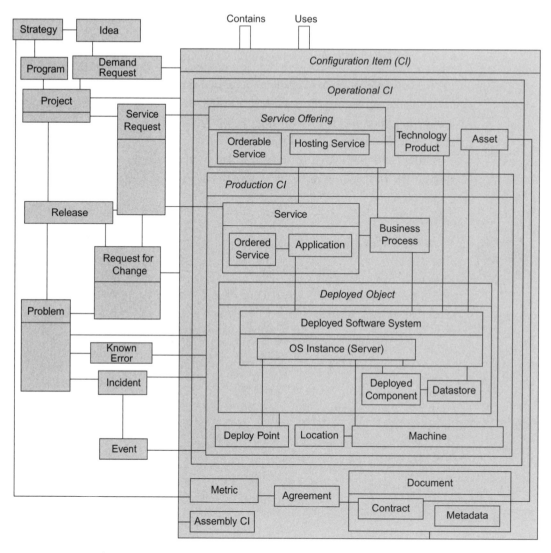

Figure 3.2 IT enablement conceptual model.

Overwhelmed?

If this model looks overwhelming to you, you might want to review the section later in this chapter titled "An Iterative and Incremental Approach to Configuration Data Maturation."

Pictures such as this only tell part of the story. They require a detailed discussion of each box (or entity), what it means, and how to interpret the lines (relationships) to the other boxes.

Figure 3.2 is a conceptual data model. It is primarily about refining language and concepts. The goal of this model is not technical precision but rather resonance with common industry usages, which overlap and are not well delineated. It's an attempt to push common usage toward more rigor and admittedly encounters a number of problems in this effort.

It also deliberately omits a number of details that would be necessary to realize a solution. Attributes obviously are not included (e.g., Serial Number on Machine or Date Signed on Contract). Omitted entities are generally intersection entities and dependent entities that elaborate on the core concepts. Some notes on possible approaches for elaborating this into a full logical data model are covered in the data definitions.

Building a model such as this for an industry that is not yet mature in its process best practices and terminology is challenging. The relationships among entities such as Release, RFC, Service Request, Project, and Configuration Item might have many permutations. This is a reference model, presented as a starting point for your own analysis. Reasonable professionals may come to different conclusions about which entities should be related to which.

This picture, technically speaking, is not the model. *It is only one view on the model.* One characteristic of a good conceptual data model is that its central concepts can be represented with a one-page view; there are always more details to add. Thus, in the subsequent sections other entities will appear, along with relationships not drawn in Figure 3.2.

DIALOG

It's All about the Language

Chris: Wow. What a picture. I'm getting a little glassy eyed.

Kelly: That's OK. Just take it a couple boxes at a time, and here are some useful reminders:

   First, it's all about the language. This picture is a long way from anything we're going to build; it's here to help us understand how our project, incident, change, monitoring, configuration, and service management systems relate.

   Second, there's a trick to reading the lines. Where you see an arrow or a box inside a box you should read it as "is a." For example, an Application *is a* Deployable Object. Where you see a number or star on either end, then you can read it as "has" or "is associated with." For example, an Application *has* Components, or an Asset is *associated* with a Machine.

Chris: That makes it easier. It's still pretty complicated though!

Kelly: Well, let's go through it in some detail.

3.3 IT Process Entities

This section is concerned with the IT entities that are *not* configuration items. Generally, all conceptual entities that are not configuration items can be thought of as "IT process entities."

We start with the first subgrouping, Strategy, and related entities.

Strategy

A Strategy is a top-level organizational direction or guidance toward the overall mission. The term Strategy is used generically here and might include concepts such as mission, goal, and objective detailed into a more concrete framework.

Strategies have two avenues into lower-level IT data: they drive Programs and Projects to implement new functionality, and they require the support of Business Processes to achieve ongoing success. (Notice that for graphical simplicity the Strategy–Business Process and Release–Configuration Item links were not drawn in the main data model in Figure 3.2 and appear as thinner lines. There will be other cases of such omissions.)

Strategies are related to other Strategies (this is the meaning of the "U"-shaped line on the left side of the Strategy entity).

Strategies should be measurable using Metrics; this relationship is critical to the establishment of digital dashboards.

Program

A Program is an ongoing, large-scale organizational commitment and corresponding investment toward meeting a major goal or objective of the enterprise. A Program typically consists of one or more Projects.

Idea

An Idea is an initial, typically business-generated, opportunity for IT services. It is minimally qualified.

Demand Request

An Idea becomes a Demand Request after going through some form of IT assessment for sizing or capacity impacts and preliminary feasibility. A Demand Request is a fully qualified request for an IT service change, awaiting full funding authorization to become a Project.

Project

A Project is a defined set of manageable activities to achieve a well-specified mission (e.g., Demand Request fulfillment), usually represented by some set of deliverables or enumerated changes, with explicitly allocated resources (time, money, staff), executed and measured within the scope of those resources. A Project has one or more Releases (see the "Release" section). Projects in many cases are constrained to a fiscal year. A Project should always be associated to a Demand Request.

Projects may be non-IT (e.g., construction projects), but that usage is out of scope for this book.

A Project before it is approved may be considered a Demand Request.

Projects relate to Configuration Items either directly or (more rigorously) through defined, named Releases. This ambiguity can be seen in Figure 3.3.

Projects may be grouped into larger Programs (not represented in the model). A Program is an ongoing, large-scale organizational commitment and corresponding investment toward meeting a major goal or objective of the enterprise. A Program typically consists of one or more Projects.

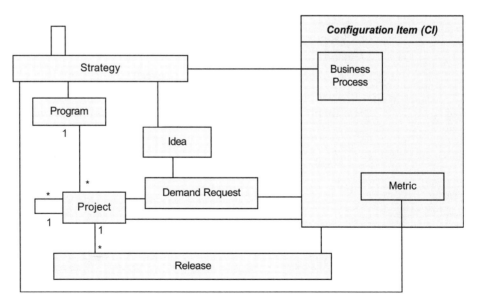

Figure 3.3 Strategy and related entities.

Strategy–Program–Project versus Idea–Demand

The model graphically depicts two competing paradigms: one from the top down, the other from the bottom up. A traditional top-down IT planning model would state that Strategy drives Program drives Project. However (especially when executed using an annual time frame), this is not an agile method for responsive IT. An event-driven, business-responsive demand process is also necessary. Aligning these two paradigms will be a different exercise for every organization; commonly, Demand Requests are evaluated against the annual strategy baseline.

(Request for) Change

A Change is a work order or authorization to alter the state of some Configuration Item.

A Change is an authorization to alter the state of some Configuration Item. ITIL defines Change as follows:

The addition, modification or removal of approved, supported or baselined hardware, network, software, application, environment, system, desktop build or associated documentation.

It defines request for change (RFC) as follows:

Form, or screen, used to record details of a request for a Change to any CI within an infrastructure or to procedures and items associated with the infrastructure.[143]

There is much additional discussion of Change in ITIL. However, the scope of Change in this framework is somewhat more limited; business-driven RFCs are Demand Requests.

This model does not distinguish between Changes and RFCs. However, an operational configuration management tool may detect unapproved Changes for which there are no RFCs; these can be considered Events and potentially Incidents.

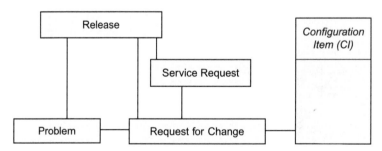

Figure 3.4 Change and Release context.

Change as Transaction

On a more architectural level, Changes can be analyzed using principles of transaction processing as a useful metaphor.[144] Changes, like transactional logical units of work, should have the following characteristics:

▶ Atomic
▶ Consistent
▶ Isolated
▶ Durable

In the context of enterprise IT, an *atomic* Change is "all or nothing"; either the Change is successfully applied or it is rolled back completely. If a Change has some part that would be rolled back and another part would stay, it should be framed as two Changes. ITIL does allow "partial rollback" but clearly indicates this is not preferred.[145]

A *consistent* Change means that the change, when deployed, leaves the item in a stable state. Characteristics no longer needed by the new version of the item should be removed as part of the change. New functionality should integrate seamlessly with the previous functionality without an undesired or unexpected effect. Any temporary states during the Change that deviate from normal practice are removed (e.g., temporary copies or parallel execution).

An *isolated* Change means (in theory) that it can go in without affecting other changes or item functionality, and is not affected by other concurrent changes. This would be hard to achieve in all cases but is nevertheless something to strive for. Achieving logical isolation of Changes is a goal for an integrated Release and Change Management process.

A *durable* Change is one that, once executed, is stable and permanent. For example, all instances of the new software in all deployment locations persist, and older software is not inadvertently reinstalled (e.g., during a system restoration process). This example requires attention to the Definitive Software Library.

Change–Configuration Item

This is perhaps the most important relationship in all of ITSM. Simply, a Change by definition affects configuration items (CIs), and CIs are objects under change control. This is far simpler to state and to model than to execute in the real world. A naïve approach to implementing this concept will result in unmanageable data. Clearly, it is not optimal for a Change record to have to be related to 1500 individual

CIs, yet this is what a simplistic approach will arrive at (e.g., in putting in an initial release of a software package with many separate binary assets).

Whether or not to inventory all binary software components in the CMDB is an important decision.

There are various techniques for mitigating and simplifying this, mostly involving encapsulation and abstraction. If a logical Application CI is defined, for example, it can be presumed to include all lower-level physical binary Components. Whether or not to inventory those binaries in the CMDB is one of the most critical decisions the ITSM implementer faces. For high security organizations this may be done, but it is questionable whether lower-criticality information systems organizations truly require it, especially in a world of purchased software where the physical architecture of a software product is less and less of a concern for the package vendor's customers.

Alternatively, the concept of assembly CI (which is also a CI) can be used. An Application plus its Datastores and Deploy Points might be a logical assembly CI. This is where the issue of Logical versus Physical CI comes in, pointing up the importance of having a defined process for maintaining logical Applications and related assembly CIs. It is *not recommended* to allow individuals the ability to create high-visibility logical CIs; this results in a chaotic environment. Everyone must *agree* that there is one Application (e.g., Quadrex), composed of, for example, these 50 Components.

Change–Service Request

Changes may require a Service Request to implement, for example, if database administration services are part of the service catalog and the addition of a new table is handled as a Service Request. This will depend on the maturity of the IT organization.

Change–Release

Changes are tied to Releases. In this framework, a Release is typically associated with a Project and results in one or more RFCs to add or alter CIs for a given IT service.

Production Change and the Software Development Life Cycle

RFCs in this architecture, and the concept of Change generally, are not applied to project deliverables. This is in keeping with the ITIL philosophy that "changes to any components that are under the control of an applications development project—for example, applications software, documentation or procedures—do not come under Change Management but would be subject to project Change Management procedures…. [The] Change Management process manages Changes to the day-to-day operation of the business. It is no substitute for the organisation-wide use of methods…to manage and control projects."[146] While the project change management concepts are similar, they are managed in a project context that is quite different from production operations and out of scope for this book because they are extensively covered in the project management literature.

Release

Release is the gateway from the software development life cycle into the ITSM world.

In this framework, a Release is the gateway from the software development life cycle into the ITSM world. It is one of the most important concepts for which to develop an enterprise approach. A Release is (if narrowly defined) a distinct package of new or changed functionality deployed to production, usually enabling new capabilities and/or addressing known Problems.

ITIL says "a Release should be under Change Management and may consist of any combination of hardware, software, firmware and document CIs.... The term 'Release' is used to describe a collection of authorised Changes to an IT service."[147]

Releases, like Changes, should be transactional, although their larger grain makes this more challenging.

The concept of assembly CI may be helpful in supporting a Release's various elements. However, some consider a Release to primarily be a dependent entity of an Application.

Note that release management as an overall capability includes planning and harmonizing all Releases in the environment, not just managing Releases for an individual Project or Program (the enterprise release managers should interface with the program or project release managers).

Project–Release

The relationship between Project and Release can work two ways: a Project may have several (smaller-grained) Releases, and a large-grained enterprise Release may coordinate across multiple Projects. This flexibility of interpretation, coupled with narrower and broader scopes for Release, make it a particularly difficult concept from a conceptual modeling perspective.

Change–Release

A Release may have a number of Changes associated with it, but a Change should be "owned by" only one Release. That is to say, two different Releases should not be cited as justification for one Change. (See the "Justify Change" pattern in Chapter 5.)

A Release usually affects multiple CIs; however, CIs can be grouped, as with the assembly CI.

Project, Release, and Change

The ITIL conception of the relationship between Project, Release, and Change is presented in Figure 3.5.

In ITIL terms, an RFC precedes the establishment of a Project.

Note that in ITIL terms, an RFC precedes the establishment of a Project, in theory.[148] The Release might also result in smaller-grained RFCs for change control (e.g., actual physical deployments); thus, there is a conceptual difficulty in distinguishing Change granularity, which ITIL calls out as a risk[149] but does not present a systematic framework for resolving.

This may be problematic in terms of language and culture for organizations with a strong tradition of change control, possibly including a function named Change Management. They will not want their process (and system) "contaminated" with RFCs more focused on Project initiation; a forward schedule of change is as far as they may wish to go.

An alternate view is presented in Figure 3.6.

The controversy is primarily linguistic. The ITIL intent behind front-loading the RFC is presumably so that it is suitably assessed by all stakeholders. This is also the objective of the demand and portfolio management processes (as well as the function of enterprise architecture), and there is arguably more maturity in their conceptions of how to do this.[150]

Whether you subscribe to the ITIL view or this book's framework, these issues should be clarified in any large IT organization.[151]

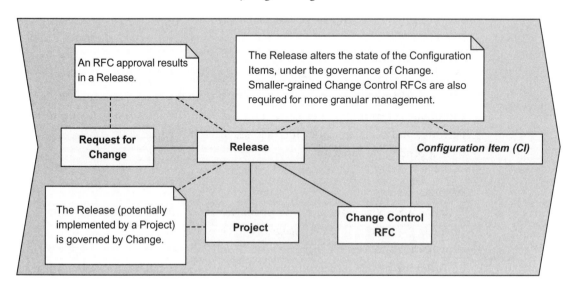

Figure 3.5 ITIL representation of RFC, Project, and Release.

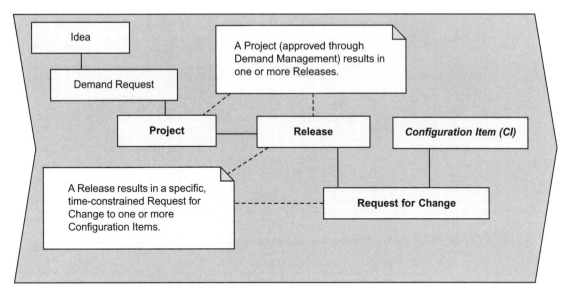

Figure 3.6 Alternate representation of RFC, Project, and Release.

Event

Events are the raw material of Metrics, which in turn drive Agreements and Contracts.

An Event is raw material. It is any operational signal emitted by any Production CI. Only a small fraction of Events are meaningful to ITSM, and an even smaller fraction result in Incidents. Events are one basis for Metrics, which in turn drive Agreements and Contracts.

One important type of Event is emitted by change control and detection systems, and that is the identification of physical change. This Event specifically indicates that for a given CI a state change has occurred that is of management interest. Change Events may be generated automatically by the CI in question or detected by active probing (e.g., tools such as Tripwire that compare the current state with a known baseline). The most sophisticated IT operations reconcile such change detection Events with the RFC process.

ITIL implies that an Event is equivalent to an automatically detected Incident.[152] Anyone who has experienced an autogenerated "ticket storm" will know that this definition is not suitable—most Events are not Incidents; extensive and well-architected correlation and filtering are required.

Of course, in the broadest sense, an Event can apply to any entity undergoing a state change of any kind. In this sense, a Contract might "raise" a logical Event when it expires. However, this is so broad that it's not a focus of this model.[153]

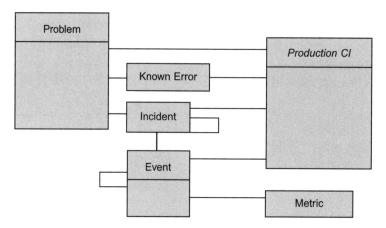

Figure 3.7 Event, Incident, Problem, and Known Error context.

Note that Events can be related to both discrete physical CIs, such as Servers and Datastores, and to logical Services. This is characteristic of monitoring correlation architectures, business service management (BSM) and end-to-end transaction monitoring. Rather than monitoring an individual, granular CI, the major Event of interest is an aggregation or derivation of multiple internal Events within the Service (e.g., expressed as overall transaction response time or customer-visible service failure).

Events are also indicators of capacity consumption and support measurements for that purpose: hardware utilization, memory, transactions, and so forth. Financial chargeback may depend on event management.

Advanced IT providers and infrastructure systems are starting to work with statistical analysis of Events, for example, to determine whether a certain repeated Problem has an identifiable Event signature that may help resolve it. This gets into cutting-edge research into pattern detection across large data sets, related to data mining.

A best practice for all operational Events is the embedding of an appropriate CI identifier. By definition, an Event must have had a CI that emitted it—it cannot arise out of the ether. This reinforces the case for managing unique and *terse* CI naming conventions, because many Event data structures will not be able to support long identifiers. See the "Application ID and Alias" pattern in Chapter 5.

The change Event is discussed further in the "Configuration Management" section in Chapter 4.

Incident

ITIL defines Incident as "any event which is not part of the standard operation of a service and which causes, or may cause, an interruption to, or a reduction in, the quality of that service."[154] ITIL also states that a Service Request is a type of Incident, which seems perverse. (A Service Request is not an interruption unless you are trying to build a culture of hostile customer service!) This line of thinking is not supported here.

Incidents are independent of their mode of detection.

Service requests may be tied to Incidents through the CI against which the Incident is reported. In this interpretation, Incidents are independent of their mode of detection; this is necessary to support Incidents that may be reported or derived through enterprise monitoring without ever being reported through the centralized service desk.

An Incident has to be experienced. It is an occurrence. This distinguishes it from the Known Error concept used for knowledge management for the help/service desk (an error being a known condition in the abstract).

A Service Request may occur in response to an Incident. Incidents (especially when generated from monitoring tools) often require correlation and root cause analysis, which are supported through the relationship of Incidents and Events to each other.

Change–Incident

A Change may be in response to an Incident, without going through the more formal and heavyweight Release process. Alternatively, an Incident might be the result of a poorly executed Change. This means that the relationship between Change and Incident should probably have a type attribute so that it is clear which caused which (see the section on intersection entities later in this chapter).

Problem and Known Error

In ITIL, a Problem is "the *unknown* underlying cause of one or more Incidents," and a Known Error is "a Problem that is successfully diagnosed and for which a Work-around is known."[155]

However, this leaves a hole for Problems with known underlying causes that nevertheless have no workaround, so the ITIL specification won't do as a data definition. The definition here is that a Problem is generally a (known or unknown) root cause of many Incidents, although in the current model it is possible for an Incident to be caused by several Problems.

ITIL further states, "A Problem can result in multiple Incidents, and it is possible that the Problem will not be diagnosed until several Incidents have occurred, over a period of time. Handling Problems is quite different from handling Incidents and is therefore covered by the Problem Management process."[156]

A Known Error is a knowledge management hook—it is an entity that can house the known resolution techniques for a given Problem.

Problem–Release and Problem–RFC

Problems may be addressed by Releases, which might solve multiple Problems. An individual Problem might also be addressed by one or several RFCs. One possible approach is to say that Problems are generally handled by Releases (using demand management), and Incidents are handled directly by RFCs (when called for). Ideally, an RFC should be able to reference both Incidents (tactical) and Problems (longer term). This will depend on the capabilities of incident management and its degree of integration with Problem and Change.[157]

Service Request

Problems may be addressed by Releases, which might solve multiple Problems.

A Service Request is a logged interaction between an individual and the service desk that requires follow-up. Service requests may have various types, such as the following:

▶ Hardware or software request
▶ Incident report (i.e., the request is "resolve this incident")
▶ Configuration change request (the Service Request is the actual work request, not the authorization request)
▶ Security request

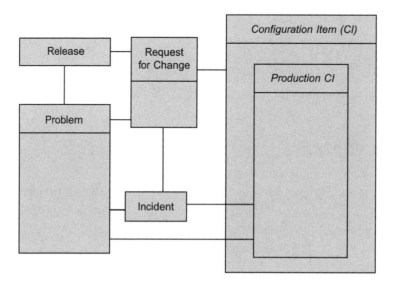

Figure 3.8 Problem, Release, and RFC context.

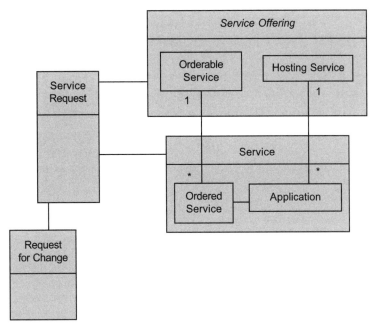

Figure 3.9 Service Request context.

Incoherent ITIL

The ITIL definition of Service Request is "every Incident not being a failure in the IT infrastructure."

The definition of Incident is "any event that is not part of the standard operation of a service and that causes, or may cause, an interruption to, or a reduction in, the quality of that service."[158]

Translation: *A Service Request is, or may be, an interruption.*

This is incoherent at best and perverse at worst. Service requests are part of normal operations. They are not interruptions.

RFCs might be seen as more closely related to Incidents, because these do pose a risk. However, changing systems is in a larger sense part of standard value chain activities, as opposed to true Incidents, which are usually understood to be unforeseen.

A critical distinction is that between Service Request and Project initiation. The service management architects will need to pay close attention to the differences among Service Offerings that may be straightforward products, Service Offerings that are more open ended (analogous to professional services or consulting), and work requests that should not be framed as Service Requests but should be routed to demand management. Alternatively, the architects might view a Demand Request as a type of Service Request and drive to a more generalized approach (the "single pane of glass" philosophy).

See the "Clarify Service Entry Points" pattern in Chapter 5.

A Service Request is not a CI. It has a defined life cycle and typically figures in only one Business Process—its own fulfillment.

Service Request–Service Offering

A common relationship pattern is that Service Requests turn Service Offerings into Services.

Service Request–Service

A Service Request may occur with respect to an already-delivered Service. See the discussion later in this chapter.

Risk

When a resource becomes essential to competition but inconsequential to strategy, the risks it creates become more important than the advantages it provides.

—Nicholas Carr[159]

A Risk is a known possibility of adverse events, usually described by 1) likelihood of happening and 2) cost of occurrence. Risks are best seen as directly applying to CIs; a deficiency of modern risk management software is that it is often designed in a vacuum, with the risk management team entering their own representations of CIs,

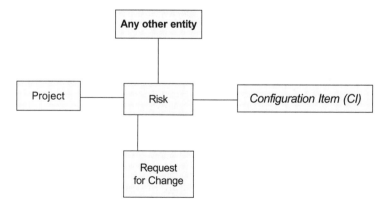

Figure 3.10 Risk context.

such as Application and Process, and not looking to a common system of record for this reference data. See the CMDB-based risk management pattern in Chapter 5.

Risk Relationships

Risks may theoretically be associated with virtually any entity in the model, but the primary targets should be CIs, Projects, and Change requests.

Account and Cost

An Account is a financial construct. According to Wikipedia, it is "a record of an amount of money owned or owed by or to a particular person or entity, or allocated to a particular purpose."[160] Other terms are "cost center" and "charge code."

The relationships of Account were not included in the main data model because of graphical complexity issues. Account is typically tied to a number of different entities, depending on the financial management approach being used (Figure 3.11).

Account might also be tied to any arbitrary CI, but this can imply considerable complexity.

Cost is an attribute, not an entity, and therefore does not appear in the conceptual model. Cost might be an attribute on any of the entities surrounding Account in Figure 3.11 and others (e.g., lower-level entities supporting Service, such as Application or database). A CMDB technically might allow any entity (not

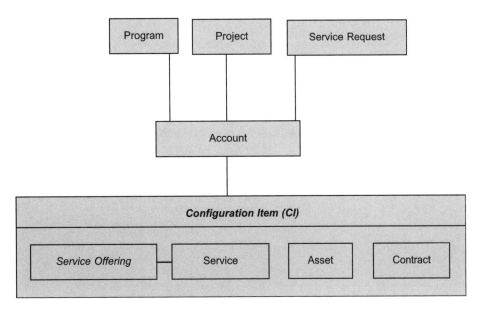

Figure 3.11 IT accounting relationships.

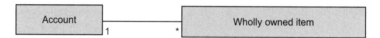

Figure 3.12 Account and wholly owned item.

just CIs as defined in this book) to have an associated cost, and determining which CIs might appropriately have a cost would be an important implementation task.

One common issue is allocation. If a given entity instance is related to one and only one Account, it "rolls up" and financial management is simpler—the account holders know that they bought the whole item. This is represented as a one-to-many relationship (Figure 3.12).

However, if the costs for a given IT item are to be split across multiple accounts, it turns the relationship into many to many, requiring resolution with a specific allocation percentage (Figure 3.13).

Attributes

Percentage, the first attribute, has appeared. This book does not go into much detail about attributes.

For example, if a network Service is shared across several accounts, a percentage allocation must be established for each Account (Figure 3.14).

Direct versus allocated (or indirect) costs are a substantial management challenge in IT. The desire for financial visibility runs into the issue of "dollars chasing

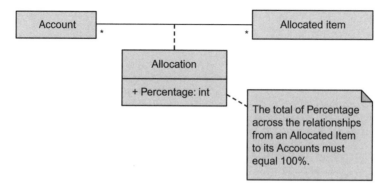

Figure 3.13 Model for allocating across accounts.

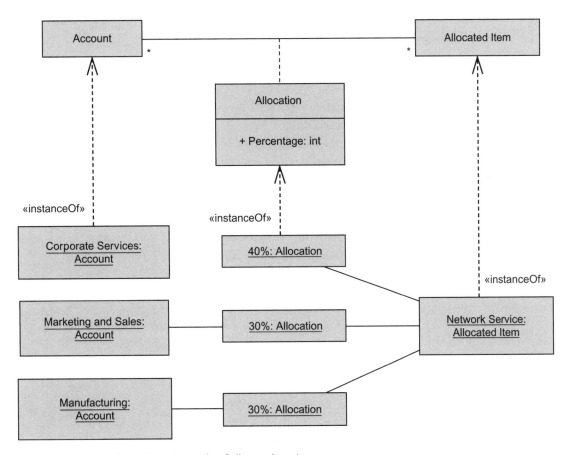

Figure 3.14 Example of allocated service.

dimes": the costs of managing the direct allocations outweigh the benefits in having granular visibility. In ITIL's words, the risk is that "the IT Accounting and Charging processes are so elaborate that the cost of the system exceeds the value of the information produced."[161] This book takes no position on what is an appropriate level of complexity but rather seeks to describe the general case capabilities needed to support a variety of approaches—one thing architects can be sure of is that requirements will change.

As Jeff Kaplan notes,

Each IT service component (development, integration, help desk, network management, data center operations, maintenance, etc.) has a unit cost. Unit cost is the cost of providing one unit of service at predetermined service levels. Examples include cost per call, cost per connection, and so on. The specific units used are less important than is measuring each service's variance from the standard cost. Using cost accounting, organizations should set a standard cost per unit for each service and project, based on the expected cost of providing an incremental unit of service.[162]

This passage, although informative, requires some thought to interpret as a requirements specification. First, the distinction between orderable and nonorderable services becomes important. A nonorderable service by definition has a large fixed cost that can be allocated arbitrarily against a user base, but doing so might not be advisable. For example, consider an investment in a high-capacity customer-facing online order system. This system must be kept running regardless of workload, and the marginal cost for heavy use as opposed to no use may be negligible. In naïve chargeback models, cost to the customer will vary *inversely* with usage, and this does not help IT credibility. (Even worse is when a unit's cost goes up—with stable consumption—because another unit has *decreased* its consumption.)

The concept of activity-based costing is a significant departure from older costing approaches. This book's interpretation of activity-based costing requirements applied to IT is that a concept of the business transaction is needed (this is the true "activity").

Role Management

The human organization will be more fluid than the core ITSM and meta-data concepts.

The core data model has no Roles or people in it. *This is deliberate.* Organizational approaches to managing the processes and their data will vary, titles will change, and in general the human organization will be more fluid than the core ITSM and meta-data concepts. Therefore, the Role structure is generalized; Parties (people or groups composed of other parties) have Roles with respect to any entity in the model.

Party, Person, and Group

A Party is either a group or a person, people are members of groups, and groups can contain other groups. The following are all Parties:

▶ Oracle Incorporated
▶ Bill Smith
▶ Support group APPL-2-CNS
▶ IT Service Management Forum

Party is a controversial concept in data modeling, because business users do not understand it. They understand concepts like "administrator" or "steward." However, these are *Roles*. (These are well-understood issues in data modeling.)

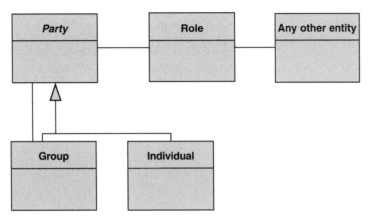

Figure 3.15 Role model.

Roles

Here are some example Role types and the entities they might interact with. Note that ITIL and other industry sources, such as the Enterprise Computing Institute, go into some depth about this, so this section doesn't include an exhaustive survey.

Role	Entity	Notes
Requester	Service request (as related to Service Offering or Service)	A requester can request a new instance of a Service Offering (which becomes a new service) or can request a Change to an existing Service.
Support group	Usually Application	A support group would usually be a group associated with one or more Applications. Sometimes, a support group might be associated with a Technology Product (e.g., a Windows Engineering group).
Developer	Project (preferably related to Release and Application)	A developer carries known expertise on a given system. For any Application, a complete record of all developers (especially at the senior level) who worked on it is recommended. To provide value, this list might be sorted by hours worked on the system; those who spent the most time on the system would be of highest interest. Other software development roles (e.g., architect, tester, and analysis) could be handled analogously.

(continued)

Role	Entity	Notes
Release manager	Project, Release, Change	A release manager is responsible for coordinating the output of a project into releases to be accepted into production.
Change coordinator	Change	A change coordinator is responsible for the successful execution of one or more Changes. They may be part of a specific capability team or part of an enterprise change team.
Operational change approval group	Operational CIs	An operational change approval group is often seen as a dynamic entity, composed of representatives from the support groups associated with the CIs in question, as well as overall change coordination from a central enterprise group. Often, the change approval group may have standing representation from major technology product areas (e.g., Unix engineering or network engineering) or other operational capabilities (e.g., security).

Here is a common Role type that may be problematic:

Change Advisory Board	Any CI	ITIL calls for a unitary Change Advisory Board, admitting that the composition of that group may vary even within a single meeting.[163] However, different CIs may have radically different stakeholders. For example, if a Contract is a CI, it should be under change control, but the change approvers would be the senior IT executives, the contract office, and legal—your engineers would not be involved. The concept of a Change Advisory Board becomes so general that its usefulness is questionable. The better understood use of change approver is with respect to Production CIs. See the "Clarify Service Entry Points" pattern in Chapter 5 and related discussions throughout.

Support roles for a Service (e.g., an Application) may be ordered, which requires an escalation path (Figure 3.16).

Escalation paths may be of several types, typically functional and hierarchical; a functional escalation path is, for example, from level 1 to level 2 to level 3 support, and a hierarchical escalation path might walk the organization chart from application manager to director to vice president. Specialized escalation paths to technical subject matter experts (e.g., database administrators and senior software engineers) may also exist; alternately, the escalation path may become a tree with decision points and not just a linear progression.

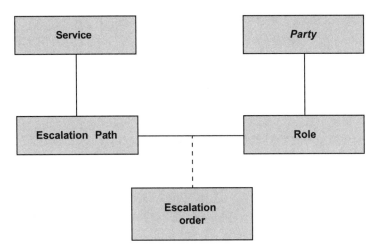

Figure 3.16 Escalation.

Figure 3.17 Classification taxonomy.

Classification

Taxonomies are used extensively in IT information management, for the same reasons they are used in science and other fields requiring knowledge management. A hierarchical tree structure is an intuitive and effective way to manage complexity. Typical taxonomies encountered in internal IT systems are functional decompositions, data subject hierarchies, application and technology categorizations, and so forth. There are commercial providers of taxonomies.

There is overlap between this entity and other treelike structures. The differentiation is that a classification taxonomy is merely a lightweight conceptual structure. Each node is of the same basic type. One does not typically establish dependencies between the taxonomy nodes or assign extensive attributes to them.

A valuable use of the taxonomy concept is to identify overlap or redundancy, for example, in an application portfolio. See the "Taxonomy-Based Rationalization" pattern in Chapter 5.

3.4 The Configuration Item and Its Subtypes

The Base Technology Stack

Before discussing the particulars of the CI and its subtypes, some discussion of the general IT stack is called for.

The concept of a "stack" has a long history in information technology, perhaps originating with the OSI networking model. In ITSM, an extended stack is often depicted something like the one shown in Figure 3.18.

Figure 3.18 shows a stylized representation of concepts present in much ITSM literature, advertising, and so on. One thing that all of these concepts have in common is that they may be seen as CIs.

> A CI is a managed, specific object or element in the IT environment. It is one of the most problematic concepts in IT governance.

CI is one of the most necessary yet problematic concepts in IT governance. It is highly abstract: any managed "thing" in the environment, from an individual computer chip to an entire mainframe, can be a CI. This high level of generality makes the concept difficult to manage from the perspectives of process, data, and Application.

The ITIL definition of CI is as follows:

[A CI is a] Component of an infrastructure—or an item, such as a Request for Change, associated with an infrastructure—that is (or is to be) under the control of configuration management. CIs may vary widely in complexity, size, and type, from an entire system (including all hardware, software, and documentation) to a single module or a minor hardware component.[164]

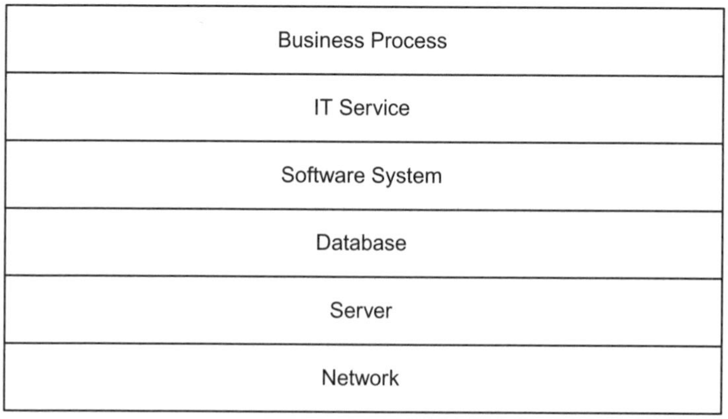

Business Process
IT Service
Software System
Database
Server
Network

Figure 3.18 The generic IT stack.

The preceding sentences are imprecise from a data management point of view. Essentially, a CI as it is viewed by ITIL could be construed as *any piece of data representing any IT concept.* The phrase "item, such as a Request for Change, associated with…" extends the CI concept unmanageably—every data element in the IT problem domain becomes a CI. There is then a paradox: if an RFC is a CI, and a CI by definition is under change management, that means the RFC requires an RFC requires an RFC, and so forth.

Here is the ITIL specification as it describes the interrelationships of CIs:

Configuration structures should describe the relationship and position of CIs in each structure.… CIs should be selected by applying a decomposition process to the top-level item using guidance criteria for the selection of CIs. A CI can exist as part of any number of different CIs or CI sets at the same time.… The CI level chosen depends on the business and service requirements.

Although a "child" CI should be "owned" by one "parent" CI, it can be "used by" any number of other CIs.…

Components should be classified into CI types.… Typical CI types are: software products, business systems, system software.… The life-cycle states for each CI type should also be defined; e.g., an application Release may be registered, accepted, installed, or withdrawn.…

The relationships between CIs should be stored so as to provide dependency information. For example,…a CI is a part of another CI…a CI is connected to another CI…a CI uses another CI.…[165]

This is again highly general. One issue in the industry is that some vendors have interpreted this specification to allow their customers too much freedom in defining CIs and their relationships. In some tools, a Server might be "a part of" a random access memory (RAM) chip; a printer might be "connected to" an extensible markup language (XML) schema—connections that obviously do not make logical sense.

More rigor is necessary. This analysis refines the ITIL representation and makes it more specific by applying data modeling (metamodeling) principles.

▶ For this book, a CI is a managed, specific object or element in the IT environment.

▶ A CI by definition is under change control *of some form.*

▶ Typically, a CI also has an indeterminate life cycle, unlike a Project, Service Request, or Incident; these are *events* and defined and tracked partly in terms of their closure.

Every data element in the IT problem domain becomes a CI.

A CI typically has an indeterminate life cycle, unlike a Project, Service Request or Incident; these are defined and tracked partly in terms of their closure.

- ► CIs are not instances of activities, although an activity definition may be a CI. They are real, not abstract.
- ► CIs typically also participate in multiple IT processes. If something is relevant only to one IT process, it is probably not a CI.

Applying the preceding principles means that certain things are not CIs, such as the following:

- ► Strategies, Programs, Ideas, Demand Requests, and Projects (Projects may have multiple CIs within them, but they themselves are not CIs)
- ► Events
- ► Incidents and Problems
- ► Requests for Change
- ► Service *Requests* (but a Service *Offering* is a CI)
- ► Data records in databases and files generally; they are under the "change control" of the accessing Application
- ► CI *records* (the representation is not the object); however, see the discussion of the Metadata CI type

This architecture proposes three major categories of CIs: base, Operational, and Production.

CIs should always be specific. "Oracle Financials," if present in the environment, would be a logical CI, containing and using many physical CIs (e.g., software Components and Datastores). A Generic "Human Resource Management Application" as a reference category would not be a CI.

CIs have subtypes, and those subtypes in turn can have subtypes. Figure 3.19 shows one representation.

The major types of CIs are as follows:

Servers and Applications can have Incidents and Known Errors—but can a Contract?

- ► (Base) CI
- ► Operational CI
- ► Production CI

They are "nested" (Figure 3.20).

This means that an Operational CI is also a base CI and a Production CI is also an Operational CI and a base CI.

Subtyping is often overapplied. An important reason to subtype (in conceptual modeling) is if a subtype can have a relationship that the parent does not participate in. Figure 3.21 shows this clearly: a Change can apply to any CI or subtype, a measurement can apply to an Operational CI or a Production CI, and an Event can only be associated with a Production CI.

Again, can a Contract have an Incident?

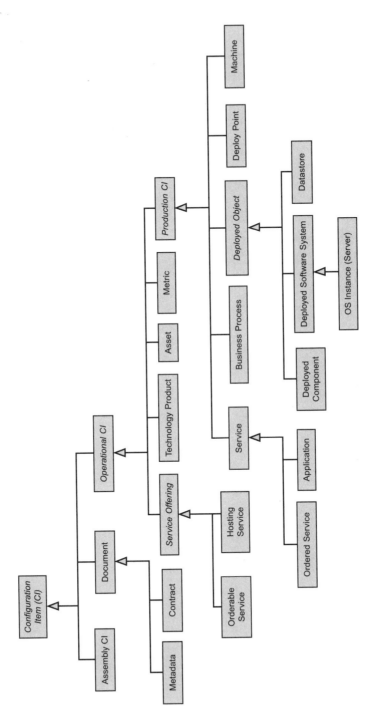

Figure 3.19 Detailed CI taxonomy.

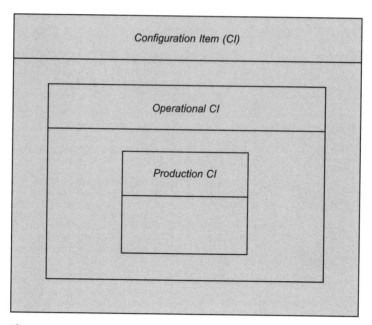

Figure 3.20 CI subtypes.

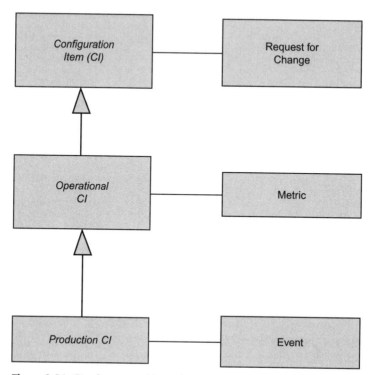

Figure 3.21 CI subtypes and key relationships.

Table 3.1 Logical versus Physical CIs

Logical CI	Physical CI
Application	Component
Process	Datastore
Service	Deploy point
Technology	Document

Logical and Physical Configuration Items

Applications, Processes, and Services in the service catalog–sense are logical CIs. Machines, Components, files, and network-addressable Web services are physical CIs.

CIs can be logical or physical. From the top down versus from the bottom up is another way to think of this distinction: logical are from the top down, physical are from the bottom up.

Physical in this case means no ambiguity about the boundaries of the CI (even if it is only transient bits on volatile storage). Logical means that some consensus is required to set the bounds of the CI.

Applications (especially those built in-house), Processes, and Services in the service catalog sense are the best examples of logical CIs. Machines, Components, files, and network-addressable Web services are physical CIs. Managing logical CIs is challenging and requires a clearly defined process to establish the bounds of this potentially blurry "thing."

Discussion of Logical Applications

Chris: What's the big deal with applications and how they're "logical"? You've been harping on that all day.

Kelly: I found a diagram in some of your system literature.

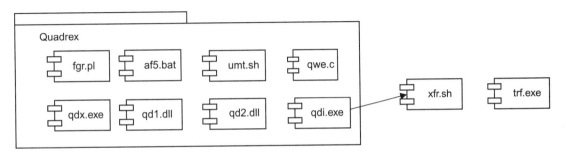

Figure 3.22 Application and boundaries.

It's the perfect example. Those little boxes with "dog ears" are a standard representation (from UML) of software Components. Notice how they are named—that's what you would see on the Servers supporting the application. The functionality as a whole is named Quadrex; that's how you refer to it in meetings and in the halls—but there is no such thing as far as your computers are concerned.

One question: Is "xfr.sh" part of the application? The Quadrex team told me that it's an extract job for data going to the TSI system. The TSI team told me they don't think they support it. Who does? Most organizations have such "gray area" questions, and clarifying the application portfolio's ownership can help reduce the risk of finger-pointing and ineffective response to service outages.

The Base Configuration Item

The next set of definitions focuses on the base CIs, as shown in Figure 3.23.

The base CI is the master category that all CIs belong to. It is any "thing" in the IT environment that requires management (usually defined as being under change control of some sort).

CIs have differing levels of involvement in day-to-day service management and production processes. The base CI includes documentation and the definitions of

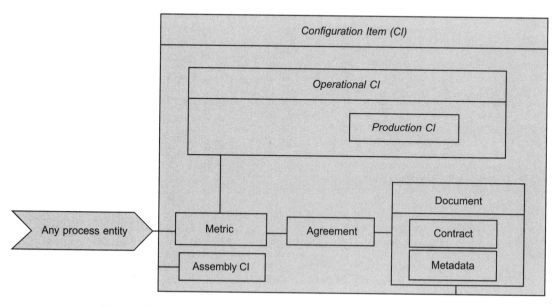

Figure 3.23 Base CIs and relationships.

service-level measurements, objectives, and agreements. Any type of CI may be involved in an RFC.

Change control for items that are not Production CIs (not operational or production) may or may not be formalized. For example, the service management group may define Service Offerings, or the asset management group may add new Assets, without going through the highest-formality change control processes reserved for Production CIs.

An Operational CI is distinguished from the other base CI types as something that is involved in day-to-day Business Processes, that can be measured, and that is a primary entity in the service management workflow.

A Production CI refines the concept of Operational CI to include the core CIs that may be involved in Incidents and have Known Errors. (Think data center, or production workstation.) Change control for Production CIs is usually a formal, high-visibility process that is what many enterprise IT people think of when referring to "the change process."

An Operational CI is something that is involved in day-to-day business processes, that can be measured, and that is a primary entity in the service management workflow.

DIALOG

Why Several Categories of CI?

Chris: So, I'm seeing that a Document is a CI—OK. And an Operational CI is a CI? What do the italics in the diagram mean?

Kelly: The italics mean that something can't *only* be an Operational CI or a CI itself. It has to be something *under* the box with italics: in this case, a Service Offering, Technology Product, Asset, or something under Production CI.

Chris: Why do we bother with these detailed types anyway?

Kelly: It's all about being precise. Suppose that we just had one category of CI that included Documents, Service Offerings, and Contracts, as well as Servers and Applications. Servers and Applications can have Incidents and Known Errors—but can a Contract? Not really. This is fundamental information modeling; people can spend their whole careers specializing in describing data structures precisely. Without this precision, your CMDB is at risk.

Assembly CI

CIs require grouping for various reasons, such as supporting a Release, a Service map, or a Service Request. The assembly CI leverages the "owns" and "participates" relationships to support this.

Document

SLAs, underpinning contracts and OLAs…should be brought under Change Management control….

—ITIL[166]

A Document may be a CI if its existence and content are significant enough to IT service delivery to warrant formal change control. It may apply to any CI or CIs, and any CI may have multiple Documents. There are of course many other types of Documents, and not all are under change control (which means they are not CIs). Another class of Documents that are usually under change control is the class of project Documents. However, this change control is usually at the project level, and ITIL specifically avoids discussing it.

Important types of Documents (not modeled) are Requests for Information (RFIs) and Requests for Proposal (RFPs).

Metadata

The contents of the CMDB are all metadata.

In this model, Metadata is *nonruntime* structured information related to the IT environment. This is a reflexive (self-referential) concept in the CMDB. A clear example would be the relationship between a data model (metadata) and the physical production data structure it represents (Datastore). The contents of the CMDB are all Metadata.

Metadata has a more general computing sense in which it is "data about data." However, because data about data exists throughout IT elements such as file systems and configuration files, this is not a useful definition for this model. There is the conceptual issue of how to distinguish Metadata from general aspects of stored-program computing architecture (taken to the extreme, all processing instructions are data about data).

Metadata can be deployed to an operational context (sometimes by transformation), which makes it runtime. In such cases, the Metadata becomes a Component or a Datastore: for example, a logical data model from which an actual database schema on a running Server is generated. In this case, the database schema as a Datastore CI might be related to the logical data model, as a Metadata CI. Another example would be a BPEL process definition generated from a visual flowchart. When such a transformation happens, the transformed runtime artifact by definition is no longer Metadata. It is computing architecture and impossible to distinguish from general aspects of stored program computing.

Keeping
Metadata in
synch with the
real processing
architecture
is a continual
problem.
Because it is by definition nonruntime, keeping Metadata in synch with the real processing architecture is a continual problem, addressed by tools such as scanners and techniques such as model–database comparison.

Some have called for "real time" or "embedded" Metadata, which would imply continuous introspection into live production infrastructure. The performance and security implications of this are nontrivial, and there are value-adding aspects to offline Metadata (e.g., verbose text definitions and logical dependencies) that will never be directly represented or identifiable in a production infrastructure.

Metadata as a CI is a riddle;[167] it suffers from the same problem noted previously if Change records were considered CIs—the Metadata has Metadata has Metadata, and if all is under change control, the infinite loop can't be resolved and no changes can take place. However, because there is precedent for Documents as CIs, it is conceivable that some Metadata (e.g., as a fixed form or structured project document) may be under change control.

This is one of the more difficult conceptual areas in this book, dealing as it does with "thing" and re-presentation of "thing." Metadata is *re-presentation*. It is not the *thing*.[168]

Contract

A Contract is
an agreement
between two
parties with
authority in the
overall IT service
context.
A Contract is an Agreement between (usually) two parties with authority in the overall IT service context. A Contract may enumerate several formal agreements, based on objectives for measurements of CIs. Contracts are often the subject of intense scrutiny, and their signing is (or should be) a visible event. However, usually a contract management office performs this particular type of change control, and it is not part of the mainstream "change process" as generally understood in most IT organizations.

Contract–Agreement

A Contract may document many Agreements (e.g., SLAs), in turn based on Metrics.

Contract–Asset

A Contract may be the source documentation for the acquisition of certain Assets, especially if the definition is broadened to include invoices.

A measurement
definition is a CI
because it repre-
sents the criteria
on which IT ser-
vice performance
is measured.
Metric

A Metric is a defined, specific characteristic of a CI or a process entity, amenable to capture and verification. Metrics are the basis for process control.

(Process entities include all the non-CI entities, e.g., Incident, Problem, and Change.)

Metrics typically vary over time. Specific means that it is one of the basic levels of measurement: nominal, ordinal, interval, or ratio. This conceptual entity encompasses both the definition of the Metric and the implication of its specific instances. Metrics typically nest in a hierarchy, moving from the more technical and specific to the more general and strategic.

A Metric is meaningless without the context of a CI (often a Process, but perhaps a Service). *Metrics have objectives as an associated concept* (not shown in the model). An objective is, with respect to a Metric, what the Metric *ought* to be. This specifically supports the concepts of service-level objective and operational-level objective, where a service provider may have informal service targets that are not the subject of an Agreement.

A measurement definition is a CI because it represents the criteria on which IT service performance is measured.

Metrics may be called for concerning the following, among other IT processes, functions, and characteristics:

- ▶ IT financial management
- ▶ Availability
- ▶ Capacity
- ▶ Integrity
- ▶ Security
- ▶ Disaster recovery
- ▶ Performance
- ▶ Training
- ▶ User support
- ▶ Change management

Specific measurement approaches will be discussed in the design patterns section.

Note that the Metric entity is the *definition* of a Metric, such as "unscheduled Changes," "transactions per second," "average response time," or "downtime." Such definitions are not themselves measurable—think about it. But they might be under change control as a basis for contractual agreements.

The ITIL section on IT financial management calls for a resource cost unit; this is a type of Metric applicable to various CIs.[169]

Metrics may use or contain other Metrics; taking this functionality to an extreme will result in the need for mathematical expression management (metric A = metric B × metric C, etc.).

Metrics are described by Metadata. See the Common Warehouse Metamodel's Expressions, Transformation, Information Visualization, and Information Reporting packages for detailed discussion.[170]

The focus in this discussion is Metric as applied to ITSM; Metric also applies more generally to business decision support. A Service may consist of delivering Metrics to an executive dashboard by a certain time every day.

Metrics are directly linked to Strategies; this linkage is essential for applying business performance management principles to IT governance and, for example, building effective digital dashboards.

Agreement

An agreement is between two parties with respect to a service level, operational level, or some other aspect of a CI.

An Agreement is between two parties with respect to a measurement, for example, a service level, operational level, or some other aspect of a CI. A Contract may have many Agreements.

DIALOG

Agreements and Related

Chris: OK, how does this all fit together? Document, Contract, Agreement, Measurement? Seems a little elaborate.

Kelly: Let's walk through a couple cases.
  ▶ An email Service where you are guaranteeing 2-day turnaround on 95% of email requests on average, as an SLA to the client
  ▶ A consolidated database farm where you are guaranteeing 99.995% uptime as an OLA to your application teams

The email account provisioning is a Service Offering, and each account request is a Service. Both are CIs; therefore, they can both have measurements. The measurement for the Service Offering might be "Aggregate % Turnaround in Days." Each individual Service has associated workflow that tells you the request date/time and the completion date/time. Those measurements are aggregated into the overall Service Offering measurement.

The objective for that measurement might be "< = 2 Days for 95%." (There are precise ways to represent this so that a service management application

(continued)

can accurately calculate it.) However, that objective is just an informal stake in the ground until it is the subject of an Agreement between two parties. And as we all know, if those two parties are within the service provider it is an operational-level agreement (OLA); if one is the client and one is the service provider it is an SLA. That particular SLA might be part of a broader Contract specifying all aspects of the relationship between client and provider. That Contract in turn is a Document and therefore a CI—and hopefully a Contract is under change control. But again, is it managed by exactly the same processes and systems that handle the deployment of software in a data center? Perhaps, but probably not.

Chris: What about the database farm?

Kelly: That's simpler. Let's assume it's a nonorderable Service (it was purpose built for a suite of applications and no more databases will be hosted there). The only thing different from the email case is that it's not a Service Offering; the measurement (e.g., availability with an objective of 99.99%) is on the Service. Aggregation is still necessary at a technical level, however, and that's where you get into the relationship between the Service-level management capability and the lower-level monitoring architecture.

As noted in the ITIL *Service Delivery* volume, agreements may be effectively managed at the corporate, customer, and service levels. See the discussion on role management, which is applicable here (any Party—organization or person—may have an interest in an Agreement).

Note that many components of an SLA would not be discrete measurements: narrative discussions on overall service scope, discussions of continuity management, chargeback formulae, and other aspects. The general problem is that of structured versus unstructured data; unstructured is easier to capture but more difficult to objectively manage, and the converse for structured data.

Configuration Item Dependencies

Allowing CMDB users the use of uncontrolled generic dependencies may result in poor data quality.

The arbitrary dependencies available on the CI concept are risky. They can enable a nonsensical connection, such as a (software) Component containing a (hardware) Machine. Arbitrary dependencies (contains and uses) are useful for CIs of the same type or for grouping CIs into manageable packages. But allowing them generally to be used by CMDB users may result in poor data quality and misalignment among different people's concepts of IT service modeling.

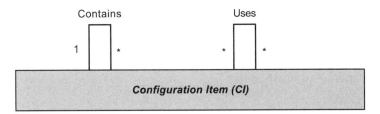

Figure 3.24 CI dependencies.

For further information, see the section on networks and trees (recursive relationships).

We Shouldn't Need Configuration Management Black Belts

From *www.erp4it.com*

More evidence that the theoretical critique of current CMDBs is reflected in people's practical difficulties.

It's been reported to me that a large firm in my area that uses a prominent CMDB tool has determined that its conceptual flexibility is hard to manage. They've had to lock data entry down to a small group of configuration management "black belts."

This is a natural consequence of an overly generic data structure; what these people are essentially doing is building a more precise, de facto consensus information model (metamodel, if you will), which they are enforcing through their group process and joint understanding. This is an unsustainable approach. They are forced into this because the tool does not allow this to be done automatically through declarative constraints, which is how we ought to manage complex data, according to well-established data management principles.

This is why a black belt team emerges when such tools are purchased: a consensus starts to build that, "yes, this service (as in SLA) is a CI, and yes, this hard drive is a CI, but we are not going to directly link the two—instead, we will put the drive in a SAN cabinet, allocate it to a mount point, deploy a database to it, assign the database to an application system, and finally create a dependency between the SLA service and that application." But no automatic constraints enforce such relationships; they are simply embedded in the group consensus that this is the way to do things. Automating such a group consensus is exactly what data architecture (or object-oriented class design) is all about.

(continued)

The scale of the configuration management problem is huge, and to capture and maintain such a mesh of data in a cost-effective way, we need a tool that will enforce sensible data relationships when being used by a variety of staff (e.g., offshore resources).

Again, the fundamental issue here is that CMDB tools vendors have taken the ITIL requirements literally as data schema requirements and are basically delivering simplistic graph metamodels. From discussing the situation with longtime ITIL thought leaders, it's clear to me that this was never intended by those who built the standard.

Usual rant: I don't think that configuration management will ever meet its goals without adopting more explicitly defined metamodel semantics, such as those the OMG (Object Management Group) has been painstakingly building.

Operational Configuration Item

An operational CI refines the base CI concept by including things that are *measurable,* which includes Service Offerings, Technology Products, and Assets. Operational CIs also are directly involved in the day-to-day provision of Services, but the documentation-oriented base CIs are not.

Some Operational CIs are also Production CIs and will be described below. The Operational CIs that are not Production CIs are Service Offering, Technology Product, and Asset.

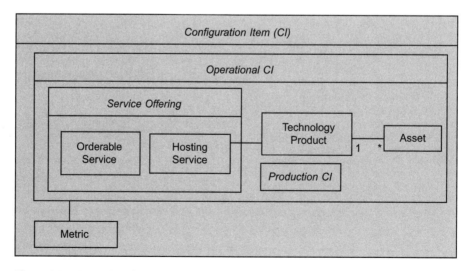

Figure 3.25 Operational CI in context.

Some CIs might not leverage the high visibility change control process that is usually focused on the production data center.

Operational CIs are under change control, but it is a different kind of change management dependent on their specific life cycles. A Service Offering goes through a different process than a change to a production application Server. Although ITIL implies that CIs all participate in a generalized conceptual RFC process, some might not leverage the high visibility change control process with its bias toward production concerns.

For example, a new Technology Product will probably go through some sort of adoption and certification process, perhaps an architectural review led by the IT organization's designated stakeholders for that type of technology. But it probably will not be a subject of change advisory board discussion, unless that Change Advisory Board has the broad ITIL scope.

Asset

An Asset is a financial concept. It shows up on the company's balance sheet and may be depreciable. The Asset concept is often one to one with Machines and Applications in terms of software licenses. However, a Machine may or may not also be an Asset. Another option may be for turnkey systems including several Machines and Deployed Software Systems to be tracked as one Asset.

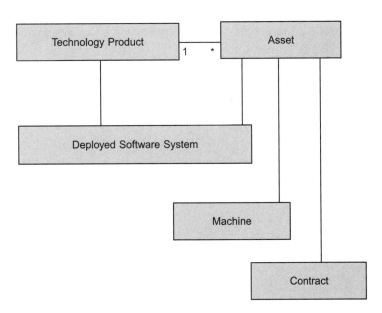

Figure 3.26 Asset context.

DIALOG

Assets and Configuration Items

Chris: All right, you got me. When is a Machine not an Asset? It can be on the loading dock and it should still show up on our books.

Kelly: Remember when we signed the deal with NexQ? Part of the arrangement was that they would locate two of their management servers in our data center. Stuff like that happens all the time nowadays. We track those servers as CIs; they are attached to our network, they are mission critical, and we even pull data off of them. But they aren't ours and don't show up on our balance sheet.

For software, the Asset is more or less equal to the software license. There is little or no industry consensus as to whether to call systems built in-house Assets—they may be built with capital budgets and depreciated, but often the expenditure is simply considered as a Project.

There's increasing awareness that systems developed in-house need to be managed as a portfolio—what relationship this portfolio management concept has to formal asset management is to be determined. Certainly, some of the background and orientation of experienced asset management staff would be valuable to the IT portfolio management objectives. Will asset management ultimately be seen as a subset of IT portfolio management?

Assets should have asset tags and formal identifiers, which should not be equated with serial numbers. Some Assets simply don't have them, and cases have arisen in which serial numbers change but the Asset remains the same, for example, if the serial number is tied to an assembly that is replaceable in the field, such as a machine motherboard.

When Assets are procured, their invoices should be provided in digital form and should enumerate all purchased products by type, model, and serial number. In this way, the incoming invoice can populate a database (asset management or integrated asset/CMDB) directly or with a little translation. One poor practice is when, for example, five Servers are purchased and appear as a single line item—this then requires further analysis and perhaps even physical inspection to determine the actual Servers and their serial numbers (which are often miscaptured when manually examined, rekeyed, or both).

Technology Product

The [IT] organization might hold the maintenance budget flat and force a 5% to 10% productivity improvement. This requirement would drive IT implementers to design efficiencies into their applications and processes to achieve this goal [which] might motivate IT managers to consider additional criteria when evaluating application concepts, such as asset utilization and projected annual maintenance cost, putting pressure on the organization to simplify the application architecture and minimize the number of new platforms.

—Jeffrey Kaplan[171]

A well-defined Technology Product database, showing dependencies on technologies, is critical for the enterprise's vendor management and technical road map.

The concept of Technology Product is crucial for enterprise architecture and vendor management. A well-defined Technology Product database, with mappings to the specific Applications and Machines that depend on those products, enables tracking the enterprise's status with respect to product obsolescence, portfolio simplification, security issues, vendor support, and overall technical road map. It also helps in Program estimation and is an input into *infrastructural drivers of IT cost.*

The context diagram shown in Figure 3.27 elaborates on the conceptual data model; there are a number of dependent entities not shown on the main diagram.

The Technology Product concept is a combination of the ITIL concept of Definitive Software Library plus the various *types* of hardware devices approved for the environment (note that this is not the same as the ITIL Definitive

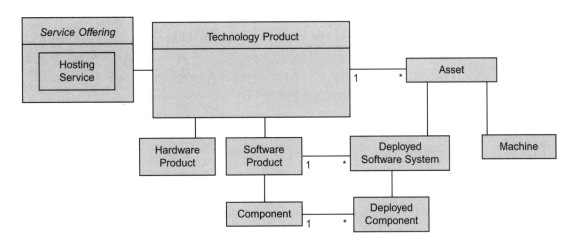

Figure 3.27 Technology Product context.

Hardware Store, a supply of spares). Because of tightly coupled hardware–software solutions (e.g., routers with embedded firmware), it is not feasible to separate Technology Products along strict hardware–software lines, although some kind of categorization taxonomy is required for enterprise architecture purposes.

New Technology Products require acceptance into the environment through some sort of defined process. Often, this may be owned by an enterprise architecture capability.

Technology products have versions; this is a complex problem relevant to many other CI classes. See the versioning discussion in the "General IT Data Architecture Issues" section later in this chapter.

One possible attribute for a Technology Product is a class of use, which might represent various levels of availability or processing power: a class 1 designation might include high availability, for example.

The concept of Technology Product would also be an appropriate place to link the skills sets of IT staff. When a Technology Product is no longer supported, this has an implication for human capital management—are those staff members with strong expertise in the product being retrained?

Technology Product–Hardware and Software Product

It is difficult to make a distinction between hardware and software for purchased Technology Products.

Note that Technology Products may aggregate both hardware products and software products; many purchasable solutions include both, with some level of independence—think of a Cisco router with its upgradeable firmware or a turnkey materials management system based on IBM iSeries (AS/400) computers.

Software products in turn contain Components; software products are logical, and Components are physical. Software products are *by definition* not deployed. Their deployments are represented by the concepts of Deployed Software System and Deployed Component. This representation in particular draws on the concise, elegant Software Deployment model from the OMG's Common Warehouse Metamodel.[172]

When a Technology Product is no longer supported, are those staff members with strong expertise in the product being retrained?

Technology Product–Asset

Technology products type Assets, which in turn are related (often, but not always, in a one-to-one association) with Deployed Software Systems and Machines. Turnkey systems combining both software and hardware will need to be carefully considered here as to data capture approach.

DIALOG

Infrastructural IT Demand Drivers

Chris: Infrastructural drivers of IT cost? You lost me there…

Kelly: We understand when the business comes and asks us to build something. Where we fall down is when Oracle decides to stop supporting Oracle 8, for example. Our business clients typically don't have any awareness of such shifts in the product landscape, but it's a really big deal for us—we have to go without support, pay an expensive (and less-qualified) third party for aftermarket support, or retest all our software on Oracle 9. Our business clients wish that these kinds of costs would just go away, but it's not that easy.

The thing is, we knew 18 months or more in advance that Oracle 8 was going off support. We were kind of in denial about it, partly because we didn't have a good handle on our exposure. Now, with a complete understanding of the technology stacks underlying our apps, we know exactly what our exposure is when Oracle 9 goes off support—we've got 3 big packages and 40 smaller applications, and we've already got the funding for this migration identified in our long-range plan.

Note that these are no different from other business infrastructure issues. Compare to "we have to move, our lease is up" or "our business card supplier is out of business and we must switch suppliers"—the same business drivers drive the same response.

Service Offering

A Service Offering is a defined entry in the enterprise service catalog. It is a measurable and specific offering of the IT organization to external clients. It should be seen as a "logical API," or application programming interface, of the service provider; everything behind it (in theory) may be opaque to the service consumer. Service Offerings are of two major types: Orderable Service and Hosting Service. (In this model, the Project orders the Hosting Service using a Service Request.)

Service Offerings and Services themselves may be created by Projects. In effect, the Project can be seen as the Service Offering of "create new Service."

The Project can be seen as the Service Offering of "create new service."

In ITIL terms, an Orderable Service might be seen as (by definition) a preapproved RFC. Access to an existing Application (sometimes termed a subscription) would be one type of Service Offering.

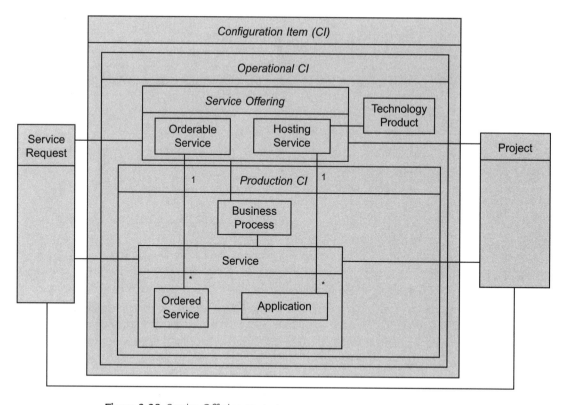

Figure 3.28 Service Offering context.

The Hosting Service is the infrastructure and support services necessary as a platform for an Application.

The Hosting Service is the infrastructure and support services necessary as a platform for an Application. Instances of a Hosting Service are Applications; the Hosting Service is a sort of approved template for how standard Applications are built.

Hosting Services are not preapproved RFCs; they require extensive validation. Ordering a Hosting Service usually implies starting an implementation Project. Hosting Services are based in turn on standard Technology Product stacks.

Projects may involve both Orderable and Hosting Services and their actual Service instances.

Notice that the service *definitions* (Orderable Service and Hosting Service) are Operational CIs. This means that although they can be measured, they do not emit Events and are thus not production concerns. However, their instances are—both the Ordered Service instance and the Application service are production concepts.

Notice the symmetry: A Service Request turns an Orderable Service into an Ordered Service. A Project turns a Hosting Service into an Application.

DIALOG

Service Catalog Confusion

Pat: We're doing a service catalog.

Kelly: So are we. How many services are you going to have in yours, do you think?

Pat: About 20.

Kelly: We're past 500 and counting!

Pat: Seems high.

Kelly: I know you have more than 20; just the other day you said you were managing 45 different SLAs.

Pat: Oh, those are mostly our applications.

Kelly: Aren't those in your service catalog?

Pat: No, of course not. Are they in yours?

Kelly: Yes, of course. They are the major things we're managing for the business. How can they not be in your service catalog? Service-level agreement, service catalog—same thing, right?

Pat: We have something called a hosting service that covers all our applications. Each application is an instance of that hosting service. We manage the hosting services as a different portfolio, but we don't call that our service catalog.

Kelly: I don't see how that can work. We "host" two enormous mainframe applications that are worlds unto themselves, a bunch of midrange stuff, and then dozens and dozens of smaller scale Web apps. I could see the Web apps being instances of a generic hosting service, but what about the bigger stuff?

Pat: Well, as you know we don't have anything quite as huge as yours—lots of medium-sized stuff. We did define several tiers of hosting, based on capacity and availability requirements. What if you took your two biggest applications, kept them as separate service catalog entries, and saw the rest as simply hosting instances? Are the rest of the applications generally comparable?

Kelly: Maybe... I'll have to think about that.

A Service Offering is not a service.

A Service Offering is not a service. The Service Offering is a template, an item *type*—but it is not the item. One Service Offering may result in many actual Services; in other cases, a Service may not even have an Offering (it is a nonorderable service). However, an Offering with no Ordered Services is like a poorly selling retail product; its reason for being is clearly in question. (This is where portfolio management comes in.)

Examples of Service Offerings might be the following:

▶ Provision new user with a workstation

▶ Set up new email account

▶ Set up new user in human resource management system

▶ The three preceding bulleted examples, all as a package

▶ Provision new remote store with wide area networking

▶ Provision Project with new technology stack (e.g., Java 2 platform, enterprise edition) standard container and Oracle database)—notice that this is an internal, IT-to-IT Service

Service Offerings in some cases will reference single or multiple Technology Products that may be composed of other Technology Products (the term "stack" may be used here).

For example, one Service Offering may be "provision HA (high availability) Enterprise Java with RDBMS." This Service might be the configuration and delivery of an enterprise Java application server using WebLogic 8.0 and Oracle 9i, load balanced across enterprise standard servers and managed for failover.

The overall stack record would have dependencies, in turn, on WebLogic 8.0 and Oracle 9i and the necessary server infrastructure to enable HA.

There is risk of making Service Offerings and Services too granular. A distinguishing feature of any Service *Offering* is that it must have a quantifiable price. (Not all *Services* must have a price. They ideally have a quantifiable cost, however.)

A Service in this sense is not a specific technical offering like a Web service; a specific Web service would be a Component and would be linked using the Application entity.

Service–Service Offering

A Service Offering may have many Service instances. See the Service discussion later in this chapter. Also see the "On the Relationship between Service and Application" section.

Service Offering–Business Process

A Service Offering may both support a Business Process and depend on one. Service Offerings in some discussions of ITIL break down into technical versus professional services; orderable professional services can be seen as Business Processes. This reference model assumes that professional services are always based on a process and not functional.[173]

Generally, any Service Offering may require a Business Process to realize it as Service.

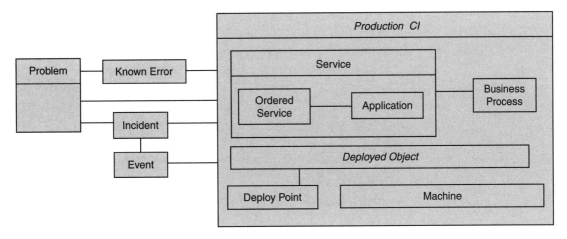

Figure 3.29 Production CI context.

Production Configuration Item

A Production CI is where the rubber meets the road. It's something that's directly involved in the day-to-day delivery of IT Services and whose failure or compromise would have an identifiable effect on the customer's value chain. Production CIs are best thought of as the data center and all its components, the networks, and the production workstations attached to those networks. A Service is itself a Production CI, a high-level logical one that serves as a sort of interface by which the consumer interacts with or gains value from the complex underlying IT infrastructure.

Production CIs

Production CIs do not have to be *in* production; just *intended for*. A quality assurance instance of an enterprise application is still a Production CI. It is the fact of being a deployable candidate for operational monitoring that makes it a Production CI.

Production CIs are often logical (Service, Process, and Application). This makes them no less important. Managing the logical CI is one of the most challenging aspects of configuration management; a clear approval and publication process is required.

The concept of "production" can be paradoxical. As the development life cycle becomes increasingly mature, a developer's workstations and lab servers are seen as "production" assets supporting the Business Process of software development.

A true nonproduction status increasingly must be reserved for pure "sandbox" research and development machines being used to evaluate products and technologies. A workstation being used to develop software upon a standard, proven Java or Oracle technology stack, to tight time frames and deliverables, is a different thing from a prototype workstation brought in to demonstrate the viability of a new 64-bit architecture or experiment with a new encryption product. In short, "development" is "production" to the IT value chain—but not to the business value chain.

Production CI–Event

One distinguishing feature of a Production CI is that it is the only CI type that may raise a monitored Event. Almost without exception, only physical Components, Servers, Machines, automated Processes, or Datastores[174] can raise Events.

Production CI–Incident

Another distinguishing feature of a Production CI is that that is the only CI type against which an Incident can be registered. Incidents can be against logical CIs (e.g., Application), either through a Service Request or through event correlation.

Production CI–Known Error

Another distinguishing feature of a Production CI is that that is the only CI type that may have a Known Error.

Business Process

A Business Process is a defined set of tasks, usually executed in sequence, that results in a specific business objective.

A Business Process is a defined set of activities, usually executed in sequence, that results in one or more specific business objectives (according to process guru Michael Hammer, it must "provide value for the customer"[175]). A Process is generally the intersection point of IT and the business.

Business Processes should be managed as distinct CIs with clear names, identities, and life cycles (e.g., pilot, production, and retired); formalizing their management is a challenge today, and most organizations have an informal process portfolio based on undocumented group consensus. ITIL states that for IT processes "…the process definition itself…should be treated as a CI…";[176] why limit just to IT processes?

It is a hierarchical concept with much ambiguity around granularity; there are various decompositions such as workflow–task–step. At the highest level, a Process is a value chain, and relatively few exist in a given enterprise.

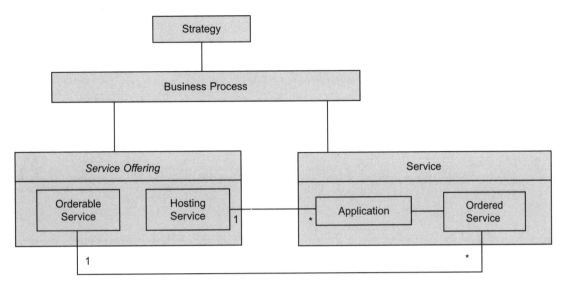

Figure 3.30 Business Process context.

Business Processes may be automated, manual, or (often) both. Many IT processes have critical manual steps, and in an IT organizational culture the importance of these manual steps and the need to make them repeatable may not be appreciated.

Computing Processes

Computing processes (such as those you can see by hitting Ctrl–Alt–Del in Windows NT/2000/XP) are different from Business Processes; they have a specific definition in operating system architectures.

IT processes are Business Processes as well.

This framework does *not* distinguish between "business" and "IT" processes; IT processes are Business Processes as well—just supporting processes, not primary value chain. They are no more special than human resources, property management, or financial processes.

Formally managing a process portfolio results in the interesting metaquestion guaranteed to glaze the eyes of executives: "What is the process to manage the processes?" (Something like, "What is the data about the data?")

For further information, see the literature on BPM cited in "Further Reading." (Note that there is ambiguity in the process management terminology; BPM is sometimes restricted to runtime process management engines. The usage here is more general, referring to the work of authors such as Paul Harmon, Geary Rummler, and Alan Brache.)

If you are enabling a capacity planning capability in your IT organization, you may have a need for transaction in your data model, for example, to map end-to-end transaction paths. This would be a decomposition or subtype of process.[177]

Strategy–Business Process

Business strategies depend on processes in many or even most cases. Business Processes are a primary vehicle for implementing strategies.

Business Process–Service Offering

Business Processes may depend on routine Service Request fulfillment; this can be seen in part as a decomposition of the process into more specific workflows. Service Offerings in turn may depend on, or be described in terms of, Business Processes (e.g., "Provision new email user").

Business Process–Service

Business Processes depend on IT Services to enable them, typically Applications. IT Services may also require Business Processes.

Service

A service is an instance of a Service Offering.

Service is a general concept with two major subtypes: Ordered Service and Application. Where the Orderable Service may be "provide email to new user," the Ordered Service is "provide email to Peter Baskerville," accompanied by the various workflow steps documenting the provision of that Service from start to finish. (In this case, the Service Offering is a Subscription.)

Services may not depend on automation. The IT organization may provide a purely human-based Process with no Application involved; it may provide a Service based strictly on the availability and performance of an Application, or it may provide both—a Service based on the human execution of a Process backed by automated Applications.

The Service aspect of Applications is distinct from Services focused on provisioning consumers. Provisioning consumers results in many Services for one Service Offering (Figure 3.32).

Service Offerings often require average turnaround times as part of their SLA (e.g., provision email within 48 hours).

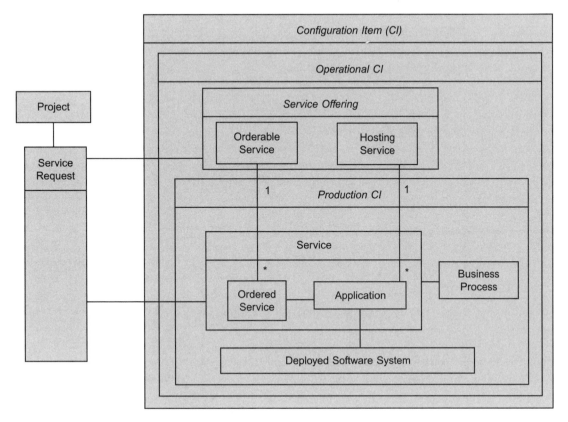

Figure 3.31 Service context.

A Service Offering of access to a given Application may be termed a subscription. However, the following are Application Services:

▶ Maintain the Quadrex system up with 99.99% availability over 12 months and 99.995% availability during the peak season.

▶ Complete the X-time batch by 8:00 AM every weekday 99% of the business days.

Another emerging term for Application services are nonorderable services. They are the subject of SLAs based on measured behavior of the Application (e.g., performance and availability).

Another term for Application Services are "nonorderable Services." This means that although they are measured, they are not requested, or to be precise, they are "ordered" through the Demand–Program–Project life cycle—a different service entry point from standard Service Requests. A current consideration in ITSM is the blurry boundary between discrete atomic services such as "order new workstation" and project-based "time and materials" requests such as "Build a new application"—see the discussion on service entry points in Chapter 2 and the "Clarify Service Entry Points" pattern in Chapter 5.

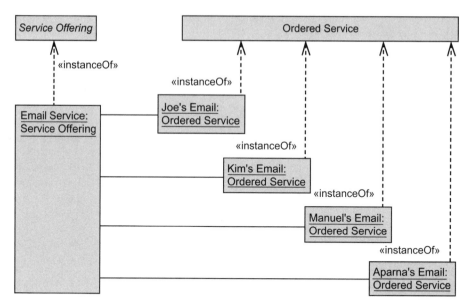

Figure 3.32 Orderable Service Offering and instances.

Their ongoing maintenance is assumed and may be the subject of SLAs, but those SLAs are not based on workflow (e.g., speed of request fulfillment): they are based on measured behavior of the nonorderable Service (e.g., availability). Nonorderable Services do not have a Service Offering entry. Note that for comprehensive service-level management, both Service Offerings and Services need to be tracked. However, Applications may offer subscriptions that *are* Orderable Services.

An Application may play a part in supporting Service Offerings, especially with respect to provisioning (Figure 3.33).

Orderable and nonorderable services are two very different types of entities.

The existence of both Orderable and nonorderable Services has implications for the Service catalog structure. Although a unified report may be desirable from a management visibility perspective, these are nevertheless two very different types of entities and will need to be distinguished in any Service catalog presentation.

Both Orderable and Application services can face inward or outward (see Table 3.2).

Is a Project an Orderable Service? This is a question the IT organization will have to answer. This model treats Projects as distinct from Service Offerings because they are neither preapproved nor fixed in cost.

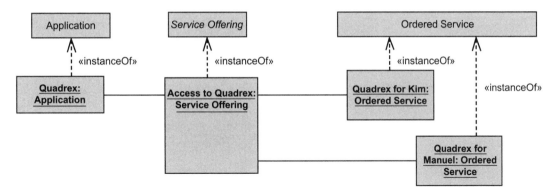

Figure 3.33 Orderable application-based Service and instances.

Services as CIs can contain other Services. This may be useful if several Application services underpin a larger, customer-facing Service concept; however, the Applications themselves should be large grained enough to be recognizable to the business. Smaller-grained, more technical groupings of software are Deployed Software Systems.

As you can see in Figure 3.34, the email Service is underpinned by mainframe and internet email logical Applications, themselves Services. Notice that although

Table 3.2 Service-Type Matrix

Type of Service	Consumer	Internal
Orderable: Fixed cost	New PC (standard configuration)	New server (standardized technology stack)
	New email account (e.g., application subscription)	New database (existing shared database farm with clear pricing model)
	Priced application enhancements (e.g., standard report requests)	
Orderable: Time and materials	New PC (custom configuration)	New server (nonstandard configuration)
	New application project	
	Application enhancements, nonpriced	
Nonorderable (application)	Existing business-facing Service with SLA	Existing infrastructure Service with OLA

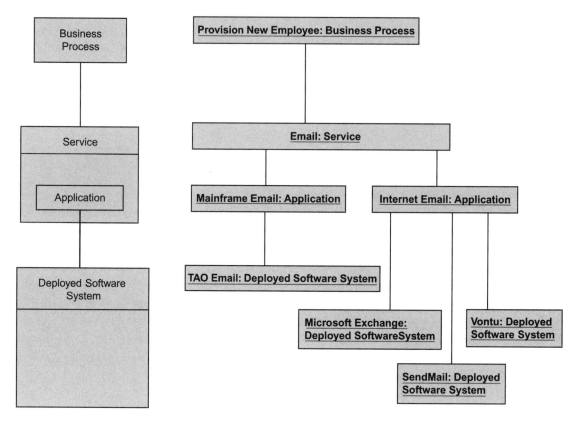

Figure 3.34 Service layering.

the email Service as a whole is the customer value proposition, the underpinning mainframe email and internet email Applications are large grained enough to be recognizable points of investment and support and are themselves managed as Services—not mere technology.

There are many variations on these concepts. In some cases, the Application is the Service—no need for an intervening layer. The critical point is that the enterprise needs to develop a coherent and universal view on these dependencies. It is not acceptable for the architects to have one representation and operations to have a completely different view—although one may be a subset of the other. Naming in particular must be based on common reference data, which in data management circles is known as a master data management problem.

One heuristic for the highest-level business-facing Service concept is that it be traceable directly to a quantifiable business value chain. Understanding the revenue dependencies of a Service is essential for correctly prioritizing the IT organization's activities, but too often this information is locked only in the heads of the most senior executives. It should be broadly available and transparent (within judicious security boundaries).

The highest-level business-facing IT Services are privileged and should be easily separable from lower-level internal Services. But both are distinct from mere Deployed Software Systems, which are purely technical in nature and do not, for example, ever have SLAs or OLAs.

API as Metaphor for ITSM

The API is a key concept to object- and component-oriented development; the implementation details of a software component are encapsulated behind a defined set of gateway operations (Figure 3.35).

The idea is that 1) the only way to access the program's functionality is through the interface and 2) it is no concern of the user how the program does its job; it can be radically revised as long as the interface still exhibits the same behavior.

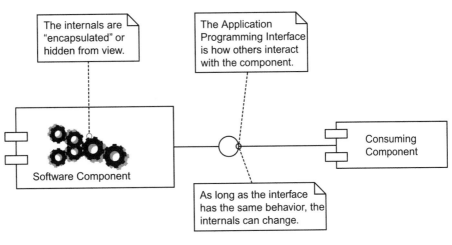

Figure 3.35 Components and interfaces.

(continued)

This is a perfect analogy for Service Offerings and Services. To carry it further, the Service Offering is the API definition, and a Service is a particular invocation of the API.

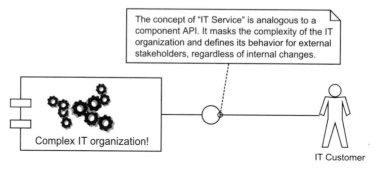

Figure 3.36 Service as API.

Application

An Application is a logical grouping of software Components. It is a consensus concept and must be carefully crafted so that it is neither too abstract nor too granular.

This is also known as product, software, software service, or middleware.

An Application is a logical grouping of software Components managed as a Service in the ITSM sense. Technologists may liken it to a "namespace." It is a consensus concept and must be carefully crafted so that it is neither too abstract nor too granular. Some rules of thumb that may be useful:

▶ An Application should be recognizable to a senior business manager. It is first and foremost a *portfolio* concept.

▶ Applications should be assigned to financial management structures. They should have clear executive ownership.

▶ Applications may be instances of a Hosting Service if the Organization has formalized these as Service Offerings.

▶ An Application usually will have been the sole product of a Project, but subsequent Projects may be managed to enhance it. (Not all projects result in the creation of an application.)

▶ An Application may be externally hosted (i.e., Software as a Service).

▶ Databases are not necessarily owned by any one application.

All CIs owned by the Application should be named using its identifier.

▶ Applications should have a unique human memorable identifier, ideally a three- or four-letter acronym. All CIs owned by the Application should be named using that identifier as a basis for a naming standard. (Vendor-delivered software is not renamed but should still have an identifier assigned for security identification.)

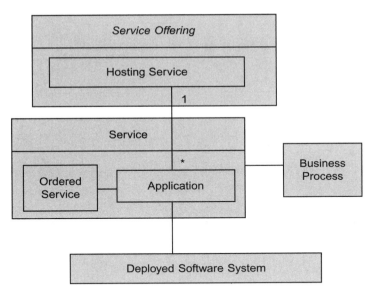

Figure 3.37 Application context.

Events emitted by the Application's Components should have this identifier, if possible.

▶ The same Application may have different informal names in the Organization; therefore, an aliasing capability is essential to manage the portfolio and eliminate redundancy while supporting legacy terminology.

▶ Applications in this model are specific instances. If an organization has two instances of Oracle Financials (e.g., for two different operating companies) supported by two different support teams, that should be two entries in the portfolio. Oracle Financials would also have one record as a Technology Product for each major version.

If no one wears a pager for it, it may not be an application.

If no one wears a pager for it, it may not be an Application, as Applications are subtypes of Service. If an Application is not part of an identifiable Service, it might be a Technology Product. For example, if an IT organization uses WebSphere Application Server for multiple different applications, WebSphere might not be in the Application portfolio—it would be a Technology Product (possibly part of a stack) and Deployed Software System on which Applications depend. However, if a shared WebSphere server farm is managed as an entity with perhaps an OLA by an infrastructure team, then that should be in the Application portfolio.

One problem
with a strict
application
taxonomy is that
actual applica-
tions often fall
into more than
one category.

Applications may have various types, with a common distinction being between "business" and "infrastructure." "Customer facing" versus "back office" is another sustainable distinction. Figure 3.38 shows a simple Application classification; more elaborate taxonomies are possible, but complexity may be hard to maintain, especially in terms of sustaining mindshare and driving effective use. There are vendors of in-depth classification taxonomies that may be useful in some cases. One problem with a strict application taxonomy is that actual applications often fall into more than one category.

Note in Figure 3.38 the question as to whether an ITSM Application is a business-facing or infrastructure Application. This is more than an academic distinction, as it may affect which major organization supports the application. Classifying such applications as "back office" is more in alignment with the IT Enablement

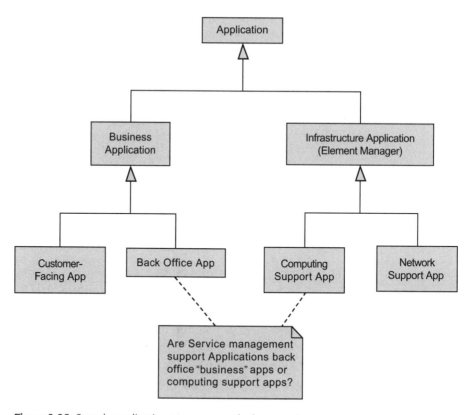

Figure 3.38 Sample application taxonomy and a key question.

Capability pattern. With this approach, all infrastructure Applications are focused on element management and may be managed by their own team. (See the "IT Enablement Capability" pattern in Chapter 5 and the discussions of element management.)

Applications as Portfolio

The Application portfolio is a key set of CIs to baseline for an ITSM initiative concerned with the data center. Physical devices will be seen as highest priority, but these usually have some attempts at management; the master list of applications, on the other hand, often does not receive explicit management.

Some CMDB efforts fail because they attempt to start with the concept of physical binary Component, which (while straightforward to harvest) is too granular and hard to manage for most organizations. The logical concept of Application provides a bridge between the overwhelming details of the technology and the business it supports.

A defined process must be implemented for identifying that something is to be tracked as a formal Application, for example, requiring the agreement of an architect and an IT line manager. Proliferation of Application identifiers (which can happen if a nonarchitectural, technical team is allowed to assign them) is a bad practice because it prevents the accurate rollup of IT operational data into larger, business-aligned hierarchies for IT performance reporting.

This model does not distinguish between Application and middleware. It's assumed that the Application entity if implemented would have a "type" attribute and this distinction could be handled at that level. Both Applications and middleware behave similarly in terms of the relationships to other entities, and the boundary between them can be blurry.

Middleware can be both a Service and a Technology Product. A middleware "hub" operated as a shared enterprise service is an Application, probably infrastructure, as well as a Technology Product and instance of a Deployed Software System. A middleware product used as a building block by many different service providers (e.g., application teams) is only a Technology Product.

Middleware as a Service, however, generally would not be business facing.

Application identifiers should be visible on all CIs where appropriate, in particular on Web pages and other graphical user interfaces. There is currently a problem in the industry with inaccurate CI identification: users do not necessarily know what Application they are even interacting with. Firm labeling standards for all Application interfaces would be a big help. This is

The Application portfolio is probably the most important set of CIs to baseline for a data center–focused ITSM initiative.

A defined process must be implemented for formally identifying Applications.

nothing new; on older mainframe green screen systems, the system and screen identifiers would typically appear in a corner. New distributed systems with less rigorous graphical user interfaces development standards were a step backward in this concern; off-the-shelf packages could easily add this as a configurable functionality.

CASE STUDY

Disparate Application Portfolios

A Fortune 100 corporation established an Integration Competency Center, which began to track the difficult subject of application interdependencies. The group tasked with this goal realized the first priority was to establish a definitive list of applications. (How can you define *relationships* between "things" when you are not sure what the "things" are?)

The application support and maintenance team had a list, but it only included applications that had been formally "turned over" and some key applications had never gone through this process. It also had poor data quality, with applications listed for which no physical evidence or owner could be found and other applications listed twice (by different names).

The production control group was responsible for assigning "system codes," three-character identifiers associated with the logical application concept. However, they never had strong criteria for doing so, and as a result the codes tended to proliferate, with one logical application sometimes having many codes. In other cases, one code would be used by a large application area for all applications.

The distributed server engineering group had a list of distributed applications and their dependencies on servers, but it did not include mainframe applications and had no defined process for maintenance.

A consulting group was brought in to reinventory all the applications, and this resulted in one more list. Lists were also compiled for compliance and disaster-planning activities. It became clear that there was significant waste and redundancy occurring.

The Integration Competency Center declared itself system of record for the application portfolio and defined a process for maintaining applications and their stakeholders and dependencies. The enterprise architecture, compliance, and security teams began to partner on these processes, which helped enable tighter controls. The application identifier assignment was seen as a key component and added to the mix, with tighter policies aimed at ensuring "one application, one code." This list then served as the basis for first-generation configuration management; databases and servers were linked to the applications and the capability took off from there, becoming recognized as a valuable IT asset.

Application–Application

Applications have many interrelationships between each other, which should be documented in the repository or CMDB. Approach issues to be sorted out here include the distinction between Application-to-Application dependencies (i.e., at the API layer) and Datastore-to-Datastore dependencies (i.e., the extract, transform, and load domain). Another issue is the danger of capturing trivial dependencies, for example, the near-universal dependency of all distributed computing on the TCP/IP system infrastructure (which should be captured as an infrastructure Application or Service in the repository).

Application–Component

Applications contain Components. For accountability, all Deployed Components should be owned by one and only one Application (although they may be used by many).

Application–Datastore

Application-to-data dependency is one of the most important production dependencies to understand.

Applications are collections of processes and algorithms at their core. They depend, in turn, on Datastores such as relational databases or flat files. Application-to-data dependency is one of the most important dependencies to maintain for CIs in the data center; many organizations spend considerable resources continually reanalyzing this dependency. One immature approach is to simply document the dependency of an Application on a database Server (without specifying catalog or database); however, database Servers are often large, shared assets and the database administrators need to know *exactly which database,* or schema, is serving an Application. (This is also needed for regulatory compliance.)

Application–Deployed Software System

Applications depend on Deployed Software Systems. The distinction between the two is subtle but crucial. Deployed software systems are all software Components that support the Application. They include the actual software Components embodying the logical Application, as well as application servers, DBMS engines, operating system services, middleware, and so forth. They should not be business visible.

A sign of an immature environment is when Projects are confused with Applications.

On the Relationship between Project and Application

A sign of an immature IT enablement environment is when Projects are confused with Applications. Projects have a defined life cycle, typically measured in months.

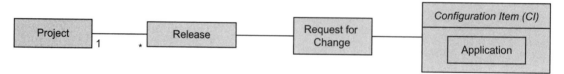

Figure 3.39 Project, Release, and Application.

Applications have an indeterminate life cycle, typically measured in years. One Application is usually the subject of multiple Projects; the first Project creates and deploys it, and subsequent Projects enhance it. *It remains the same Application throughout*, unless a conscious decision is taken to manage a major new version as a distinct new Application. There are various approaches here; the important point is that they be managed and agreed to.

The relationship between Project and Application in the model is mediated through Release and Change (Figure 3.39).

This is a purist approach, and it may be desirable for your IT enablement tooling to simply relate Project and Application—there's quite a bit of value there, even if you haven't sorted out Release yet (Figure 3.40).

For example, if an Application has a known Risk having to do with regulatory compliance, the Project making changes should be held to high standards for process adherence and software quality. That kind of focused emphasis is difficult to achieve consistently without a rich and well-managed IT enablement system that clearly distinguishes between Application and Project. It also speaks for the integration of demand management with ITSM tools to more objectively assess risk and impact (cf. the generalized ITIL Change concept).

Application–Process

The alignment between the IS [information system] view and the customer view gains value when IS is able to identify the relationship between the technologies and the business processes they support.

—ITIL[178]

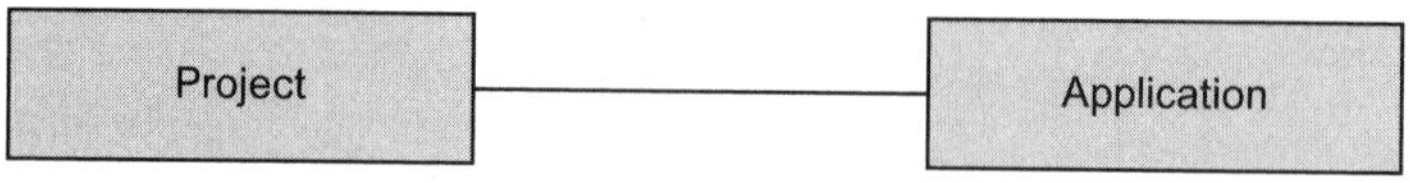

Figure 3.40 Project–Application direct relationship.

Processes are supported by Applications (as Services) in a many-to-many relationship. For example, the pricing process at a large retailer may involve a merchandising system and a point of sale system, provided by different vendors. The merchants set the prices, which are then replicated down to the point of sale terminals. Value is not derived from the process until it runs from end to end, so one process depends on two Applications.

Similarly, it is common for one Application to support two distinct processes, such as a customer relationship management system that supports both operational customer interactions and analytic planning purposes.

Processes can be decomposed into constituent steps, depending on the granularity of the analysis required. One constituent of a process would be a transaction, and understanding the major transactions supported by an Application and/or an underpinning Deployed Software System is useful for portfolio management, capacity planning, financial chargeback, and other purposes.

Deployed software systems increasingly may directly support processes as well, especially in the emerging world of SOA. There may be no concept of an Application—just process choreographies interacting directly with technical services. This is an emerging area and this representation is preliminary.

See also Figures 3.32–3.34 and 3.37 and related discussions.

On the Relationship between Service and Application

Although the IT industry has traditionally made a distinction between Application Development (creating a service) and Service Management (delivering the service), that has not always worked well.

—ITIL[179]

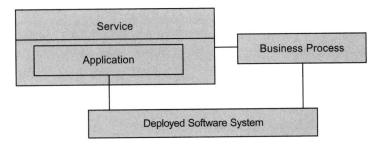

Figure 3.41 Service, process, and Application: complex and subjective.

The relationship between Service and Application is subtle, so subtle that many Organizations may wish to *not* distinguish the two. ITIL is strong on distinguishing the two because its view of Application is technical—it's simply the binary software executed for the customer. However, in many large IT organizations, an Application team is concerned with customer service issues and effectively is supporting a Service or system—not just technology but people and process as well. Such customer-oriented application management teams would be surprised to learn that they are "invisible to the Customer," as ITIL states.[180]

There is great variability in the industry: in some organizations the application teams are indeed merely technical, and in yet other organizations there is no consistency. Some application teams are truly service managers, and others are merely technicians. The inconsistencies erode IT credibility.

However, at least for a first cut inventory, *the enterprise Application can serve as a reasonable surrogate for a Service.* This starts to break down in enterprise applications that are so large they support multiple distinct Business Processes and have multiple stakeholders (perhaps expecting different SLAs). An example might be an ERP system for which the operational customer negotiates 99.99% uptime and a planning group negotiates decision support batch completion by 8:00 AM every day. (Of course, an overall contractual SLA may have multiple specific agreement points in any case—the distinction here is that there are two different customers expecting notification for different types of service breach.)

Conversely, if a set of smaller Applications has been developed with all managed by the same team, these distinct pieces of functionality may be managed increasingly as a unitary Service.

For example, an organization may have a legacy email system on its mainframe and a distributed email system such as Microsoft Exchange. Both may be supported by the same team, and a request for "email access" may result in the customer receiving accounts in both environments. Nevertheless, they should remain two distinct entries in the application portfolio so that there is visibility into the portfolio's complexity and enterprise progress toward simplification (e.g., stopping support for the mainframe email system).

Service versus Application

One way of managing the distinction is linguistic. Where the Application is "Oracle HRMS," the Service might be "human resources application management."

Where the Application is "Oracle HRMS," the Service might be "human resources application management."

This has an advantage of conceptually decoupling the Service to some degree from the Application; however, the added value of this linguistic distinction may be suspect, if all involved (wink, wink, nudge, nudge) know that it simply translates into the same set of services the Oracle HRMS team has provided all along.

The introduction of a layer of abstraction also poses maintenance issues: now *two* logical CIs that are hard to manage must be maintained, with a mapping between them.

See further discussion under the Service Request description (e.g., Figure 3.44) and in the ITIL *Service Delivery* volume under "Service Level Management: What Is a Service?"

DIALOG

What's an Application Manager to Think?

Natalie is an application manager for a large midwestern manufacturer. Her responsibilities include both the development of new functionality for her system (the enterprise customer relationship management system) and its ongoing operations. One day she is called into a meeting at which a senior ITIL consultant is discussing service management.

Gary: The thing you folks need to do is get out of a technology-centered approach to interacting with the business. The business doesn't care about things like "applications"!

Natalie: Excuse me, why do you say that?

Gary: Well, it's clear. The business doesn't know what an application is. You shouldn't even talk about it with them. What they need is a service!

Natalie: I'm not providing a service?

Gary: Not if you are calling yourself an application manager. All that application managers do is build technical stuff.

Natalie: Hmm. I just got out of a meeting with the senior VP for marketing. We were talking about my application's availability level. We even used the term SLA. But this term "service" you're throwing around, we don't talk in quite the same way.

Gary: That's because you are too technical in your approach. See, you need to get out of the bits and bytes and talk in business terms!

Natalie: Like discussing the business objectives of the next major release with the SVP? How the application—excuse me, service—is going to help improve customer retention and sales force productivity?

(continued)

Gary: Right... Say, I thought you said you were just an application manager.

Natalie: I did... Oh, never mind....

Relationship among Service Offering, Service Request, and Service

Now that I have introduced all of these concepts, I will examine how they work together and hopefully clarify why we need them.

The concept of service is tricky; it is used quite freely in the ITSM literature. It's therefore not surprising from a data perspective to find that the term is badly overloaded and requires considerable clarification, including five distinct entities in this discussion. This is not even including "service" as used in SOA (Figure 3.42).

Figure 3.43 shows the interrelationships of the service-related entities for a simple scenario of email provisioning. Note that email provisioning in this enterprise consists of configuring the user's accounts on two different email systems, a good example of one Service being supported by two Applications.

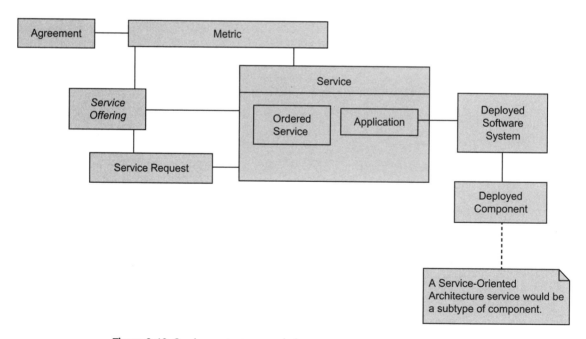

Figure 3.42 Service context: expanded.

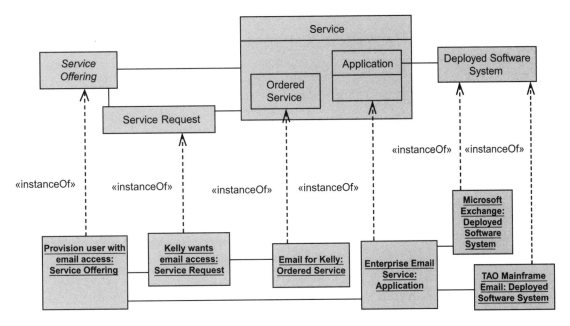

Figure 3.43 Service instance example.

Again, an individual provisioning of the email service to a customer might be called a subscription.

Why Is This So Complicated?

Well, it's really not. It's just unfamiliar. Think about ordering a book from your favorite online retailer.

Say that I log into my favorite online bookseller. It offers in general a Service of selling books, but that is not what I am *ordering*. I am ordering *one book* in the bookseller's equivalent of a service catalog. However, the ongoing performance of that bookstore is a Service as well—a nonorderable Service. (It's as simple as a store keeping its doors open—you don't *purchase* that, but it's *necessary* if you are to enter the store and see what's on the shelves.) The bookstore Service itself is supported by underlying Applications; for example, its own order management system and a delivery logistics system that might be outsourced (e.g., to UPS). I need all of these things to get my book.

(continued)

The one thing that seems a little elaborate is the distinction between Service Request and Ordered Service. However, this is necessary because of the ongoing production nature of ordered IT Services; the bookstore delivers my book and doesn't care about supporting it once I have it, but an IT organization delivers a computer (or email account or disk storage) and then has to provide ongoing support for it.

Deployed Object

A Deployed Object is a Deployed Software System, a Component, or a Datastore. Figure 3.45 attempts to represent an extremely complex space concisely. More elaborate representations are possible,[181] but these core concepts can serve as a basis.

Deploy Point

A deployable object is tied in turn to a Deploy Point, which is usually a file system directory.

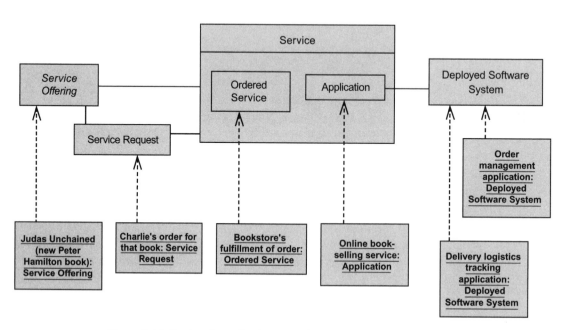

Figure 3.44 Book order as Service example.

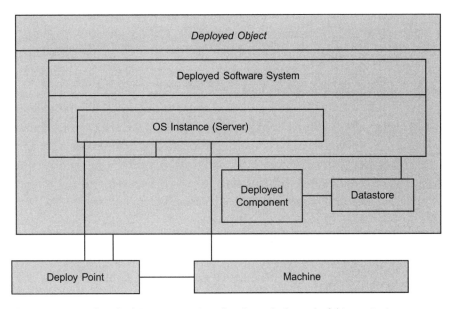

Figure 3.45 Deployed Object context (applies through the end of this section).

A Deploy Point is a major type of CI.

The concept of Deploy Point as a type of CI is an innovation proposed in this analysis and comes from my experience with configuration management and supporting an integration competency center. There are several reasons for this:

► The need to identify "root" directories to facilitate interaction between infrastructure and applications teams (root in this sense not being the base file system object but the top directory allocated to the application team)
► The sensitivity of certain directories when used as exchange points for moving data
► For configuration management approaches that do not enumerate distinct Components but rather perform broad integrity checks across large blocks of storage
► Capacity management of centralized storage and its traceability to application services

The application root directory is a key interaction point for the infrastructure team managing the server and the application team.

The Application Root Directory

A large, complex application may have dozens or hundreds of directories, in some cases appearing and disappearing dynamically. However, with few exceptions the application's scope of activity is constrained to one or a few master directories that contain myriad subdirectories used by the application. These master directories are a key interaction point for the infrastructure team managing the server and the application team (assuming that the IT organization has moved toward the best practice of segregating these teams and moving the application teams out of the business of server management).

Shared libraries complicate this arrangement, but multiple applications updating shared libraries have been proved to be poor practice in Microsoft Windows. This touches on core computing issues around component reuse and operating system services and architectures, and it will never be a simple matter. Arguably, the move toward server virtualization is in part a response to the complexity of managing shared libraries in a single operating system instance.

The Shared Exchange Directory

Shared directories that facilitate Application interaction are important points of control and need to be treated as CIs.

A problematic design pattern in integration architectures is the shared directory. This is typically a directory in which one application deposits files and another picks them up for further processing or to consume their information.

The trouble with shared directories is that sometimes the consuming application will be built with logic that states, "Do X for all files in the directory." Thus, if an incorrect file is placed in the directory, unexpected results may occur. (An architecture of this nature resulted in the complete failure of the replication feed for all pricing data at a major retailer, costing many hundreds of thousands of dollars and spurring an interest in configuration management.)

Shared directories that facilitate application interaction are therefore important points of control and need to be treated as CIs.

This whole concept may seem obvious; the key point being made here is that *these directories should be explicitly tracked as CIs in the CMDB*, and the stuff they contain is not necessarily individually tracked.

Deployed Software System

A Deployed Software System[182] is a more technical concept than an Application. It is a specific set of computing Components that can be managed as a unit. Applications (which in this model are seen as subtypes of Service) depend on Deployed Software Systems.

Deployed software systems are often the instantiations of Technology Products. They are the *real, running instances*. They support Applications, which in turn figure in SLAs, may have Incidents, and so forth. Technology Products in contrast show up on invoices and Contracts, and the complete list of *software* Technology Products is the Definitive Software Library.

As you can see in Figure 3.46, Applications as Services depend on a great deal of technology they do not own. Maintaining these relationships is essential for understanding the effect of external forces on the IT organization.

One result of the model's distinction between Technology Product and Application is the apparent duplication in some cases of information across the Technology Product, Deployed Software System, and Application entities, which in simple cases may all have the same informal name.

Technology Product includes "undeployed software" generally, and this is useful in the case of both externally and internally developed products, especially those that have multiple production versions. Again, if a piece of software is to be considered part of the Definitive Software Library, it must be registered as a Technology Product.[183]

A question to consider is whether the custom module entity in Figure 3.46 should also be a Technology Product.

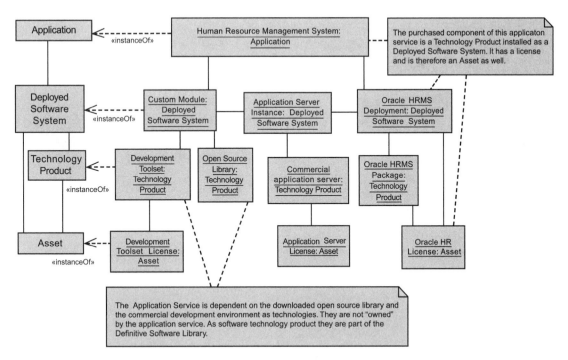

Figure 3.46 Application Service, Deployed Software Systems, Technology Products, and Assets.

Deployed Software Systems do not have SLAs or OLAs. Those concepts are reserved for the Application entity as a subtype of Service.

Operating System Instance (Server) and Machine

Servers and Machines are not the same thing.

A precise definition of Server versus Machine is increasingly critical. Server is becoming an ambiguous term because of virtualization, but as one of the most commonly heard words in IT, it must be addressed in this model, which sees Server

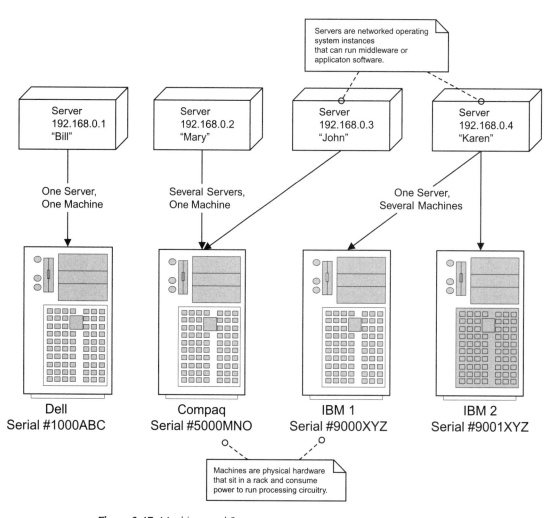

Figure 3.47 Machines and Servers.

(and workstation) as an *operating system instance, almost always networked.* An operating system instance is a special case of a Deployed Software System.

A Machine is a physical computing device that can be equated to an Asset. One Machine may host multiple Servers (virtualization and partitioning), and one Server may be hosted by multiple Machines (failover and load balancing). Server is the bits and the process (often linked to a software license as an Asset); Machine is the atoms and the serial number, linked in turn to a physical Asset tag.

Machines may have subassemblies, including well-recognized components such as disk drives and memory chips but also including full computing devices (blade systems).

Common asset management solutions are just beginning to support these requirements, and in many companies the reality of the computing infrastructure has already outstripped their asset management solutions' capabilities.

Component

A Component is a physical piece of executable code that can be objectively inventoried.

A Component is a physical piece of executable code. Even though it is only magnetic bits and bytes, it is common practice to call a Component "physical." Calling it "physical" in this context means that there is no disagreement about what and where it is; Components are unambiguous assets that can generally be objectively inventoried without debate about their boundaries.

UML "Component"

During the writing of this book I became aware that the UML definition of Component had changed considerably between UML 1 and 2. This book retains the UML 1 sense of the word; the new UML term is "artifact," which I find too general and nonintuitive—it is not a commonly heard industry term in IT operations.

Again, the purpose of this conceptual model is to rationalize commonly heard industry terminology, not to develop a completely precise model, which would require the use of less familiar terms (such as artifact) in support of more rigorous normalization.

The use of Component here is not in a pure object-oriented sense. In the object-oriented world, a Component also has a well-defined interface that encapsulates its behavior and provides an effective contract for anyone who chooses to use it. However, Component as defined here applies to any piece of executable code, regardless of whether it has a well-defined interface.[184]

A Web service, shared object, or other similar addressable, distinct piece of functionality *in this model* is a Component—not a Service. This is quite a point of confusion because of the overloading of the term Service.

Modern discovery tools discover Components in many cases through their associated computing process evident in the operating system. (The concept of computing process is not represented in the model—this is *not* a Business Process.) Computing processes have interesting technical metadata, including the specific command line used to invoke the process by launching an executable. This area moves into more technical concerns out of scope for this conceptual model.

Component Relationships

Components, like Applications, can be related to Datastores and Deploy Points. However, doing dependencies at this level for the general case of a large enterprise IT organization is usually not practical or useful given current industry capabilities—the objects and their dependencies would quickly amount to millions, and the information might not even be available in many cases (e.g., packaged software). Instead of inventorying all the detail of Components, some configuration management approaches focus on overall integrity checks across large blocks of storage. In such cases the deploy point becomes a fundamental CI to manage.

> Capturing Component-level dependencies is a recommended best practice for all aspects of EAI.

Capturing Component-level dependencies *is* a recommended best practice for all aspects of EAI.

Datastore

> The most well-known example of a Datastore would be a relational database catalog.

A Datastore is a distinct, addressable source of data, usually structured. The most common examples would be database catalog (sometimes imprecisely called an "instance"; this model uses it in the DB2 sense of a query space containing schemas) and flat file; message queues may also be represented here (Figure 3.48).

A Datastore should have one and only one data definition. As a Deployed Object it depends directly on Servers and their underlying Machines. Note that as a CI it can depend on and contain other Datastores. Again, generalized CI containment is frowned on in the model—you don't want Datastores containing Machines!

A database would further decompose into the well-known stack of schema, table, and column (Figure 3.49). Metadata attributes specify the data types, lengths, and so forth of the columns.

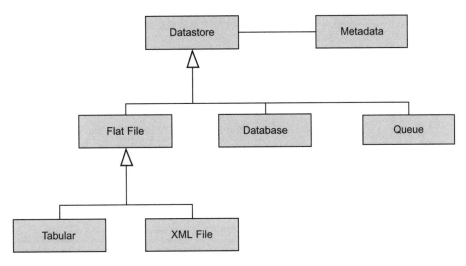

Figure 3.48 Subtypes of Datastore.

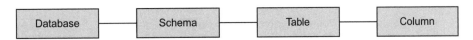

Figure 3.49 Simple data dictionary.

Datastores should have data definitions, which are by strict definition *Metadata*—data about the data.

The data definition tells you whether a given Datastore contains customer or supply chain information. More elaborate representations exist: distinctions between entities, attributes, tables, and columns; the structure of keys and indices; inheritance; and other fundamental information modeling concepts. Making sense of these elaborations requires attention to the issue of what is a Datastore (physical CI) and what is Metadata (its offline representation in a structured format). As noted in the Metadata section, this is one of the more difficult conceptual areas in the book.

See the OMG's Common Warehouse Metamodel and other metamodels and the work of David Marco, David Jennings, and Dave Hay (among others). References are noted in "Further Reading."

Datastores are often equated with their relational database management system (RDBMS) instances in casual architectural sketches. Precisely, an RDBMS is an instance of a Technology Product installed as a Deployed Software System, and the Datastore is merely a passive container managed by the RDBMS. However, this level of precision is sometimes not necessary in earlier phases of configuration management.

Process and Data

The separation of process and data has both a conceptual and a physical driver. Conceptually, it is convenient to think of data as orthogonal to process, a distinction carrying through into fundamental computer science. Practically, the distinction of data and process has been reinforced by the "access time gap": the difference between real-time, processor-driven access to solid-state memory (the province of programming languages) and slower media such as hard disk and tape (the focus of data management as it's evolved over the past 50 years).[185] This distinction is eroding because of advances in hardware capabilities and economics (solid-state memory continues to decline in price, making "in-memory databases" increasingly common). It is also eroding because of ongoing efforts to incorporate persistence semantics directly into higher-level computing languages and eliminate the "object–relational impedance mismatch." The continuing amalgamation of data into the processing realm will have implications for configuration management practice.

However, data reuse, capacity, and regulatory drivers will push the continued distinction of data as a separate asset from (or at least a manageable and distinct subcategory of) purely processing elements. How this plays out for the CMDB of the future will be an interesting question.

See also Figure 5.8, "Metadata-based risk management."

Location

A Location is the physical site at which a Machine may be located. The Location–Machine relationship can be elaborated for the purposes of facilities management, including concepts such as rack and grid. Power and HVAC systems present significant information modeling challenges that will not be directly addressed here.

An Iterative and Incremental Approach to Configuration Data Maturation

An Iterative Approach

"Love the reference data model. We're not going to get it done for years. What to do in the meantime?"

"Well, let's look at how to build it up over time."

Depending on the business objectives the configuration management capability is to meet, it's strongly recommended that the architects consider its evolution incrementally and iteratively.

The configuration management problem is a large and varied challenge, and different patterns and approaches will be discussed in subsequent sections. From a data perspective, I describe a maturation process.

Stage 1

First, the association of Applications to Servers is often the top priority when assessing the business value of configuration management. This is a relatively simple data structure (Figure 3.50).

Note that in this data structure there is no distinction between Applications and Deployed Software Systems or between Servers and Machines. The Application dependency on the Server may be due to a database, but that is not called out as a separate entity, so certain data privacy requirements will be poorly handled. The challenges of tracking Technology Products as distinct from IT services will not be met, nor will the issue of Server virtualization be covered.

However, as an incremental step, it is a solid achievement and may present significant challenges in itself.

Stage 2

This adds the concept of Datastore to the model. Databases are now called out specifically but are simplistically related to Servers (Figure 3.51).

A Datastore requires an intervening DBMS deployed to the Server, but this can be disregarded at early stages of configuration management. There is now potential to tie in Metadata, for example, as relevant to data privacy issues.

Immediately attempting the full scope of the reference models outlined in this book would be sure to fail.

Figure 3.50 Configuration iteration 1.

Figure 3.51 Configuration iteration 2.

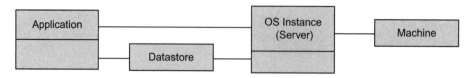

Figure 3.52 Configuration iteration 3.

Stage 3

This stage distinguishes between the Server as a logical instance of an operating system, as distinct from a physical Machine (Figure 3.52). Being fully mature in this area may require further elaboration, as there may be host and guest operating systems and machines containing machines. (Technically, you may have to institute a recursive relationship on the operating system instance and Machine entities. This is tricky to manage consistently, especially if multiple engineers are inputting data manually. Fortunately, this level of the stack is amenable to discovery tools, not that they are all that mature as of this writing.)

Stage 4

This distinguishes between Application and Deployed Software System (Figure 3.53).

This is a *big* job, probably one that requires discovery tools to get it right. It also can become annoying, as now you have to navigate through the Deployed Software System concept to reach the Server. (It's possible to still relate Application directly to Server, but the potential for ambiguity arises and it's not recommended. See your local data architect if you want an in-depth discussion.)

Note that each of these iterations will require data refactoring; see the refactoring literature for assistance here.[186]

Further Stages

Deploy point and Component might be considered next, and generally there are many options once this basic framework has been built. Depending on the organization's priorities, they may include more focus on networking, storage, metadata, messaging, or many other concerns.

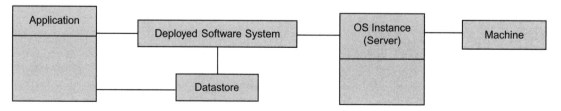

Figure 3.53 Configuration iteration 4.

This discussion only scratches the surface of the iterative approach to the ITRP problem domain. However, it's highly recommended that you approach your project in this way, because immediately attempting the full scope of the reference models outlined in this book would be sure to fail. Implementing an iterative approach within the constraints of vendor products will be particularly challenging but still more likely to succeed than a "boil the ocean" approach.

3.5 Process and Workflow: A Data Perspective

In this data-centric section, I haven't talked a lot about workflow and process. Let's turn to these from the data perspective.

The CRUD Matrix: An Old Standby

The CRUD, or create–use matrix, tells us the relationship between data and process.

A well-known technique for understanding data's relationship to process is the unfortunately named CRUD matrix. CRUD stands for the following:

▶ Create
▶ Read
▶ Update
▶ Delete

I'm going to modify the old CRUD standby to the following matrix:

▶ Create
▶ Use
▶ Aggregate

Note the following about this modification:

▶ Use includes both read and update.
▶ Delete isn't really of interest for high-level architecture.

An aggregate usage always means a Metric is being derived.

▶ Aggregate means that a given process depends not on *single instances* of a given data entity but rather on *summarizations* such as counts and averages. An aggregate usage always means a Metric is being derived and often implies some sort of underlying data mart or warehouse capability, which is important to know when considering systems architectures.

Creating such a matrix is a key reason for doing a conceptual data model. With the data on one axis and the processes on the other axis, the intersections are used for understanding how the data and process relate; it's an important alternative to spaghetti process models. Table 3.2 shows a high-level create–use–aggregate matrix for the book.

Table 3.3 Data and Process Cross-Reference

Entities / Processes cross-reference (values: C = Create, U = Use, A = ...):

Primary Value Chain / Supporting Activities	Process	Strategy	Idea	Demand Request	Program and Project	Release	Request for Change	Service Request	Event	Risk	Incident	Problem	Known Error	Orderable Service	Hosting Service	Service	Ordered Service	Application	Technology Product	Business Process	Deployed Software System	Component	Deploy Point	OS Instance (Server)	Location	Machine	Datastore	Asset	Assembly CI	Measurement Definition	Agreement	Contract	Account
Manage Demand	Manage Customer Relationship	C	C	C	C	U		A		U	A	U	U	U	U	U		U		U										A	C	C	U
Manage Demand	Fulfill Demand Requests	U	C	C	C							U	U	U	U	C		C		U											C	C	U
Developed Solutions	Manage Project	U	U	U	U	U	C			U					U	U		U	U	U	U	U		U	U		U		U	U			U
Developed Solutions	Manage Requirements	U	U	U	U	U				U		U	U		U	U		U	U	U	U		U							U	U	U	
Developed Solutions	Design and Build Solution		U		U	U	U			U		U	U		U	U		U	U	U	U	C	C	C		U	C		C	C	U		
Developed Solutions	Ensure Solution Quality				U	U	U			U		U				U				U	U	U	U	U	U	U	U	U	U	C	U		
Developed Solutions	Manage Releases				U	C	C			C	U	U	U		U	U		U	U	U	U	C	C	C	U	U	C	C	C	U	U	U	U
Developed Solutions	Manage Production Change				U	U	U	U	C	C	U	U	U			U		U	U	U	U	U	U	U	U	U	U	U	C	U	U	U	U
Developed Solutions	Manage Production Configuration				U	U	U	U	U							U		U	U		C	U	U	U	U	U	U	U	U	U			U
Support Services	Fulfill Service Requests					U	U	C			C		U	U	U	U	C	U	U	U	U		U	U	U	U	U	U	C	U	U	U	U
Support Services	Sustain Services					U	U	U	U		U	U	U	U		U	U	C	U	U	U	U	U	U	U	U	U	U	U	U	U	U	U
Support Services	Resolve Incidents and Problems					U	U	U	U	C	C	C	C	U		U	U	U	U	U	C	U	U	U	U	U	U	U	U	U	U	U	
Manage Architecture	Develop IT Strategy	C	C	C	A	A	A	A		U	A	A	A	A	A	A	A	A	A	A	A	A	A	A	A	A	A	A		A	A	A	A
Manage Architecture	Manage IT Portfolio	U	U	U	C	C	A	A	A	U	A	A	A	C	C	C	U	C	C	U	A	A	A	A	U	A	A	C	U	A	U	U	U
Manage Architecture	Manage Capacity	U	U	U	U	U	A	A		U					U	U	U	U	U	U	A	A	U	A	U	A	U			A	U	U	U
Manage Architecture	Manage Availability	U	U	U	U	U		A	U	A	A	U	U	A	U	U	U	U	U	U	U	U	U	U		U	U		U	A	U		
Manage Architecture	Manage Service Levels	U	U	U	U			A	A	U	A	A	A	U	U	U	U	U	U	U				A					U	A	C	U	U
Manage Architecture	Manage Process	U	U	U	U			A						U		U	U			C										C	C	C	
Manage Architecture	Manage Data	U	U	U	U											U		U	U	U						U	U						
Manage Architecture	Manage IT Finances	U	U	U	U	U	U	U		C				U	U	U	U	U	U	U	U			U	U	U	U	C			U	C	C
Manage Architecture	Manage Sourcing, Staff, and Vendors	U	U	U	U	U		A			A	U				U	U	U	U			U	U		U	C					U	C	U
Manage Architecture	Manage Risk, Security, and Compliance	U	U	U	U	U	U		U	C	C	U			U	U	U	U	U		U	U	U	U	U	U	U	U		U	U	C	C
Manage Architecture	Manage Facilities and Operations		U	U	U	U	U		U	U					U	U	U	U	U	U	U	U	U	A	C	U	U	U		U	U	U	U

The Matrix

This is a "reference matrix" based on my industry experience and research. It's presented as a method example more than a normative reference (although I did devote considerable thought to it).

If you are rationalizing your internal IT systems, consider doing your own matrix for both your current and your desired target states. Don't just take this version as gospel. Map it out yourself.

Another 100 pages could have been devoted to analyzing every cell, elaborated out to all intersection entities. As the academics say, this will be "left as an exercise for the reader." It will be different for every organization. The primary goal of this section is to demonstrate the analysis principles.[187]

A Document and its subtype of Metadata can be created by any of the process areas, and the IT enablement process area, because it is a miniature of the entire value chain, similarly can create and use anything—hence they are not shown.

A matrix like this is a distilled view of information that could also be drawn in dozens of diagrams. For example, Incidents and Problems go through a life cycle that may feed back into the demand process (Figure 3.54).

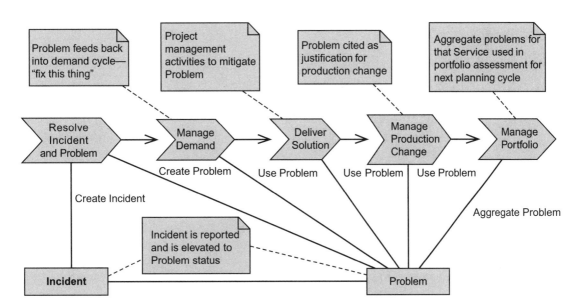

Figure 3.54 Graphical representation of a process or data create–use matrix.

This create–use matrix is presented as a starting reference model. There are lots of interesting questions generated by such a matrix.

Is a Problem created in the Incident process, or is it created in the Problem process? (Incident Management refers one or more Incidents to Problem Management for further analysis, but Problem makes the call as to whether to create a new Problem record.)

An RFC can be created by the release manager in the system development process or by some team attempting to respond to an Incident. When an entity can be created by more than one process, this deserves special attention. Ditto for Service Offering, Process, and Contract. Contracts might be created as the result of outsourcing service agreements, for vendor product purchases, or between the IT organization and its clients—three different origination processes.

Notice how many processes use the Application entity. This is typically one of the most poorly managed entities in all of IT governance.

The primary value chain activities are the most reliable data origination points. Although data also can originate in the supporting processes, these processes may be underfunded and not scrutinized effectively for quality. Therefore, it's a best practice to focus on core value chain activities and the data that they produce and consume.

For example, asking the risk management or business continuity activities to generate a list of all Business Processes dependent on IT is bound to fail. That is core IT value chain data, and the systems underpinning those processes should have the process dependencies documented as part of their construction and release.

If a supporting process needs data to achieve its mission, efforts should be made to capture that data as part of the primary value chain activities. If resistance is met, either the matter should be escalated or the supporting activity's need for that data should be questioned and perhaps abandoned.

The primary value chain activities are the most reliable data origination points.

Intersection Entities and Process

Most entity relationships in the conceptual data model are many to many. As noted later in the material on intersection entities, these relationships must be resolved with an intermediate table. Such intersection entities require the same CRUD analysis as the major IT concepts, and some of the most challenging problems emerge in attempting to manage them.

For example, an Application may have many Servers, and vice versa (Figure 3.55).

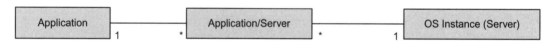

Figure 3.55 Application to Server.

Table 3.4 Intersection Entity Analysis

	Manage Application Portfolio	Provide Infrastructure	Document Application Dependencies
Application	C		U
Application/Server			C
OS Instance (Server)		C	U

(See the earlier section "An Iterative and Incremental Approach." Note that this example is actually using the third iteration for simplicity.)

When analyzing process to data, include all three entities as in Table 3.3. Note that in this example the processes are more granular—the process framework as presented in this book needs to be drilled down further to enable this level of detailed analysis.

Workflow

One requirement for IT enablement tooling in general is rigorous tracking of all changes to any entity: *who* changed *what, when.* There are a surprising number of tools that do not do this and should be ruled out as possible product choices for any enterprise. Common terms will be "effective dating," "timestamping," and/or "audit trail" (use these in vendor discussions).

Business Process meets the entity through these techniques, especially when audit trails are collected on the changing roles and responsibilities for an entity (see the "Role Management" section earlier in this chapter). A trail of who "owns" an Incident and where it has been referred is a feature of most incident management tools; this is a specific example of the general principles here. Timestamping of status changes is (in part) how SLAs are monitored for workflows like Incident, Service Request, and Problem resolution.

Similarly, IT enablement tooling should manage audit trails on other entities and their Role assignments:

Timestamping of status changes is how SLAs are monitored for things like Incident, Service Request, and Problem resolution.

▶ Who have the application managers been for this Application?
▶ What Projects have built upon this Application? Who has been on these Projects?
▶ Who has approved this Change?

3.6 General IT Data Architecture Issues

Mapping the Business to IT

The goal of mapping IT to the business is implicit throughout the data model; one representation of often-encountered concepts can be seen in Figure 3.56.

If the preceding concepts (or equivalents) are understood and formally inventoried, with dependencies mapped and maintained, this can be of great service in understanding business–IT alignment. (Business–IT alignment is also a matter of perception, which no amount of data can address.)

Some of these concepts are highly subjective and require clarification for a given organization's context and culture. There are various methodologies, out of scope for this book. See Appendix A for a detailed discussion of function *vis-à-vis* process. Capability is another concept sometimes encountered.

Enterprise architecture efforts should map IT services to the enterprise value chain, including quantified revenue data.

Such analysis is typically the domain of enterprise architecture. It can degenerate into ivory tower efforts and must remain aligned with business objectives. Enterprise architecture efforts would be well advised in particular to analyze and document the role of any particular IT Service, Business Process, or Function with respect to the enterprise value chain, including quantified revenue data. Mapping architecture to the enterprise financial model is not often done and would help the enterprise architecture practice immeasurably if undertaken. Such data has

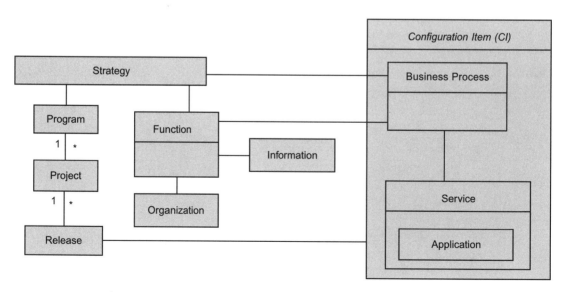

Figure 3.56 Essentials of Business–IT mapping.

applicability in ITSM efforts such as prioritizing Incident and Problem resolution and continuity strategies. Unfortunately, many enterprise architects do not have the requisite background.

Versioning

For a given product, any unique combination of the base software plus patches is a version.

Versioning is a challenging area in IT data management, especially with respect to application software. Technically, for a given product, any unique combination of the base software plus patches is a version. For many complex enterprise software products, patches are applied on an as-needed basis—they are not cumulative, so the number of potential combinations can be large. This means that naïve approaches to tracking IT components (such as a simple version field on a CI) are not robust enough.

Fully elaborated patch and version management should be considered an element management problem area and left to the specialized tools emerging (e.g., provisioning systems) optimized to handle this complex domain. The consolidated CMDB is probably best served by keeping version and patch management information at a relatively high level, with traceable links to the provisioning or patch management systems if that level of detail is required.

CMDBs and metadata repositories also run into some conceptual issues with versioning and life cycle state; there is a need to distinguish between the following:

1. The life cycle state of the *object in question*—for example, purchased, in service, or retired—and the relevant versions
2. The life cycle state of the *CMDB record pointing to the object*—for example, planned, discovered, or confirmed

As noted in the discussion on the Metadata entity, this is a core problem of "thing" versus "re-presentation of thing." This is further discussed in the "Configuration Management" section in the next chapter.

Related to the concept of versioning is current versus target analysis. An enterprise architecture is essentially a set of high-level dependencies distinguished from an operational service model by 1) how low in the technology stack it extends and 2) the presence of future-state data.

An ideal solution would be a robust as-is model of the IT configuration (including logical concepts such as Process, Service, and Application) upon which future-state scenarios could be based, modeled in an area logically separated from the critical current-state data. These scenarios, once elaborated, can be compared with the current state and change initiatives derived.

Collaboration

Any entity in the model might serve as a basis for collaboration. The ability to have a threaded discussion on any item would be highly desirable, as would be the ability to easily exchange links (e.g., Uniform Resource Identifiers).

Portfolio

A portfolio is a collection of objects with like attributes across which meaningful comparisons can be made for decision-making purposes. It has a further connotation of a financial resource pool or account of some sort, but portfolios can also be measured and managed on nonfinancial bases.

There is no portfolio entity.

As discussed in Chapter 2, there are various approaches to portfolio segmentation. Portfolio is not a straightforward concept to model; there is not a single abstract portfolio entity. It is better to conceive separate portfolios based on the objects to be comparatively managed:

▶ Project portfolio
▶ Service portfolio
▶ Application portfolio
▶ Technology product portfolio
▶ Asset portfolio

These classes of objects might further be distinguished into different portfolios based on an organization (i.e., as a Party) having a defined portfolio interest in them. For example, organization A might have 15 projects in their portfolio, and organization B has 23. These are truly separate portfolios with different assessment metrics.

Each class of item has different metrics. For example, a Service portfolio may have comparison metrics based on SLA adherence, perceived quality, intensity of use, and life cycle of underpinning technology, and a Project portfolio might have metrics based on business alignment, anticipated return on investment, and so forth.

Granularity is a key issue in portfolio management. Some theorists call for an ideal of "no more than 30 to 50" applications,[188] for example, but the number of applications in a large company may easily top 1000 (depending on the methodology by which they are counted). This is a classic rollup or aggregation issue amenable to the same techniques used to construct dimensions for business intelligence purposes.

Should Applications Be Managed as Projects?

Every product and every activity of a business begins to obsolesce as soon as it is started. Every product, every operation, and every activity in a business should be put on trial for its life every two or three years. Each should be considered the way we consider a proposal to go into a new product, a new operation, or activity—complete with budget, capital appropriation request, and so on. One question should be asked of each: "If we were not in this already, would we now go into it?" And if the answer is "no," the next question should be: "How do we get out and how fast?"

—Peter F. Drucker[189]

Having emphasized earlier that an Application and a Project are different things, I want to contradict this. How do you track TCO for Applications? This question gets to the heart of IT portfolio management, which in some representations has a project-centric bias—project in the sense of having a defined end date. But what if we relaxed that requirement and accepted the concept of application as a sort of open-ended Project? (This will give anyone schooled in formal project management pause; having a defined end date is typically seen as essential to the definition of a Project.)

The portfolio of base activities should include the application portfolio as a subset.

However, pragmatically, the time-tracking tool may be first brought in to support project management. Implementing a separate time-tracking tool for nonproject staff hours (e.g., time spent supporting the operation of an Application) clearly makes no sense, so the list of chargeable elements in the time-tracking tool needs to include both Projects and other activities. The portfolio of base activities thus should include the application portfolio as a subset. (It won't be a complete match because there are base activities that don't correspond to either Projects or Applications).

The overall population of "buckets" thus should look like this:

► True, defined-scope Projects (typically incremental, sometimes base)
► Ongoing maintenance activities tied to defined Applications or Services
► Other valid activities (e.g., training)

Without integration, visibility into project versus maintenance activities will remain elusive, and integrated staff resource planning will remain difficult.

This can present practical consequences if a project management office controls the time-tracking tool; its members may not understand the concepts of IT Service or Application well and may implement charging structures that do not align with the IT Service portfolio. Determining the master system of record for steady-state elements (i.e., the Application or Service portfolio) to be used as a basis for time tracking and where necessary building data feeds will be critical.

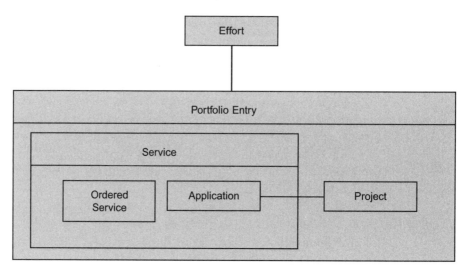

Figure 3.57 Effort tracking based on portfolio entries.

Figure 3.57 shows a conceptual fragment illustrating the commonality of service, Application, and Project within an overall portfolio management structure. Note that, although they are similar elements in this representation, for other purposes they are radically different concepts, Service being a CI with an indeterminate life cycle and Project being a defined-scope, finite effort.

Because effort can be expended on either, their data must be rationalized and integrated to some degree; there would be several technical means of doing this. Without this integration, visibility into Project versus maintenance activities will remain elusive and integrated staff resource planning will remain difficult.

The concepts of Program and product are sometimes used in Project portfolio management in solving these issues. An Application might be seen as a longer-lived Program in the project management sense (not the computing sense).

See the "Justify Change" pattern in Chapter 5.

Intersection Entities

The intersection entities are where the devil emerges from the details.

This is a high-level conceptual data model. Most of the relationships (all the unadorned lines) are of the many-to-many type. For example, an Application may use many Servers and a Server may support many Applications (Figure 3.58).

Figure 3.58 Unresolved many-to-many relationship.

Figure 3.59 Resolved many-to-many relationship.

(This is from iteration 1, so it doesn't track with the full reference model.) To turn these language concepts into an operable system, an *intersection entity* is required[190] (Figure 3.59).

If you look at the main data model and imagine all many-to-many relationships being elaborated with their intersection entities, you'll see that it would be far too complex to represent as one diagram. That's the beauty of a well-scoped conceptual data model; it should be able to represent a substantial problem domain on one page.

The intersection entities are where the devil emerges from the details. For example, it is likely that your database administration team has a list (or at least a spreadsheet) of all the team's databases. Perhaps you have an application management group with its own spreadsheet. Therefore, you might be able to say that you can populate the Application and Datastore entities. But who is responsible for the relationship, as represented by the Application–Datastore entity? Questions of this nature permeate the problem of configuration management. As with any entity, documented processes are required for the creation, reading, updating, and deleting of data in the Application–Datastore intersection entity. Would it be your application team? Your database administration team? A separate team of configuration analysts?

The current state of most IT organizations is much less formal. What you often see is uncoordinated spreadsheets, which do not handle the challenge of many-to-many data well.

DIALOG

Spreadsheet Silos

Chris: What's so bad about people maintaining their own spreadsheets?

Kelly: Well, let's look at your Organization. Here are some extracts from spreadsheets maintained by your application support, database, and server teams:

(continued)

Server team:

Server name	Notes
WNAPPLO1	Supports FirstTime and X-time Batch
FRED	?
UXPLVO1	PLV server. See Scott Armstrong
WINWEB03	External Web server
UNXDB001	PLV databases
WINDB2	SQL Server
TXEMLA	Email server
QDXAPPO2	Quadrex App server

Applications team:

	Servers	Databases
Quadrex	QDXAPPO2 UNXDB001	Oracle
X-Time	WNAPLO1	SQL Server
PLV	UXPLVO1 UNXDB001	Oracle

Database team:

Database	Server	App
PDBXO1	UNXDB001	Quadrex
LVDBXO1	UNXDB001	PLV/X-Time
ARGDBXO2	WINDB2	Argent
GDBXO1	WINDB2	GuardSys

Chris: Ouch. This data makes my head hurt.

Kelly: Well, stick with me. There are some serious issues here. Let's focus on Quadrex. The server team knows that Quadrex uses QDXAPPO2 as an application server but doesn't seem to realize that Quadrex also uses UNXDB001 through its use of the PDBXO1 database. They think that UNXDB001 is only used for PLV. (Perhaps there was surplus capacity on that server and Quadrex came later.)

The application team knows that Quadrex is using QDXAPP02 and UNXDB001, but it doesn't have the level of detail that the database administrators do, that Quadrex is using specifically the PDBX01 database on that server. Quadrex does not own that server—the PLV team is also using it. This is important from a cost allocation and support impact standpoint.

Chris: Actually, no application team "owns" their server according to our VP for systems engineering, even if that server is currently allocated 100% to them. It's a "hosting" relationship. But some of them haven't quite bought into that point of view.

Kelly: Right... Common argument nowadays! Now, the database team knows that Quadrex is using the PDBX01 database on UNXDB001—but isn't tracking Quadrex's use of QDXAPP02, as that is an application server that they don't manage. Finally, notice that someone fumble fingered the Quadrex name on the first row of the database administration spreadsheet, misspelling it "Qaudrex." This means that when we go to consolidate all this data into one database, we're going to have to manually identify and clean that up.

Chris: Why didn't the database administrators pick from a list of application names?

Kelly: Has that list been shared with them? Do they agree with how those applications are represented? Is there confidence in the process for keeping the list up-to-date? (For that matter, is there even a process?) Do they have a technical approach on how they can integrate that list from another system? Excel can pull a list from a live database, but you start to get into advanced features—too far down that road and you're looking at real system development.

The same issues need to be thought through for every many-to-many relationship, such as the following:

► Event–Incident–Problem
► Application–Technology Product
► Application–Process
► Change–CI
► Change–Incident

The complexities of doing this are why vendor products are recommended, but it's not impossible to build your own.

This is also the most critical area to review the vendor product—a common vendor mistake is to put in a one-to-many relationship where a many-to-many relationship is required. For example:

▶ A Problem might be addressed by several Releases, but your problem management tool only allows you to identify one Release that fixes it.
▶ A Datastore may be shared by many Applications, but a configuration management tool only allows you to identify it with one.
▶ A Machine may support multiple Servers, but your asset management tool only allows you to associate it with one.

These are the kinds of details critical to review in assessing any vendor product—and it all starts with having good, specific, clear requirements for what you need to track and how it needs to relate. Even when purchasing a vendor product, a conceptual data model is needed. (Emphasis on conceptual. The physical data model is irrelevant; the purpose of asking for a data model is to assess the business rules that the application is based on—not to assess their technical architecture.)

The purpose of asking for a data model is to assess the business rules that the application is based on.

Networks and Trees

IT configuration management data (or metadata) presents unique problems compared with the data that IT manages on behalf of its partners.

Metadata, or IT configuration management data (this book sees them as synonymous), presents unique problems compared with the data that IT manages on behalf of its customers. Financial, logistics, and human resources data has deep roots in paper-based history; a purchase order or hiring authorization message can be traced directly to its origins in the forms once routed by interoffice mail to "IN" baskets throughout preelectronic corporations.

One difference is the "recursive relationship," a common occurrence when managing IT data.

If you look at a sales journal or a stack of invoices, you will generally see consistency: the data model is the same for all the information. The data also has limited interconnections: one invoice does not typically reference another in simple models; invoices do not have *dependencies* on one another. An invoice references common customer lookup tables and product tables, resulting in data models that are relatively straightforward to understand (Figure 3.60).

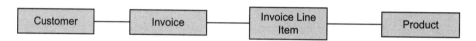

Figure 3.60 Basic data model.

With configuration management, everything becomes more complex. Applications depend on other applications, data flows from one database to another to yet a third, and network devices are by definition embedded in a web of interconnections. The data (and its required modeling) starts to take on new characteristics. In mathematical terms, it becomes graph-based; that is, it looks as shown in Figure 3.61.

This kind of data presents well-known problems in storage, querying, and presentation because it requires "any-to-any" data models and can rapidly become complex to the point of incomprehensibility.

This kind of data is not typically encountered in the business-centric systems that are successors to forms-based paper processes. It *is* encountered in manufacturing and supply chain systems in the well-known "bill of materials" problem. It is the kind of data stored by CMDBs and metadata repositories, when they move into managing technical metadata such as interconnections among network devices, integration flows, and so forth. It is also seen in computer-assisted design and manufacturing tools, and CASE tools.

The recursive relationship enables complex data. This is a relationship when one type of thing can be connected to other instances *of the same thing*. There are two basic types of recursive relationship:

▶ Tree
▶ Network

The tree relationship is a relationship where one thing "contains" other things. A taxonomy is a tree; so is a hierarchy. Common examples of trees in ITSM are CIs containing other CIs, organization hierarchies, and process steps

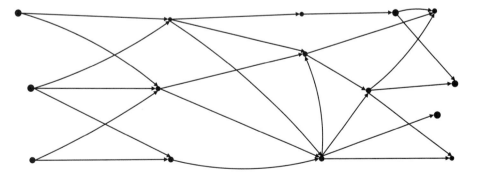

Figure 3.61 Graph-based information.

decomposing into finer-grained activities and tasks. A tree often looks as shown in Figure 3.62.

Notice how it is always possible to say that one box owns and/or is owned by others. A tree can be recognized in a data model by the notations in Figure 3.63.

While simpler than networks, trees can be troublesome to report on if they are of indeterminate depths; that is, if one branch of the tree is five levels deep and the other is only three, it's hard to create a consistent, sensible report. A common strategy of data architects when dealing with treelike structures is to *fix the*

A common strategy of data architects when dealing with tree-like structures is to fix the number of levels.

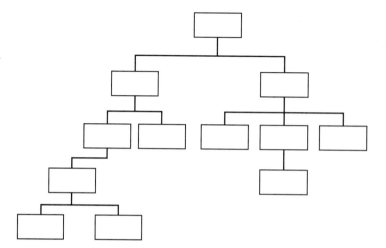

Figure 3.62 Indefinite-depth tree.

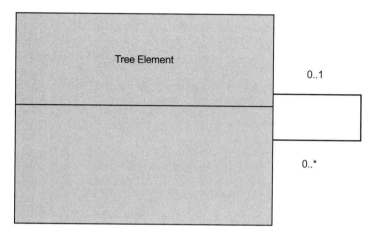

Figure 3.63 Tree data model.

levels and establish that all branches of the tree have the same number of levels (Figure 3.64).

But this may have problems in dealing with the real world—what if the organization (or whatever) is just not structured that way? Organizations may decide to structure themselves, and adapt their business processes, to fixed-level hierarchies, as you see in retail Organizations with their typical store–district–region hierarchies.

A network is characterized by things related to other things, not necessarily containing other things. A diagram of a redundant wide area network, an Organization chart with "dotted-line" relationships, or a mapping of how systems interrelate would probably be a network. A network often looks as shown in Figure 3.65.

Although there are treelike structures in it, the difference is that it is no longer possible to say that one box owns or is owned by others. A network can be recognized in a data model by the notations in Figure 3.66.

This is also often called the "any-to-any" relationship.

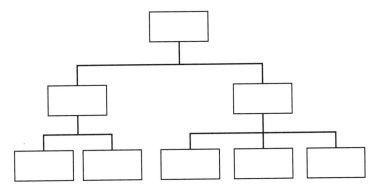

Figure 3.64 Fixed-depth (level) tree.

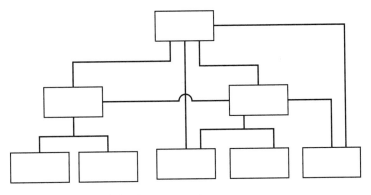

Figure 3.65 Network (no longer a tree).

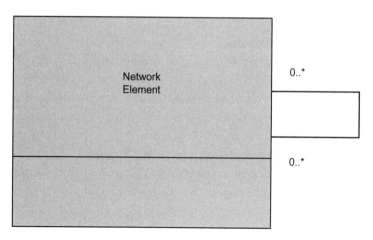

Figure 3.66 Network data model.

One issue in service dependency mapping is that a service map is often presented as a tree but in reality is a network because infrastructure elements often support more than one Service.

Trees and networks make ITSM data much harder to deal with compared to sales or financial data. Why is this? Start with a (now somewhat dated) picture of my son (Figure 3.67).

[n.b.: Thanks, yes he's cute. He's a happy boy :-).] What I want to draw your attention to is the Skwish toy he's holding (Figure 3.68).

Now, a regular business data is like a deck of cards (Figure 3.69).

You can say,

"Show me all the red cards between 3 and 8."

"Show me all the jacks."

"Show me all the hearts and spades."

It's a pretty simple problem. The hearts don't have much to do with the spades, and there's not a lot of ambiguity.

What if you say "show me every-thing connected to the small red sphere"? What do you mean by that?

The Skwish toy represents interconnected, indefinite-depth, recursive data. It's troublesome. You can say, "show me a small red sphere," but what if you say "show me everything connected to the small red sphere"? What do you mean by that? The whole toy? Or just things immediately connected to the red sphere? By elastic? By wood? Where do you draw the line?

What does this have to do with reporting for ITRP (and ITSM)? Much mainstream business reporting is of the deck-of-cards variety. You can handle this with the same tools your business users use: relational databases and reporting or business intelligence tools such as Crystal, Brio, Microstrategy, and Actuate.

Figure 3.67 Keane Betz and Skwish toy.

Using these well-established techniques, one can answer all of the following questions (assuming the data is consolidated into a data mart):

▶ What Services do I have?

▶ Have I met my service levels for a Service?

▶ What is the history of changes associated with a CI?

▶ How many Projects do I have running right now?

▶ Which Projects contributed to building this system, and what did they cost?

▶ What does this system cost to run?

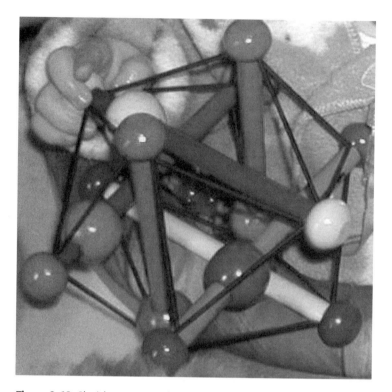

Figure 3.68 Skwish toy: network example.

Relational
databases and
query tools don't
handle recursive
data well.

But those tools don't handle reporting on recursive data. Although a relational database will *store* recursive data just fine, with relational databases and query tools, it's hard to answer the following questions:

▶ What is this Service dependent on (other Services, Applications, hardware, network)?

▶ What depends on this infrastructure piece, directly or indirectly?

▶ Is the Project on schedule? On budget? (This requires traversing an unknown depth of project tasks and subtasks—obviously, project management tools do it, but a customer is hard pressed to deal with this data in raw form. A project management office, in configuring the project management tool, may "fix the levels," only allowing, for example, four levels of project, phase, task, and subtask.)

▶ For a Project, which tasks are on the critical path? (Ditto.)

▶ What is the complete lineage of this data item in this report? Where did it come from? What systems did it flow through? (An important compliance issue.)

Figure 3.69 Deck of cards.

▶ What are all the downstream destinations for this data element? What middle-ware infrastructure does it flow across? (Important security questions.)

Basically, if you have language like "direct or indirect dependency" in a requirements specification, you probably are into the Skwish type (tree or network) problem. The problem is that although the theorists have been kicking this around for a while, no standard approaching SQL has been implemented across multiple platforms.[191]

Recursion in internal IT data is an immediate challenge to the application of business intelligence–based performance management principles.

Practical Use of Recursion

The recursive relationship can easily be abused and can enable nonsensical connections.

The recursive relationship can easily be abused and can enable nonsensical connections. One of the problems with the CI concept as framed by ITIL is that it calls for any-to-any relationships between CIs generally. (Actually, it calls for both the "contains" and "uses" relationships for any CIs.) However, some connections don't make sense. For example, a Datastore should not "use" a wide area network circuit, and a RAM chip would have nothing to do with an XML schema—yet some configuration management tools allow the customer to put in such relationships. Being more precise is why we go to the trouble of building a data model.

It is usually the case, however, that any CI *of a given type* can both use and contain other objects of the same type, especially in a high-level conceptual data model such as this.

For example, a Server might contain hard drives; both would be types of machine. A Machine might be connected to other Machines using a network. A Process can both contain and depend on other Processes. Datastores contain other Datastores, and with mechanisms like linked databases they may depend without owning. A Deploy Point (i.e., a file system directory) can certainly contain other Deploy Points and through mechanisms like directory linking (common in Unix) can depend on them without owning.

It's OK if the configuration management tool allows the any-to-any relationship as a controlled administrative option.

Finally, it's also the case that the IT world is not well understood and new dependencies present themselves. Therefore, it's OK if the configuration management tool allows the any-to-any relationship as a managed, controlled administrative option. It's important to be clear about how this differs from bad practice CMDB tools: in the recommended approach, an administrator can decide that "well, we do need to track a dependency between XML Schemas and RAM chips." They specifically allow *just this additional dependency* to be permitted by the tool and created by customers. In a poorly engineered tool, the *user* gets to decide what is related to what. That is a recipe for chaos.

Partitioning the Data Model

There are no vendor products on the market that cover the entire scope of this conceptual data model. The IT organization will therefore need to integrate two or more products. These integration points can be understood by simply drawing boxes around the entities, representing systems of record, and then observing where those boxes are crossed by relationship lines—that is where interfaces must be built.

For example, if service request management is handled by a different system than service management (a common industry pattern), some Service Requests may result in true, formal RFCs (Figure 3.70). This in turn requires some sort of interface between the two systems to handle the relationship between Service Request and Change. The interface may be one of several types:

▶ Service requests requiring RFCs are moved from the Service Request management system and automatically moved to the service management system.
▶ The Service Request is assigned an unambiguous identifier, and this is manually entered into the RFC system (potential for human error).

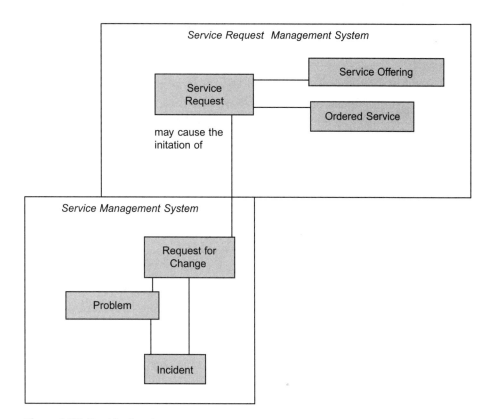

Figure 3.70 Partitioning data across systems.

▶ The Change is created and its identifier is manually entered into the Service Request (again potential for human error).

If no cross-reference is created, the Service Request is at risk if RFC approval is needed to complete it.

Don't underes-
timate the costs
of integrating
several best-
in-class systems.

The creation of data silos that do not interoperate is one of the most pervasive architectural failures in modern IT systems, and it is recommended you don't do it to yourself. But interfaces are expensive to build and run, so don't underestimate the cost of integrating several best-in-class systems.

Data Implications of Operational versus Portfolio Configuration Management

As noted previously, there are two types of configuration management: operational and portfolio. (Drift control is a type of operational configuration management.)

Portfolio configuration management is where data models are applicable. Operational configuration management, with its bit-level concern for change, can't be easily translated into a metamodel—there are too many variations. Data models would be necessary for all file formats for starters, which is impossible.

Operational configuration management therefore becomes concerned with the Deploy Point concept, which is a defined block of storage across which integrity can be ensured and changes detected. It also might be applied individually to the Document, Component, and/or Datastore concepts, but this may be inefficient in the case of large-scale Applications with dozens or hundreds of Components and Datastores.

For example, an Application may be deployed to a given Server, situated in a Deploy Point. Portfolio configuration management tracks the fact of deployment and the Application's other dependencies on databases, other Applications, and so forth.

The operational configuration management tool runs a nightly scan on the Deploy Point (filtering out data processing directories) and through analyzing checksums identifies if anything has changed. (A simple listing of files will not do; their size and internal characteristics need to be examined and compared.) Although this could conceivably be integrated with a portfolio CMDB, there are also tools that decouple the change detection management from the portfolio and dependency management problems.

3.7 The Business Case

Making the business case for data architecture and analysis is notoriously difficult. It is often seen as overhead on projects, busy work to be gotten out of the way so that the real work of system construction can commence. The problem with this attitude is that the data model is a fundamental consensus point for many (if not most) complex IT undertakings. Hammering out the shared definitions of the major "things" in the problem domain is essential for project efficiency and effectiveness. Without consensus on the data model, the project runs the risk of integration problems, unfulfilled expectations, conflicting reports, and so forth.

Building a data "view" on the IT enablement problem domain can assist with identifying and aligning conflicting or redundant processes, identifying opportunities to reuse shared data, and minimizing the capacity consumption of internal IT enablement systems.

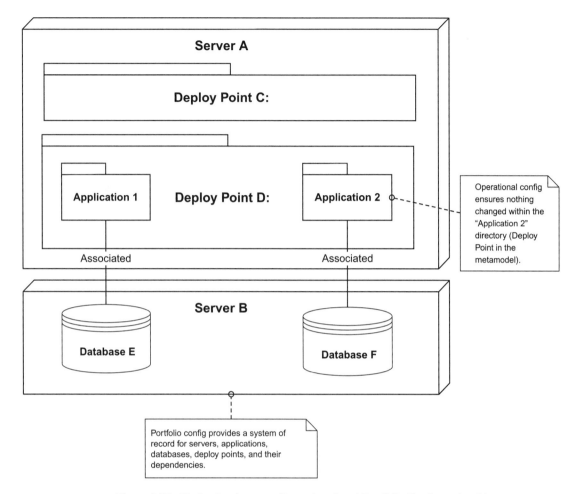

Figure 3.71 Distinction between Operational and Portfolio Configuration Management.

3.8 Making It Real

▶ Do you have an inventory of all the datastores containing internal IT data? What major subjects and entities are contained in each?

▶ Does every data element in your production IT enablement infrastructure have a defined maintenance process? Are data quality metrics defined and measured?

▶ Do any represent "multiple master" situations in which the same data is being maintained in two different places by two different processes or owners? (The core list of Applications is a common problem. Application to Server dependency is another example.)

▶ Do you have the ability to formulate dependency queries? That is, can you report on an Application dependency chain such as Application A is dependent on B is dependent on, and so on, to any number of links in the chain? Can you constrain and filter this query to make it usable (limit the number of links, limit it to only certain data topics, etc.)?

▶ For a given element of infrastructure, can you identify instantly what business Service or Process it supports?

3.9   Chapter Conclusion

The definition and normalization of conceptual entity models is an essential part of any full process analysis.

One of the unfortunate extremes encountered with today's process-centric thinking is the idea that data is some mere technicality whose consideration can be deferred to vendors or developers. The definition and normalization of conceptual entity models is an essential part of any full process analysis and is a key bridge between the process framework and the technical systems supporting it.

This discussion of the essential, process-independent data concepts has clarified the core concept of CI, essential to the maturation of IT enablement. This concept will reappear often in the system and pattern discussions. The management and interactions of these data structures are concerns to be further elucidated in the following material.

The objective of this chapter was to create a controlled vocabulary.

Again, the objectives of this chapter were to create a controlled vocabulary reflecting current IT management discourse and to start to explore some of its implications. The objective was *not* technical design, although the degree of precision required in the vocabulary analysis required the use of modeling notations and matrices.

3.10   Further Reading

This discussion is by no means the first coverage of internal IT data analysis. The most sophisticated efforts are generally found under the heading "metadata" and "metamodeling." Significant work has been done by the OMG, the Distributed Management Task Force, the Tele-Management Forum, and authors such as Adrienne Tannenbaum, David Marco, Michael Jennings, and David Hay. This chapter, as with the process framework, sought to distill much of this effort down into a digestible chapter focused on essentials and terminology in common use.

An early systematic matrix of IT data to process is seen in *A Management System for the Information Business* (IBM 1980). However, the data representation was not as a normalized conceptual data model but rather as data "classes" corresponding to what would be called subject areas today. Although this work was reportedly an input into ITIL, the rigorous data-based approach was lost to the overly general CMDB and CI discussion.

For data modeling generally, see Reingruber and Gregory (1994), Teorey (1994), Hay (1996), Carlis and Maguire (2001), Halpin (2001), and Simsion and Witt (2005). For the OMG specifications on metadata and metamodels, see OMG (2002a and 2002b) and *www.uml.org*.

For the DMTF work, see the Distributed Management Task Force (2000, 2002a, 2002b, and 2003) and Bumpus (2000). Other views of IT domain (meta)data models can be seen in Marco and Jennings (2004) and Hay (2006).

Data Center Markup Language is another standards effort, notable for its advocacy of Semantic Web technology to solve the CMDB data Problem. Although the Semantic Web approach will present significant skills challenges, the promise of that standard seems to fit well with CMDB data requirements: partial knowledge, multiple representations, discovery based, and so forth. I encourage you to investigate this avenue—but the learning curve for any hands-on implementation will be significant.[192]

For IT metrics and measurements with respect to SLAs, see Ruijs and Schotanus (2002), Brooks (2006), and Aitken (2003), Chapter 5. For the classic discussion of dimension management and modeling, see Kimball (1998) and Kimball and Ross (2002). Dennis Gaughan of AMR Research (paid subscription required) is actively developing a comprehensive metrics hierarchy for IT.

For an overview of the history of transaction-based processing in the context of end-to-end response management, see Tsykin (2002). For further information on the Integration Competency Center concept, see Schmidt and Lyle (2005). For discussion of the Application–Service relationship, see the ITIL *Application Management* volume (Office of Government Commerce 2002a). For further information on events and application management, see Sturm and Bumpus (1999) and Bumpus (2000).

4

A Supporting Systems Architecture

> If you look at the glossy brochures and listen to the sales talk, Service Management tools are indispensable. However, good people, good process descriptions, and good procedures and working instructions are the basis for successful Service Management.
>
> —ITIL[193]

> We've seen best-in-class portfolio management processes implemented on a shoestring software budget, using spreadsheets and document templates. We've also seen worst-in-class practices implemented with million-dollar portfolio management applications.
>
> —Jeff Kaplan[194]

VARIATIONS ON THE PRECEDING quotes are *de rigueur* in most discussions of IT enablement. However, at some point the process architecture is defined and it becomes clear that manual approaches usually won't work in IT organizations of any size. As discussed at the outset of this book, companies then turn to the research organizations, the vendors, or both. However, the vendors are clearly self-interested, and the research organizations receive much of their funding from the vendors and are not articulating a comprehensive vision for how IT enablement tooling must interoperate. Hence, this chapter. Enablement tools and architectures *are* important and must be given their due.

An application system is a fixed-form combination of computing processes and data structures that support a specific business purpose.

First, what is an application "system"? The definition this book will use is a fixed-form combination of computing processes and data structures that support a specific business purpose. Fixed form means that the system is stable in functionality (relative to its context) unless explicitly changed through a controlled process. A specific business purpose in the context of this book would mean one or more processes from Part I and the individuals and groups involved.

This chapter has several goals. First, it discusses the generic categories of internal IT enablement systems and potential interactions and overlaps. One issue in particular in this area is the proliferation of single-point systems. Most readers may be confronted with a variety of legacy investments that need to interoperate better in support of enterprise IT processes; "rip and replace" is rarely an option. Providing a framework to support such efforts is a primary goal of this chapter.

Although the "ERP for IT" concept evokes the idea of a single, massively integrated system on a common data repository, this idealistic vision will probably never encompass all systems functionality described here. There are strong practical reasons to maintain loosely coupled systems; having the same architecture supporting source code control and IT financial planning would make a lot of sense. However, in analyzing what a true ERP for IT system might look like, it is necessary to consider all systems that might be related to it.

The ERP for IT concept may be completely virtual in many organizations for years to come. However, this chapter also discusses ideal, more integrated future-state architectures.

A Story of Too Many Tools

From *www.erp4it.com*

Author's note: This is a fictionalized composite of a number of organizations I am familiar with. What is distressing is the number of comments I received after writing it confirming its similarity to many other organizations that I have no experience with. *A story from a large IT shop not too far from here…*

Bill and Sandy were having lunch in the cafeteria. Bill was in the IT financial planning group, and Sandy was from the project office.

Bill said, "It seems like we go through this every year, and it's gotten much worse since the tech bubble popped. We can't explain nearly well enough how we support the business!"

Sandy pointed out, "Well, in terms of project funding it's pretty clear—the business sponsors sign up for what they want, and we deliver it."

Bill replied, "Yes, that might be the one area we're doing somewhat right. But what I'm more concerned about is how foggy everything gets when the system is in place and running for a while. We don't have good visibility into the total cost of ownership."

Sandy asked, "Well, can't you get reports out of the operations side of things?"

Bill answered, "Yes, that's the problem. There are several different areas and they don't report on the same things, or even look at the environment the same way. It's all on spreadsheets and in people's heads."

Sandy said, "You know, that's similar to what I hear from the project managers. They are always complaining that their teams don't have the information they need to fix, enhance, or integrate systems."

Bill replied, "Well, maybe we need some systems of our own."

Bill and Sandy weren't the only ones feeling the pain; their problems had become widely appreciated, and as a result the IT executive committee authorized an unprecedented investment in internal systems just to run the IT organization's business processes. This caused some raised eyebrows on the business side, but the CIO made a persuasive case that this investment would result in far better bang for the IT buck.

The money was allocated among various stakeholders.

John in enterprise architecture purchased a leading enterprise architecture tool and started building functional, system, and information models.

Jeff in the engineering group purchased a sophisticated discovery tool and started mapping the as-is connections of deployed technologies.

Chris's operations group continued to work with a management framework, receiving some incremental investment to add that vendor's CMDB.

Terry, running the help desk, continued to use an old but powerful mainframe-based tool for day-to-day operations.

Jane in the project office purchased a portfolio management tool and started defining IT portfolios. However, the time tracking was still done in a different system (a human resource management system module of the central ERP system).

Joe in the asset management office purchased a dedicated asset management tool and started entering all servers, licenses, and so forth.

In the meantime, Sheila in the data group had been running a metadata repository for about 10 years, but had never quite been able to get the funding to fully populate it or the buy-in from the other IT areas to contribute to and leverage it—it was always seen as a "data dictionary," although it was capable of representing virtually every element in the IT environment.

(continued)

Project managers were deployed across the board to drive all of the initiatives to completion. Although there were a few hallway conversations in which people started to wonder about the possible redundancy of these projects, the timeline-focused project managers always said "out of scope" and discussions were quickly halted.

When these projects were completed, reports started to filter up to the senior executives. Although each area seemed to have made some progress, the meetings were increasingly spent in unproductive "spreadsheet wars." In particular, even though the concept of "total cost of ownership" for the enterprise's systems was a key issue for the CIO, it wasn't something anyone really seemed to own.

Joe said, "Well, I can tell you how much we're spending on servers and licenses, but the support costs would have to come from the time-tracking system."

The CIO said, "Joe, in your asset management report, you have all your hardware expenses rolling up to engineering. Don't projects actually pay for some?"

Joe answered, "Well, we discovered we need an interface to get the project definitions into the asset system, and now we're out of money to build that integration."

Jane said, "And aren't some servers shared across projects? Can your system handle that?"

Joe answered, "Actually, I think it only can track an asset against one project. The vendor is tracking this as a future enhancement. That requirement got by us; our RFP process was a little rushed and these integration requirements actually came up pretty late."

The CIO said, "I'm still not hearing how we get to TCO. Servers and software bought by projects are all very well, but what about maintenance and support? We're spending three-quarters of our budget there. And are we talking TCO for a project, or something else? It seems we need to be tracking things by system, but some of these tools think it's all about the project. What about the help desk?"

Terry said, "Unfortunately our software is all structured around supporting the client, not classifying the service request for TCO. What we need is to tie our call types into a master list of our systems, but this is going to be tough on this legacy ticketing system."

The CIO was pretty frustrated. He had come from a data warehousing background and had seen this same sort of thing on the business side: spreadsheets and reports filtering up to the senior level that just didn't agree. "Do you mean to tell me we've done the same thing to ourselves we've been trying to fix for our clients for the past 15 years?" he asked. "How could this happen?"

Some of the architects noticed that the discovery tool looked something like an enterprise architecture tool, but no one seemed to have a clear idea of how it related to the product the architects were using. There were significant differences—the discovery tool didn't have a real modeling capability—but the overlaps in the system description and decomposition space were troubling.

Each team seemed to think the other should be providing it with an interface, and the vendors were no help—they could support interfaces going either way, but each vendor wanted its system to be primary and none could provide the all-important data mapping. A couple of software engineers looked at the problem on a technical level and were disturbed at the complexity involved; "these are some of the hardest interface requirements I've ever seen," said one very senior engineer. "Aren't there some standards that could help here?"

The problems went on. The management framework's new version had a nice service dependency mapping capability integrated with the monitoring tool, but the engineering staff didn't have a firm grasp of which business areas consumed what infrastructure service or even how to define something so nebulous.

The enterprise architecture staff members had an understanding of what a service was and the overall relationship with the business but didn't have access to the management framework and were wondering why their enterprise architecture modeling tool couldn't play a part here—after all, it was the system of record for applications and services and their interdependencies.

The relationship among the management framework, the discovery tool, and the enterprise architecture tool started to consume a lot of time and conversation. The interim solution was dual (and in some cases even triple) maintenance of quite complex system hierarchies and interconnections, which started immediately to have accuracy problems. All three systems pulled data from the asset management list of servers, which also caused questions from the leadership.

The vendors in the meantime were doing their best to increase the scope of their licenses. Lunches and rounds of golf helped entrench each IT area more into its chosen software.

Finally, a consultant was brought in. The CIO didn't quite know where to look, so he asked around for someone with ITIL credentials and some enterprise application implementation experience. Al was pretty in demand lately.

His first assessment: "You folks have bought way too many toys, and not spent nearly enough time working out what your processes and requirements are. This is the same problem I've seen over and over again in ERP projects for human resources and finance: the senior executives who need to define the requirements haven't had the time to really focus, so their staff just goes out and buys stuff based

(continued)

on vendor interpretations of what the requirements are. The trouble is in IT, everything overlaps even worse than in finance or HR."

He went on, "The other area in which big application projects fail is just building agreement among the stakeholders! When you've decided to integrate multiple systems, there are all kinds of politics baked into seemingly simple issues like how you are going to roll up your reports. Seems like no one took ownership of this."

The CIO agreed. "From what I can tell, no vendor emphasized the need for us all to agree on what the 'things' were in the environment we're trying to manage."

Al responded, "That's like setting up a financial system and not agreeing on the chart of accounts. You know, you could have started some of that work in a spreadsheet—and it's probably the most important thing!"

4.1 Systems and Families

There are few systems that provide an integrated, end-to-end value chain view of IT.

IT systems categories have a functional flavor. There are systems for planning and controlling, systems for building, and systems for running. There are also a number of systems that focus on information management and some systems that bridge the functional boundaries. However, there are few that provide an integrated, end-to-end value chain view of IT—you have to integrate a variety of off-the-shelf solutions to create such a capability.

The tool categories include the following:

▶ Portfolio management systems
▶ Project management systems
▶ Capacity management systems
▶ Various types of IT-optimized business intelligence systems: dashboards, scorecards, portals
▶ Risk and compliance systems
▶ Software development enablement systems
  • Requirements management
  • Issue management
  • Modeling or CASE tools
▶ Software configuration and build management
▶ Configuration management systems
▶ Provisioning systems
▶ Incident management and help desk systems

- ▶ Change management systems
- ▶ ITSM suites, covering some set of incident, problem, change, configuration management, and sometimes release
- ▶ Business service management systems
- ▶ Service request fulfillment systems
- ▶ Monitoring and element management systems

There have been various frameworks proposed for categorizing them; for the purposes of this analysis, the value chain is wrapped into a circle and segregated into functional areas, around a core of information management (Figure 4.1).

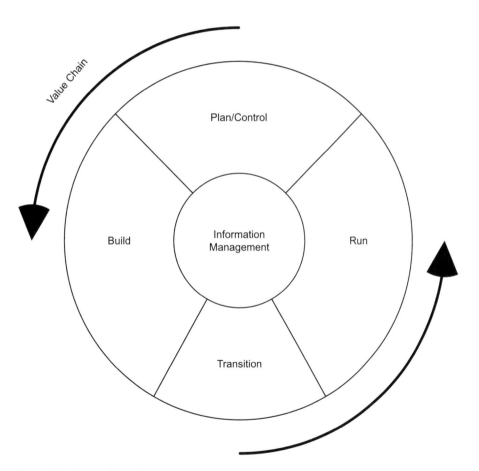

Figure 4.1 System domains.

Currently available IT systems are functional silos, and it is the task of the consumer to integrate them into a value chain semblance.

We do this because there are few examples of full value chain ITRP systems. Instead, the currently available systems are functional silos, and it is the task of the consumer to integrate them into a value chain semblance.

One purpose of this section is to provide a larger grouping and sense of order to the myriad classification schemes and reference categories of systems proliferating in the trade press and from the research vendors. This is not an attempt to replace the ongoing work of research firms in tracking various categories and the systems in them.

Here is a simple systems integration model (Figure 4.2).

This is a simplified representation of a subset of the systems described in this chapter and their relationships. More comprehensive depictions on one diagram become complex and start to tax human comprehension; additional systems and relationships thus will appear later in this chapter.

Minimally, a large IT organization needs to have most or all of the preceding systems in some form or other—either as standalone products or as logical

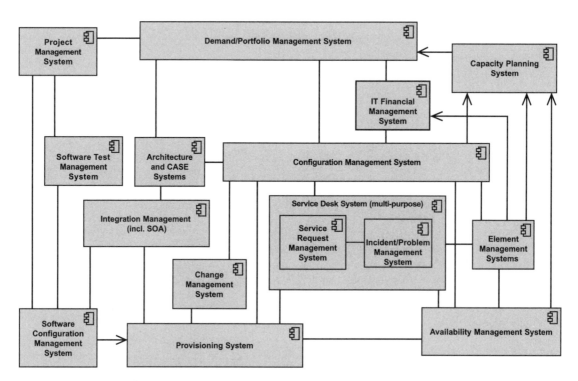

Figure 4.2 Simplified IT system integration model.

functionality within other products. More detailed context diagrams are presented throughout the next section.

4.2 Cohesion and Coupling

The manner in which we physically divide a system into pieces (particularly in relation to the problem structure) can affect significantly the structural complexity of the resulting system.

—Edward Yourdon and Larry Constantine[195]

The objective of this chapter is to clarify, using the preceding process and data analysis, the types and interactions of the IT enablement systems, with an eye toward understanding their needed evolution and consolidation. To this end there are two concepts from software engineering that become useful: "cohesion" and "coupling."

In the context of systems analysis, coupling is a measure of the interdependence of one system on others. A tightly coupled set of systems is a set of systems that have many interconnections and/or strongly depend on one another for services—if system A is not functioning, system B is typically compromised. Loosely coupled systems have fewer interdependencies, and the interdependencies they have are more forgiving—if system A is not functioning, system B may be able to continue providing services.

Cohesion is a measure of the strength of the association of elements within a system and its singleness of purpose. A system should do one thing, and do it well. This is easier to establish at the lower technical levels of software engineering but becomes more subjective as you move into higher levels of abstraction such as the concept of "application system" generally. Nevertheless, cohesion is still a useful filter; you don't want network monitoring and project management in the same system!

Obviously, the concept of an ERP system provides some challenges of cohesiveness. ERP systems aggregate much diverse functionality and might be seen as poorly cohesive. However, this functionality is always subdivided into modules, and the modules overall share common data structures, which makes a cohesive framework a logical solution.

SOA in some respects has emerged as a response to the limitations of ERP's monolithic, shared data approach. However, there are sound technical and practical reasons for centralized datastores; SOA with its implied increase in data replication and heterogeneous system dependencies is inherently harder to achieve.

> You don't want network monitoring and project management in the same system!

The ITRP system should treat the primary IT value chain as a cohesive problem.

Use these concepts as appropriate and not as dogma. They give further refinement of the ERP for IT, or ITRP principles.

The ITRP system should treat the primary IT value chain as a cohesive problem. This does not mean that every activity within that value chain is automated by the large-scale system (that would be impossible); it simply means that the system sees the value chain as a whole and interoperates as needed with the tactical and operational systems to monitor and control the overall IT objectives.

The ERP for IT system should interoperate with, but not assimilate as a first priority, those other cohesive problem areas that can be loosely coupled to the core system.

The core system should be system of record for all cross-process reference data.

The coupling points (process handoffs and reference data) should be explicitly identified and managed; the core system should be system of record for all cross-process reference data.

The cross-functional nature of the value chain becomes apparent in this analysis.

4.3 Systems for Planning and Controlling

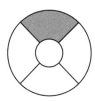

This section includes tools for planning and controlling IT activities, such as the initial customer relationship management, ideation and demand management, and risk management, as well as high-level feedback tools from the development and operations areas.

Demand/Portfolio Management System

Description

A demand/portfolio management system is a planning and controlling tool.

Although demand and portfolio management are conceptually distinct, the reality is that their product families have converged. At its base, a demand/portfolio management system is a planning and controlling tool for making informed investment decisions across baskets of similar IT elements, including the following:

▶ Planning ideas
▶ Projects
▶ Assets
▶ Services
▶ Processes
▶ Applications

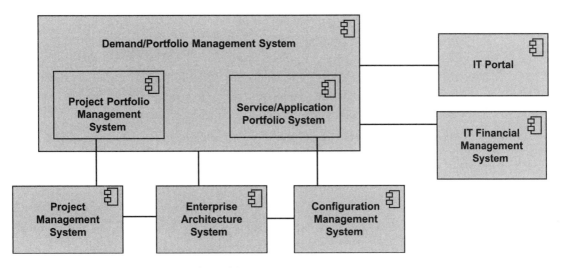

Figure 4.3 Demand/portfolio system context.

▶ Data
▶ Human resources
▶ Technologies
▶ Hardware

This is a functionally oriented system type, optimized for supporting steady-state, calendar-driven, and event-driven activities requiring information for various purposes. It is characterized by the ability to define a set of metrics for a given set of portfolio elements and display such metrics in characteristic visual formats such as bubble charts and heat maps.

The demand management functionality provides a front-end intake system for requests for changes to IT services themselves. There's ambiguity here; what is the relationship between a demand management system and a service request management system?

Demand management typically implies one or more of the following:

▶ A new service or change to a service
▶ Incremental investment (not base)
▶ Project management methods

A request for a new workstation, or access to a system, is not demand management. A new $50 million ERP system is. There is a gray zone in the middle,

The demand management functionality provides a front-end intake system for requests for changes to IT services themselves.

however; what about requests for new Web content? Some organizations might provide such services as a base, with a well-defined service request process.

Demand management implies prioritization and often will leverage portfolio management techniques to assess the suitability of a proposed investment; however, it diverges from portfolio management conceptually in that true end-to-end portfolio management will also monitor the ongoing progress of a project and the final service product delivered. Demand can be seen as the front end to portfolio.

See the "Clarify Service Entry Points" pattern in Chapter 5.

Subtypes

Subtypes are project portfolio management system and application portfolio management system.

Gotchas

Applications are notorious for having multiple representations of the same logical "thing."

Portfolios of logical assets such as services, processes, and applications depend on well-controlled procedures for defining their members. Applications are notorious for having multiple representations of the same logical "thing," and without a controlled system of record the portfolio cannot be managed.

IT portfolio management in general has many overlapping definitions, and the scopes of tools marketed in this sector are similarly diverse.

Note that the process area "manage portfolio" includes enterprise architecture activities that would be primarily supported by the enterprise architecture system modeling tools.

Some application portfolio management tools provide no means for linking applications to other elements in the infrastructure. This will ultimately be an unacceptable limitation. If the application portfolio tool is distinct from the CMDB, it must be clear which is the system of record for the application or service concept.

Overlaps/Consider Platforming On

Because portfolio management has significant overlaps with and depends on information from other systems in the IT value chain, portfolio management as a function may not require its own system. The characteristic analytics of portfolio management (bubble charts, heat maps) can be created using off-the-shelf business intelligence tools against a back-end data mart, possibly replicated from information sources such as the financial management system, asset management system, service-level management system, CMDB, and/or project tracking system—perhaps all consolidated in an IT data mart (described later). Outbound integrations are especially important if the portfolio tool is a master source (system of record) for reference data (e.g., master list of applications).

Application portfolio management is relevant for both in-house (bespoke) applications and externally developed packages and Software as a Service (SaaS); application portfolio management does not depend on having access to application source code. In this taxonomy, source code analysis is the domain of the "reverse engineering/code analysis" system type, not "application portfolio management."[196]

Interactions with the IT capability can be channeled through a central service desk that might use a workflow-based service request tool. However, a true demand management tool provides some rich self-service capabilities for customers to outline the new or changed functionality they seek. It would be possible to build such functionality on any standard workflow-based engine.

Most project portfolio management systems also handle demand management. Application portfolio systems are more aligned with enterprise architecture and configuration management. See the "Portfolio" section in Chapter 3 as well for discussion of the relationship between application and project portfolios.

The demand management tool requires access to current metrics on IT resource consumption; integration with the service request, incident management, and project management systems would be required to fully enable this (perhaps using the centralized IT data mart).

Project portfolio management and project management are two different reference system types.

Note that project portfolio management and project management are two different reference system types. One focuses on *all* projects and their investment decision and status; the other focuses on executing individual projects (e.g., from the point of view of an individual project manager) and tracking their day-to-day activities. Vendors are combining the functionality, but it doesn't have to be seen as inherently tightly coupled. In many cases, they will be the same product; however, in some cases time tracking may be handled in a different system.

Service Management System

Description
ITSM is a broad concept, so systems professing to support service management are similarly broad. Roughly speaking, they span a space that starts (from bottom

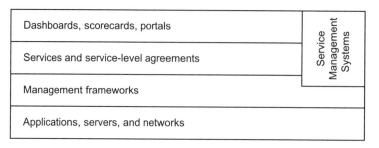

Figure 4.4 Service management system domain.

to top) at the high end of enterprise management frameworks and ends at the contractual SLA enforcement and executive dashboards and scorecards, shading into portfolio management concerns (Figure 4.4).

Subtypes

Subtypes include management framework–based systems and standalone systems.

Gotchas

Business service management requires the involvement of enterprise architects and business analysts, as well as operational staff.

This is a poorly cohesive system type because of the overall breadth of the ITSM concept. One implementation issue with business service management–type tools is that, although the intention is to provide links between the business and the IT operational elements, the definition of business functions and processes is something that the service management team may not be versed in. Correctly implementing business service management thus requires the involvement of enterprise architects and business analysts, as well as operational staff.

Business service management is an outgrowth of the management frameworks and therefore implies *instrumented* dependency mapping, in which the components involved in the service map are actively monitored. Of course, not all services in a large IT organization merit such active monitoring.

The CMDB data will be a superset of the instrumented dependencies managed in the business service management tool.

If dependencies are maintained in a business service management tool, these dependencies need to remain aligned with the dependencies in a CMDB or repository. The CMDB data will be a superset of the instrumented dependencies managed in the business service management tool. The Assembly CI entity would be appropriate as a basis for service maps.

Overlaps/Consider Platforming On

The more robust management frameworks are incorporating much of the higher-end display and SLA adherence functionality characterizing standalone

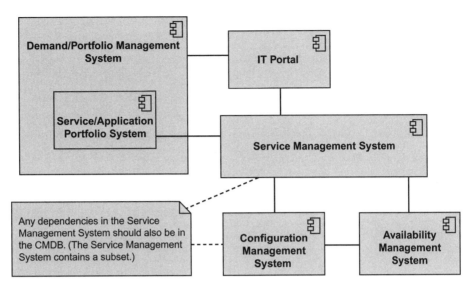

Figure 4.5 Service management system context.

service management systems. Dependency mapping (seen in business service management systems) is available also as add-ons to management frameworks (e.g., HP Service Navigator for HP Openview). The portfolio management system has clear affinities but a more strategic focus. Determining the relationship between IT operational reporting and IT business intelligence is part of the question.

Capacity Planning System

Description
A capacity planning system consists of a large-volume datastore containing historical performance information, coupled with specialized analytics and modeling to project various consumption scenarios (bandwidth, storage, and processing) and their financial and technical consequences. This is a fairly cohesive system type.

Gotchas
There are *big* storage requirements to do this right.

Overlaps/Consider Platforming On
Although the base datastore is amenable to commodity storage approaches, there really is no substitute for advanced capacity analytics. This is not something you want to try writing on your own.

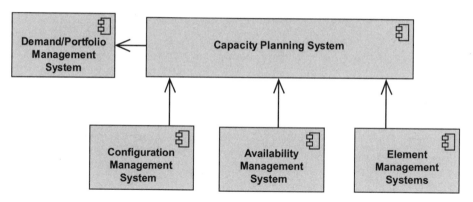

Figure 4.6 Capacity management system context.

As ITIL notes, "The CMDB and CDB [capacity database] may be the same database, but even if not a single database, there is a data set that is common between the two databases."[197]

The capacity system needs reference data from the configuration management system (e.g., applications and their dependencies) and detailed monitoring of capacity trends from the availability management system and element management systems. (Element management systems information may be routed through the availability system or directly sent to capacity.)

The capacity system in turn feeds demand management with recommendations and information regarding capacity-driven requirements for new or increased capacity.

Enterprise Architecture System

Description

Enterprise architecture can be (provocatively) summarized as portfolio management implemented through graphical modeling.

An enterprise architecture "system" can encompass a variety of purposes. Portfolio management with graphical modeling is one way to summarize this category. Architecture is particularly concerned with dependencies, categorizations, and modeling techniques:

▶ Functional
▶ Process
▶ Data
▶ System
▶ Matrices
▶ Scenario

Some architecture methods stress the creation of various "views" on a problem domain; others look to the Zachman framework and its systematic identification of metadata types throughout an enterprise context.

Achieving traceability from high-level concepts such as business objectives down through organizational functions, processes, systems, and infrastructure is typical of enterprise architecture modeling. Definition of current and future-state scenarios is another common activity, anticipatory to demand and as a precursor to project initiation.

Integration between enterprise architecture, portfolio management, metadata, and configuration management is highly desirable but not well supported by any products today. For example, if an architect is modeling a system architecture and drops an application system icon from a palette, a picklist of existing applications could appear for selection (with a "create new" option) based on the defined enterprise portfolio.

Gotchas

Enterprise architecture must take its own medicine in designing its enablement systems.

Enterprise architecture is a function, not a process, and architecture modeling efforts often have no defined maintenance process. Integrating enterprise architecture with some version of change and configuration management processes is advisable, which will require careful discussion as to process scope and handoffs. Full-blown configuration management efforts have been built on enterprise architecture capabilities, but it's not clear that this is desirable.

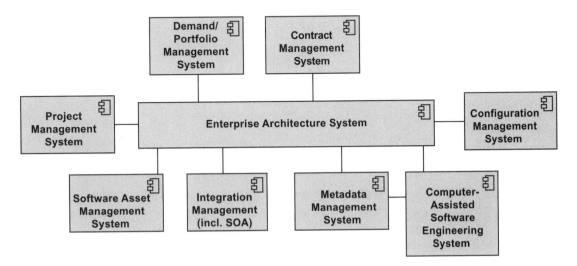

Figure 4.7 Enterprise Architecture System context.

Overlaps/Consider Platforming On

Architecture modeling, when primarily a graphical exercise (and less concerned with portfolios), can be done with off-the-shelf UML tools.[198] Such tools may have limitations in repository support and reporting and analysis capabilities (e.g., creating a dependency matrix as done in this book). UML also does not natively contain business architecture domain concepts such as strategy, mission, goal, objective, capability, and so forth.

Visio is a particularly inexpensive tool with a rich API that a number of third-party vendors have leveraged to create rich repository-based solutions.

The poor cohesiveness of the enterprise architecture system concept is evident from its many possible interfaces. Most commonly, enterprise architecture "systems" are seen as some variant on CASE modeling (e.g., data, process, and system modeling). However, if the enterprise architecture team is responsible for process-based workflow, such as systematic review of demand requests, projects, product evaluations, and contracts, this may also be reflected in their tools. Enterprise architecture groups are often concerned with driving component and now SOA reuse, involving further distinct system types. Metadata may directly interface with enterprise architecture and may be an aggregation point for information from integration and CASE systems. Data architecture, with its particular tooling requirements, may be part of the enterprise architecture teams' responsibilities, further expanding the system scope into areas such as data standards and profiling.

In general, there are many variations on how this area may be architected, and the intention and business purpose of the enterprise architecture capability must always be considered first. It is truly a case of taking one's own medicine.

Business Continuity Management System

Description

Provisioning systems' precisely scripted installation and configuration capabilities provides increased confidence in service restoration in the event of an outage.

Systems in this category focus on the process of certifying that a given service, process, or application is recoverable (analysis and approach has been completed), as well as that of performing knowledge management for the business continuity planning, or BCP (a.k.a. IT service continuity) function. One unique aspect is that these tools need to manage restoration sequences, not just static dependencies; some manual BCP efforts, for example, have documented recovery plans in Microsoft Project. This is an area ripe for further tool support and integration with the software development life cycle, because such recovery plans are best established when the initial install scripts are developed and documented. Instead, they are too often done after the fact. One of the justifications for automated provisioning systems is that their precisely scripted installation and configuration capabilities provide more confidence in service restoration in the event of an outage.

Generally a continuity plan—wherever and however it is expressed—is a sequenced list of CI activations. Any element (CI) in a continuity plan not in the CMDB is theoretically an exception, and CIs not appearing in any continuity plan would be another potential exception report—for high-maturity organizations.

Gotchas

These systems have a big potential problem if they do not interoperate with CMDBs. The same dependencies needed for BCP are needed for support and portfolio management purposes. However, some of the consultants in this sector advise against this approach for unclear reasons.

Overlaps/Consider Platforming On

Service effects must be determined with respect to the business functions and processes depending on the IT infrastructure.

This class of system requires visibility into IT assets and dependency management—that is, a CMDB. Determining the effect of an outage (and therefore the priority of service restoration) is typically done with reference to the business functions and processes supported by the IT infrastructure. Such business analysis should be done in a unified, maintainable way and not as a continuity-driven one-off—hence the recommended integration with the enterprise architecture system. As noted previously, basing a system on an automated provisioning system decreases risk (as

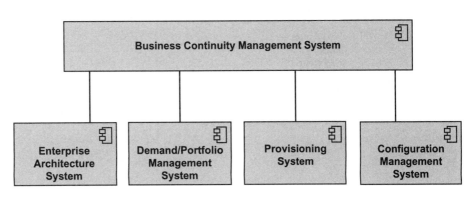

Figure 4.8 Continuity system context.

opposed to relying on manually documented installation procedures that may be incorrectly executed during a stressful crisis).

Risk Management System

Description

A risk management system is similar to a BCP system in that it is focused on both risk and compliance priorities and workflow, as well as enough IT element knowledge to have something to tie risks to. For example, a risk management system might focus on processes as risk elements.

A related class of system is the "compliance system." Compliance to regulations such as Basel II, Sarbanes-Oxley, and HIPAA can take so many forms that vendor marketing of "compliance" systems borders on disingenuous. Compliance initiatives can often be well handled through diligent application of BPM principles; vendor solutions based on a general-case BPM tool (perhaps tied into a CMDB) might be a better approach.

> Vendor marketing of "compliance" systems borders on disingenuous.

Gotchas

Risks do not stand alone; they are always with respect to some *thing*—CIs, projects, changes. Are the risk components or elements redundant with other datastores, for example, the CMDB?

Overlaps/Consider Platforming On

A CMDB framework that can manage IT elements and dependencies effectively may also be able to handle the basic status determination or workflow

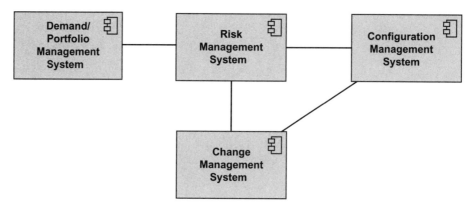

Figure 4.9 Risk Management System context.

necessary to ensure that the risk identification process is carried out thoroughly and systematically.

IT Financial Management System

The IT financial management system is a logical grouping of some combination of the systems shown in Figure 4.10. As ITIL notes, it includes core accounting functions usually handled by enterprise financial systems. IT-specific financial functionality is often handled in spreadsheets. In larger organizations, there is opportunity to further automate this, especially through integration with a CMDB or element management tooling that might become the system of record for resource unit costs. Financial metrics might be derived through usual reporting approaches based on the IT data mart (sourced in turn from project management, service request management, and service management capabilities).

Purchasing System

Description

A purchasing system is used to track defined vendors and purchases from them. This system category overlaps broadly with non-IT functions and may be a primarily non-IT system, supporting IT as one of many areas needing structured vendor management. These systems overlap with accounts payable and purchasing functionality on the enterprise financial side; however, an accounts payable system may not include vendor product catalog functionality.

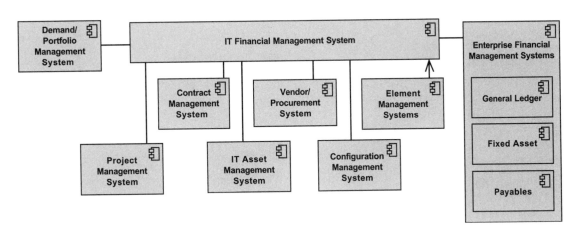

Figure 4.10 IT Financial Management System context.

Such systems are a control point for expenditures on information technology and should (as with the contract management systems) be governed by appropriate architectural checkpoints to minimize the acquisitions of redundant and unsupported technology.

Overlaps/Consider Platforming On

Such systems are often separate from contract and asset management systems. Seek integration. Also, they are origination points for the technology product entity, data about the "building blocks" currently in use for delivering an organization's IT services (see the Technology Product entity in the conceptual data model).

Contract Management System

Description

A contract management system is optimized for the management and storage of documented contractual agreements. Beyond simple document management, contract management systems overlap with vendor management systems, filling such requirements as ensuring that negotiated discounts are reflected in actual charges. Much money can be saved through the correct implementation of contract management.

Gotchas

Contract management systems need to be integrated with configuration and asset management, to answer questions such as the following:

▶ What contract covered this asset or CI?
▶ For what project was it negotiated?
▶ What else was purchased with this contract?
▶ Where is it now? What is it being used for? Who "owns" it?
▶ What are its performance and utilization measurements?

Overlaps/Consider Platforming On

Contract management systems have a document management aspect, but document management systems have a focus on managing unstructured data. To answer the preceding questions, the contract must have a tie into the structured world.

Such systems are a control point for expenditures on information technology and should (as with vendor–procurement systems) be governed by appropriate architectural checkpoints to minimize the acquisitions of redundant and unsupported technology. This may imply an interface, for example, with enterprise architecture technology approval processes.

Some vendors are offering integrated contract and asset management systems.[199]

Asset Management System

Description

An asset management system tracks organizational investments in tangible property considered valuable enough to maintain records for. This record keeping activity needs to enable the following:

▶ Optimal asset allocation and usage
▶ Asset depreciation tracking and refresh and reinvestment activities
▶ Asset security and loss prevention
▶ License management and reuse

Subtypes

Subtypes are facilities, desktop, and data center.

Gotchas

Is the IT asset management system highly redundant with configuration management? Contract and vendor management?

Overlaps/Consider Platforming On

When data center assets become a significant investment, simple tools no longer suffice.

Small and midsize businesses may find their central asset concern is workstations, whose management challenges are becoming well understood. But when data center assets become a significant investment, simple asset management tools no longer suffice. Configuration management becomes essential to answer questions such as "who is using this device" and "what are the consequences/migration cost/risk of replacing it," information necessary in turn to enable chargebacks and asset refresh activities.

It is recommended therefore (at least for larger organizations) that the asset management system be considered a logical function or subsystem of a broader configuration management or ITRP system. The marketplace is quickly converging, and integrated systems of this nature will probably become the standard.

Vendor and contract management systems may feed the asset management system, and in some cases these systems are evolving to cover asset management internally, which poses interesting questions as to their relationship with configuration management. There may also be a corporate fixed assets system requiring interoperation with a dedicated IT asset system.

Facilities Management System

A facilities management system is a specialized type of asset system concerned particularly with building management. Some examples have specialized functionality in representing a data center and its power, HVAC, and cabling plant and can be used to optimize new physical machine provisioning. They have financial, provisioning, and configuration management responsibilities.

Bridging the Plan—Build Functional Boundary

The major vectors from plan or control to build are as follows:

▶ Demand/project portfolio management
▶ Enterprise architecture

Demand/project portfolio management systems handle the identification of requests for new functionality, the management of resources allocated to create the new functionality, and their delivery progress.

Enterprise architecture tools may include modeling tools that might be used in a planning mode by enterprise architects and then subsequently in a design mode by project architects.

Controlling the acquisition of new technology platforms might be handled by either a portfolio or an enterprise architecture system.

IT Portal, Performance Management, and Related Systems

Description

Finally, there is a logical presentation layer that may go by various names:

▶ IT portal
▶ IT digital dashboard
▶ Business performance management

These systems include business intelligence capabilities and rich graphical frameworks. There are a variety of emerging products and approaches, but the most advanced are drawing on the concepts of business activity monitoring and business performance management.

The IT portal may include "workbench" capabilities integrated with, for example, the service request management system. The idea is to create a single interface to structure the activities of all (or most) IT staff. Higher-level users will be presented with dashboards, traffic lights, and drilldown reports.

Gotchas

Some vendors are attempting to "skim the cream." That is, they sell attractive front-end systems that claim to provide powerful insights into the status of an IT organization. Such systems often do reflect some sophistication in IT metrics development. However, the trouble with these systems is that they are too lightweight, requiring expensive integration to obtain the necessary data. This integration is wasteful given that the source system vendors are also moving in the direction of integrating and providing dashboards and other business intelligence analysis capabilities, often based on industrial-strength reporting tools. Basing IT governance on core systems is more in keeping with the principle that data should be managed as part of primary value chain activity.

If internal IT data is well understood and of high quality, the construction of digital dashboards is a relatively straightforward exercise, given the power of modern reporting software packages. The primary value-adding activity for a vendor is assisting in the precise definition of organization-appropriate IT metrics in support of process control objectives—not in building a proprietary reporting framework and claiming some competitive advantage in this commoditized endeavor.

On the other hand, they are first steps and may help enable a more federated approach. The determining factor in any case is the maturity of the organization considering implementing such tools. As in most other areas of business, it is often necessary to integrate data and metrics from multiple systems, and a dedicated system for this purpose may be necessary.

Portals may be useful for IT enablement systems; they enable presentation-layer integration of data, rather than requiring back-end data integration. However, without common IT master reference data (conformed dimensions), a portal infrastructure may add little or no value, being just a bunch of windows ("portlets") from different applications with no conceptual integration.

> If internal IT data is well understood and of high quality, the construction of digital dashboards is a relatively straightforward exercise.

> Without common IT master reference data, a portal infrastructure may add little value.

4.4 Systems for Solutions Delivery

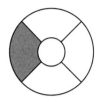

Each stage of solutions development has been accompanied by increasingly richer frameworks and supporting tooling.

For the build functional area, you will find tools supporting the software development life cycle and project management after the initial project approval. This includes system and software development and can go all the way down to granular products of software engineering craft scaffolding. The management of nonproduction environments is also in scope for this functional area.

The history of computing can be seen as the evolution of enablers to better support analysis, design, and construction. Binary gave way to assembler, in turn superseded by third-generation and modern object-oriented languages. Each stage has been accompanied by increasingly richer frameworks and supporting tooling: integrated development environments, proprietary libraries, and a variety of developer enablement tooling, including the following:

▶ Source code control
▶ Automated build management
▶ Code quality analysis tools
▶ Automated testing harnesses

CASE tools have persisted in the guise of data modeling, UML tools, and others. The open source movement continues to provide increasingly rich contributions to software development infrastructure.

Additional to the software craft tooling is the matter of enabling project management, including its gateways into the production world: release and deployment management.

Overall, this area (and its borders into release management) is consolidating under the term Application Lifecycle Management (ALM), which is perhaps equivalent to (or at least a subset of) the broad ITIL concept of Release Management.

Project Management System

Description

A project management system may be the first piece of ITRP or IT enablement tooling purchased by a growing IT organization. Its scope is the management of resources, timelines, deliverables, and dependencies within a project—project being a defined-scope, time-bound set of activities to achieve a specific business objective. A project management system may provide a means of modeling the project's activities and how they must flow, including identification of critical paths and resource bottlenecks. It also may provide a system of record for project staff to track their time and activities, data that in turn drives project metrics such as EVA.

Gotchas

Project managers prefer Microsoft Project.

One of the biggest issues in project management tooling (evident in every IT organization I have worked in) is the preference of project managers for Microsoft Project, with its superior usability and analytic capabilities, versus the preference of project management offices for repository-based project tools that typically have inferior modeling and usability characteristics. Various attempts have been made by vendors to integrate Microsoft Project with repository-based tools, with mixed success.

Overlaps/Consider Platforming On

There is really no substitute for a project management system; however, examples of integration between demand, project portfolio, and project tracking are emerging from the likes of Mercury and CA. The integration of these systems with configuration management and operational systems is the next priority for the industry.

Overall, the project management system (as shown in Figure 4.11) can be seen also as a logical family including requirements, estimation, and issue management.

Requirements Management System

Description

Requirements management is the most critical activity in the project life cycle.

Requirements management has repeatedly been shown to be the most critical activity in the project life cycle in terms of risk reduction and eventual project success. A requirements management system has two major concerns: traceability and audit. There are a number of frameworks and approaches for structuring a requirements management activity, but generally they move from the more general and conceptual to the more specific, with crosscutting aspects such as risk management. Traceability comes in mapping across the general–specific divide so that a specific requirement ("the system must store tax data") may trace to a general requirement ("the system must comply with applicable laws"). It also includes mapping requirements to the project deliverables by which they are fulfilled. Requirements must also have an audit trail, as changes and new requirements drive project scope and risk. When was this new feature asked for, by whom, and who approved it? The general activity of project change control is a stakeholder in requirements tool functionality.

An interesting twist on requirements capture is the recent emergence of graphical user interface simulation tools targeted at business users. Such tools allow users to

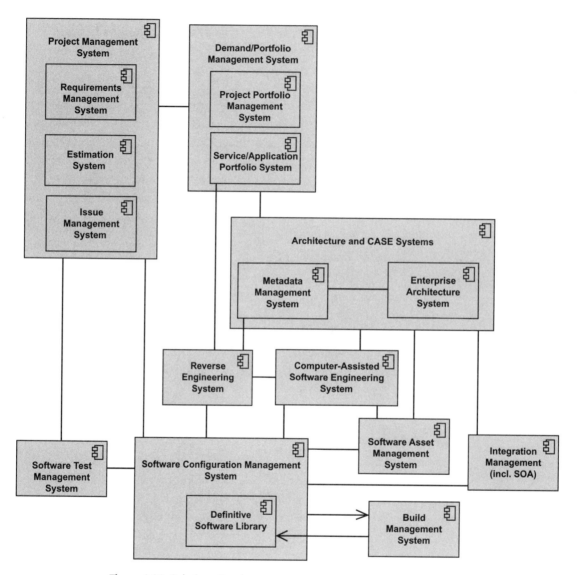

Figure 4.11 Solutions Development context.

mock up screens and rudimentary behavior with a high degree of fidelity, as input into solutions development.

Overlaps/Consider Platforming On

Requirements are often managed in spreadsheets stored in source code management systems. However, this does not provide much granularity in managing them and their changes in particular (depending on how well the spreadsheets are set up and their format honored). Some CASE modeling systems have requirements modules, often starting at the UML use case level. UML use cases, however, are more granular than higher-level conceptual requirements (depending on how they are used). Adopting a development methodology will help clarify these matters and is recommended.

Estimation System

Description
This is a system for modeling the costs associated with either a project or a steady-state capability. The most common examples are project estimation systems based on methodologies such as COCOMO. A current gap in the industry is solutions to assist in TCO or run-rate modeling for ongoing IT services.

Overlaps
Capacity planning tools provide some related services, in particular for determining ongoing run-rate modeling with respect to defined technical elements (storage, bandwidth). More integrated solutions that also included labor forecasting would be welcome.

Issue Management System

Description
This is a project management concept, not to be confused with the ITSM concept of operational incident management. It is the process (in the true BPM definitions) of identifying, tracking, and resolving difficulties that may have been unanticipated in project planning. (Project risk management is similar but sometimes distinguished in project methodologies.)

Overlaps/Consider Platforming On
The core database and forms for issue management systems are trivially simple to build; I have seen several hacked together in a few days by project personnel. If workflow integration (e.g., by email) is added, they become somewhat more complex.

Break-fix issues often are first identified through service support processes.

Software or project issues are always with respect to some *thing*: deliverable, task, bug, and so forth. As with risk systems, standalone issue systems therefore have less value proposition than those integrated with some larger system, usually project management or possibly software configuration management. Fully automated integration with incident and problem management is not common, and this would be a big plus, as break-fix issues often are first identified through service support processes.

A best practice for system changes is requiring traceability to defined requirements, incidents, or problems, and integration between incident and issue enables this. See the "Justify Change" pattern in Chapter 5.

CASE Tools

See entry in the next section.

Software Asset Management System

Description

This system type has two quite divergent connotations: managing the base of installed software licenses and managing internally developed software as costly, reusable intellectual property. This definition is for the latter.

Code reuse is a Holy Grail among development organizations, and enabling this is the primary goal of software asset management systems. The initial versions of these systems came of age during the industry focus on component architectures (CORBA and COM), before the rise of SOAs. The first-generation software asset management systems therefore show awareness of software assets as represented by compiled binaries, as well as defined interfaces, and usually can interface with source code control systems. These vendors are moving rapidly to support reuse of SOA components.

The OMG's Reusable Asset Specification is a relevant industry standard in this area.

Gotchas

The use of the word "asset" in this class of system can lead to confusion with general asset management systems.

There is convergence between software asset management and metadata management systems.

Overlaps/Consider Platforming On

There is clearly convergence between software asset management and metadata management in the eyes of research firms, although the actual data subjects being stored differ considerably (data dictionary versus component information down to the API level). An enterprise architecture modeling tool, especially if based on UML, can represent software components as well and, because enterprise architecture is often charged with enabling reuse, may need integration with the software asset system.

SOA Management System

Description

SOA, as represented by the UDDI, SOA, and WSDL standards, is essentially an attempt (enabled by today's more powerful processing and network architectures) to finally realize the promise of component-based development through eliminating the debate over middleware binary wire formats (the standards are based on ASCII over HTTP). As with previous efforts of this nature (dating back at least to efforts at enabling reusable transactions in CICS and other transaction processing environments) defining semantics and thus enabling reuse is a concern. (There are technical aspects to managing SOA as well, such as security and load balancing; these element management aspects of SOA are of less interest to this book.) As noted previously, SOA registries (which generally look to the UDDI standard) are being incorporated into more general software asset reuse repositories. What will be the relationship between the Reusable Asset Specification (RAS) and UDDI in such tools? (A question to ask your vendors.)

Subtypes

Some tools in this area focus specifically on documenting the metadata for XML schemas, which define the structure of messages exchanged over SOAs.

Overlaps/Consider Platforming On

If an enterprise architecture organization is attempting to drive reuse and service rationalization, it will need access to the SOA repository.

Possibilities include software asset management systems, UML tools, or dedicated metadata repositories. (General purpose metadata repositories are just starting to support this space.) Again, if an enterprise architecture organization is attempting to drive reuse and service rationalization, it will need access to the SOA repository.

Software Configuration Management System

Description

A critical capability for any organization actually developing software, the software configuration management (SCM) tool provides a managed environment for containing source code and its derivations (including executable binaries), as well as other project documentation. (It is also known as "source control.") "Managed environment" in this context means that changes to the items under control are tracked and an audit trail (in this case known as a version history) is maintained.

Subtypes

Subtypes are source code control and build management.

Overlaps/Consider Platforming On

There is really no substitute for SCM; it's a fundamental requirement for many if not most forms of IT project management, although free open source tools are quite robust.

The use of the word "configuration management" causes confusion with configuration management in the ITSM sense. While it is true that the configuration management function and related change control processes are similar conceptually between development and operations, the actual functionality of an SCM tool versus a CMDB is quite different. A CMDB is more of a card catalog, showing records *about* IT assets, and an SCM tool is a repository that actually *contains* an important class of IT asset—software in its various forms—and possibly unstructured project documentation. Furthermore, the SCM tool contains work in progress and human-understandable representations of software (i.e., source code), and a production-focused CMDB typically might only concentrate on the final executable code deployed to production.

Build management is a separate, related class of tools. Mature environments use build management tools as a bridge between the source repository and the provisioning system (Figure 4.12).

ITIL calls for the SCM tool to be interfaced with the CMDB. This is not widely supported in today's market; the road map for achieving this will involve the SCM–build–provisioning relationship, with the provisioning system feeding the CMDB.

ITIL also suggests that the Definitive Software Library may be a logical partition of the SCM system.

Software Test Management (a.k.a. Quality) System

Description

This class of tooling supports quality control for systems development. Testing is (or at least ought to be) an activity universal to all IT projects, and there are various

> A CMDB is a card catalog, showing records about IT assets, and an SCM tool is a repository that actually contains an important IT asset—software.

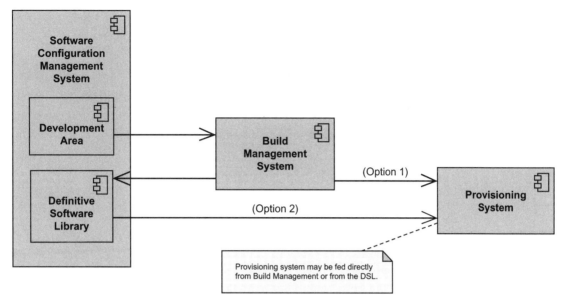

Figure 4.12 Source code, build, and provisioning systems.

approaches to managing it, usually integral parts of a given software methodology. Test management systems support the activity of testing through organizing the complexity of test conditions, scenarios, execution cycles, and expected versus actual results. They also may support the automated execution of some types of tests, generally anything scriptable.

Agile "test first development" has driven the integration of automated unit testing capability into integrated development environments.

The emergence of "test first development" as a core part of agile software development has in turn driven the integration of automated unit testing capability into commercial and open source integrated development environments. However, automated unit testing approaches usually do not cover higher-order, more functional testing requirements such as system testing and user acceptance testing, which require more human judgment.

Subtypes

Subtypes are test case management, automated test harnesses, and load-testing tools.

Gotchas

Test automation tools are not trivial to set up and run, and in particular load testing tools can require substantial investments in both hardware and staff expertise. The agile emphasis on "test first" development has promoted a beneficial growth of integrated unit test scaffolding for the modern programming languages.

Overlaps/Consider Platforming On

Test control can be done quite successfully with spreadsheets, although the implicit data structures are relational and a database is optimal. Test automation can be to some extent covered by open source tools, but there is no substitute for load testing where required.

Reverse Engineering/Code Analysis System

Description

This class of tooling analyzes source code artifacts in support of reengineering or maintenance efforts. Forrester Research calls this "application portfolio management," which is a more technical interpretation.

Gotchas

Internal application complexity is owned by package vendors, but enterprise application integration is inevitably owned by the enterprise.

These systems are nontrivial to set up and interpret results. Although these tools are sold as a means to understand complexity in an enterprise IT environment, they do not typically address the issue of interapplication communication, which (especially in a package-centric organization) is critical. Internal application complexity is increasingly owned by package vendors, but enterprise application integration is inevitably owned by the enterprise, unless it has outsourced large sections of its IT development and operations.

Overlaps/Consider Platforming On

Metadata repositories historically had rich source code scanning. Some of the newer code analysis tools are based on the OMG standards, reducing vendor lock-in and providing more options for using the generated analyses. Some products are being marketed under the term "legacy modernization." The primary value proposition of such tools is reducing complexity and therefore improving programmer productivity.

They may integrate with enterprise IT portfolio management systems, CMDBs, and metadata repositories.

There might be synergies between design-time code analysis and runtime configuration discovery tools, but no vendors have gone down this road yet.

4.5 Cross-Boundary Build–Run Systems

There are several types of tools that cross the build–run boundary:

▶ CASE tools
▶ Release management tools
▶ Security tools

CASE System

Description

CASE has only failed in its most high-reaching goals.

CASE as an overall tool category is quite broad and difficult to model.[200] This book uses the term deliberately, in some defiance of vendors and analysts who are squeamish about the mixed reputation of CASE and its perceived "failure" in the

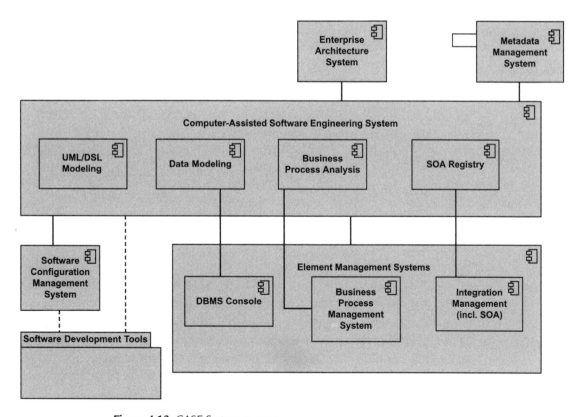

Figure 4.13 CASE System context.

mid- to late-1990s. This book takes a contrarian view: that CASE has succeeded and prospered across a variety of domains and really only failed in its highest-reaching goals (still being pursued by a number of players today, with arguably increasing success).

To have a rational discussion about CASE, consider the acronym: Computer-Assisted Software Engineering. Read strictly, this term can be applied to all software development tools starting with the first compiler, which "assisted" the software engineer by converting human understandable symbols into the binary code required to this day by Turing–Von Neumann stored-program computing architectures. (Yes, we are still using those :-).)

In this sense, all the digital scaffolding and jigs used by developers are CASE tools: linkers, source code control tools, integrated development environments, and so forth. An even broader interpretation would include project and requirements management tools and essentially the entire application life cycle management domain, which has considerable market activity.

The core controversy in CASE comes in the area of graphical versus grammar-based software construction.

Typically, CASE tools use visual formalisms to translate complex processing semantics into more human-readable forms, and most allow for some translation from abstract visual forms down to machine-executable forms or at least skeletal elements suitable as a basis for further software engineering.

The core controversy in CASE thus comes in the area of graphical versus grammar-based software construction. Some domains in software lend themselves well to being described with boxes and lines, static structures (e.g., data, class, component, and deployment models) in particular. The features of limited-function electronic devices such as appliances and basic cell phones also lend themselves to visual formalism (e.g., state machines).

Other domains, however, such as complex activities and processes, are much less amenable to graphical modeling, and the CASE movement of the 1990s did arguably run into these limits to its detriment. Full-fledged graphical specification of software resulting in "push button" generation of executable code may never succeed (although some BPM systems are yet again attempting this, as well as the OMG with Model-Driven Architecture[201] and Microsoft with Domain-Specific Languages[202]).

One CASE success story is the extract–transform–load (ETL) tools, which are frameworks for designing and implementing large-scale data transfers with no (or minimal) use of procedural code. Other examples would be BPM tools, batch schedulers, and business rules management systems. All of these systems cross the build–run gap, with environments that interoperate seamlessly across designing and running, and in some cases enable the administrative implementation of quite significant functional changes.

Controlling such environments through the enterprise change process may require in-depth discussions, given their potential blurring of build–run boundaries.

CASE has also been interpreted as computer-assisted *systems* engineering. That interpretation would cover all enablement systems in this chapter.

As with the rest of this chapter, the representations here are a reference model and food for thought that will need to be reinterpreted for any given organization's environment.

Subtypes

One distinction is between CASE tools that only operate with the software development life cycle and those that bridge the build–run boundary in some form (Figure 4.14)

On the way to attempting the ambitious goal of full life cycle CASE, the industry has developed a number of core technologies and approaches that can be seen as essentially CASE systems:

▶ Application life cycle management (ALM) tools
▶ Database ETL tools
▶ BPM tools
▶ Data modeling tools
▶ Object-oriented modeling (i.e., UML) tools

BPM Tools

BPM and workflow tools are of particular interest. They are not only sources of metadata about the larger business operation but also increasingly critical enablers

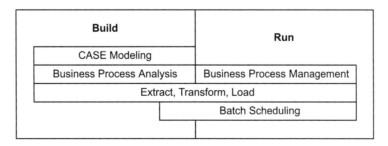

Figure 4.14 CASE system types.

of IT processes internally. It is advisable to invest resources in determining your IT organization's approach to BPM techniques and tools both externally (BPM for the business) and internally (BPM for IT, which as noted elsewhere is simply composed of business processes itself).

Overlaps/Consider Platforming On

Look for convergence among all the categories listed previously, and seek out vendors who are well positioned to benefit from such convergence. The OMG's UML and related specifications is emerging as the dominant standard here, but Microsoft is pursuing its own agenda as well.

Job Scheduling System

Description

A job scheduling system manages batch (periodic) processes, such as nightly extracts of data for import into a data warehouse. These tools can be highly sophisticated; their abilities to define conditional workflows across multiple platforms is analogous to basic BPM system capability. Some include event-driven capabilities and rich APIs enabling a variety of processing control. They are important sources of information, especially in heavily data-oriented environments dependent on bulk transfers and updates; understanding the schedule sequencing is often the first step in many troubleshooting activities.

Overlaps/Consider Platforming On

Modern BPM
systems may
eventually
converge with
job scheduling
systems.

Modern BPM systems may eventually converge with job scheduling systems; the occurrence of a clock cycle is an event just as much as something human initiated, and there are many similarities in the architectural requirements of these mission-critical distributed control systems.

Provisioning System

Description

This is also known as a release management or software deployment system.

Provisioning systems[203] are a broad class of systems used for the general activity of deploying an IT service either internally to other IT stakeholders or externally to business partners. Provisioning systems include the following:

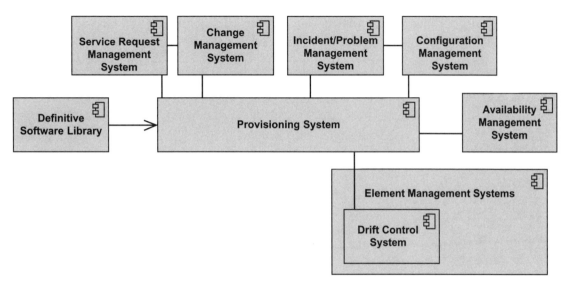

Figure 4.15 Provisioning System context.

- ▶ "Bare metal" server build tasks: create (and re-create) standard server images (a.k.a. templates) on demand, including operating system, patches, middleware, and any other core services
- ▶ Software deployment (and redeployment)
- ▶ Other on-request service delivery, such as access rights

The deployment of code to production environments is often handled casually.

Once software is developed and tested, it must be deployed into a production state (this book is written for enterprise IT purposes, not for packaged software product development). The deployment of code to production environments is often handled casually through "whatever works" approaches: developers mapping drive shares from quality assurance and production environments to their workstation and manually moving the new code into production would be one characteristic approach.

With the increased attention to IT risk management, the actual installation of production code is now under considerable scrutiny in larger organizations. The principle of segregation of duties prohibits developers from having access (especially update access) to production systems. Old practices such as migrating code using a workstation with simultaneous access to multiple environments no longer are acceptable to corporate auditors, who are demanding higher standards of predictability, security, and control.

These tools provide an interface from the software development life cycle to production operations. Developers build code, test it, and once it is approved, use a release management framework to place it into production; when mature, such tools integrate with change management and/or service request management.

Provisioning systems provide an automated means for promoting software assets from one environment to the next. These tools can provide scripting capabilities, automated rollback, and positive confirmation of migration success; they also are typically integrated with an organization's source code control and change management functions, providing a critical bridge point between the development and the operations worlds.

The more general capability of these systems to instantiate entire technical stacks leads to an implied integration with and interest in the technology product entity and portfolio and vendor management generally. Their "templates" should reflect the current approved enterprise software infrastructures available for application support in the enterprise. The use case of understanding what the enterprise implications are of a major software product's end of life would be enabled through data kept in the provisioning system.

Provisioning systems are a concrete step toward "on-demand" and utility computing.[204]

Subtypes

Subtypes are infrastructure, application, and desktop.

Overlaps/Consider Platforming On

Software deployment tools may also include tools intended for deploying software to consumer desktops—a problem similar in nature. If an organization chooses not to invest in this class of tooling, the more important safeguard is the strict segregation of duties between developers and operations staff. Some organizations have written their own tools in this area, where vendor products have been a bit immature (focusing more on desktops and less on the production data center).

These tools should integrate with the change and configuration management systems seamlessly. One function is the management of a release calendar, possibly integrated with (or identical to) the change management system's forward schedule of change. The major releases for an application system are also relevant to the portfolio management system.

However, provisioning systems generally do not understand or handle logical dependencies, which are critical to configuration management in the broad sense.

COBIT calls for the automated restoration of configurations. This implies a drift control system interfaced to the provisioning system; when the drift control system detects a change in an element configuration, the provisioning system steps in and restores the configuration from the current approved template.

Element Management

Description

Element management tools are the control consoles and utilities used by operations and infrastructure staff. A detailed discussion of element management tools would considerably expand the scope of this book; this is one of the broader categories and includes a variety of tools.[205] The common characteristic of such tools is their support for the most detailed nonprogramming work in IT management: network administration, security administration, database administration, middleware administration, storage administration, operations management (where not otherwise covered), and so forth. Element management tools are important sources of information and visibility into complex IT operations, including resource unit costs, and the ability to integrate them is desirable.

Element management tools support the most detailed nonprogramming work in IT management.

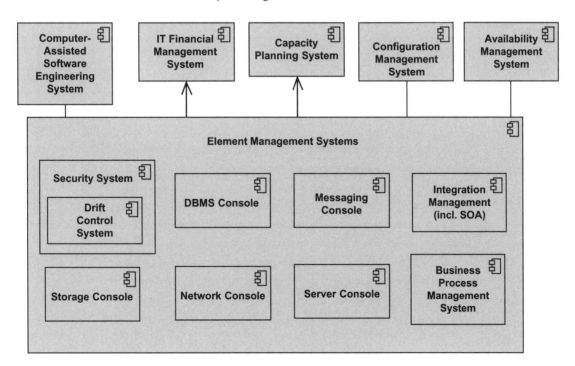

Figure 4.16 Element management system context.

Metering

The ability to track unit costs is known as metering. Some metering occurs at the element manager level (e.g., bytes of storage or network packets); some occurs at the application level (e.g., transactions). Application-level metering is more difficult to set up but provides a more business-oriented view of capacity consumption.

Element management systems are by definition production oriented.

Element management systems are by definition production oriented (although preproduction environments often will have extensive element configuration for testing purposes). Element management tools overlap with CASE tools at the build–run boundary. One distinction is that CASE tools can use graphical models for input and element management tools typically only use graphical displays for information communication.

Subtypes

Subtypes are network management tools, database management tools (vendor-specific and multiplatform third-party tools), middleware management tools (e.g., for managing message queues or file transfers), batch schedulers, SOA management tooling, and storage area network management tools.

Overlaps/Consider Platforming On

Purchasing any major class of IT infrastructure always brings such tools with it; the consideration is usually whether to stick with vendor-supplied tools (e.g., Microsoft SQL Enterprise Manager or IBM's delivered MQ manager software) or to use value-adding third-party software (e.g., BMC's tool for multiple database platforms or Nastel's products for MQ administration). Also, the relationship between silo element managers and management consoles that may integrate with, or replace, some of the element managers' functionality must be determined.

As seen in Figure 4.13, CASE systems may be the originating point for detailed element management configurations, especially when those configurations lend themselves well to graphical representation.

SNMP (Simple Network Management Protocol) is a common standard in element management systems; its future at this writing is unclear.

Security Tools

Security is a deep and complex domain, and this book's coverage is necessarily abbreviated. Topics such as intrusion detection and cyberattack defense are not addressed here.

Security tools are a type of element management tools. Security departments rely on a variety of tools to perform their duties, tools that can be grouped into two general classes:

▶ Management tools
▶ Control tools

The management tools are generally more proactive and concerned with matters such as identity management and provisioning (authorizing) access to securable resources. Common tools in this area are directory services tools and more specialized identify management tools. These tools are generally out of scope for this book, although it's a gray area.

Control tools are those tools that through passive or active scanning provide actionable security information on the IT environment.

In a passive scanning approach, once an environment is set up it will be scanned. An initial install of a new technology stack might result in a "gold master" designation, so similar machines with similar software configurations can then be released. The issue with this is that the state is a singularity in time. With any change to the environment, there are security implications (ports opening, new code, etc.) Typically, security departments will simply rescan passively throughout time on set schedules and provide reports of changes that are treated as incidents, which must then be rectified.

In an active scanning approach, an agent on the server monitors all changes to managed elements (file systems, registries, and more specialized infrastructure). These systems are closely related to intrusion detection systems but may also be deployed simply to control unauthorized changes by well-intentioned personnel. They impose overhead on servers and are not well liked by systems and database administrators, or anyone concerned with host capacity.

Description

Security activities also cover both the build and run activities; nonproduction environments are often secured by the same measures as production environments.

Security management is closely related to configuration management; the inventory of CIs in the environment contains the inventory of securable resources, generally speaking. Risk assessments rely on dependency understanding—a security team may be one of the earliest and most enthusiastic users of a CMDB.

The inventory of CIs in the environment contains the inventory of securable resources.

Overlaps

A drift control tool should integrate with the availability management system so that alerts of unplanned changes can be raised, perhaps as incidents. It should also integrate with the provisioning system so that configurations can be automatically rolled back if called for.

Integration Management

Description

Integration management software, or enterprise application integration (EAI) software, is related to SOA management tooling; it includes functionality for message routing, workflow, and various forms of application communication enablement. It is relevant to this book because (like database management system software) it is an important source of information regarding complex IT dependencies. Mapping such managed integration information to higher-level business drivers is a challenge for these types of tools.

Gotchas

If a heavyweight EAI tool turns into just one more integration option, not much may be gained.

When used pervasively EAI can reduce complexity in an enterprise, but it requires a mature organization dedicated to getting maximum value from it—if a heavyweight EAI tool turns into just one more integration option, not much may be gained. Techniques like topic-based publish and subscribe require strong organizational commitment, willingness to incur analysis costs, and defined methodology.

Overlaps/Consider Platforming On

Many organizations integrate applications using custom-built code, which works fine but tends to become unmanageable because there are many technical methods by which data may move from one application to another, and developers when left to their own devices will choose the means most familiar to them personally.

4.6 Systems for Service Support

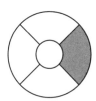

This general category of tooling represents the capabilities required to run IT services once they have been developed. Included are tools for managing various human-driven processes that proactively and reactively interact with the automated IT infrastructure and interface with the plan and control tools particularly concerned with visibility into the operational world.

Change Management System

Description

Change management is a true, event-driven IT process and one of the most important concepts in all of IT governance. Change management systems at their

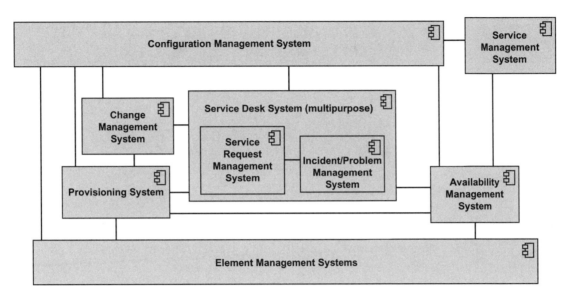

Figure 4.17 Service support context.

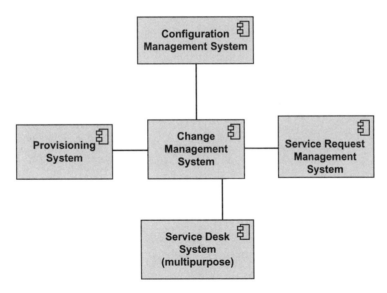

Figure 4.18 Change Management System context.

most basic track an RFC, which is a defined statement of some alteration to a managed IT infrastructure (including quality assurance and production environments). RFCs fundamentally are cross-functional items; by definition they must have enterprise visibility so that all interested parties may comment on the possible effects and advisability of the change.

Change Management systems often include some form of risk assessment; various information regarding the change is collected (possible effect on customers, time to execute change, risks or consequences of failure) and manually and/or automatically assessed.

More advanced change management systems (as with incident management earlier) relate changes not merely to categories but to CIs with all their richness. This is an essential part of the ITIL vision.

Note that change *detection* tools are discussed under Configuration Management and Security Management.

Is the change management system also a request management system?

One question is whether the change management system is also a request management system. They may be implemented both ways. In some cases (e.g., in organizations with a separate service request management tool), the change request is simply an approval vehicle, with no relationship to tracking the work of the change (Figure 4.19).

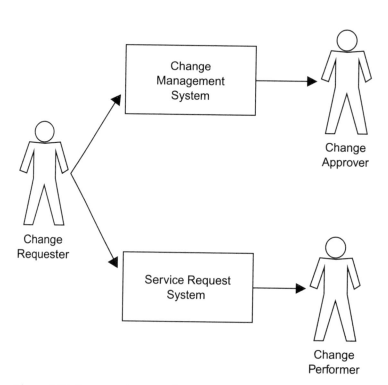

Figure 4.19 Separate change and request systems.

In other cases, the change request drives the actual allocation of resources (e.g., a database administrator needed to create a new table) and their completion of the work request (Figure 4.20).

Gotchas

Automated change impact analysis is the major direction for the next generation of these tools. If a server is supporting an IT service that in turn underpins a critical business process, proposed changes to that server should be considered in light of that potential effect (Figure 4.21).

The depiction here is common in vendor literature and could easily be assessed through automated means, *if* the dependency data is up-to-date. (See the "Service Integrator Responsible For Dependencies On Consumed" pattern in Chapter 5.)

However, robust dependency mapping can become more complex. Figure 4.22 shows a more realistic representation of applications and dependencies. Again, an automated change impact tool could walk all the dependencies—but the result might be a plethora of stakeholders required to approve the change, resulting in loss

An automated change impact tool could walk all the dependencies—but the result might be a plethora of stakeholders required to approve the change, resulting in loss of agility.

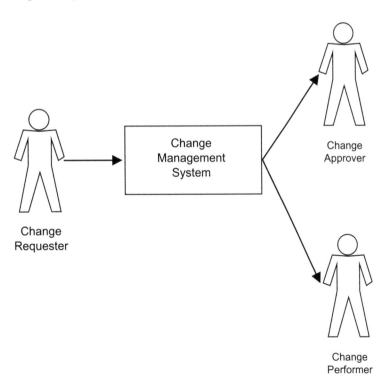

Figure 4.20 Change system driving work request.

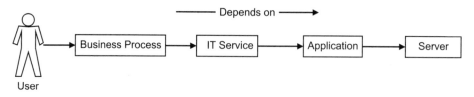

Figure 4.21 Change impact (simple).

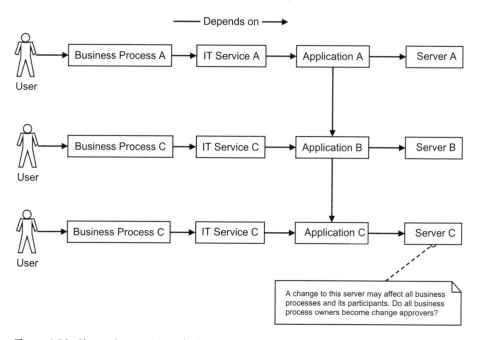

Figure 4.22 Change impact (complex).

of agility. The question will be, What is the nature of the dependencies between the applications? Are they tightly or loosely coupled? If Applications A and B are loosely coupled to Application C, it is a different matter than if they are tightly bound such that a failure in application C results also in the failure of Applications B and A.

Drawing such dependencies therefore requires care and common enterprise standards. Distinguishing between synchronous (e.g., through Web services and component APIs) and asynchronous (e.g., file transfers and message-based interactions) dependencies is a first-cut distinction. Automated dependency-based change impact analysis may always require some human intervention for "sanity checking."

One approach is to insist that the service dependency maps have a final manual treatment. Automated discovery tools and more general dependency data are used as inputs, but the final versions are tweaked using the staff's professional judgment as to which dependencies are germane and which are not.

Overlaps/Consider Platforming On

This is critical IT enablement functionality, and organizations that have not centralized change management are advised to do so. Integrated ITSM suites provide functionality that includes change, as well as incident, problem, and other areas. A generalized workflow tool in theory could be used to support change management as one of several processes.

Availability Management System

Description

An availability (a.k.a. enterprise monitoring) system is among the first sought by the operational team.

This is also known as a monitoring framework or enterprise framework.

Just as a project management system is the first system sought by the project management office, an availability (a.k.a. enterprise monitoring) system[206] is among the first sought by the operational team. These tools provide a variety of mechanisms for monitoring and controlling operational IT systems, generally through

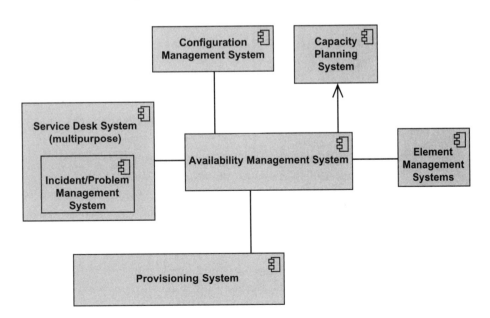

Figure 4.23 Availability Management System context.

small software "agents" deployed to computing platforms. These agents may monitor processes and their return codes, performance metrics (e.g., memory and CPU utilization), events raised through various channels, network availability, log file contents (e.g., with standing filters for messages indicating problems), interactions with other elements in the IT infrastructure, and more. Some tools issue "synthetic transactions" against operational systems to gauge whether response times are within acceptable parameters. All of this data is then forwarded to a central console and integrated with the objective of supporting the organization's SLAs in priority order.

Controlling the runtime (as opposed to design-time) activities and monitoring of element management systems is a critical aspect of a general availability management system.

Subtypes

Subtypes are overall management frameworks and transaction monitoring systems.

Gotchas

Enterprise monitoring tools are notorious for requiring agents on servers; although some things can be detected without such agents, having software running on a given computer still provides the richest data. Because licensing is often agent based, this becomes expensive.

As noted in the discussion of service management tools, the combination of operational monitoring with dependency mapping gives rise to the concept of business service management, or service impact modeling, in which managed infrastructure elements (e.g., those actively monitored by agents) are hooked together in hierarchies with business process or SLA as a top element. Understanding the business processes dependent on IT operations requires the involvement of those architecture and development areas tasked with modeling and analyzing business processes; the operations team alone should not attempt this.

> Service impact modeling ties managed infrastructure elements into hierarchies with business process or SLA as a top element.

Instrumented dependencies are only a subset of all the dependencies requiring tracking. New tools are emerging that can discover dependencies based on a transaction's path end to end; however, such approaches will only be useful for transactional applications—batch and middleware-mediated applications may present challenges. Such applications are optimized for troubleshooting known transaction paths, not performing exhaustive inventories. Automatically inferring all dependencies for a portfolio will probably remain intractable; some manual intervention will be required.

Overlaps/Consider Platforming On

Management frameworks overlap with element management and service-level management tools; performance metrics captured for incident resolution and problem mitigation are also important for capacity planning (and should be collected once and reused by these various stakeholders).

Given the pervasive need for monitoring frameworks and their infrastructure characteristics, it is perhaps surprising that they have not had more attention from the open source community.

Vendors of specific computing platforms at the higher end have always provided direct monitoring services themselves, as part of standard support. This helps ensure that proactive maintenance flags especially are heeded before the system is in crisis.

Incident and Problem Management

Description

An incident is defined as an unanticipated interruption to a defined IT service. Incidents require tracking and resolution, minimally. The interruption of an IT

An incident is defined as an unanticipated interruption to a defined IT service.

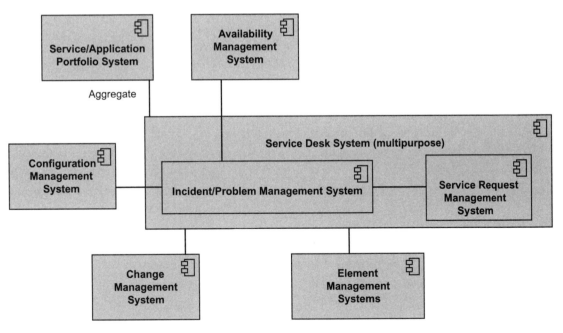

Figure 4.24 Service Desk context (applies to next two sections).

service may result in numerous incidents (both human-reported and automatically reported), so a next level of sophistication in these tools includes the ability to correlate many reported incidents with one resolution effort (trending). More mature features include integration with configuration management so that incidents are tracked not only to overall categories but to defined, managed IT elements with their own identities, relationships, and dependencies.

Incident management also implies the management of resolution techniques at some level; resolutions may be known and repeatable (in which case the incident may be a Known Error in ITIL terms), with corresponding documentation on what to do when it occurs.

ITIL is concerned with the operational distinction between incident and problem management for good reasons of proactive–reactive balance of activities. However, the technical requirements of Incident and Problem are largely the same—a Problem is similar to an Incident in terms of the data structures and workflow requirements necessary to support its resolution, and traceability between the two is required. Therefore, both process areas should be supported with the same tool set.

Gotchas

Manual correlation of incidents is troublesome, both in terms of enabling staff to perform effectively and in terms of process efficiency. Managing resolution techniques (scripts) shades into the problem of unstructured knowledge management. Knowledge management techniques are needed for both.

Overlaps/Consider Platforming On

Incidents and Problems can be seen as special cases of more general workflow problems.

Incidents and Problems can be seen as special cases of more general workflow problems. Incident management overlaps substantially with service request fulfillment, but (as discussed in the data section) this book takes a different tack from ITIL and does not see routine service requests as "interruptions." Managing service request life cycles is also a substantially different problem in terms of process and approach; for further information, see the section upcoming on service request fulfillment systems. Nevertheless, because service requests and incident resolutions can morph into each other, the idea of a consolidated service desk serving as an initial point of user–IT contact is sound.

Incidents and Problems are important indicators of system quality and therefore relevant to the portfolio management system.

See the "Clarify Service Entry Points" pattern in Chapter 5.

Service Request Management System

Description

Performance metrics for work-flow-based IT service processes may be part of SLAs.

The service request management system is similar to incident management, as it serves as an intake point for consumer requests (e.g., new PC or security authorization). This type of system must have capabilities for defining and managing workflow (setting up the order of tasks and forwarding notifications to responsible parties). Performance metrics for workflow-based IT service processes may be part of SLAs as well as service availability and performance. Service request management may require integration with a Provisioning system if it is used for internal IT purposes (e.g., facilitating the relationship between applications developers and infrastructure teams or between project and operations teams).

A Service Request Management system should integrate with automated telephony (call routing) for both initial capture and status inquiries.

The generic workflow requirements imply integration with identity management tools (e.g., LDAP).

Overlaps/Consider Platforming On

Service request management is so workflow oriented that a generic workflow or BPM tool can certainly handle it (the major additional part is support for the request intake, which requires scalability and possibly integration with interactive voice response and customer-facing Web forms). The added value of more specialized products comes in their particular adaptation for the IT environment, including templates for standard IT services and processes.

The demand for services should be aggregated and input into the portfolio management systems.

The demand for services should be aggregated and input into the portfolio management systems. Service requests may apply to element management tools as work orders associated with RFCs.

See the "Clarify Service Entry Points" pattern in Chapter 5.

4.7 Information-Centric Systems

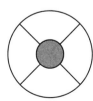

This central class of tools includes all the various forms of repositories used to provide insight into complex IT infrastructures, including enterprise architecture, knowledge management, metadata management, and configuration management. It covers both top-down and bottom-up capture, analysis, and management of complex concepts.

The concept of "repository" has a long tradition in IT management. Simplistically, it means a database. The term, however, has had specific meaning in describing databases of internal IT information, or at least implying a certain level of richness: metadata repositories, CASE repositories, document repositories, and so on. Repositories may have complex data models, versioning capabilities, check-in and check-out capabilities, and other features that distinguish them from basic database systems. They usually take on some characteristics of object-oriented databases in their frameworks (while remaining based on relational databases).[207]

Configuration Management

Description

Along with Change Management, Configuration Management is a central theme of this book; therefore, its enabling systems merit extended discussion.

A CMDB provides centralized management of the various forms of data used to run the IT capability itself. As a data management capability, it only is useful insofar as true IT business processes leverage it (e.g., release management, change management, and incident and problem management). The scope of the ideal CMDB is that of the conceptual data model presented in Chapter 3, and products are moving in this direction.

In viewing Figure 4.25, you may think, "But I have both change and configuration management in the same system." The architectures presented here are logical and modular. Many vendors are integrating more and more functionality, supporting many different logical functional modules in unified product sets. The architecture here is presented in part to provide a framework for comparing and assessing such integrated suites. The two most important modules to have a common platform are change and configuration management.

It's also tempting to be overwhelmed by all the interfaces. These are only potential interfaces for consideration. It would be expensive, and probably unnecessary, to implement all of them for a given organization. But they all should be considered to ensure that master data is aligned.

One of the most important aspects of the configuration management system is distinguishing it from deeper element management systems and discovery tools. There is an ocean of data available from IT management tools; the CMDB's value proposition is in relationships. If someone needs to know the particular configuration of a database or message queue, that person should go to the appropriate team with the deep element management console. The CMDB's job is to show how the database and message queue relate to each other, which neither element manager will be able to handle.

The two most important modules to have a common platform are change and configuration management.

One of the most important aspects of the configuration management system is distinguishing it from deeper element management systems and discovery tools.

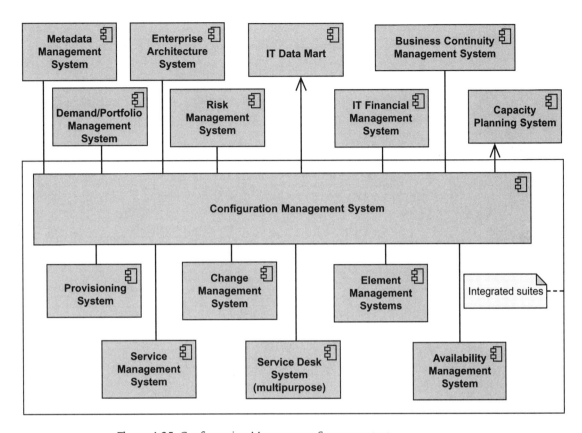

Figure 4.25 Configuration Management System context.

As discussed in Chapter 3, configuration management presents significant changes in data management, such as deep inheritance, complex data models, frequent recursive structures, and more. The ideal CMDB system can save defined reports and supports reporting on network and tree structures. It has URL–based addresses for all objects in it so that its data can interoperate easily with other processes and tools. The complex structures within it can be used in what-if analysis or other representations of alternate states (e.g., discovered versus planned), requiring branching and merging functionality similar to that of source control tools (except implemented in a structured data paradigm).

Presentation of complex metadata structures can effectively use a design pattern that might be called "focus–collection," in which a primary object is the focus of a screen, with collections of links to the other items it is related to; navigating to one of those links makes that link's corresponding item the new focus object. (See "The

Ideal Architecture" section for a discussion of enterprise application architectures, and "Further Reading" for more technical references.)

As noted previously, there are two general concerns of configuration management: operational and portfolio, with operational configuration management controlling baselines and detecting change (no matter how small) and portfolio configuration management focusing more on dependencies and usage.

Both of these aspects are supported by scanning and discovery tools. CMDB collectors can either directly scan IT resources or interface with intermediate collection points such as management frameworks or specialized discovery tools. Scanning functionality varies, with major areas being element inventory, dependency discovery, and change detection. Drift control and change detection is positive assurance that nothing has changed on a given device; such tools use checksums and maintain accurate, comprehensive records at a detailed level that can, for example, show that parameter file A on server B was changed January 5, 2007.

At the other extreme are tools that attempt higher-level inventories and correlations between IT elements, such as inferring from network traffic that code running on application server D is binding to database server E. (See the related "Gotchas" section.) Many tools tend toward one or the other; some are beginning to attempt both.

To support change management the repository needs to incorporate baselining and audit functions, and any piece of data may have multiple identities or perspectives. What if the scanning tool discovers an element that has not been authorized for deployment to a given machine? How is this data managed and a process enabled for resolving the anomaly? How can complex CI hierarchies be built *before* their production deployment so that they can be inspected for accuracy? What if a complex set of CI dependencies is being restructured so that the new version has both similarities to and differences from the old? Because CIs are *representations* of reality, and come in using different channels, it is necessary to manage their states carefully, for example, as follows:

▶ Planned or proposed
▶ Current approved state
▶ Discovered but not confirmed
▶ Discovered reconciled with approved state
▶ Discovered but not approved

Actually maintaining multiple copies of CIs (e.g., approved and discovered), to be merged when their status is confirmed, may be necessary. Clear naming

Major functions of scanning are element inventory, dependency discovery, and change detection.

conventions for CIs are essential because these naming conventions will enable the easy categorization and merging of discovered items.

These kinds of requirements lead to technical requirements such as perspectives, versioning, merging, and delta compare, making the ideal CMDB a difficult tool to build—it is far more than a simple relational database. The advanced metadata repository vendors have many years of experience in such matters, and CMDB vendors mostly do not.

Low-level scanning of IT infrastructure can return too much data.

CMDBs must handle the concept of abstractions; low-level scanning of IT infrastructure can return too much data (e.g., every piece of executable code in a data center). Such details must be mapped into overall reference structures; a useful analogy is the fact–dimension structure of data warehouses. The problem is, how is a given physical software component (fact) mapped to a logical application (dimension)? This is a central problem of configuration management from a data perspective. The best practice used for many years in mainframe environments is to establish a portfolio of official "application identifiers" and require all physical software assets to embed those identifiers (typically as the first characters in any object name, sometimes followed by a delimiter).

A reporting module may be needed to simplify complex object/relational data structures into more user-friendly reporting structures.

Finally, the relationship between the CMDB and an IT data mart is still undefined. A CMDB should be considered an operational, transactional system; however, typical CMDBs do not approach the volume of large-scale operational systems (e.g., for sales). Because of their smaller volume, it is debatable whether a separate reporting instance is justifiable on the basis of scale; however, a reporting instance may be needed to simplify complex object/relational data structures into more user-friendly reporting structures. Current practices in data warehousing and business intelligence may be able to shed some light here, but the problems of IT data management are unique. (See the data model discussion in Chapter 3 and "Further Reading" in this chapter.)

More on Discovery Tools

The trouble with relying on discovery is that it can only tell you what is there—not whether it should be there.

Tools have always existed that can inspect an IT processing environment and analyze the inventory of programs, files, processes, and the like. These tools are becoming an important point of discussion as configuration management becomes more mature. Too often, however, they are presented as a "silver bullet." The trouble with relying on discovery is that (even at its best) it can only tell you what is there—not whether it should be there. (Just like your bank statement—it tells you what the transactions were but not whether you intended them.)

A capability any discovery tool requires for relevance in enterprise IT is the concept of fingerprinting or footprinting. This is an ability to infer from the presence of some physical component that a logical application dependency exists.

For example, if the executable file is qdx.exe on a server, you can infer that the logical application Quadrex depends on this server. (However, it cannot determine whether Quadrex should be there.)

Footprints must be maintained—if a new Quadrex module consisting of newly named executables is deployed, the discovery system's database will need updating. This needs to have an explicit process step, probably as part of the overall Release process—the concept of a system manifest (an assembly CI) is used here.

Even the maintenance of footprints is not a silver bullet. Once you have established that an application is running on a server, should it be there? Mainframe autodiscovery tools may detect reports, job control language, batch jobs, customer information control system transactions—all nice to know about, but *should* they be there? Are the reports being used? Are they being sent to bewildered offices where they are promptly recycled? This is where the discipline of portfolio management is required.

See the "Application ID and Application Alias" pattern in Chapter 5 for more details on increasing discovery tool effectiveness.

Change Detection

Discovery tools optimized for change detection (e.g., Tripwire) do so by maintaining baseline configuration information. This may not be very granular; one approach is to manage checksums across blocks of storage expected to remain static (e.g., the directories containing the binary executables for an enterprise application). As mentioned in the conceptual modeling section, the detection of change by such a tool should be treated as an Event; if security or process control procedures warrant it, that Event should become an Incident, which (in the model) might be reconciled to a known Change—or an indication of an unauthorized Change.

Tools that announce their significant changes to an enterprise event bus (e.g., a management console) are desirable; this eliminates one potential need for separate scanning infrastructure. Notice that a segregation of duties requirement emerges—the person with the ability to turn that change announcement functionality on and off perhaps should not be the same person who can make other administrative configuration changes.

The most realistic solutions to configuration management (especially in a world of loose coupling) may be far more manual than technologists would care to admit.

Finally, discovery tools are limited in their ability to detect application-to-application data transfers, which are some of the most critical dependencies in a large enterprise. Because of the variety of means by which application data can be transferred, no discovery tool yet exists that can comprehensively map all the different flows: file transfer protocol, file shares, middleware, ETL, EAI, Web services, shared databases, and so forth. Files renamed en route, parameter-driven

EAI adapter architectures, dynamic binding of process to data resources, and similar difficulties make this an extremely difficult configuration management challenge.[208] The near-term realistic solution may be far more manual than technologists would care to admit.

It should, however, be a goal for the enterprise's application architects to specify an integration architecture that is as transparent as possible so that this notorious problem becomes easier to manage. Providing greater visibility here is one of the justifications for centralizing an enterprise Integration Competency Center.

Grid and on-demand computing also may completely alter the possibilities of configuration management; for better or for worse is unclear.

IT Finance

As noted elsewhere in this book, IT finance should be supported by the CMDB. Many IT financial efforts are based on spreadsheet models, which could be further automated if fully integrated into CMDB functionality. Because the financial models must be based on the service dependencies, this is clearly the most efficient approach, given the expense and pain of dependency management documented in this book.

This is an advanced topic in the industry, and vendor offerings are not sophisticated.

Subtypes

Subtypes are portfolio configuration management, operational configuration management and change detection, and dependency mapping tools.

Gotchas

Some CMDBs use an overly simplified "any-to-any" relationship to represent the entire range of CIs in an environment. This approach can lead to considerable confusion about what are appropriate relationships between types of CIs. (Should a business process be directly dependent on a router?) A more refined data model is highly desirable; the OMG and Distributed Management Task Force have done significant intellectual work in this area free for industry use.

Dependency mapping by scanning can deliver some interesting data, but there are many important types of dependencies it cannot discover, so use caution. Something as simple as a flat file being extracted, transferred using scripting, and loaded after being renamed en route is typically beyond the capabilities of such tools; if that extract represents a dependency between applications A and B, the tool (and its users) will not understand this.

If a middleware
adapter can bind
to 1 of 10 data-
bases depend-
ing on a given
message's con-
tent, how do you
interpret such
dependencies
from a CMDB
perspective?

The configuration management goal of tracking dependencies is particularly challenging with application integration, which includes highly complex architectures such as message queuing. Current direction with tools in this space is to make integration increasingly parameter driven, which makes deterministic understanding of interapplication dependencies even more difficult. If a middleware adapter can bind to 1 of 10 databases depending on a given message's content, how do you interpret such dependencies from a CMDB perspective?[209]

Again, discovery tools fall short here. The best sources of dependency data are application architects, and their knowledge should be directly captured for the CMDB during the software development life cycle (see the patterns discussion later in this chapter).

Overlaps/Consider Platforming On

As noted in the discussion that follows, CMDB functionality can be based on a metadata repository. (It is more difficult to manage metadata with a CMDB because most CMDBs draw the line at describing a data dictionary or handling CASE models.) The drawback to doing this is integrating the ITSM process tools (e.g., release, change, and incident management) so that they interoperate with the metadata repository; many of these tools are part of integrated suites with their own CMDB. However, metadata repositories are more mature in some of the framework features required for managing highly complex data.

CMDB functionality has also been based on enterprise architecture modeling tools.[210] Expect convergence in these tools in the next 3–5 years.

The "Federated CMDB" Concept

From *www.erp4it.com*

"Let's put all of IT's data into one database and call it a CMDB."

"OK. Wait, this is too hard!"

"Then let's keep it in several databases and call it a 'federated CMDB.'"

"OK. That's easier. Wait—why are we calling it a CMDB at all?"

That's my summary of the current discussion around the latest wrinkle in ITSM, the so-called federated CMDB. Having realized that it's difficult to consolidate and rationalize internal IT data (just as it's difficult in any line of business), various folks are now putting the brakes on the monolithic, totalizing CMDB concept.

This is an unsurprising development. As I've noted elsewhere, the problem generally is one of the overall rationalization and convergence of all systems enabling

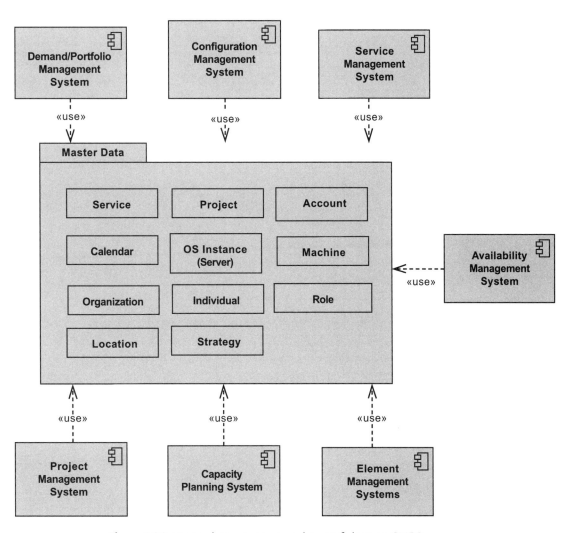

Figure 4.26 Master data management: how to federate a CMDB.

the IT supply chain. CMDB is just one particular theme in many ongoing discussions of how to better manage IT; it's a provocative concept, and now the scope challenges are biting back.

In discussing "federation" with respect to a database of any sort: even in the case of loose system coupling (i.e., federation), it is necessary to determine the means by which any coupling can occur.

Take two databases. They are federated if you can cross-reference the data in them and run an integrated report; if not, they are just two ships passing in the night.

(continued)

The best insight into how to federate a CMDB is to be found in the work of Ralph Kimball and his concept of "conformed dimensions" in data warehousing. If you are trying to rationalize your internal IT databases but not necessarily physically centralize them, then Kimball's work is a starting point. In addition, the concept of "federated data warehouse" has received much attention over the years, and this material should prove useful in the federated CMDB discussion.

Kimball's primary insight is that although you can have physically separate data "marts" they must share common reference data, or "dimensions." In the ITSM and IT governance space, these common dimensions include the following:

▶ Organizational hierarchy
▶ Application portfolio (rolling up into both the organizational hierarchy and SLAs)
▶ Program or project portfolio
▶ Data subject areas (hierarchical, not relational)
▶ SLAs
▶ Enterprise calendar
▶ Enterprise operational locations and hierarchy

Conformance means no difference. Even if they are in five different databases, they are always identical, and process is in place to keep them so, backed by strong senior executive support.

You may unearth intractable process and political difficulties in your search for conformance.

Some of these will be well understood by your data warehousing group (e.g., calendar and location); others will be new ground. You may unearth intractable process and political difficulties in your search for conformance. You'll probably also be confronted with the challenging topic of slowly changing dimensions if any part of your federated CMDB is historic and being used for analysis.

Suppose you have incidents rolling up by application portfolio and organizational hierarchy and you've developed some nice trending reports over the years. Then reorganization happens. How do you handle it? There are three approaches, all with pros and cons that need to be understood in depth.[211]

The application portfolio has proved to be most important and difficult. I have seen up to 10 different lists of applications in one organization, causing no end of confusion around what IT was really doing and who owned it. Your enterprise architects should own this particular dimension; they are best suited for managing this slippery consensus concept of "application." Note that reconciling so-called discovery tools (and their welter of physical IT data) to a master "application" or "service" dimension (of logical concepts with an often-tenuous relationship to discoverable assets) is a problem still not well understood in the industry.

The project portfolio can also be a source of pain. Just as with systems, people tend to refer to projects by myriad imprecise names. What is the system of record for your projects? Does every federated CMDB database that references project do so using an unambiguous project identifier or a picklist derived from the system of record? Or is the project name just casually typed in with no check for accuracy?

Even though a federated CMDB would look somewhat foreign to practitioners of Kimball's federated data warehouse (because data warehousing is mostly about analytics, and a CMDB has a significant operational component), the principles for alignment are identical. Learn from the experiences of your professional colleagues in data warehousing!

Metadata Management System

Description

The metadata repository is the system of record for all aspects of the business intelligence and data warehousing application portfolio.

Metadata management is perhaps the original attempt to structure knowledge about IT, starting with data definitions and moving into data about the programs and systems that used the various data structures. The most well-known use of metadata repositories are as adjuncts to data warehouses, where they serve as enablers for consumers who would otherwise be overwhelmed by thousands of tables containing terabytes of data. In robust implementations, the metadata repository is essentially the system of record for all aspects of the business intelligence and data warehousing application portfolio.

Metadata repositories serve as integration and presentation points for various CASE tool artifacts, in particular data models; they also have scanners that can inspect RDBMS and older data management architectures, as well as source code and many types of mainframe elements. They historically have *not* integrated with enterprise management frameworks.

Robust metadata repositories have handled many problems emerging among CMDB tools, including issues of object/relational mapping, complex metamodels, and versioning. CMDB vendors at this writing have some catching up to do.

Metadata in the classic sense is purely about an organization's data resources (e.g., logical entity and attribute definitions). They also are optimized for capturing ETL feeds between datastores, an important class of CI dependency. However, most metadata repositories also have varying abilities to capture "technical" metadata, and this data in particular (e.g., application, physical database, and server) clearly overlaps with the scope of CMDBs and emerging application portfolio management approaches.

Subtypes

Subtypes are data-centric (classic), software asset management, and data profiling.

Gotchas

Metadata as an enterprise function has historically not paid much attention to the question of maintenance: how is the metadata kept current? The assumption has been that there are accurate metadata sources and the repository's role is simply to integrate them and provide analytics. This is not a safe assumption in the distributed world, where there may be no defined source of record for concepts like Application, Process, and Service. In such cases the metadata repository may become the system of record for one or more data subjects, and being a system of record implies a defined maintenance process.

Overlaps/Consider Platforming On

Does this server contain sensitive customer data?

You can see the ambiguous position of metadata repositories in Figure 4.27. Metadata repositories today cover a variety of subject areas and overlap with configuration management, software asset management, enterprise architecture modeling, and IT portfolio management. However, if one goal is to track data assets to a granular level (e.g., tables and columns) there is no substitute for a metadata repository. Relating specific data definitions to IT infrastructure (i.e., does this server contain sensitive customer data?) is an important compliance

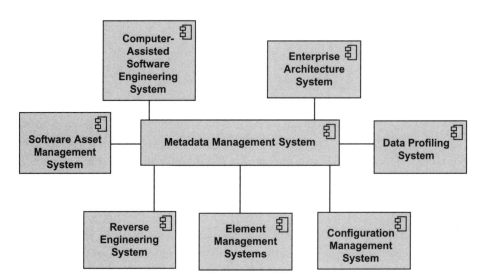

Figure 4.27 Metadata Management System context.

goal and further evidence that IT data management needs to converge on one platform.

A data profiling system is a specialized tool for examining actual data instances and analyzing their data quality. It can examine poorly architected data and infer a clean logical model, a useful technique in some cases.

IT Data Mart

Description

An IT data mart is a different perspective on the metadata and configuration management space. It has the following assumptions:

▶ The data mart is generally a stock RDBMS.

▶ The data model is (more or less) intelligible to users.

▶ All data in the mart is mastered elsewhere and replicated into the RDBMS—it is read only.

▶ A standard business intelligence tool will be used to derive information.

There is one important advantage of commodity data warehousing: scalability.

The IT data warehouse concept may seem to have limitations compared with CMDBs or metadata repositories, but there is one important advantage: scalability. Architectures of this nature routinely support terabyte-level data sets; another advantage of this approach is enabling the use of off-the-shelf reporting tools.

Event, capacity, and performance metrics are the major class of IT information requiring such capacity, and an IT data mart would be expected to serve as consolidation point for such data; however, its possible scope could include IT portfolio and dependency data as well, assuming some of the technical issues can be handled (e.g., lack of an object/relational mapping architecture and dealing with complex inheritance and with network and tree data structures). See "Further Reading" for a citation describing Merrill Lynch's approach to this.

Gotchas

How do you simplify intricate metadata structures (e.g., for reporting) without losing information?

Overlaps/Consider Platforming On

The IT data mart might pull from any or all of the system types discussed in this chapter. This functionality would be built using an organization's defined business intelligence or data warehousing infrastructure, for example, Oracle/Microstrategy or Teradata/Business Objects.

Knowledge Management System

Description

Knowledge Management (KM) is a difficult domain to describe; it contains aspects of document management, training and human change management, and structured data management. One of the best known KM frameworks was Lotus Notes, an environment optimized for storing unstructured documents in a rich context of structured information, with easy collaboration and basic application development tools. The current smorgasbord of KM products covers the historic Lotus Notes domain and more.

AUTHOR'S NOTE

Metadata and Knowledge Management

From *www.erp4it.com*

The problem with most KM solutions I have seen is that too much depends on the Taxonomy Gods. That is the all-powerful committee tasked with subdividing the knowledge domains and coding the knowledge resources so that people can retrieve documents. Although this is a necessary function, it has hardly proved sufficient—the uptake of KM as a capability is pretty dismal in a lot of organizations that have tried it.

The problem here is the inherent subjectivity of taxonomy creation and people's unwillingness to invest time in climbing the learning curve of another's knowledge categorization philosophy.

There may not be a general solution for this, but there is a particular section of KM that dovetails with metadata: how to manage the volumes of unstructured documentation generated in building and running IT systems. Source control repositories don't cut it; they are no better than file systems as far as retrieval goes. However, a metadata repository can be an ideal solution. Because metadata is generally objective and unambiguous, and does not have to be shoehorned into a hierarchical taxonomy, it provides a more robust framework on which to hang knowledge assets.

For example, a metadata repository might have a record for a given server (assuming the repository is handling technical metadata). This server is a known fact, one that everyone in the IT organization can agree on. Therefore, its record is an ideal consensus point on which to hang documentation, because people will go looking for the server by an unambiguous name and will probably be interested in whatever they can find pertaining to it.

People will go looking for the server by an unambiguous name and will probably be interested in whatever they can find pertaining to it.

The same goes for databases, queues, components, batch jobs—all the major elements of the IT infrastructure.

Like I said, it doesn't solve the general crisis of KM. But for IT organizations trying to leverage their masses of Word and Visio documents, a metadata-driven KM framework is an intriguing possibility.

Overlaps/Consider Platforming On

KM overlaps with document management if the more ambitious Notes-like features are not required.

Document Management System

Description

A document management system is an application that stores and controls unstructured data such as Microsoft Word or PowerPoint files. It includes change control and versioning for these assets and usually some form of document metadata: author, keywords, and so on. (In some cases the tool will draw the metadata from the document itself; in other cases the tool may have a database allowing more metadata to be attached to the document record, independently of the document's actual contents. Many tools allow both approaches.)

Overlaps/Consider Platforming On

As noted previously, an SCM tool can also manage documents. Some repositories and IT portfolio management tools can import entire documents as well; however, they may not support change control and versioning.

CMDBs versus Enterprise Architecture and Metadata

Seek integration and reuse. The investment pool for all such tools is limited.

Perhaps the most difficult issue in this area is determining the proper relationship among the CMDB, enterprise architecture, and metadata tools. The portfolio management systems are also relevant here. As indicated by the preceding "Overlaps/Consider Platforming On" notes, there are significant overlaps here. Further insight is provided by a matrix, which cross-references these system types against functional and process concerns (Table 4.1).

Table 4.1 CMDB, Enterprise Architecture, and Metadata Comparison

	Configuration Management Database	Enterprise Architecture System	Metadata Management System	Portfolio Management System
Directly tied to change and incident processes	Yes	No	No	May summarize
Production systems scanning	Yes	No	Sometimes	No
Source code scanning	No	No	Yes	Application portfolio management, depending on definition
Data models	No	Yes	Yes	No
Process models	No	Yes	Yes	No
System models	Yes	Yes	Yes	Partial
Planning views	No	Yes	No	Yes
Financial view	Sometimes partial	No	No	Yes

Even though the three tool types have current differences in how they are used, they have significant similarities in architecture and data topics and there are potential synergies here. (Note that they all can handle system models.) For example, a key question with metadata is how it is kept up-to-date, a concern that arguably the ITSM-based change process answers. Simply resigning to the fact that they currently address different functions and processes (and therefore have different market segments) seems shortsighted, given that the investment pool for all such tools is inherently limited.

Security and IT Information

Is your CMDB a road map for hackers?

Many information-centric IT systems (metadata repositories, enterprise architecture systems, CMDBs) have minimal if any security. These systems have often had such problems gaining support and mindshare that *preventing* people from looking at the data has been a low priority.

However, there is another view of such systems: as road maps for hackers. A person bent on stealing sensitive customer data or compromising a core system could hardly do better than to gain access to a complete CMDB or actively managed enterprise architecture tool, with listings of business processes, applications, data, and networked servers.

Because of this aspect of internal IT data, internal security organizations are starting to take serious interest in the security implications of CMDBs and related tools. This in turn drives a need for both vertical and horizontal security: vertical being the protection of fields and attributes across the system and horizontal being the restriction of access to particular data elements (i.e., rows) based on the credentials of the user. (Analogous requirements are seen in other enterprise software, such as financial systems with charts of accounts and human resource systems with organizational structures.)

Systems supporting the concept of multitenancy have horizontal security at a high level, at least.

Closing the Circle

The operational systems finally need to feed back to the planning and controlling systems. The major vectors from operations back to the plan/control world are as follows:

▶ Service-level management
▶ Capacity planning

Service-level management systems aggregate operational data primarily for the purpose of client relationship management and assessment of SLA adherence. Business service management is a related capability based on the mapping of dependencies underpinning a business-facing service.

Capacity planning systems aggregate operational data primarily to support modeling and forecasting of capacity utilization scenarios that may drive various investment approaches.

These systems may generate data used for planning processes for platform direction, investment scenarios, and process improvement.

4.8 General Issues

Enterprise Architecture and Portfolio Management

Enterprise architecture and portfolio management tools at this writing have troubling overlaps. It is helpful to see them primarily as two different views on the same problem.

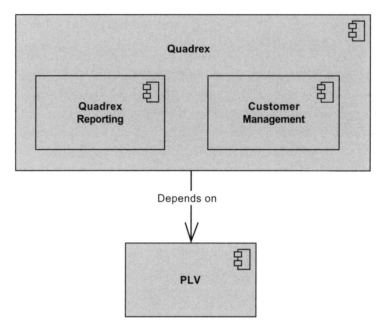

Figure 4.28 Enterprise architecture portfolio representation.

An enterprise architect may build a representation such as the one in Figure 4.28. The same information might be represented in text format in a portfolio system as follows:

> Application: Quadrex
> > Subsystem: Quadrex Reporting
> > Subsystem: Customer Management
> > Depends on: PLV
>
> Application: PLV
> > Depended on by: Quadrex

Cultural differences, if anything, may be the primary determinant of which representation is preferred. However, technically it is easier to derive a textual format from the graphical format than vice versa.

System to Data Entity

An integrated enterprise architecture requires cross-referencing data to both process and system.

Again, as mentioned regarding Table 4.2, this is a method example and a reference model; it's recommended that a comprehensive IT reengineering effort for a

Table 4.2 Data Entity to System Matrix

	System \ Entity	Strategy	Idea	Demand Request	Program and Project	Release	Request for Change	Service Request	Event	Risk	Incident	Problem	Known Error	Orderable Service	Hosting Service	Service	Ordered Service	Application	Technology Product	Business Process	Deployed Software System	Component	Deploy Point	OS Instance (Server)	Location	Machine	Datastore	Asset	Assembly CI	Measurement	Agreement	Contract	Account
Plan/Control	Demand/Portfolio Management	C	C	C	C	U		A		C	A	U	U	C	C		A	U	U	U	A			A		A	A	A		A	U	U	U
	Service Management	U	U	C	U			A		C	A	A		U	U	C		U	U	C				U	U	U	U			C	C	U	U
	Capacity Planning	U	U		U		U	A		C	A	A			U	U		U	U		A	U		U	U	U	U	U		A	U	U	U
	Enterprise Architecture	U	U		U										U	U		U	C	C	U	U	U	U	U	U	U	U	C	A	U		U
	Business Continuity	U			U					C					U	U		U	U	U	U	U	U	U	U	U	U			A	U	U	
	Risk Management	U	U		U					C				U	U	U		U		U	U			U	U	U	U	U			U	U	
	IT Financial Management			U	U	U								U	U						U				U						U	U	
	Contract Management				U					C			U	U		U		U	U		U	U	C	U	C	C		C	C	A	C	C	U
	Asset Management				U													U	U		U	U	U	C	U	C	U	C	U		U	U	U
	Vendor/Procurement				U					C			U		U			U	U	U	U			U		U		U	U			U	U
Build	Project Management		U	U	C					C								U	U	U	U	U		U		U		U			U	U	U
	Requirements Management			U	U								U		U				U	U	U	U		U		U		U			U		
	Estimation		U	U	U	U				U					U						U	C											
	Issue Management				U													U	U			U	C	U	U				U	U			
	Software Asset Management				U											U		U	U		C	C	C	C	C	C	U	C	C	U			U
	SOA Management				U													U			C	C							C				
	Software Configuration Management				U	C												U	U		C	C		U					C		U		
	Software Test Management				U	U												U				C		U					U				
	Reverse Engineering/Analysis																		U			C							U		U		
	Computer-Assisted Software Engineering																				C	C	C						C				
Build/Run	Job Scheduling				U	U	U	U	U		C	U	U	U	U	U	U	U	U	U		U	C	U	U	U	U		U	U		U	U
	Provisioning		U		U	U	U	U	C		C		U		U	U		U	U			U	U	U	U	U	U		U	C			U
	Element Management				U		U	U	C		C	U			U	U		U	U			U	U	C	U	U	U		U	C	U		
	Security Management				U	C	U	U	C		U				U	U		U	U	U	U	U	U	C	U	U	U		U	U	U		
	Integration Management				U	U	U	U	C		C				U	U	U	U	U	U		U	U	U	U	U	U		U	U			
Run	Change Management			U	U	U	C	C	C	C	C	U			U	U		U	U	U		U	U	U	U	U	U		U	U			U
	Availability Management		U		U	U	U	U	C		C	U	U		U	U	U	U	U	U	U	U	U	U	U	U	U		U	U	U		U
	Incident/Problem				U	U	U	U	C	C	C	C	C		U	U	U	U	U	U		U	U	C	U	U	U		U	U	U	U	U
	Service Request Management			U	U	U	C	C			C	C	C	C	C	C	C	U	U	C		U	U	C	U	U	U		U	U	U	U	U

given enterprise completely redo this matrix (current state and target) as part of their analysis effort.

Note that the information management systems (metadata, CMDB, etc.) are not included in this matrix. That is because *they may contain any or all of the data entities listed.*

Insights from this matrix include the pervasiveness of the application and service concepts, which need to be managed as key reference data and not allowed to become disparate (i.e., multiple masters).

4.9 The Ideal Architecture

Figure 4.29 presents application portfolio recommendations for IT enablement systems. In planning a large-scale IT enablement systems architecture, it is most important to minimize the plan/control and information management system

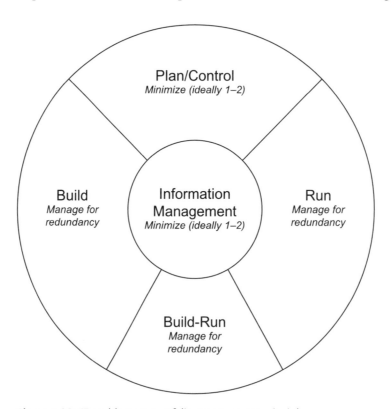

Figure 4.29 IT enablement portfolio management principles.

domains and centralize that data. As this systems analysis has demonstrated, there is much redundancy in the products being sold as solutions for various categories; focus on the overall function. If it is governance or core information management, aggressively seek to consolidate and challenge your vendors on integration. If necessary, seek out third-party vendors with integration expertise or perhaps construct additional modules on a given vendor's framework.

The other system areas (build, build–run, and run) should be managed for redundancy. This can be achieved through the use of a reference taxonomy; prospective system acquisitions should be mapped onto that taxonomy and evaluated for overlaps. Research firm services can be of great use here.

Simple application architectures require too much effort to add new capabilities.

Finally, as internal IT systems continue to amalgamate and increase in size, it is useful to consider the evolution of generic systems architectures. The simplest systems look something like Figure 4.30: code built in a programming language talking to a database. Such systems are not terribly durable or flexible, nor easy to integrate. (They may scale perfectly well, and the question of whether they are physically two, three, or *n*-tier is not relevant here.) The primary issue is that they require too much effort to add new capabilities. The actual source code for the product must be opened up, either by the vendor or (in undesirable scenarios) by the customer.

Figure 4.31 shows (highly simplified) enterprise application architecture as it has evolved over the past 20 years. Presentation, workflow, and persistence (data storage) are configurable by developers versed in the product's internals; development

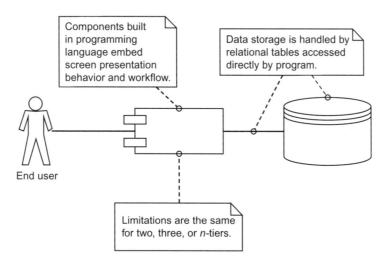

Figure 4.30 Simple application architecture.

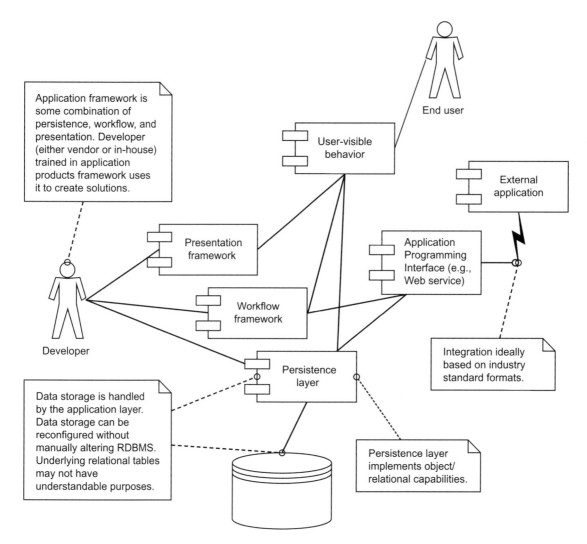

Figure 4.31 Enterprise application architecture.

consists of working within those constraints and often not even using full-fledged languages such as Java or .Net (many different models exist). Vendors with these types of architectures typically have several development teams, one to maintain the framework and one or more to build user-facing solutions with the framework. A (now out of favor) term for the early versions of these types of architectures is fourth-generation language (4GL).

Examples of products built on such architectures include SAP, Oracle–People-Soft enterprise applications, and BMC–Remedy. There is little question that IT requires this level of sophistication for its internal applications, but too many new products continue to be released upon architectures closer to that shown in Figure 4.30. You may want to show the two graphics to prospective vendors and ask which is a closer representation of the vendor's product line.

Newer products may be open source products wired together in various configurations—for example, Struts for presentation, Hibernate for persistence, and JBoss jBPM for workflow, using XML and XSLT as the primary interchange mechanism between the building blocks.

Unfortunately, it is too often the case that systems with the weaker architecture have the superior apparent functionality (because that is where they have been focusing their time), and systems with the better foundation are functionally less strong. If you find a vendor with a workable balance of functionality and framework, it may be a good choice.

Beware of the seduction of enterprise software with rich frameworks.

Finally, beware of the seduction of enterprise software with rich frameworks—it is far too easy to overcustomize such packages with these powerful internal tools, making upgrades tough. Some organizations adopt a strict "no customizations" approach, even if the tool has the capabilities. On the other hand, it can be difficult to even define the difference between "configuration" and "customization" with such tools.

4.10 The Business Case

The business case for infrastructure tools is notoriously difficult to make on financial terms but not impossible. In particular, true "hard dollar" savings are difficult to come by; the typical benefits are too diffuse. (100 positions have 10% effort reduction, rather than 10 positions being completely eliminated.) However, these diffuse productivity benefits can be coupled with regulatory justifications that may require improvements in IT systems management visibility and tracking.

Another way of making the business case is indirectly, through focusing on IT initiatives with real dollar saving potential and examining them for information gathering and change management implications. For example, if a reduction in operational costs is desired, one alternative is to consolidate computing capacity for better utilization. Such a consolidation project has nontrivial information gathering and coordination requirements; servers cannot be retired until the services and

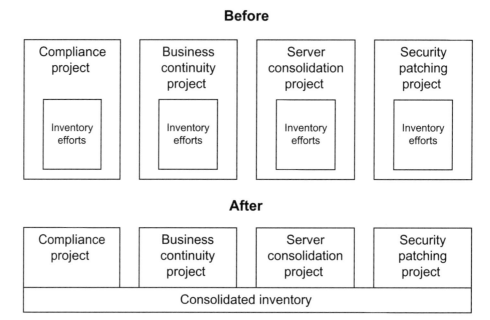

Figure 4.32 Business case for inventory (CMDB) consolidation.

applications running on them have been successfully redeployed to a new platform. In a large and complex IT environment, doing this at speed can be quite difficult because of the unknown dependencies. The consolidation project may not be able to justify a full CMDB investment, but if other stakeholders (e.g., continuity planning) are identified (Figure 4.32), a joint business case for an enabling CMDB might be constructed. Of course, coalition-supported efforts incur substantial risk of scope creep.

4.11 Making It Real

How much are we spending on configuration management today, including decentralized, inefficient, and partial solutions?

A well-optimized IT governance system ideally results in *no net new effort*. This is one of the hardest but most essential points to communicate, and it requires attention to setting the terms of the debate. Rather than allowing the question to be "do we need to spend money on a new CMDB?" the question must be framed as "*how much are we spending on configuration management today, including decentralized, inefficient, and partial solutions?*"

The emphasis must be on redirecting current efforts into a harmonized process, data, and system architecture. The high levels of redundancy and rework most large IT shops experience internally makes this a plausible strategy, although incremental investment will be necessary.

▶ Do you have an inventory of all your major IT systems?
▶ Do you apply portfolio planning and architecture principles to them, as well as to your business-facing systems? Do you have a road map?
▶ Do you understand what IT functions and processes each support? What major data entities they manage? Their interfaces (direct and batch)?

Avoid Shadow Systems

IT enablement data is expensive to collect and keep current. Driving out redundancy is key. The way to do this is to persistently ferret out offline, "shadow" data systems and partner with their owners to meet their needs using enterprise means.

The processes that consume IT data need to have feedback loops to the central datastore and incentives to support its accuracy.

This means that the data needs to be considered both in terms of the core processes collecting and maintaining it and in terms of *the processes it enables.* The processes that consume IT data need to have feedback loops to the central datastore and incentives to support its accuracy. The reemergence of shadow systems must be avoided at all costs, which will require an internal customer relationship capability for the IT enablement organization.

Avoiding shadow systems is a goal for traditional ERP systems and will be likewise for IT for ERP systems as well. However, rather than attempting to "control" shadow systems punitively, it is better to see them as automatic demand requests.

4.12 Chapter Conclusion

The application systems required to run a large information technology capability are becoming more robust and specialized. Their interoperation is an area of concern; comprehensively integrating all the system types outlined in this section would be an expensive proposition, and this is why there is such a rush of acquisition and consolidation among the vendors of these systems.

Just as current ERP systems still must interoperate with many other point solutions that will remain separate for the foreseeable future, so an ERP for IT system will never incorporate all functions and tasks performed by the large IT organization.

The evolution of such capabilities will take place over time and be largely virtual in many organizations, where the critical question of integration looms. The use of a common logical process and data model can assist in the integration of the vendor packages available, and in particular the master data subjects (services, applications, databases, servers, projects, etc.) must be clearly established with defined systems of record so that the diverse systems can be aligned.

Looking Ahead: ERP Consolidation

Ultimately, I predict that the major ERP vendors will incorporate ITRP capabilities (probably through acquisition) in their suites, as the IT area needs strong integration with other back-end corporate systems such as corporate finance, vendor management, and human resources.

4.13 Further Reading

There is surprisingly little book or journal coverage of IT enablement systems. Most of the in-depth work is undertaken by commercial research firms such as Gartner, Forrester Research, and AMR Research. The professional practitioner is urged to invest in memberships to these companies; they can provide clear benefits in helping one avoid suboptimal tool strategies.

However, bear in mind that any classification or taxonomy scheme is arbitrary and has limitations; unspoken assumptions should be critically considered. In particular, research firms may be overpartitioning the IT enablement space based on their perception of the current market and not systematically identifying commonalities and integration points between the different classes of IT enablement systems.

The classic discussion of cohesion and coupling is in Yourdon and Constantine (1979).

Sturm, Erickson-Harris et al. (2002) provide a detailed overview of the service-level management system products available. This guide has been updated and is now available as an ongoing service from Enterprise Management Associates.

If you are considering building a CMDB, or want to understand the technical drivers that make building them hard, see Fowler (2003) and his discussion of the metadata mapping, query object, and repository design patterns (core to the problem of object/relational mapping).

Goldberg (2004) is a case study of Merrill Lynch's use of pure data warehousing approaches for a large section of its CMDB and ITSM objectives.

Metadata repositories and their data dictionary precursors are discussed in Narayan (1988), Wertz (1989), Tannenbaum (1994 and 2002), Marco (2000 and 2003), and Marco and Jennings (2004). Overlaps with CMDBs can clearly be seen in Marco and Jennings (2004), Chapter 6.

Linthicum (2004) covers EAI, SOA, and many related issues.

Patterns for IT Enablement

In software engineering, a design pattern is a general solution to a common problem.... A design pattern isn't a finished design that can be transformed directly into [program] code; it is a description or template for how to solve a problem that can be used in many different situations.

—Wikipedia[212]

THE CONCEPT OF PATTERNS, originating in building architecture and city planning,[213] has been applied in computing for almost two decades. This book also uses a pattern language, but it does so at a higher level than the software engineering pattern literature; patterns of process, organization, data sourcing and flow, and human motivation are discussed.[214]

5.1 Why Apply Patterns?

If the scope of this book were 10 times larger, the material at this point might continue with an exhaustive survey of recommended IT processes, all the way down to specific workflows, tasks, and responsibilities, mapped to an attributed-level, fully elaborated data model in turn associated in detail with candidate systems. Some of the major IT service providers and research firms have detailed material at this scale, and it's not the purpose of this book to replicate such efforts.

My view is that there is not a lot of added value in yet another workflow analysis of incident management. Again, the focus of this book is on the less obvious questions raised in stitching together seemingly disparate functions in IT. To recall the blind men and elephant analogy, the goal is just to sketch the elephant—not an exhaustive anatomy but some of the more salient features: systems, organs, joints, appendages, and how they work together—or alternate ways of making them work. And the goal is to do so with precision, covering questions of data and application architecture, as well as the process and workflow aspects.

Having covered data and systems architectures, we are now far from the value chain outlined in Chapter 2. The objective of the pattern analysis is to tie the systems architecture, data, and processes together across the functional barriers so that the value chain (and its governance) is enabled.

Optimizing IT Processes

The greatest opportunities for process improvement often lie in the functional interfaces—those points at which the baton...is being passed from one department to another.

—Geary Rummler and Alan Brache[215]

If process improvement is a goal of the pattern analysis, what do I mean by that? Roger Burlton[216] proposes several methods for questioning and optimizing any process, techniques that can be applied to IT processes themselves. These include the following:

▶ Move workloads to the front
▶ Eliminate handoffs
▶ Work in parallel
▶ Eliminate low value-add work
▶ Do the right things earlier

These approaches are refined with great precision in modern BPM methodology. Many of the patterns here are proposed in support of such objectives. Achieving even one of these objectives in the context of a particular workflow or intraorganizational relationship can represent significant progress.

How Patterns Are Organized

There are three major categories of patterns:

▶ IT value chain
▶ Configuration management
▶ Supporting processes

Each pattern generally discusses the problem it is intended to address, the overall concept of the pattern, and implementation issues, including possible risks and difficulties.

5.2 Core Value Chain Patterns

Pattern: Clarify Service Entry Points (a.k.a. Front-End Demand Distinction)

Intent

The intent of this pattern is to rationalize *all* customer and user contact with the IT service provider. This is done by distinguishing all possible classes of contacts:

▶ Ideation/exploration request
▶ Project request
▶ Service request
▶ Incident report

These sort themselves nicely into a hierarchy.

From the senior executive down, the business–IT interactions can be defined as in Table 5.1.

Table 5.1 Service Consumers and Entry Points

Business	What	IT Entry Point	Form
Senior executive	Discussions of largest-grained needs. Final escalation of most serious issues. Ideation or exploration.	Senior IT leader.	Usually personal interactions and unstructured documents (emails, presentations, etc.). Request for information.
Unit executive	Requests for major new systems. Large project level.	IT CRM. Demand management system.	May start with personal interactions, moving into process driven. Request for proposal. RFC (high level).

(continued)

Table 5.1 *(continued)*

Business	What	IT Entry Point	Form
Functional area owner	Requests for new systems, additional functionality	Demand management system.	Process driven. Demand requests or RFCs. Development requirements.
User	Requests for orderable IT services. Reporting of incidents.	IT service request system. Incident management system. Change management system.	Process driven. Service request, incident report, RFCs (operational). New system requirements.

(For further information see Hertroys and van Rooijen.)[217]

These service entry points need to be broadly understood in the IT organization, and every IT staff person should be educated that *any* contact with business customers or users should be assignable to one of these categories.

Any IT staff in a consumer contact position should be carefully vetted for customer service abilities. Technologists tend to consider such work "entry level," which is a dangerous misconception. Nothing can help or hurt an IT organization more than its public, day-to-day face.

Ideation or Exploration Request

This picks up where the highest level of customer relationship management leaves off. At this point, no funding has been authorized for the exploration of possible development, so it is covered from base services. The "happy path" life cycle for the ideation request is that it becomes a funded, approved project.

Project Request

Not all projects must go through an exploratory phase, but all start as proposals requiring evaluation and prioritization against competing uses of resources.

Service Request

The distinction proposed here between a project and a service request is the following:

▶ A project is a request to create a service or change an existing service.
▶ A service request is something that can be fulfilled by the capabilities of an existing service.

"Provision email service for one user" is a service request; "establish enterprise email service" is a project request.

One limitation to this approach is that although one service request may be just that, a thousand identical service requests may need to be treated as a project. Usually, the kind of large-scale organizational change initiatives that might result in a thousand services requests are treated as a project regardless.

Incident Report

An incident or problem management workflow is simply a special case of a general workflow, and there are systems that can do either.

The idea of an incident report is well understood; what isn't well understood is whether to use separate service request management and incident management systems or put them into one consolidated service desk system. Incident management tends to have fewer process permutations, and a generic service request management system requires a flexible workflow capability. It's not clear that purchasing the generic system gives all the functionality of a dedicated incident system. For example, a dedicated incident or problem system should have a CMDB at its back end, with each incident and problem tied to the CI in question. This may be harder or impossible to do with a generic service request system.

Incident management tends to have fewer process permutations, and a generic service request management system requires a flexible workflow capability.

Discussion

When viewing IT as a single value chain, the incoming stimuli that initiate the end-to-end process are of primary concern. They need to be captured as early and systematically as possible to eliminate missed handoffs, redundancy, and rework.

This is applicable to large, centralized IT organizations. Highly distributed organizations may not need this.

It's conceptually simple to think of requests as essentially one generic type, but the systems supporting various types of requests are also varied (see Figure 5.1). ITIL's generic RFC model would look more like Figure 5.2.

The overlaps in the systems provide several insights:

The relationship and scope between the demand and portfolio system and the project management system (if separate) need to be carefully considered.

There is clear distinction between strategic–tactical interactions, and operational interactions. There has been some discussion of a "single pane of glass" universal contact mechanism for all IT requests (the general ITIL RFC concept seems to call for this). However, it's not clear that an integrated platform would provide much value, given the different audiences and workflows for demand management versus service request management. Demand and portfolio management *do* require current aggregate metrics on IT resource consumption and therefore

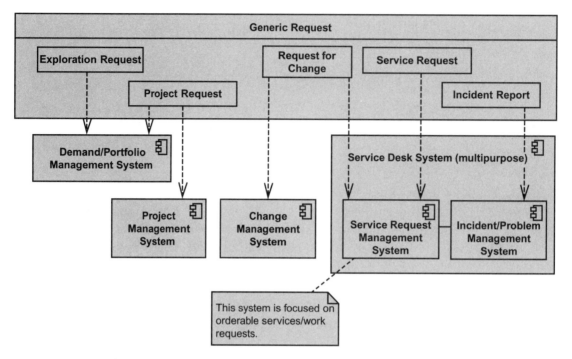

Figure 5.1 Demand subtypes and supporting systems.

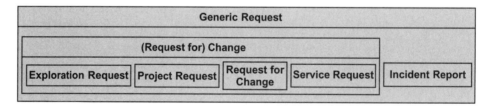

Figure 5.2 ITIL RFC.

need at least integration with service request management and any other systems that can provide such information. However, this does not require a common platform.

Service requests may be distinguished from incidents and have different systems. Service requests require general-case workflow capability, and incidents generally have a single, higher-volume workflow that may be embedded in enabling tools. The solution is to have a generic workflow-enabled service desk system, in which incident management is merely one of the defined workflows (albeit high volume and visibility). This also accommodates the occasional situation in which an Incident is actually a Service Request ("it's not a bug, it's a feature!") or Service Request is actually due to an unrecognized Incident.

(ITIL is ambiguous about the true nature of service requests, in some places seeing them as preapproved RFCs and in other places categorizing them perversely as a form of incident.)

Another complicating factor is what to do with the narrower RFC concept typical of data center operations, which also is workflow based and in some ways resembles a service request. Some ITSM writings seem to see these particularly risky IT activities as comparable to routine service requests, such as adding a single new workstation to a location. Generally, a service offering might be seen in ITIL terms as a preapproved change.

Distinguishing them is difficult, however; while one new workstation may be a service request, 100 new workstations perhaps should be an RFC given the capacity implications—so where do you draw the line?

Software development is an interesting service entry point. The icon for this section can be read to imply that customer interaction only occurs in the first and

third major areas of the value chain. This is untrue; the primary service entry point of concern to the software development capability is requirements capture. The agile movement in particular sees this as an ongoing interaction; the preceding representation implies a dysfunctional stage-contained (commonly called "waterfall") development process, with no developer interaction with the customer throughout a large section of the development life cycle.

However, this interaction does not seem to fit comfortably as a "request." The structured interactions characteristic of requirements engineering (in both lightweight and heavyweight methodologies) are distinct areas of concern and are the subjects of much-detailed study by others.

The consequences of this pattern are essentially a factoring out of the generic ITIL RFC concept into more manageable subsets. However, the (apparent) reason for the highly general ITIL RFC framing is enterprise visibility into all change initiatives, broadly defined. Preserving, for example, the ability of infrastructure groups to see and respond to proposed new applications' capacity implications remains essential regardless of the process clarifications.

While one new workstation is a service request, 100 new workstations should be an RFC given the capacity implications—so where do you draw the line?

The primary service entry point of concern to the software development capability is requirements capture.

Pattern: Standard Technology Stack

The intent of this pattern is to reduce complexity in the IT environment and improve estimation accuracy for IT projects. One current trend to improve estimation accuracy, as well as operational stability, is the definition of approved technology stacks in an environment. This capability requires tooling to manage the Technology entity (described below in the logical data model) and the dependencies of services and applications on these technological building blocks. For example, an IT organization may declare a preference for a certain application server package paired with a specified operating system version and DBMS software; applications based on this stack will receive preferential costing and perhaps some degree of infrastructure subsidization, and applications requiring nonstandard combinations may pay a penalty.

IT projects since the advent of distributed systems have often implemented architectures that are heterogeneous from a technology portfolio point of view. For example, database and application servers (increasingly a commodity) from several vendors may have accumulated over 10 years of distributed systems development.

Complexity is costly to manage.

This complexity is costly to manage; it also represents an opportunity to improve confidence in the solutions development life cycle. Implementing novel infrastructure services adds considerably to a project's risk and cost, and if these services can be bundled as commodity packages with standard pricing to be leveraged by multiple projects in the enterprise, estimation accuracy can be appreciably improved.

Figure 5.3 shows a refinement of the Technology entity from the logical model, with subtypes of Software and Hardware.

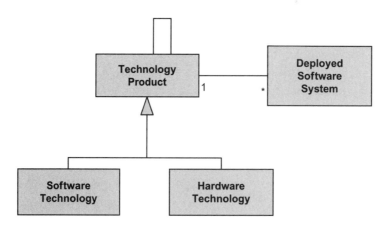

Figure 5.3 Technology data model.

A standard technology stack based on this model is shown in Figure 5.4.

One useful implication of this approach is using it as a basis for segregating the infrastructure and applications portfolios. Investments in the infrastructure portfolio by definition should result in standardized stacks with established costs of acquisition and maintenance.

This general approach has variations: a basic starting approach might be to not formally define "stacks" but to start with the simple capture of application or service dependencies on particular technologies. (This helps with managing complexity and eventually enabling simplification, but it does not provide a basis for improving solution estimation.) Standard stacks can then be derived from the existing real-world data, filtered through pro-active technology architecture planning.[218]

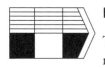

Pattern: Justify Change

The intent of this pattern is to use the RFC not only as a control point for managing risk but also as a control point for managing IT demand and expenditure.

IT activities often lack transparency, a point that should be well established by now! RFCs imply that resources have been spent in preparing the change, will be spent implementing the change, and potentially are being committed long term to supporting the change (e.g., in the case of a new system with operational requirements).

If the goal is greater visibility into IT's cost drivers, the RFC is much too important a control point to disregard. That is why every RFC should be traceable from a

The intent of this pattern is to use the RFC not only as a control point for managing risk but also as a control point for managing IT demand and expenditure.

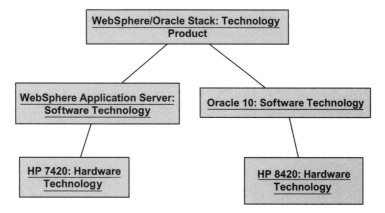

Figure 5.4 Standard technology stack.

management and budgetary standpoint to an approved project release, a problem, or an incident.

This pattern is applied to the change management process area and supporting data and systems.

A logical model of the data structures is shown in Figure 5.5.

(Technical note: The change justification entity is a purely logical concept, and implementing any sort of true inheritance from it is not the point of this pattern. It's intentionally not shown in the main logical model in Figure 5.2.)

This pattern highlights one of the most difficult issues in IT governance: what to do about so-called maintenance releases or requests expected from base funding once all projects have completed. This is a financial and organizational discussion that touches on some of the most sensitive issues in the large IT organization today.

Too much money can easily disappear into unplanned changes to the portfolio executed by application support staff.

This pattern assumes that base-funded changes to a system are still tracked as "projects." This is a recommended best practice, as too much money can easily disappear into unplanned changes to the portfolio executed by application support staff. Such staff may be nominally tasked with keeping the application running, but their duties all too often expand into continually adding new functionality with no reference to the approved project life cycle, software development process, or release management. Application enhancements become more of a discussion around permanent head count assigned to a standing application team (and a corresponding sense of entitlement) and less transparent to the question of whether the application is still aligned with evolving business strategy.

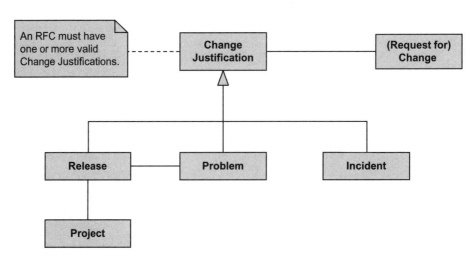

Figure 5.5 Change justification.

This is a dysfunctional situation, and it undermines the concept of IT portfolio management as a planning activity. On the other hand, there are legitimate small requests (e.g., defining a new report format) for which a heavyweight project process would be overkill.

The solution is both carrot and stick: continually question and seek to reduce the base application expenditure, but also reward application teams (and their customers) for honestly enumerating the enhancement requests that might otherwise be handled under the table. If the application team and their customers perceive that documenting application enhancements formally (in terms of demand, projects, and releases) results in budget cuts, the application support staff will suddenly be consumed with "critical production support activities" and transparency will be lost.

The consequences of this pattern can include the perception or reality of bureaucratic obstacles. Clearly, changes required to mitigate severe incidents should be expedited, and in those events, RFC completeness may be deferred; exception reports should be run to identify those "critical" RFCs for which justification was not available at the time. This sort of activity is what a central change management staff is for.

Implementing this pattern assumes that automated systems exist to track all forms of demand, release, incident, and problem and that the change management system can integrate with these other systems at least in terms of references.

For example, an RFC might be tracked to a given Incident by number. One of the issues that arises is whether an invalid incident number might be entered; this can be handled through direct integration (so that the Change system always has a current list of Incidents to pick from) or through exception reporting (which takes more staff effort). SOAs are ideal for this type of real-time, event-based integration involving relatively small amounts of cross-reference data.

Pattern: Integrate Risk, Configuration, Change, and Metadata

A typical change management tool asks a number of questions of the change requester, including the following:

▶ Can the change be backed out? If so, how long will this take?
▶ How many users will the change potentially affect?
▶ Does the change involve customer data?
▶ Was the change tested?

The responses to these questions are then processed by a defined function that calculates a risk rating for the change; higher-risk changes receive more scrutiny from the change advisory board and may be held to higher standards in a variety of areas.

Enterprise risk management is also concerned with other classes of risks; for example: Does the change affect any processes material to Sarbanes-Oxley compliance? Does it involve a system that handles sensitive customer data?

In some cases, such questions find their way into the change management tool. However, this is problematic in that risk assessment is then too much in the hands of the change requester. Yes, the requester should answer these questions honestly, and most do. But some don't, and others are put into an awkward position if they don't know the answer. "Hmm, I don't *think* I have any SOX impact—so I'll just check 'No.'"

With increasing regulatory and audit pressure on publicly traded companies, the discipline of risk management is increasingly applied to IT governance. The concept of a Risk is nebulous, however; a Risk is always with respect to some "Thing."

In the IT world you can see in Figure 3.10, Risks may relate to Projects, Changes, or CIs. (Projects may be seen as a subtype of enterprise change in some organizations, depending on the ITIL interpretation.)

When this pattern is implemented, it becomes possible to objectively assess the Risks that may apply to a proposed change to a given CI. This is more effective than Change approaches that require the change requester to identify all Risks at the point of requesting the change, an approach fraught with conflict of interest.

If changes are linked systematically to CIs, and the CIs are in turn linked to the risk management activities, the change requester is no longer in this position. For example, whether a system is material to Sarbanes-Oxley compliance is an objective fact that should be determined by the corporate auditors, not an IT project manager or other typical change requester.

Typical change assessment questions invite a conflict of interest on the part of the change requester.

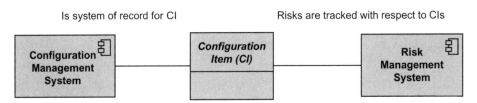

Is system of record for CI   Risks are tracked with respect to CIs

Figure 5.6 CI-based risk management.

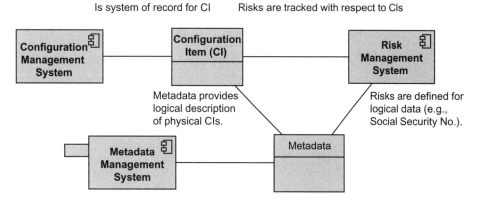

Figure 5.7 Configuration and metadata risk management.

Similarly, the number of users of a given system (another change risk driver) is an objective fact, one usually tracked for a variety of portfolio-related purposes.

This pattern thus calls for the change risk assessment to be based (to the maximum extent possible) on preexisting data in the CMDB. An additional reinforcement for this would be to *treat unspecified data as an automatic risk increase.* For example, if there is a "number of users" data element tracked for applications and it is not filled in for a given application being changed, the risk of that change would automatically go up a level.

Note that many risks today concern the privacy and confidentiality of data. Meeting such requirements requires the integration of metadata and configuration management systems, which is not done well today.

In this scenario, the metadata system is seen as primarily containing logical data definitions, and the CMDB is seen as containing information about the physical environment ("technical metadata"). The integration challenges here are not trivial, as many metadata systems also store technical metadata, resulting in overlap with the CMDB. Solving this problem requires a precise representation of the various forms of technical and logical metadata (Figure 5.8).

Figure 5.8 shows the relationship between metadata and CIs. Again, this representation assumes that the metadata is primarily logical documentation, and the technical metadata is the domain of the CMDB. (See the Metadata entity definition.) Risks should be tracked with respect to given attributes (e.g., Social Security number and credit card number) or combinations thereof. These attributes appear

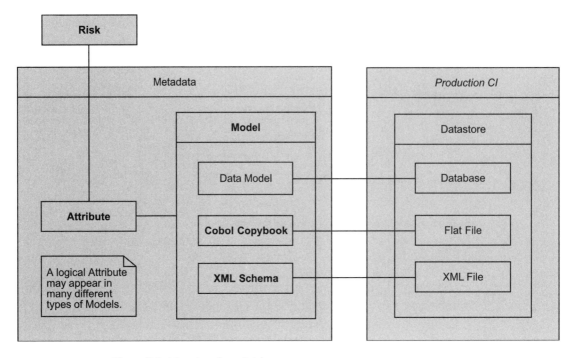

Figure 5.8 Metadata-based risk management.

in a variety of models that in turn may describe multiple instances of deployed CIs (one data model may describe several database instances).

When managing metadata, it is important to identify CI-analogous artifacts, which in the representation here are the concepts of data model (i.e., relational), COBOL copybook, and XML Schema. These are atomic units of work or deliverables at a suitable level for tracking.

5.3 Configuration Management Patterns

 Let's return now to configuration management, a recurring theme throughout this book, with many patterns and antipatterns. Consider the following skeptical quote from one thought leader in the ITSM professional community:

Often, an ITIL "implementation" will start at an early stage, setting up and fleshing out a configuration management database. According to developers, this CMDB should serve many purposes, such as configuration management, asset management, resource management, cost management, etc., and should support practically all processes. This creates a database full of detailed information that contains many interrelationships. Maintaining such a database is often time-consuming, making it almost impossible to verify data. The problem is aggravated further by the fact that *those who are responsible for the detailed maintenance of changes, i.e., system managers, operators, and/or change support staff*, do not see the full benefit of their efforts in their daily work. Proper maintenance of a CMDB, therefore, requires a great deal of discipline and effort. The returns are further diminished as, in the case of many of the larger actions, the CMDB often does not contain the information required, making further stock-taking necessary. The CMDB offers limited support for activities, while its maintenance requires a disproportionately large amount of effort.[219]

The emphasis is added. This quote will be referenced in the discussion that follows. To delve more deeply into the problem: the entities in Figure 5.9 are perhaps the core of production data center configuration management.

(Figure 5.9 is a simplification of the more precise representation in Figure 3.2, reprinted from the maturity model illustrated in Figure 3.50 through Figure 3.53.)

There are many variations and refinements on this basic problem area; for example, the DMTF has extensive specifications, and large parts of the OMG's modeling languages also cover it.[220]

In many organizations, this data is fragmented into small, incomplete spreadsheets and databases. Often, there is no defined process for keeping these data sets up-to-date, and each point solution takes a particular point view at the expense of related data.

> In many organizations, configuration and portfolio data is fragmented into small, incomplete spreadsheets and databases.

Centralized attempts to maintain this data have proved to be ineffective as well. There are three areas that historically have attempted this mission:

▶ Metadata management (the oldest)
▶ Enterprise architecture
▶ Configuration management (the most recent)

> Central maintenance of complex dependencies usually fails.

The trouble in all of these cases starts when a centralized team attempts the data maintenance with little or no distribution of process steps and (often) no defined process. History has not been kind to such attempts, which usually wind up abandoned.

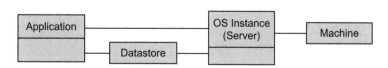

Figure 5.9 Core configuration management.

Configuration management challenges include the following:

▶ Continual reanalysis is needed of items and dependencies (data fragmentation).
▶ The service provider is responsible for consumer dependencies.
▶ Configuration management does not replace existing processes or artifacts.

Continual Reanalysis of Items and Dependencies

In this antipattern, the lack of configuration management results in the repeated re-collection of inventories: servers, databases, and applications in particular. This is an expensive antipattern, given the compensation levels of the staff usually required to provide inventory information and the opportunity costs of their participation in such redundant efforts.

Technical (ICT) Service Provider Responsible for Consumer Dependencies

The infrastructure team does not have primary responsibility for the business-facing application service definition.

In this antipattern, engineering capabilities are responsible for understanding what depends on them. For example, the server engineering team is responsible for maintaining the data about which applications depend on a given server. This responsibility pattern is dysfunctional in that the infrastructure team does not have primary responsibility for the business-facing application service definition. Application teams can partner in unexpected ways, and new dependencies can be introduced on infrastructure that are impossible for the information and communication technology staff to detect. SOA is only making this worse, with its call for dynamically recomposable applications—this translates to dynamic dependencies, changing perhaps *outside the scope of the change process.*[221]

Configuration Management Does Not Replace Existing Processes or Artifacts

In this antipattern, configuration management is implemented but its potential to enhance and even replace other IT deliverables is not recognized. For example, a word-processing document may still be generated as a run book for production turnover, with manually drawn diagrams representing the same items and their dependencies managed in the CMDB. Achieving cultural change in such matters is difficult but essential to gaining value.

I will turn now to positive responses to these configuration management challenges.

Would you
rather sign up for
a process that
costs you five
full-time staff
members or one
full-time staff
member?

Pattern: Capture Data at Appropriate Level

The intent of this pattern is to capture data related to IT assets at the most efficient level. It is essentially a pragmatic application of data normalization.

DIALOG

Data Normalization?

Pat: Data normalization? Boy, that seems academic. Let's just capture the data and be done with it.

Kelly: Sigh—that's so often the response I get. Yes, the data architecture theory is called normalization, and it was first established by Ted Codd, an IBM scientist. It's the basis for our relational databases, and Oracle CEO Larry Ellison is a very rich man because of it.

So let's put it in practical terms. A data model is a process commitment. An application screen is a process commitment. We want to minimize the number of data entry points as much as possible. Would you rather sign up for a process that costs you five full-time staff members or one full-time staff member?

Pat: Data architecture can make that much difference?

Kelly: Yes, it can. Data modelers are your friends. Even if you are going to go out and mainly purchase packages, they can help you identify packages that may be impossible to maintain or give you insights into how to implement the package. There are always decisions to be made in setting them up, and many of these decisions have to do with how you're going to treat the data.

Consider an organization with a list of hardware devices and their costs and depreciation information (a typical asset management function). Such a capability may increasingly be called on to answer questions such as, "But who really benefits from owning this hardware (e.g., a server)?" Subsidiary questions such as risk tracking (does the server have confidential data?) may start to appear. All become attributes of the device, which is a violation of well-established data architecture principles.

The resulting inefficiency can be seen in Figure 5.10. Capturing data at the wrong level could mean 10 times as much work!

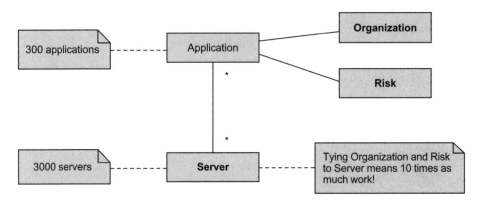

Figure 5.10 Appropriate data capture level.

Pattern: Consumer Manages Dependency

The intent of this pattern is to find an effective combination of people, process, and technology to ensure the viability of configuration management and its complex portfolio and dependency management implications.

Van den Elskamp states that the following staff members are responsible for updating the CMDB: "system managers, operators, and/or change support staff" who "do not see the full benefit of their efforts in their daily work." This leads to the situation in which the "CMDB offers limited support for activities, while its maintenance requires a disproportionately large amount of effort."[222]

Clearly, configuration management will not be a viable concept in the modern enterprise under these circumstances. The primary issue with the preceding quote is that *the wrong people are named as CMDB maintainers.*

The data center team is often hard pressed to understand the dependencies on a given device.

Most organizations have split server (data center) engineering and operations from the application development and maintenance teams; beyond making sense from a functional perspective, this is required to meet audit objectives regarding separation of concerns. The data center team is often hard pressed to understand the dependencies on a given device (the classic "can of Coke" problem—if I spill one on a machine, what business process is affected?). This leads to continuous issues when servers need to be patched for crosscutting system reasons (e.g., antivirus measures) or when 20% of the servers in a data center must be retired for lease refresh reasons.

The application teams find themselves reacting to unplanned outages and reboots and having to scramble because a server must be decommissioned. Neither side in this equation is particularly happy with the other.

It is therefore critical to distribute the maintenance of complex system dependencies to the application and support teams. This is not as hard as it sounds.

The solution is to require the application team to document its dependency on the server. *It owns the task of data entry.* The understanding must be that if the application team does this, it will be notified of server impacts. If it does not do this, the application team has no expectation of notification. Because application teams are generally more customer facing than the engineering or data center teams, they have the higher incentive to do this.

The service integrator is a recommended ITSM organizational approach that well supports the pattern that "dependencies should be maintained by the consumer." The service integrator takes on the role of general contractor, responsible for the service package, and the actual business customers then only need to understand their dependency on the service, not its underlying internals.[223]

Because the service integrators are directly accountable to the business customers, the service integrators are more highly motivated to maintain the dependency documentation. The service integrators therefore are the best choice to be responsible for updating the CMDB, and the accuracy of their data should be directly tied to the service they receive from their subcontractors.

> Customer-facing application service teams have a higher incentive for accurate CMDB data.

Who's Responsible?

A large corporation undertook an initiative to increase server utilization in the data center, in conjunction with a massive lease refresh. This required the removal of large and complex applications from the current servers, which in turn required a complete understanding of those servers' current usage. Multiple meetings were held (driven by the infrastructure team) for each group of servers, which still did not necessarily accurately identify all dependencies, resulting in outages.

The CIO decided to leverage an enterprise repository (effectively a CMDB) and made it known that the application teams would be responsible for doing their own data entry. The vice president for infrastructure engineering supported this by announcing that any servers with no documented dependencies were at immediate risk of being either decommissioned or reprovisioned to new tasks.

Table 5.2 Contrasting RASI Approaches

	Application Team	Infrastructure Team		Application Team	Infrastructure Team
Identify app–server dependency	I	R	Identify app–server dependency	R	I

Table 5.2 shows two RASI (responsible, accountable, supporting, informed) matrices summarizing the key insight of this pattern. The first matrix shows what doesn't work; the second matrix gives the recommended approach.

The Psychology of the IT Process

One of the most critical aspects of process design is psychology. The correct harmonization of IT processes with the psychological leanings of IT practitioners is a rich field of inquiry; careers could be made here. This process is based on a win–win relationship between the application and the infrastructure teams, and it places accountability on the service integrator, who has the stronger, customer-facing motivation to get the data right.

Participants

Note that this pattern calls for "service providers," not just "application owners." That is because it is a more broadly applicable pattern. This pattern includes the following responsibilities:

▶ Database administrators would be responsible for documenting their database-to-server dependency
▶ Server engineers would be responsible for documenting their server-to-switch dependency and server-to-storage area network dependency
▶ Business process owners would be responsible for documenting their process-to-application or -service dependencies

Again, the general assumption is that the consumer depends more on the provider.

Service Integrator and Customer Service

Pat: What about the goal of customer service? Why wouldn't we expect the service provider to know their customers?

Kelly: Let's say you are a caterer. You're responsible for organizing a wedding banquet, on a certain day without fail. You need to know your local merchants, when they are open, and so forth. There is no way that they can anticipate your particular needs as you put together that banquet. They should extend you good customer service by honoring their posted hours of operation, selling high-quality merchandise, and keeping it in stock. If they know you personally and go the extra mile, all well and good.

But *you* are ultimately the accountable service provider "integrating" that banquet, and your clients are not going to care if one of your suppliers is causing you problems. You need to know that you are going to stores X, Y, and Z the day of the banquet; what their hours are; and whether they will have what you need. It's not the merchants' job to know this; therefore, you have the most accurate knowledge of your dependencies.

This is an important principle, and often things are attempted the other way.

The consequences of this pattern ideally will be improved ownership of the configuration data and concern for its accuracy. Again, data is only as good as the business processes that produce and consume it and the owners of those business processes must have clear incentives to update the data.

If no application team has seen fit to document a dependency on the server, it may be assumed to be excess capacity.

This leads to perhaps the most controversial aspect of this pattern: the recommendation that application teams' notification of infrastructure effects be based on this data. This can be extended to the consequence of servers being reprovisioned if they have no documented dependency. If no application team has seen fit to document a dependency on the server (or database or technology), it may be assumed to be excess capacity or functionality. The same principle applies to applications considered for retirement: dependent application teams must document their dependency or the application relied upon may be removed without their being notified.

The same principle could and should be applied to application teams' dependency on a given product license being renewed annually.

Obviously, such measures are somewhat draconian and should be implemented cautiously (e.g., after much systematic, broad-spectrum communication and starting with development and test environments). However, you who are skeptical of this approach should examine just how well your organization is managing infrastructure effects currently. If the approach is to semirandomly gather staff and guess at what is running on the server, or who is using a given software product license, *you are risking operational impact regardless.* (Don't fool yourself.)

Discovery tools and service dependency mapping tools may alleviate this issue to some extent, but these tools only present what is in the environment, not whether it should be there. That determination requires human intervention. They also only present physically detectable evidence and require human intervention to define even basic logical concepts such as "application."

The effect of this pattern is quite broad and may involve dozens of application teams. With such a large user base, attention to organizational change management is essential for success. The items and dependencies to be tracked must be clearly identified at the outset of implementation; changing or adding items or dependencies after rollout will be difficult and may provoke the user base.

Furthermore, the items to be tracked probably have different owners than the dependencies (see example).

It is important to limit the transactions for which the server owners are responsible. These should be specific maintenance of defined dependencies, for example:

▶ Application to Server
▶ Application to Database
▶ Application to Application
▶ Application to Technology Product (or deployed software system)

Table 5.3 shows one possible approach, with the items, dependencies, and responsible areas. The data, server, and architecture areas may already be accustomed

> Discovery tools and service dependency mapping tools only present what is in the environment, not whether it should be there.

Table 5.3 Configuration Data Responsibilities

	Database Management	Server Engineering	Enterprise Architecture	Application Management
Application			R	
Technology			R	
Database	R			
Server		R		
Application/Application Dependency				R
Application/Server Dependency				R
Application/Database Dependency				R
Database/Server Dependency	R			
Application/Technology Dependency				R
Technology/Server Dependency		R		

to maintaining their own configuration data; the salient feature of the matrix is the assignment of significant dependency management responsibilities to the application management area. This may be a rollout of unfamiliar responsibilities.

See the intersection entities discussion in Chapter 3 regarding dependencies.

Related Patterns

Application portfolio management.

Pattern: Security–Configuration Management Synergy

The intent of this pattern (like many in this section) is to strengthen the centralized configuration management capability by basing processes upon the data maintained therein. The configuration data will never be up-to-date unless its accuracy is a gate standing in the way of other desired outcomes.

The motivation for this pattern is the increasingly strong position of information security as a functional area in the modern enterprise. There is mutual benefit for security and configuration management partnership. The CMDB (or repository more generally) can be a powerful tool for security teams to understand dependencies and risks in the complex IT environment. Conversely, if security processes require complete CMDB data to execute, this will drive good data quality, as security authorizations are a frequently encountered gate in the solutions development life cycle.

This pattern is applicable to most production CIs; anything requiring access controls to interact with.

The structure enabling this pattern is the core Party–Role–CI set detailed in the conceptual data model.

Taking Figure 5.11 as an example, no user would be able to gain access to the application until it is registered in the CMDB and acceptable Parties and Roles are populated (e.g., application support team and application business customer). This principle can be applied to the beginning of the software development life cycle and to all secured CIs.

Do not confuse the maintenance of Party–Role–CI, which is a low-volume, low-volatility data problem, with the actual maintenance of security rights for CIs. Access management is a high-volume, high-maintenance process usually supported by a defined set of directory services tools in partnership with various element management systems and/or the security architectures internal to applications.

The configuration data will never be up-to-date unless its accuracy is a gate standing in the way of other desired outcomes.

Do not confuse the maintenance of party–role–CI, which is a low-volume, low-volatility data problem, with the actual maintenance of security rights for CIs.

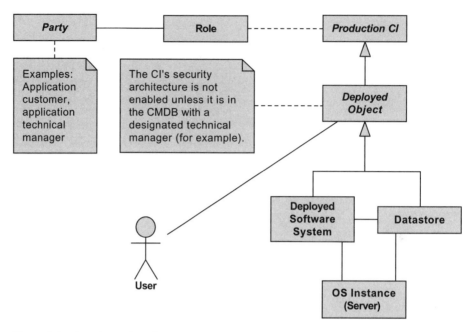

Figure 5.11 Security and configuration management.

The participants are the security team and especially those parties seeking *the first instance of authorization* to a CI in a particular context.

Potential consequences of this pattern, as with many in this area, are the perceived or real establishment of bureaucratic obstacles in the primary IT value chain. Efficiency and responsiveness of the security and configuration management process are paramount; they should be measured and optimized with continuous improvement techniques.

The implementation will require strong partnership with the security organization and a well-established application identification process. Securable CIs to start with might include applications, databases, and servers. Basing the naming convention of runtime security accounts upon the application ID concept has been shown to work.

A new application server is provisioned as a development environment for a new application. Before the application team can gain access to the new server, the application name and identifier (ID) must be established, as the ID is part of the naming convention for the resource security account. This requires the application team to initiate the process of establishing a new application ID, which will in turn lead to the visibility of this new application to other enterprise IT processes (architecture, capacity, etc.).

> Security and configuration management processes should be measured and optimized with continuous improvement techniques.

Pattern: Integrate IT Knowledge Management with Configuration Management

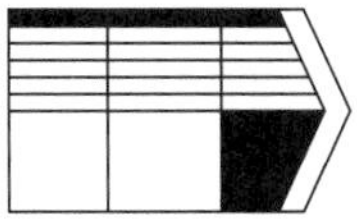

Knowledge management is a difficult challenge, troubled in many organizations. One difficulty is the inherent subjectivity of classification taxonomies. Categorizing information is never simple, and many users of a knowledge base leave frustrated because their mental "maps" are different from those of the knowledge base's architects.

This book proposes no general solutions for the problems of knowledge management, but the specific problem of IT knowledge management has some advantages: the unambiguous names of physical CIs and the importance of standardizing the names of logical CIs. Although customers may disagree about whether an application is a "customer service" or "customer relationship" application, there should be no disagreement that it is deployed on server X and uses database Y. Those unambiguous data points provide a structure for managing unstructured data, assuming that the CMDB can store documents and their metadata, along with the configuration metadata (most can).

Maturing a configuration management capability often involves a gradual shift from less structured to more structured documentation. Even a mature IT organization will use unstructured documents extensively and require an effective means for categorizing and retrieving them.

The core structure for this pattern is shown in Figure 5.12.

Notice that Document is a CI and can be associated with CIs (remember the unspecified association line means many to many). As a CI, it can have multiple

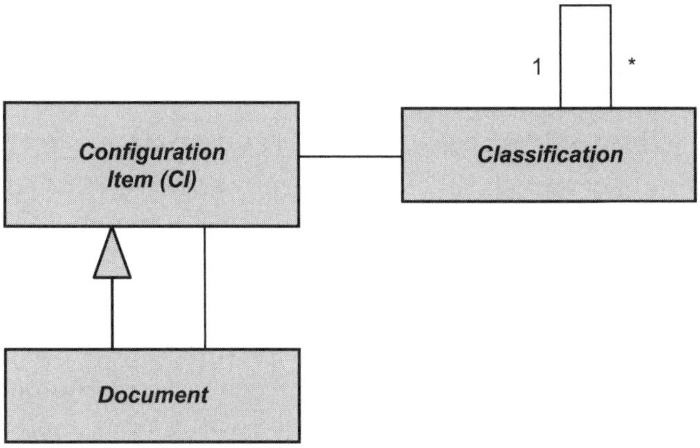

Maturing a configuration management capability often involves a gradual shift from less structured to more structured documentation.

Figure 5.12 Knowledge management.

Classifications (Classifications are reference taxonomies). If the taxonomies are ambiguous or not well considered, the document can still be located based on its relationship to CIs—for example, Applications, Datastores, and Servers.

A positive consequence would be easier location of unstructured documentation in the IT environment. One issue to take into consideration is the possible need to formalize the document life cycle; are the documents associated with CIs up-to-date and accurate? Finally, this pattern should be balanced against the goal of moving IT information generally from an unstructured paradigm to a structured one. Can word-processing documents and standalone graphic diagrams be replaced with CMDB data? (See the "CMDB as the System of Record for the Run Book" pattern.)

The relationship between the structured CMDB and any unstructured document management capabilities will need to be formalized. This can be achieved through the use of URIs (uniform resource indicators), an excellent means of maintaining a loosely coupled relationship across systems.

For example, an architectural design is created for a new system and updated throughout its development. It is associated with the Application CI, which is in turn associated with Servers and Databases. Subsequently a capacity-driven server consolidation effort is considering the application's servers for consolidation and wishes to understand the potential consequences for this application; that effort can quickly find the architectural design as an input for their analysis. The downside to this is that many of the dependencies in an architectural design should also be available directly through the CMDB, for example, through a defined report. The architectural analysis may be more of a point-in-time snapshot, not guaranteed to be accurate.

Proposed Pattern: Model-Driven Configuration Management

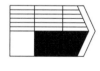

Complex system dependencies are carefully mapped by architecture and development teams.

A basic BPM principle is that data should be captured when it is first identified and maintained (not recaptured) afterward. This is especially critical to the success of configuration management, which is one of the more difficult data management challenges.

Vendors of ITSM tooling, and some commentators on the topic of configuration management, do not seem to recognize that complex system dependencies are carefully mapped by architecture and development teams as an essential part of the systems development life cycle. Much of the literature about configuration management[224] assumes that the CIs and their dependencies will be reanalyzed and recaptured at the point of production change (i.e., deployment), which is highly inefficient. This approach also causes a technical bias in the understanding of large IT systems, especially when discovery tools are relied on.

The problem is that the mappings done by development teams are too often done in a format (e.g., PowerPoint, Visio, or even just a temporary whiteboard sketch) that cannot be consumed by a configuration management capability. This is simply a matter of standardization and tool alignment. To mitigate the typical last-minute "over the wall" dysfunctional handoff from development to operations, CI identification should be driven as far upstream as possible. In its section on configuration management, ITIL argues:

Support tools should allow control to be maintained, for applications software, from the outset of systems analysis and design right through to live running. Ideally, organisations should use the same tool to control all stages of the life-cycle.... The IT infrastructure Configuration Management tool should at least allow Configuration Management information to be transferred from a software development Configuration Management system into the CMDB without the need for rekeying.

However, this seems to imply some sort of interface between the source code control tool (a.k.a. the software configuration management tool or repository) and the CMDB. Source code control tools such as PVCS, VSS, and CVS play an essential role in the software development life cycle, but they are just specialized file management systems with the ability to compare text files. The overall structure of an application is not represented in the source code control system, which is hierarchical and focused on the source code—basically, just a managed directory structure with audit trail and text comparison capabilities, by no means a modeling tool.

A modern distributed system's complexity comes in the interconnections and dependencies on things like databases and middleware, which the version control system does not represent. A simple distributed system, for example, might have a database with stored procedures, several interlinked components on an application or Web server, and dependencies on other systems through message queues. These dependencies cannot be derived directly from a text-based software configuration management system.

Component and deployment diagrams should be mandatory outputs of the solutions delivery life cycle.

This pattern is applicable to the software development life cycle and the transition of production systems to operational (production) status. Note that this book does not call for the detailed modeling of software structure or behavior, which is a controversial issue in software engineering. The component and deployment diagrams, however, are valuable for a variety of enterprise stakeholders and should be considered mandatory outputs of the solutions delivery life cycle. Most application teams already create documentation covering these higher-level system characteristics as a turnover requirement. See the "CMDB as the System of Record for the Run Book" pattern.

The most obvious development artifacts are those based on structured semantics, in particular the OMG's UML. This language encompasses various semantics for describing software systems, including both their internal structure and their larger-grained architecture, such as deployment to runtime environments (the Component and Deployment diagrams).

UML is a flexible tool and will require a defined implementation approach specific to an organization's requirements. Figure 5.13 shows a trivial example with a logical software component, its instantiation as a runtime Java Server page, and an associated database on a separate server. Note that all of these elements can be composed (nested and associated) with arbitrary complexity.

The singular advantage to UML is that the preceding diagram is not merely a picture; it is based upon a sophisticated data model and therefore can be exchanged among a variety of tools through a standard known as XML metadata interchange (XMI). Because XMI is based on XML, all the standard XML tooling can be used. (XMI is a verbose standard and out of scope for this book; see the OMG's Web site, *www.omg.org,* for further information.) XMI provides everything needed to feed a configuration management system: objects with names and unique IDs and a precise representation of their interconnections. Connections can be represented between servers and switches, between components and databases, and between virtually anything else imaginable in the modern IT infrastructure. A competent extensible stylesheet language transformations programmer could convert this structure into whatever format a CMDB required; far preferable would be a CMDB that accepted this industry standard directly.

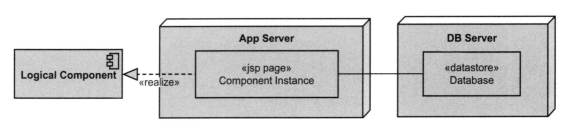

Figure 5.13 UML deployment diagram.

Microsoft also has created a Domain-Specific Language for modeling data center dependencies.[225]

A simple approach to distilling configuration information is depicted in Figure 5.14.

UML is not an out-of-the-box solution to this problem. The organization will need to define standards for stereotyping the UML elements and parsing them out of raw XMI. The problem is generally not limitations of the UML and its related standards; the problem is more often their richness, in that there are usually multiple ways to solve a given problem. Further standards work in defining more targeted, intuitive profiles for this problem is needed.

There is considerable depth in the UML and XML talent pools, and finding resources to build this integration should not be difficult.

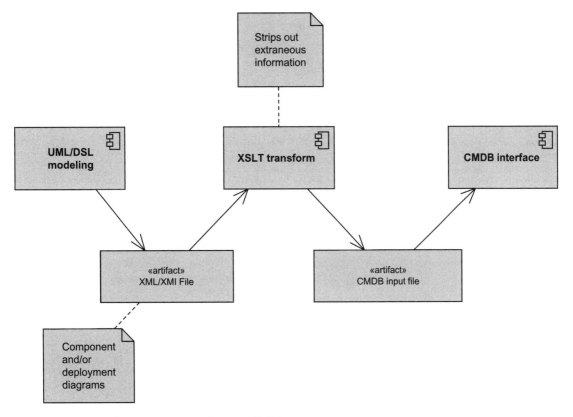

Figure 5.14 XMI as input to CMDB.

Pattern: Scalable Dependency Entry

One of the more onerous tasks associated with maintaining a configuration management capability is the entry or research of significant numbers of dependencies. The following data entry use cases all have this as a common challenge:

▶ Associate a Change with 150 network switches

▶ Associate an Application with 25 servers

▶ Associate a Technology Product with 400 machines

▶ Notify the owners of 50 applications dependent on 500 servers

▶ Associate 20 entities of various types with 30 dependencies between them of various types.

Naïve tools require a separate, low-performance search for each association to be made or require the consumer to scroll through lists of thousands of items with checkboxes. Neither is acceptable; richer tool support is required, which can take a couple of forms.

First, a dynamic search capability with the ability to quickly retrieve and incrementally build a list of objects to be associated is essential. The specifics of how search is implemented become critical and need to be considered in detail.

Figures 5.15 and 5.16 show an efficient and an inefficient approach to dependency entry. Although the sequence diagrams show a particular approach to a two-tier architecture as an example, the key requirement is that the customer needs to be able to quickly navigate a large collection of CIs and down their search efficiently, while building a set of selected objects without having to save each one individually. This can be achieved through means such as:

▶ Instantaneous parsing of entered object names, resulting in dynamically filtered lists

▶ Hierarchical tree navigation structures

▶ Finding objects through other known dependencies on them (e.g., "I want all servers supporting application A").

Most of these approaches are more efficient with some in-memory caching of data, although this is not technically required.

Dependency entry and analysis capabilities should also be able to accept lists as an input, with the system validating the entries and accepting the valid ones while flagging any invalid ones. It is possible to build a front-end data capture tool using spreadsheets with data entry constrained to predefined lists, which fulfills the twin requirements of user acceptability and rigorous data quality.

> One of the more onerous tasks associated with maintaining a configuration management capability is the entry or research of significant numbers of dependencies.

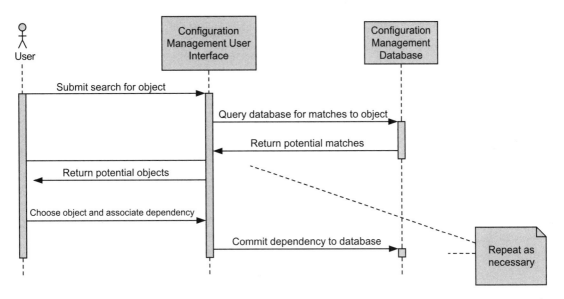

Figure 5.15 Inefficient dependency entry.

On Notation

The UML sequence diagram is presented here for the first time; it is read from top to bottom and is analogous to a process swimlane diagram.

CIs are often changed by broad initiatives covering hundreds or more, each in turn possessing its own complex dependencies. If the work request and task documentation covering this effort is not integrated with the configuration management system, entry into the CMDB will be seen as rework, with potential for inaccurate data capture. This implies that certain types of work requests (e.g., server patching and lease refresh) should be as tightly integrated with the CMDB as possible. Tactical integration (e.g., using SOA) with office automation tools such as spreadsheets would be a desirable capability for the CMDB system.

A related pattern is Model-Driven Configuration Management, which discusses graphical artifacts as inputs into the CMDB.

Pattern: Configuration Accounting Processes

The perpetual question with complex configuration management is how to keep the data up-to-date and ensure confidence in it. One of the means for doing this is

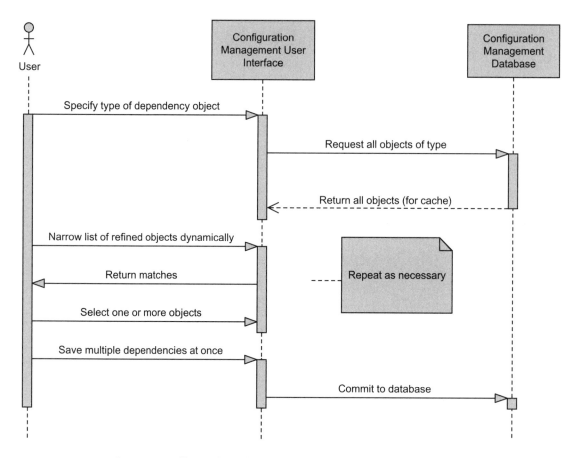

Figure 5.16 Efficient dependency entry.

a periodic process by which owners of configuration data are called upon to validate its completeness and accuracy.

This is a cyclic process, essentially a configuration accounting implementation.[226] Using current tools, it should be email driven. It requires several diagrams to describe:

In the scenario described here, it is assumed that a role titled service architect is responsible for responding to the configuration accounting process. In other models, it could be a support group, or a different individual role title.

Security best practices (e.g., the ISO 17799 standard) indicate that IT assets should be assigned a "nominated" owner for security, as well as other purposes, so the assumption that someone holds this role for a given application service is

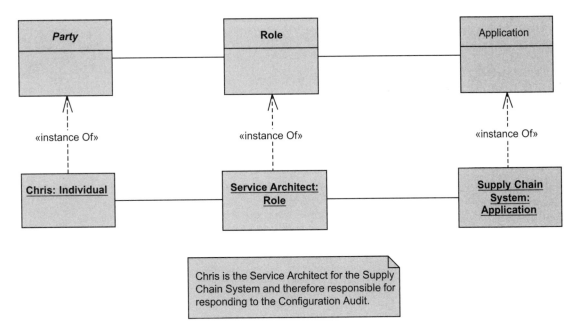

Figure 5.17 Configuration Accounting role.[227]

reasonable. (Note that asset ownership is more valuable and more easily managed for larger-grained logical constructs.)

Figure 5.18 shows the periodic correspondence that each nominated asset owner would receive.

This is not a pretty process; it is a brute-force approach. However, it is a necessary part of keeping a CMDB up-to-date.

The configuration management system should be as self-service in this respect as possible. The initial contact should be by email, and the recipient should be able to confirm or make the necessary changes simply and efficiently using a Web interface.[228]

However, there will be those who do not respond to the accounting correspondence, for which an exception report should be generated and followed up by staff, perhaps driving a Configuration Audit. Such follow-up is where a configuration management capability starts to incur ongoing operational spend.

Staff may choose to select some systems for more intensive audit activity (Figure 5.19), such as in-person interviews with application support staff and reconciliation with discovery tools. (A manual configuration audit might be the consequence of nonresponse to the automated configuration accounting process.)

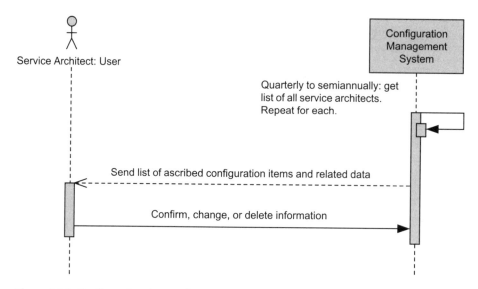

Figure 5.18 Configuration Accounting process.

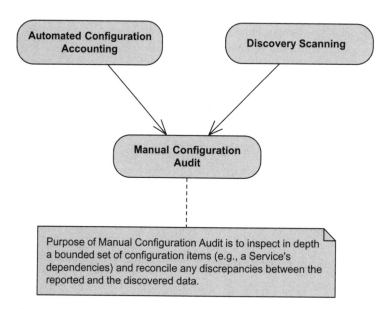

Figure 5.19 Manual configuration audit.

Pattern: Interface System

The intent of this pattern is to integrate the system interaction diagramming at an architectural level with configuration management at a component level.

Both architectural and operational views are often required on the same configuration management data set.

The motivation of this pattern is the complexity of maintaining system interaction documentation and the need to have both architectural and operational views on the same core data set. Often, multiple views on the same data are maintained independently, which is inefficient but given current approaches is often the only practical alternative.

This pattern is especially applicable to organizations that have centralized integration management (i.e., through an Integration Competency Center), an increasingly adopted best practice.[229]

Figure 5.20 shows a simple application association representing a data feed between applications A and B.

The problem with this approach is that the association arrow cannot be associated with any data structures or more detailed components, so its use for configuration management is limited.

Figure 5.21 shows an "interface system" interpolated between Application A and Application B. This additional component provides more flexibility in describing system integrations. Data structures and lower-level components can be associated with it to any level of detail, enabling the complete support of integration configuration management. The naming convention is based on the source application ID, the data topic being exchanged, and the target application ID.

The pattern can be extended to publish–subscribe architectures through the use of a logical "topic system." This increases the complexity. Content can even be routed between applications based on its content, resulting in a highly dynamic system and interesting implications for configuration management and dependency analysis.[230] This starts to approach the concept of an enterprise service bus.

Figure 5.20 Simple application association.

Figure 5.21 Interface system.

Ideally, this pattern is supported by tools that can suppress the viewing of interface systems, which add graphical complexity. (The view shown in Figure 5.20 should still be available.)

This pattern relies on application portfolio management and application ID.

It would be possible to create an analogous pattern for the concept of Datastore, in which the interface system would be ETL jobs dependent on an ETL platform.

Pattern: CMDB as the System of Record for the Run Book

[The] production acceptance…process is also an operations runbook, service-level agreement, and a working document defining everyone's roles and responsibilities for each new client/server application…. [It] will provide development and operations with the adhesive needed to bring the development and support parties together through structured communication.

—Harris Kern[231]

The intent of this pattern is to maximize the use of the CMDB by turning it into a structured system of record for the concept of an operational "runbook."

> For a centralized repository or CMDB to gain acceptance, it must replace legacy alternatives of all kinds.

The motivation for this pattern is the potential lack of acceptance of a centralized datastore for IT data. For a centralized repository or CMDB to gain acceptance, it must replace legacy alternatives of all kinds. The operational runbook is a long-accepted practice of system turnover, and basing it upon the CMDB will increase the CMDB's legitimacy.

This pattern focuses on the notorious "over the wall" part of the IT value chain, where a developed system transitions to a production, steady-state service.

> The operational runbook is a long-accepted practice of system turnover, and basing it upon the CMDB will increase the CMDB's legitimacy.

The information model supporting this pattern is essentially an application-centric subset of the overall IT logical model. The information required for a classic turnover runbook[232] includes the following:

▶ Business description of application
▶ Technical description of application
▶ Servers
▶ Databases
▶ Data feeds (batch and event-driven)
▶ Data description
▶ SLAs
▶ Stakeholders (business and technical)

▶ Participants

▶ Collaborations

Another key element of the runbook concept is interaction scripts used by support personnel, both for at-console troubleshooting and for defining user support interactions. These scripts are typically unstructured narrative but could conceivably be captured in more structured formats (e.g., workflow representations); however, the return on investment of doing so would need to be carefully considered (might be overkill).

The positive consequences of this approach are eliminating one more non-value-adding documentation activity, capturing data instead only once.

Potential negative consequences of this are that the CMDB becomes a highly critical piece of infrastructure, requiring a high-availability architecture.

Starting with existing templates for application turnover is a recommended approach; those templates should be viewed as requirements statements to the CMDB team, whose objective is to re-create them as structured reports. The production "runbook" simply becomes the current version of the report for that application or service.

5.4 Supporting IT Process Patterns

Pattern: Integrate Application Portfolio and Configuration Management

The planning practice uses the assessments of quality and service, and the bottom-line impact of the lights-on applications portfolio, to develop the IT strategic plan.

—Benson, Bugnitz, and Walton[233]

Much of the information required for application portfolio management derives directly from configuration management.

Configuration Management and Portfolio Management

"What gets measured, gets managed." Without an accurate inventory count, retailers do not know their net worth—and there is simply no substitute for walking the aisles and counting. The analogous requirement for enterprise IT is the alignment of configuration management and portfolio management.

Configuration management has several levels of granularity and several overlapping objectives. One characteristic of mature configuration management is leveraging the application concept as an organizing structure. Applications are assigned application IDs, which serve as the default naming standard for a large percentage of all CIs in a given IT operation. This is often done by an operational team without reference to higher-level considerations of enterprise architecture or portfolio management. However, much of the information required for application portfolio management derives directly from configuration management, such as the answers to the following:

▶ How complex is this application?

▶ How many interfaces does it have?

▶ How many servers does it depend on?

▶ What depends on it?

▶ How many batch jobs does it have? How long do they run every night?

▶ What databases does it depend on? Do they have high-criticality data in them?

▶ How many incidents, on average, does it have a month? What are their first-call resolutions? What is the overall trend?

▶ What is the capacity trend in terms of CPU, memory, and disk for a system? For a family of systems? For the entire application portfolio?

▶ What vendor products were used to build a given system? What systems depend on vendor product X?

These numbers are primarily aggregations of information that at a granular level should be in the CMDB and related systems. They are needed in portfolio and architecture discussions as essential information for higher-order questions such as the following:

▶ What is the overall technical profile of System A? Is it well-managed, technically sound, and at a reasonable TCO? (Portfolio management would also want a business profile, but that isn't something configuration management can help with.)

▶ If we propose a replacement for System B, what are the downstream effects and a first-order approximation of their costs?

▶ If vendor product X is going off support, do we understand the effect of that? If we wish to switch our Java application server vendor, how feasible is this?

▶ Is there an opportunity to move System C to virtualized or grid architecture? Where in our portfolio of 100 applications is the best opportunity to do this?

▶ What servers are due for lease refresh, and what are the effected applications?

▶ What application teams are directly responsible for handling customer data, and do they have sufficient training?

Implementing this pattern assumes that the CMDB and the IT portfolio management system are aligned to the same common set of reference data (see the discussion of federated CMDB in the Chapter 4).

Pattern: Application Portfolio

The intent of the application portfolio is to provide an alternate control point in the IT organization, essentially a counterweight to the concept of Project. The intent of this pattern is to provide transparency to this often-ill-defined concept and provide the framework necessary to drive the systematic leveraging, improvement, or elimination of applications from an IT environment, based on objective criteria.

Projects are relatively short lived, with defined life cycles and end points. Applications are long lived and have life cycles of an arbitrary length, sometimes measuring in decades. When coupled with the concept of "base funding" or "base staff," the application and its team become a driver of IT cost, often outside of the purview of project management (depending on how an IT organization defines "project").

This long-lived concept of "application" is a major expense driver. It is therefore surprising how little attention is paid to application end of life. How are suitable candidates for retirement identified?

Lack of alignment between financial and IT views on the IT resource are a significant obstacle to IT transparency. The application portfolio (or its cousin the service portfolio) is the basis for aligning these two perspectives. (The term "service portfolio" may become the preferred nomenclature.)

Application portfolio management is applicable to any IT organization large enough that the complete set of applications can no longer be understood by one or a few people.

In terms of the conceptual data model, an Application is an important subtype of CI. Much information is best tied to the application level; this is simply an application of basic normalization principles. For example, rather than identifying for each of 25 servers that they are critical to Sarbanes-Oxley compliance, the identification can be applied to the application that *uses* those servers and then the list of 25 can be derived through simple reporting techniques.

With infrastructure in particular, there is a blurry boundary between Application and Service; note that in this book Application is a subtype of Service. Infrastructure applications and services therefore merit their own portfolio entries and corresponding IDs.

At a process level, the Application portfolio should be pervasive throughout all IT activities; it is difficult to think of any IT process area indifferent to the concept (although there is an ongoing debate about the respective roles of Application and Service in the ITSM community).

This long-lived concept of "application" is a major expense driver.

At a data entity level, the participants in application portfolio management are Application, Datastore, Technology Product, Deployed Software System, Server, Project, various Parties with Roles, Service, and Process.

Most (nondesktop) technical elements in the environment should be traceable to an "application" as a Service subtype.

Most (nondesktop) technical elements in the environment should be traceable to an "application" as a Service subtype, even if it is an internal infrastructure application (e.g., the Domain Name System servers core to network services). In this way, the application portfolio serves as an IT chart of accounts (and in some implementations may actually be mapped into the chart of accounts in support of activity-based costing—a recommended practice, especially if there is a good understanding of the end-to-end transactions supported by the major systems). Whether or not true chargeback is desired, this management concept provides much greater transparency and flexibility.

The Application entity itself may require a variety of attributes depending on the types of portfolio comparisons desired. Here are some of the attributes that might be useful:

► Narrative business description
► Narrative technical description
► Number of authorized users
► Maximum concurrent users
► Computer programming language(s)
► Built, bought, or both?

Many other attributes might be associated with the application that are in reality attributes of related entities; one aspect of maturing the IT enablement capability is refining the normalization of such attributes. For example, an application might have an attribute of "SOX," meaning that the application supports critical financial reporting. However, this would more correctly be associated with the *process* of financial reporting, which would in turn be supported by the application. See the "Capture Data at Appropriate Level" pattern.

At a system level, the system of record for the master application list must be clearly identified. Unlike better-defined processes such as incident and change, there is no clear system type focused on managing the concept of application; instead, at this writing there are several possibilities:

► CMDB
► Portfolio management system (if it includes applications)
► Metadata repository
► Enterprise architecture system

The pros and cons of each are noted in Table 5.4.

Regardless of the chosen platform, some basis in change, configuration, or release management processes is essential to keep the data up-to-date; such data sets are too often managed as point-in-time snapshots, which limits enterprise confidence in them and decisions based on them.

Processes are called for in ensuring that the "application" concept is systematically captured and tracked; this is an imprecise consensus concept, and determining exactly when an application comes into being may not be obvious. In the absence of a defined, objective event, it is necessary to define a process that relies on a checkpoint being taken between qualified staff (e.g., a line manager and a staff architect) as to whether the project in question is creating something that should be tracked as an application. This will be obvious 95% of the time and quite difficult the other 5%.

Table 5.4 Possible Systems of Record for the Concept of "Application"

Possible System of Record	Pro	Con
Configuration management database	ITIL compliant. In theory, tied to Incident and Change processes. Applications are logical CIs.	May not be well aligned or used by some process stakeholders (developers and architects). May be focused more on desktop management, not data center or production application management.
Portfolio management system	May explicitly have a purpose of "application portfolio management," making it in theory a sound system of record.	Less common system type. Some weak "portfolio management" systems only manage projects (incremental spending, not base).
Metadata repository	Commercial products usually have the concept of "system" or "application." Historically is a well-established system for this purpose.	May be seen as strictly for data management by stakeholders and supporting team. Not typically well integrated with processes—metadata repositories are often maintained just by passive scanning.
Enterprise architecture system	Richest environment for describing application dependencies and interactions.	Modeling tools are not typically systems of record for production data. (Boundaries are blurring in this regard.) Stakeholders may be reluctant to put change control in place. Tools almost certainly will require some complex integration to share the master application list.

An additional challenge here is the identification of rogue or shadow IT systems, owned directly by business staff. These are often treated as process violations; a more constructive alternative would be to treat them as automatic demand requests.

The consequences of this pattern are formalization of a critical management concept, one that is typically pervasively used throughout the modern IT organization without crisp definition.

The baseline application data set needs to be compiled; a variety of data sources may be involved, and a sophisticated business analyst is recommended to rationalize them. Because "application" is a consensus concept, a heuristic-based approach is required. For example, a majority of "yes" answers to a set of questions like the following might be one criteria:

▶ Was the application the primary output of one project?
▶ Have there been subsequent projects to modify this application?
▶ Is there an identifiable support team?
▶ Is there an identifiable customer or business sponsor?
▶ Is the application generally recognizable as such to senior IT and business leadership?
▶ Do an enterprise architect and the application's line manager agree that it is an application and should be managed as such?

See the antipattern section later in this chapter for a discussion of application list reconciliation.

Many large organizations are defining or have defined their application portfolios; a number of vendor products exist to support the concept. Some portfolios are based on lists of production acceptance application IDs that have successfully been transitioned from mainframe to distributed systems.

Forrester Research sees application portfolio management as *requiring* source code analysis. This perspective is not reflected in this book; an application portfolio can be managed without measuring the complexity or characteristics of its source code (e.g., in the case of packaged software), although this may be desirable in many cases.

Service-Oriented Architecture and the Application Portfolio

The emergence of SOA presents interesting questions for traditional application management. If IT functionality is increasingly to be implemented by choreographies of encapsulated services, how can these be managed? The key here is to realize that the application concept, again, is subjective. It is simply a management framework of a certain granularity imposed upon a complex reality to make sense of it. Whether the underlying technical reality is COBOL with CICS, C++ with

CORBA, or BPM choreographies of Web services is not really relevant—there is a certain level of granularity, continuity, and sunk cost that will remain a sweet spot for management attention, and the need for financial accountability will continue to play a big part in driving this.

The Business Intelligence Application Portfolio

Business intelligence (BI) and data warehousing activities can be particularly difficult to rationalize with the concept of application portfolio, but doing so is possible. It's important to distinguish between the infrastructure services of the BI capability (core data warehouse DBMS, ETL, and reporting tools) and the various solutions developed on those tools (suites of reports, metrics hierarchies, etc.). Shared services with unclear cost allocations will probably appear, as well as more clearly business-owned functionality. For example, the core system may require a large and expensive set of ETL jobs to move the data from the online systems into the data warehouse and aggregate it, data which is then used by four or five distinct business areas for their own purposes.

The metadata repository may be the primary system describing this portfolio.

Pattern: The Application ID and Application Alias

Because different teams may have inconsistent yet entrenched terminology for a given application, the portfolio management capability must support legacy terminology.

Application aliasing is a required capability when consolidating and rationalizing multiple lists of applications. Because different teams may have inconsistent yet entrenched terminology for a given logical application, it is critical to the portfolio management capability to support legacy terminology. If this is not done, individuals will search a corporate repository, CMDB, or portfolio tool by a given application name, not find it (because the "official" name is something else), and conclude that the portfolio management capability is incomplete or inaccurate.

For example, if an application was always called "Beta" by a particular group but the larger organization knows it as "Baker," the former group should be able to search for "Beta" and find a link to the official application name, "Baker."

The application alias is applicable in application portfolio management and service support processes that involve user interaction.

The Application ID is a specific case of the general application alias capability. Great value derives from the application portfolio when it is aligned with the concept of the system code or application ID. The application ID is a terse, memorable identifier used as a basis for configuration management, and it provides traceability from low-level, objective technical resources to the higher-level abstraction of the application portfolio and its associated finances.

There is a longstanding history of application IDs being the basis of configuration management in the production data center; some service support organizations will accept no executable code or data files unless the first string of characters in the file name is a valid application ID. This does not work with vendor packages; it is also problematic with respect to data, as some data should be shared across applications and may not necessarily have a designated owning application.

Note that application IDs are a point of *tight coupling*.

Note that application IDs are a point of *tight coupling*. Changing them can be extremely painful. Some might argue that they should not be embedded into architecture but rather managed logically. This, however, requires mature processes to ensure that the logical–physical map is accurate; the risk is the appearance of "mystery components" in the operational environment. ("What does this do?" "Don't know—let's turn it off and see who screams.")

The application ID is essentially a configuration management concept. As noted in ITIL, "Naming conventions should be established and applied to the identification of CIs.... Identifiers should be relatively short, but meaningful, and should reuse any existing conventions wherever possible."[234] The ITIL *Application Management* volume calls for the "application ID" as one of the primary attributes of the application concept.[235]

What if the CI is not understood at the time of the reported Incident?

ITSM calls for the association of incidents, problems, and changes with their respective CIs. What if the CI is not understood at the time of the reported Incident? For example, consider an environment that highly leverages portals and other Web frameworks to present application functionality. It may be unclear to both the user and the help desk analyst taking the call exactly what application or service is having an issue, and this is only going to become more difficult with the emergence of SOA and portlet technologies.

Many mainframe systems had a straightforward approach for this: the screen and application ID would appear as a small code in the corner of the screen. There was therefore never any doubt as to what CI the user was experiencing difficulty with. The system code (a 2–5 character identifier) was key to this; it might be applied to 50 screens, 40 batch jobs, 15 CICS transactions, 20 VSAM files, and 25 JCLs, all grouped under the same overarching "application" concept, which is as much a management concept as a technical one. Incidents, problems, and changes could all be reported by this grouping, which enabled greater understanding of the IT organization's services rendered. Today, the application concept is more diffuse and often unmanaged.

The application ID should therefore be applied to all CIs unambiguously owned by one and only one application.

Two Uses of Application ID

One large corporation used the concept of application ID, starting with its mainframe systems. All program files, CICS transactions, JCL, batch jobs, and data files required an application ID, mapped ultimately into the accounting system. When distributed systems and applications started to be deployed, the infrastructure team simply applied the same principle—all new "applications" required an ID. All components (in-house built) and at least the main application directories (in-house built or package) required the system code as a basis for naming. A master list of all applications was maintained, and through this cross-referencing it was possible for the support teams to quickly identify the application and its owner for any given file in the environment.

Another corporation had had the same approach on the mainframe. However, the batch scheduler team was responsible for assigning the codes and decided that it would not extend the principle to distributed systems except for those requiring batch scheduling services. This led to a lack of necessary information on application deployments to servers; because there was no enterprise naming standard, it was not possible to determine which applications were using which servers.

Application IDs can be an enabler for discovery tools, which are becoming popular in supporting configuration management. The trouble with these tools (as mentioned elsewhere in this book) is that they are limited to discovering physical technical evidence, which does not always map easily to the logical concepts upon which IT management is based.

If raw discovered data contains an application ID, the mapping from physical to logical is automatically enabled.

Raw discovered data can be installed software packages, processes currently running on the machine, and physical files in directory structures, as well as a host of other artifacts. If the raw discovered data contains an application ID, the mapping from physical to logical is automatically enabled.

Application Alias

The data structures necessary to support application alias are generally the same structures needed to support Application ID (see Figure 5.22). The application ID, as a subset of application alias, requires further refinement of its business rules. Primarily, a given application must have only one current ID, although it may have any number of legacy and withdrawn IDs.

Figure 5.22 shows a data structure representing the relationships between applications and aliases, with application id a specialization of alias.

The structure for application alias is straightforward but has some requirements that may not be obvious at first.

An application many have many aliases; less commonly, one alias may refer to several true applications. (An example of the latter is the generic use of a vendor name to refer to distinct applications within that vendor's product line; ERP suites often have this issue—people just call it "Oracle" but don't distinguish between Oracle Financials and Oracle HRMS.)

In addition, an application should have only one active application ID. (If it has more than one, it is an application group of some sort.) Over time, IDs may be misassigned or several applications may be merged into one. Another scenario is when two sets of IDs must be consolidated, perhaps because of a merger or acquisition. These matters must be handled with some delicacy because these IDs are baked into object names and can't easily be changed. (Renaming production software simply because a naming standard has changed is usually not a good idea.)

The means of handling such matters is to explicitly allow for the concept of deprecation.

IDs are baked into object names and can't easily be changed.

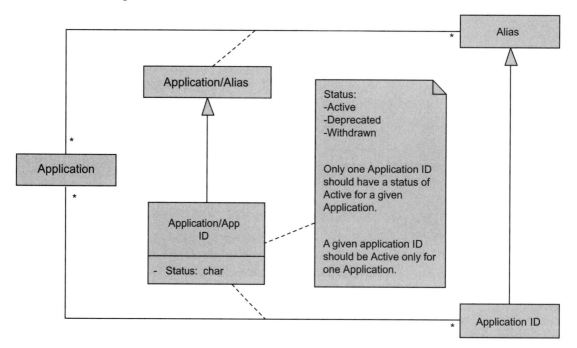

Figure 5.22 Application alias and ID.

Deprecation

In computer software standards and documentation, deprecation is the gradual phasing-out of a software or programming language feature.[236]

A given application ID has a status *with respect to an application.* "Active" means that it is the preferred application ID for all current uses for that application; all CIs should use it. "Deprecated" means that there are probably still CIs in production using that identifier but no further new CIs should be named using it. "Withdrawn" means that, as far as is known, there are no CIs in production using that code (the deprecation phase has ended). The withdrawn status provides a permanent audit trail, so it is known that at one time this application did use this application ID; this will prove useful when dealing with old documentation or orphan CIs.

An antipattern is the proliferation of application lists as data silos, which is often the starting point for implementing true application portfolio management. Lists may originate from the following, among other areas:

▶ Production control
▶ Enterprise architecture
▶ External consultant efforts
▶ Security
▶ Application support and maintenance
▶ Integration management
▶ Business continuity or disaster recovery

When these lists are not unified, the usual data quality problems emerge:

▶ The application is on one list but not on another
▶ The application has different names on each list and can't be reconciled without manual inspection (and sometimes not even then)
▶ What is represented as one application on one list is multiple applications on another list (granularity)

Reconciling multiple application lists into one is a nontrivial exercise.

Reconciling multiple application lists into one is a nontrivial exercise and requires determined data analysis and a reconciliation tool. Maintaining an audit trail of all eliminations, consolidations, and reconciliations is key; stakeholders will lose confidence in a reconciliation process that has "lost" its application (e.g., by consolidating it with a better-known representation).

Figure 5.23 shows an information model supporting application reconciliation. It is far easier to just "bless" one list as the master and avoid the reconciliation problem. The risk there is missing applications and losing credibility.

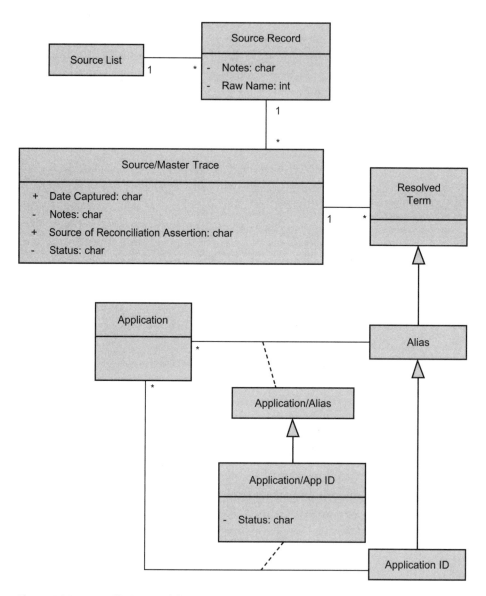

Figure 5.23 Reconciliation model.

Pattern: Taxonomy-Based Rationalization

"Rationalization" is a frequently encountered cost-cutting strategy. For example, Iain Aitken in *Value-Driven IT Management* calls for rationalizing suppliers, servers, software products, platforms, data centers, office space, services, product and service tariffs, and activities.[237]

What does it mean to "rationalize" in this sense? There are two steps:

1. Take an inventory of the items to be rationalized.
2. Categorize them to identify redundancy.

The data architecture necessary to take an inventory has been discussed in Chapter 3, but that is only part of the problem. The idea of taxonomy-based rationalization is the creation of some categorization schema to which real instances can be assigned and redundancy then identified. In this book's model, it would be implemented with the Taxonomy entity.

The subject of the rationalization is any large-grained CI, for example, process, service offering, application, datastore, or technology.

For each rationalization subject, a categorization hierarchy is defined. This hierarchy is an abstraction of the concrete instances. For example, sample categorizations for Application might include the following:

▶ Supply chain management system
▶ CRM system
▶ Internet-based order capture system
▶ Order fulfillment system
▶ Human resource management system
▶ Payroll system

Existing Applications would then be mapped into this hierarchy. Important point: an existing application might fit under two different categories. For example, a system might be both a human resource management system, concerned with recruitment and performance management, and the payroll system controlling pay disbursement.

When the application portfolio is enumerated and then classified in this way, the planning capability can run reports identifying categories with multiple systems. This is valuable planning and portfolio management data, which can directly contribute to simplification initiatives.[238]

A data subject area taxonomy may also be developed. Such a taxonomy might look somewhat similar to the system taxonomy, but it should be maintained separately:

- ▶ Supply chain data
- ▶ Customer data
- ▶ Sales data
- ▶ Order fulfillment data
- ▶ Employee data
- ▶ Corporate financial data

Data subject areas can in turn be linked to producing and consuming systems; a matrix analysis similar to that seen in Table 5.2 is often used. Determining which is the approved system of record for a given data topic is a common exercise in enterprise architecture analysis.

Taxonomies by definition are lightweight reference constructs and simple conceptual hierarchies. A more complex approach is to rationalize the as-is portfolio against a full reference model, showing system interactions and data subjects. This can become methodologically complex, but it is a rich approach if well managed.

Proposed Pattern: Application Points Costing

System Points

As traditionally defined capacity becomes "too cheap to meter," what are the emerging drivers of the IT spending?

As traditionally defined capacity becomes "too cheap to meter," complexity is the emerging driver of IT spending.

A mature configuration management environment would enable the creation of a "system points" measurement framework. Unlike function points, which are notoriously difficult to establish, system points would be based on simple, objective data in the CMDB, with weighted rankings applied. They would probably be most effective applied to the concept of service or application, and an example implementation might be:

Application	20 points
System of record	10 points
Database	10 points
Table in database	0.5 points
Column in database	0.1 points
Discrete executable	5 points
Interface from another application	3 points

Incoming entity	3 points
Incoming data attribute	1 point
Runtime dependency on other applications	3 points
Sensitive data	10 points
SOX significant	10 points
Technology product dependency	2 points
Physical server dependency	5 points
Virtual server dependency	3 points
Message queue	1 point
Batch job	1 point
Disk consumption	5 points per gigabyte

The weightings could be adjusted. The points would be used as a basis for chargebacks and performance incentives; the overall objective would be to minimize them. The incentives reflect such principles as the following:

▶ The basic fact of having something called an "application" is a significant statement in a large-scale computing environment. There is a base cost of entry into the data center, regardless of capacity consumption.

▶ Complexity drives cost, as well as capacity, and needs to be measured. With the increasing power of IT infrastructure (cf. Moore's law), complexity may become the largest driver of IT spending.

Such a model would need to be carefully adjusted and might provide incentives for nonconstructive behavior; this concept is presented simply as food for thought. (For example, if you are creating incentives against complexity, such as interfaces, would that result in a drive to overly monolithic applications and multiple systems of record for data?)

This can be seen as an architectural approach to unit cost modeling, with incentives for architectural soundness. A related ITIL concept is resource unit cost.

An accurate CMDB can provide complexity metrics that (especially in light of Moore's law and analogous progress in disk and solid-state storage) may become the key drivers of measurable IT cost.

There are many cautions against overly detailed chargeback throughout the IT management literature, and there is no recommendation here as to if and how much any of this would be presented back to the customer. But an accurate CMDB can provide complexity metrics that (especially in light of Moore's law and analogous progress in disk and solid-state storage) may become *the* key drivers of measurable IT cost.

Again, the point values presented are purely arbitrary. Furthermore this is a primitive model conceptually because it is essentially linear. Nonlinearity is what makes complex systems interesting and troublesome (e.g., if a given row's point allocations dynamically changed as a function of other rows' point assignments).

Attention Researchers

To my friends in the academic community, especially those of you with connections in the military and governmental domains: Further research is recommended here—if we had some years' worth of data from multiple similarly structured CMDBs tied to actual costing, we probably could start to derive some rich models. CMDB data from corporations and the corresponding detailed financials will probably be difficult to obtain. But large military and governmental units are starting to address the same problem, and if you can find several organizations using the same CMDB product and obtain access to their financial and IT service data, there might be some fascinating research possibilities.

Pattern: The IT Enablement Capability

It is surprising how many IT functional organizations believe they can manage the substantial architectural and software engineering challenges associated with IT enablement tooling.

It is surprising how many IT functional organizations believe they can manage the substantial architectural and software engineering challenges associated with IT enablement tooling. Just as with (occasionally) ill-advised business organizations that choose to build and run their own services, this approach too often results in low-maturity heroics, with the functional organization compromised if key staff members leave. Another consequence is badly disparate data, as functional IT organizations owning their own tools often have little motivation to integrate them (and may lack technical capability in this particularly tricky engineering challenge).

This pattern represents a unified, data- and technology-driven single engineering team for IT enablement, segregated from all internal IT process owners. Engineering in this case is defined, for example, as follows:

▶ Definition of architectural principles and models of the functions and processes requiring automation
▶ Requirements elicitation and analysis
▶ Solutions architecture design
▶ Vendor and product selection and management
▶ Software engineering
▶ Operational application (i.e., service) design, building, installation, configuration, testing, data conversion, and production deployment
▶ Integration of disparate systems in which common data subjects require it
▶ Production operations, monitoring, availability, and capacity planning
▶ Incremental evolution of the application service

The IT process owners become the customers, little or no different from customers on the business side.

The IT process owners become the customers, little or no different from customers on the business side. The principle is that IT must take its own medicine in how it builds and runs its internal systems, applying sound service management principles with segregation of duties.

The proper way to manage this nontrivial class of tools is to allocate them to a deep engineering capability, leaving functional organizations to focus on the processes they manage. (There are limits to this principle, which are described later in this chapter.)

This pattern has two primary motivations: building a center of excellence attuned to optimizing the IT value chain through superior technical architecture and avoiding conflict of interest through segregation of duties. IT process owners should not have operational control over their technical infrastructure any more than business process owners should.

An excellent technical architecture for IT enablement has the following characteristics:

▶ Low TCO
▶ Minimal process and data redundancy
▶ Defined systems of record for all data subjects
▶ Clear road map for system evolution, including acquisitions, integrations, and retirements

DIALOG

Internal Conflicts of Interest?

Pat: What do you mean by internal conflict of interest? I've not heard that discussed regarding IT often.

Kelly: It's the same principle applied in the financial world, for example, a person who sets up a vendor in the accounts payable system should not also be able to authorize payments to that same vendor—if they could, it would be possible for them to send money to anyone.

In IT, we apply that principle to say that developers should not have access to production systems. Beyond wanting to ensure that software is fully tested before it is deployed and that changes are planned and have stakeholder visibility, developers have unique skills enabling them to manipulate production systems and data, and we want a layer of control preventing them from temptation. Even worse is when the developer works for the process owner and has access to the production system.

Pat: What's wrong with that?

Kelly: In such cases we essentially can have no confidence that the system has integrity. The process or business owner may have performance incentives

(continued)

Pat: But what does this have to do with internal IT systems?

Kelly: A couple of different aspects. First, there is the simple temptation of bureaucracy avoidance. If the internal IT team owns a change or incident management system, its members may feel that they have a privileged right to change it without adhering to the same policies to which business-facing systems must adhere.

Pat: …in which case the change management team might change its system without a change request?

Kelly: Precisely. Who watches the watcher? Perhaps a more serious issue is in the area of SLA reporting. Real money often rides on SLAs, and if I were a customer of an IT service provider, I should be concerned about the integrity of the SLA data on which the contract is measured. Ideally, the team responsible for reporting SLAs should have no incentives based on those SLAs. That's a clear conflict of interest. If that's not possible, then at least the technical access to the SLA measurement system should be segregated from any service management functional group and its leadership. One way to do this would be to have the service-level management group reporting into an office of the CIO and the corresponding technical team reporting through the corporate systems application support area.[239]

This pattern is applicable primarily to the following IT enablement systems:

► Service management system
► Portfolio management system
► Demand management system
► IT data warehouse
► IT portal or dashboard
► Project management system
► Requirements management system
► Software modeling system
► Nonproduction environments (development, quality assurance, testing, etc.)
► Source code control system
► Release and deployment system
► Configuration management system
► Change management system
► Incident or problem management system

Notice that all of these systems may have reasonably broad user bases across functional areas. This is a key criterion for any system to be managed by the IT enablement capability. Some criteria may be more controversial than others; distributed development teams, for example, have long owned their own preproduction environments, but there is clearly an industry trend toward centralized management in response to capacity underutilization and security issues among other drivers.

This pattern is not recommended for deeper element management tooling. For example, database administrators use specialized console tools to manage an organization's DBMSs. These tools are typically installed and supported by the database administrators themselves (perhaps a junior member of the team) in much the same way that a carpenter spends significant time setting up shop and keeping tools in order. Other examples of such tools include network management frameworks, middleware management, provisioning, and capacity modeling tools. The distinguishing feature of all such tools is that they require significant domain expertise and are not directly used by a large, cross-functional user base.

Notice that these element management tools do not typically manage the dependencies of their element domain on other areas. That is the role of the CMDB, which should be owned by the IT enablement capability.

This is a tricky boundary to manage.

> Element management tools require significant domain expertise and typically do not serve a large, cross-functional user base.

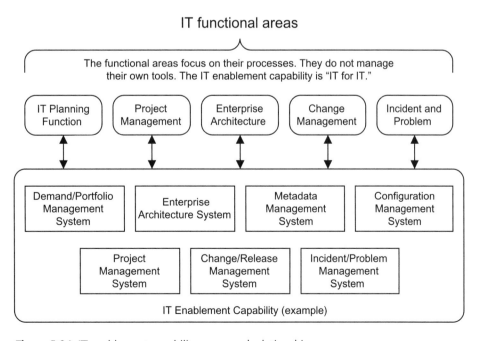

Figure 5.24 IT enablement capability scope and relationships.

The participants are the IT functional areas and the new "IT enablement capability." The group may be positioned as a subcapability under an overall "corporate systems" group, which also may have responsibility for human resources, financial, legal, compliance, and related systems. Because IT enablement systems need to interact with other back-end corporate systems (e.g., HRMS and financials systems), this positioning is optimal.

The collaborations between the IT functional areas and the IT enablement capability mirror the overall collaboration between the IT customer and the IT service organization.

The consequences of this model will optimally be greater coordination and alignment of internal IT enablement systems and exploitation of opportunities to rationalize and integrate them.

The negative consequences may be perceived or actual loss of agility for IT functional areas, as changes to systems may become more difficult in an integrated environment and with an IT enablement capability committed to "taking IT's own medicine" and working through the standard project and change management processes.

This needs to be an engineering capability.

This needs to be an engineering capability, committed to a center of excellence in the particular architectural, development, and operational challenges posed

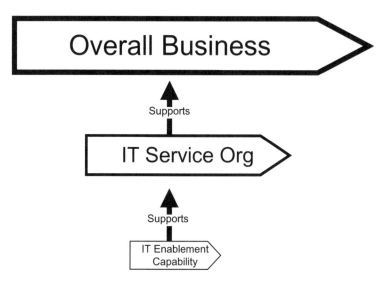

Figure 5.25 IT enablement is to IT as IT is to business.

by cross-functional IT enablement tooling. Adherence to standard software engineering and project management techniques will be essential, and generally this team should not be seen as a career path for staff members without formal training in some kind of engineering.

Service support still provides career opportunities in which staff members may work their way up from the help desk or operations center. This is a good thing; however, problems may arise when staff members with primarily operations or IT process management backgrounds work on systems implementation or integration efforts for which they do not have the requisite technical or project expertise. Staff members for this team instead should be drawn from applications development and systems architecture capabilities.

Process owners who also have their own enablement tools are subject to temptations and conflicts of interest. The classic example is the story of the change management team that brought down its own system by executing an unapproved change. (It happened!)

This can be a difficult pattern to explain to IT functional areas and process owners; there tends to be a blind spot preventing understanding. The core principle is that "you no longer own your own system," which may generate resistance.

5.5 Chapter Conclusion

This section on patterns has only scratched the surface by focusing on breaking down the functional boundaries between IT planning, solution development, and service management and enabling the accuracy of the core information store at the heart of well-managed IT. The concepts of demand and portfolio management cross these boundaries and are highly advisable places to start. The CMDB concept also is a tricky area, and I hope that the patterns described here will assist the many organizations pondering how to keep such a comprehensive datastore current.

Many more patterns will hopefully surface as IT management begins to truly mature. Even more optimistically, they will start to find their way into vendor products. Everything described in this chapter is achievable, although it may discomfit some vendors who have become overly comfortable in their chosen functional silo.

5.6 Further Reading

For the core patterns literature, see Gamma (1995) and Buschmann (1996). Fowler (2003) offers an application of pattern principles to enterprise architecture, which is highly relevant for this work. The pattern approach in this book also draws on Fowler (1997) as a model for using patterns in business analysis. For antipatterns literature, see Brown (1998); Brown, McCormick et al. (1999 and 2000); Dudney (2003); and Laplante and Neill (2005). There are also Web resources too numerous to count.

PART III

CONCLUSION

THESE FINAL SECTIONS COVER A variety of current trends that may affect the concepts discussed here. You are also encouraged to not skip the appendices, which cover both the architectural foundations of the approach used here and a discussion of the impending professionalization of enterprise IT—which I predict will prove to be a critical success factor for the vision of integrated IT governance.

6

Epilogue

THE IT WORLD IS AN INTRICATE, multidimensional landscape. Consider this image from cyberpunk pioneer and *Neuromancer* author William Gibson, describing a virtual reality representation of a complex enterprise systems landscape, in his classic short story *Burning Chrome*:

Ice walls flick away like supersonic butterflies made of shade. Beyond them, the matrix's illusion of infinite space.... Trying to remind myself that this place and the gulfs beyond are only representations, that we aren't "in" Chrome's computer, but interfaced with it, while the matrix simulator in Bobby's loft generates this illusion.... The core data begin to emerge, exposed, vulnerable.... This is the far side of ice, the view of the matrix... that fifteen million legitimate console operators see daily and take for granted. The core data tower around us like vertical freight trains, color-coded for access. Bright primaries, impossibly bright in that transparent void, linked by countless horizontals in nursery blues and pinks.[240]

"Bright primaries ... linked by countless horizontals"—that is, databases linked by feeds. Although the preceding scene has lurid connotations—the protagonists in this scene are hackers trying to rob or "burn" an organized crime boss virtually—the visual interface described might be a reasonable goal for systems administration in 2015. More intuitive, visual formats are needed that leverage a broader entire spectrum of human cognition in understanding complex interrelationships. "Metadata meets first person shooter" may be an exciting direction for innovation in systems administration.

6.1 Human Constraints of IT Enablement

Too Complex?

Pat: I hate to say this, but you're a dreamer. You've laid out an architecture and an approach that simply can't be achieved. The complexity implied in any one of your patterns or architectural areas could require millions in investment. There's a lot of focus on data, but the data is enormously complex and keeping complex data up-to-date through the collaborative efforts of hundreds or thousands of people is a challenge that I think will ultimately doom this effort.

Kelly: Well…the important thing to remember is that this book is a reference architecture. It needs to be implemented iteratively and incrementally, based on defined use cases. I'm just trying to provide a framework so that the use-case-based efforts don't result in needless redundancy.

One issue of concern is that fully automating and enabling IT management is less a technical than a human issue. The ability of humans to comprehend complex dependencies is limited, and one of the fundamental implications of this work is the need for managing dependencies at scale.

This means making the capture and maintenance of dependencies a scalable and repeatable process, which is easier at lower levels in the technological stack than at upper levels, where it is still quite subjective.

For example, suppose that a CMDB documents that dependencies exist between two systems. Later, the representation of those systems is refined into subsystems, and it is determined that the dependencies are between two subsystems. Does the higher-level dependency remain documented? Can it be derived?

IT is often criticized for a "lack of transparency." However, would real transparency be comprehensible? When one considers the myriad of dependencies and silo-breaking dotted-line relationships in the modern IT environment, one wonders if full transparency would simply be disempowering. Certainly key abstractions, rollups, and metric hierarchies are needed to make the transparency transparent.

The very nature of "ownership" is problematic in IT. Applications, as units of discrete functionality usually implemented by funded projects, have provided the clearest "ownership" hook in the modern IT organization. Processes and data have been far more troublesome, as they cross organizational boundaries and need to be managed from an enterprise perspective. Any number of strategies for managing matrixed relationships have been proposed over the years, but the bottom line always comes down to a need to effectively share power, which human beings are not particularly good at—especially in dynamic environments requiring prompt decision making, not endless deliberation.

6.2 The Next-Generation IT: MDA, SOA, BPM, Portals, and Utility Computing

A recurring theme in technology evolution is "the end of programming." Fifteen years ago it was CASE tools and fourth-generation languages, and now business rules and BPM tools are being portrayed as empowering consumers and disintermediating traditional IT.

Along similar lines, Nicholas Carr (echoed to some extent by research firms) predicts the end of the centralized IT organization, pointing out that at the beginning of the 20th century, businesses had vice presidents of electricity, an infrastructure concern now subsumed into the operational fabric.[241]

The most cogent critique of this line of thinking can be inferred from Fred Brooks ("no silver bullet").[242] Assume for a moment that no central IT organization exists or that its sole concern is infrastructure. Programming logic and business process support is entirely owned by the business organization, and sophisticated process visualization tools and business rules engines front ended by portal frameworks have virtually eliminated all traditional development (a nirvana I am skeptical about, but let's continue the thought experiment).

The fundamental complexity does not go away.

The fundamental complexity does not go away. A misconfigured business rule could cost millions in an instant. A poorly conceived business process could make hundreds of customers unhappy on its first implementation.

New processes, component services and their choreographies, business rules, and portal capabilities will still require testing, and it will still be prudent to manage changes to them, assess the risk of new configurations, and provide for change rollback. The need for quality assurance and extensive testing of proposed new functionality will not go away, and in general the same problems that have dogged IT through the decades will remain, albeit with a different face.

This complex infrastructure will still be subject (perhaps even more so) to the entropy of complex systems and will require portfolio management principles that should be centrally coordinated—just as corporate departments may control their own financial resources but still be accountable to centralized financial discipline.

In general, the IT industry still seems fixated on shiny new objects and in fundamental denial about the rising legacy swamp waters of obsolescing systems threatening to overtake all innovation. The point is not BPM, SOA, portals, or autonomic computing—the point is the overall run rate of IT and how to truly drive it down. Achieving this will not be quick or easy; it will simply require much hard work and many painful decisions in the typical large, long-lived IT organization.

SOA in particular has interesting implications for the concept of IT and specifically application portfolios. Although there is much controversy about how "fine grained" SOA services should be, it seems that they may be at least somewhat more fine grained than the traditional "application" concept. (However, even this is a matter of controversy. What if the IT Service in the ITSM sense was equated with Service in the SOA sense?)

Applications often are mapped directly to cost units with clear business allocation. The vision of SOA is to share IT application functionality more efficiently, but it is not clear that the financial models and incentives are in place to do so effectively.

How do we enable configuration management, or IT chargeback, in a world of systems continually reconfiguring themselves?

On the whole, the problem seems to be that technology in its current phase of evolution continually outstrips our ability to manage it. The trends are clearly toward increasingly dynamic systems, which pose challenges to established practices across the IT value chain. On the other hand, mainframe disciplines are reemerging throughout the distributed systems world, especially in terms of application, capacity, security, and change and release management.

Capacity management in the days of centralized mainframe systems was a significant discipline, one now experiencing something of a renaissance. Mainframe capacity consumption was tracked through the use of application IDs. How do we enable configuration management, or IT chargeback, in a world of systems continually reconfiguring themselves?

It's a major concern as to whether the new dynamic provisioning infrastructures emerging from the major computing vendors are going to be coupled with effective governance models. In theory, dynamic provisioning could provide the same level of cost transparency found in mainframe environments. However, the technology will not do this on its own. The nature of application service-to-infrastructure dependency will need to be tightly specified for the provisioning architecture to be manageable.

SOA and Autonomics

How SOA and autonomic or utility computing (the 21ˢᵗ century faces of Development and Operations) interact—not just technically but also organizationally and in terms of process—may well be the critical question of the next 20 years for enterprise IT.

6.3 In Closing

As this book draws to a conclusion, the infancy of IT management is still apparent. The premise of an integrated IT value chain, supported by defined data and systems architectures, seems obvious on its face. Many devils lurk in the implementation details, however, and fundamental industry consensus is still in progress on the IT equivalent of generally accepted practices.

The most critical issues in retrospect seem to be the following:

▶ IT's continuing mistreatment as an exceptional and unique set of enterprise activities, with corresponding gaps in the application of established management controls (e.g., performance management and process improvement)

▶ The functional gaps and thick silo walls between planning, building, and running IT services, which are reflected in misaligned and redundant processes, data, and internal IT systems

▶ The resulting lack of visibility into one of the largest consumers of capital and expense funds in any organization, in turn causing business skepticism and continuing searches for silver bullet fixes

I hope that this book has done its part to advance past these issues in preparation for the next set of problems not even visible from today's vantage point. In the meantime, I wish to extend my appreciation to all readers who got this far, and I wish you well.

Of all the money e'er I had, I spent it in good company.
And all the harm I've ever done, Alas! it was to none but me.
And all I've done for want of wit, To mem'ry now I can't recall
So fill to me the parting glass—Good night and joy be with you all

—*The Parting Glass,* Irish traditional[243]

Appendix A
Architecture Methodology Used in This Book

Influences include old and new methodologies: structured analysis and design, information engineering, object orientation, pattern languages, and BPM.

IN DISCUSSING THAT QUESTION OF "how," the focus of this book is on achievable systems architectures, down to a detailed function, process, data, and systems representation. This also required careful thought as to methodology. The approach here was to mix older methodologies deriving from structured analysis and design and information engineering with newer representation techniques based on object orientation, pattern languages, and BPM. The works of Ed Yourdon, Meilir Page-Jones, James Martin, Clive Finkelstein, Martin Fowler, Geary Rummler and Alan Brache, Paul Harmon, and the "Gang of Four" (Erich Gamma, Richard Helm, Ralph Johnson, and John Vlissides) all contributed to the analysis, as did the enterprise architecture work of Stephen Spewak.[244]

For those wondering how such a gumbo of methodologies might lead to something useful, let me clarify their usage briefly.

I give credit to the early structured methods[245] for their focus on "top-down analysis," which as you read the literature, circa 1975, was a novel concept in a world where programmers were building things from the bottom up with little awareness of design.[246] They also were concerned with the interrelationship between function and data as separate concerns, with (arguably) more of a focus on the former than the latter.

Information Engineering[247] moved data into the position of primacy, with attention to issues of relational normalization (RDBMSs had started to emerge, and the relational model was becoming more established). The information engineering material is also where you will first encounter systematic matrixing of data and process as an analysis and design technique and the "clustering" of logical groupings of data and function—a most important and overlooked technique. Stephen Spewak provided a valuable offshoot in his application of information engineering principles to enterprise architecture, which also relies on matrixing.[248]

Information engineering (as the intellectual underpinning of CASE) held out the hope of automated generation of executable systems from the analysis and design phase. This hope never quite panned out (although some large and valuable mainframe systems were indeed created with CASE tools, systems remaining in production to this day in banking, insurance, and retail). Information engineering also was not aligned with the then-emerging philosophy of business process management (or reengineering). The evolution of software languages and engineering techniques produced the next generation of methodology, object orientation, which remains the dominant paradigm to date, with SOA emerging as the latest trend.

However, despite the perceived failure of CASE, the earlier analysis methodologies (in particular the information engineering work) remain highly relevant for understanding wide-scope problem domains; software engineering–focused object orientation has proved insufficient as an "analysis" methodology *at the IT portfolio level.*

Object-oriented analysis and design are appropriate within the boundary of a given system, but when you are trying to understand the logical scope of multiple large-scale systems and their interactions in supporting activities with a financial footprint in the hundreds of millions or billions of dollars, different techniques are required.[249] The object-oriented move toward encapsulating data and behavior has clear benefits in program design and construction, but in higher-level enterprise analysis it begs the question, Why are we associating this particular data with this particular process, and who else needs this particular data? If you keep the information structures (data) separate from the activity semantics (e.g., in UML), there is no idiomatic object-oriented method for managing their large-scale cross-referencing—you rarely see matrices of any sort in object-oriented "analysis."[250] Nor is object orientation particularly friendly to data flow analysis, another important tool in the enterprise architect's chest. Therefore, the "classic" methods have a prominent place in this analysis.

A significant and useful contribution from the object-oriented world is the concept of patterns.[251] Patterns provide a concise and well-accepted paradigm for describing frequently recurring problems and their solutions. Used often at a detailed level for discussion of program design and construction approaches, design patterns also can be used, as demonstrated by Martin Fowler in his excellent *Analysis Patterns,*[252] at higher levels of conceptual abstraction. Patterns are therefore used in this book to discuss common issues of interapplication coordination in the IT enablement domain and are traced to the higher-level matrixing analyses—hopefully providing an example of how both old and new software engineering methodologies can coexist and solve a modern problem of high complexity and significance.

Information Engineering techniques remain highly relevant for understanding wide-scope problem domains and system interactions.

Patterns provide a concise and well-accepted paradigm for describing frequently recurring problems and their solutions.

Finally, neither the legacy methods nor object orientation completely encompass BPM, which is both an important movement for managing enterprise business objectives and a valuable discipline for describing and modeling IT activities.

Other enterprise architecture frameworks include Zachman and The Open Group Architecture Framework. This material is hopefully at least spiritually aligned with these.

Process, Function, and Organization

To quote Karen Lopez:

▶ A process is an activity that has an identifiable start and stop. It normally repeats and can be measured.

▶ A function is a collection of activities that starts when an organization comes into being (or when an organization adopts a new function) and continues for the life of the organization (or when an organization drops a function).

▶ A bank manages humans always, but it hires an employee each time it manages a new person.[253]

Functions are specific areas of activity, often aligned with a particular organization. Their boundaries are usually well understood, and they can become "silos"; that is, they can develop an insular perspective and become divorced from the larger enterprise value chain they are serving. A consistent theme is that functional boundaries must be broken down in service of cross-functional business processes.

Processes are usually fewer in number than functions; at an enterprise level there may be on the order of five or ten. They are sequences of activities that add value for the customer (internal or external). To quote Roger Burlton, "A true *business process* starts with the first event that initiates a course of action. It isn't complete until the last aspect of the final outcome is satisfied from the point of view of the stakeholder who initiated the first event or triggered it."[254]

For example, "human resource management" might be a function with defined organization and mission. However, value is not added by this function. A primary process it is concerned with might be "fulfill staffing needs"—the end-to-end process of identifying a need, locating a suitable person, and bringing that person to a productive working status. Notice that a human resources function does not cover all aspects of that value-adding process: input from the hiring business unit, facilities, training, IT (for equipment and access), and other areas is required. The process is therefore distinct from the function.

IT services may include processes, which are repeatable. Including IT functions as services is more problematic because of ambiguity, and the model does not support (this may be controversial and feedback is welcomed).

When analysts model function and process, functions usually are nouns, often with some verb recast as a noun:

▶ IT *governance*
▶ Software *development*
▶ Operations *management*

(Note the derivations from, or *nominalizations of,* the verbs "to govern," "to develop," and "to manage.")

Processes begin with verbs:

▶ *Establish* standards
▶ *Resolve* incidents
▶ *Develop* software

In data modeling terms, the concepts relate as shown in Figure A.1.

Organization, function, and process all *decompose,* indicated by the recursive relationship or "fish-hook" connectors back to themselves—this indicates that organizations may contain organizations and likewise for functions. The decompositions and many-to-many relationships make for a tough subject area.

Another way to view this (essentially what UML does) is to consider both function and process as subtypes of a more general activity concept (Figure A.2).

There is much criticism in the industry of an overly functional view and a desire to drive to cross-functional processes. However, this is not made easier by the current lack of distinction between function and process, even at the level of language. For example, ITIL emphasizes that it is documenting process areas, not functions—and then proceeds to use a functional naming convention (incident

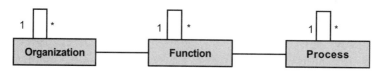

Figure A.1 Organization, function, and process metamodel.

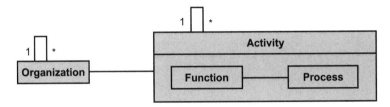

Figure A.2 UML activity concept.

management, capacity management, etc.). The relationship of ITIL process areas to true processes is well described by Alex Sharp:

Recently there has been a different sort of problem: defining cross-functional work (which is good!) that doesn't yield a business process (which is bad!). These structures are "areas" or "horizontal silos." For instance, Customer Relationship Management is a popular term (along with Supply Chain Management and Demand Chain Management), and is often referred to as a process, as in "our CRM process." It is cross-functional, the way a business process should be, but it is not countable, so it's like a function. You cannot say how many Customer Relationship Managements you did yesterday. And if you try to map, assess, and improve Customer Relationship Management, you might find it to be a very frustrating endeavor following all the paths. The underlying problem is that the CRM area includes multiple cross-functional business processes such as Secure New Customer, Resolve Customer Inquiry, and Complete Customer Communication, each of which can be studied as a separate process.[255]

Substitute Capacity or Availability Management for CRM in the preceding paragraph, and it still holds true.

Appendix B
Some Thoughts on the
Professionalization of Enterprise IT

It is surprising that the path to professional status is still so varied.

THE OBJECTIVES OF RATIONAL IT management discussed in this book will require generally higher standards of professional practice. The complex processes, data structures, and systems described here must be understood holistically and within an historical context so that their criticality is appreciated. Otherwise, the temptation to "just deliver it" and pay attention only to short-term objectives will continue to suboptimize the value chain and render ineffective the important supporting processes.

Given the compensation levels and technical requirements for those working in large-scale information technology, it is surprising that the path to professional status is still so varied. There is no question that IT is a professional field in a casual sense; however, it has not been professionalized in the same sense as law, medicine, architecture, and engineering. These fields have educational, licensure, and certification requirements enforced both by legal means and by powerful, nonoptional professional bodies.

There are three impulses of professionalization apparent for enterprise IT in the United States:

▶ Software engineering based
▶ ITIL and its International Organization for Standards/International Electrotechnical Commission (ISO/IEC) 20000 manifestation
▶ Information system audit and security-based

Software Engineering–Based Impulse

Licensure and/or certification of software engineers has been discussed periodically (and with great controversy) in the software industry for many years. The two main approaches here are as follows:

▶ Achieve professional engineer status as a software engineer (a difficult road, one that may not be available in many states—certification as an electrical engineer may be the closest possible alternative). David Parnas is a noted advocate of this approach.

▶ Achieve the IEEE Computer Society's certified software development professional (CSDP) certification.

Both of these certifications are biased toward software construction, and neither provides any support for issues of large-scale IT service planning, budgeting, and governance.

(There are a multitude of product certifications irrelevant to the broader-scope professional issues discussed in this book.)

ITIL and ISO/IEC 20000 Impulse

ITIL has long been offered as an individually certifiable credential; a 3-day foundations course and certification is easily achievable, and a 3-week masters' course with written exam is more challenging. For organizations, ITIL has recently been translated into an ISO standard, which means that (just as with the ISO 9000-1 quality certification) IT organizations will be able to seek ISO/IEC 20000 certification.

As noted elsewhere in this book, the core ITIL material is strongest in the service support area. (Service support and service delivery are the scope of the available certification and the ISO standards; the other ITIL volumes are not part of any certification scheme, which sends a message about the relative faith placed in those volumes.) Portfolio management, process improvement, data management, project management, core software development life cycle, enterprise architecture, and other important IT concerns are not well covered by ITIL in any volumes.

Security and Audit-Based Impulse

Another pathway to professionalization is the convergence of security and audit roles. The COBIT framework is gaining increasing acceptance in this area, with the corresponding certified information systems auditor and certified information security manager credentials.

This is an interesting avenue to IT professionalization, and the jury is out at this writing. COBIT is a comprehensive framework, covering virtually all of the IT value chain (but not with a value chain perspective). Certification in it would certainly give the individual a deep perspective on many core IT issues, but the audit perspective might be limiting.

Related but distinct certifications in information security (CISSP, SSCP, CAP) present similar opportunities and challenges. There seems to be significant demand for such certifications from enterprises, where they carry more weight for their respective fields than, for example, the CSDP certification carries for developers. See the International Information Systems Security Certification Consortium.

When you look at the qualifications and professional activities of IT auditors, you will see more of a traditionally professionalized field, with frequent participation in industry–government liaison bodies, academic adjunct positions, and the like. Most come into the field with accounting or finance degrees, not computer science or management information systems.

Appendix C
IT Professional Organizations

Here is a brief listing of some major professional organizations in the United States that an IT professional may consider participating in or interacting with. It deliberately omits pure technical standards bodies, which rarely see participation by enterprise IT practitioners.

Individual and Chapter-Based Professional Membership Organizations

- Association for Computing Machinery (ACM)
- Association for Information Technology Professionals (AITP)
- Configuration Management Institute
- Data Management Association (DAMA)
- Institute of Electrical and Electronics Engineers (IEEE)
- International Information Systems Security Certification Consortium
- Information Systems Audit and Control Association/IT Governance Institute
- IT Service Management Forum (ITSMF)
- Society for Information Management (SIM)

Academic and Research Institutes and Consortia (Nonprofit)

- Carnegie Mellon Software Engineering Institute (SEI)
- Massachusetts Institute of Technology Center for Information Systems Research
- IT Process Institute

Industry Consortia

▶ Distributed Management Task Force (DMTF)
▶ Object Management Group (OMG)
▶ TeleManagement Forum

Endnotes

1. (Krutch 1959)
2. (McConnell 1999)
3. (Snopes.com 2006)
4. (Sharp and McDermott 2001), p. 4
5. See *www.itil.co.uk*.
6. See *www.isaca.org*.
7. (IBM Corporation 1980)
8. For example, there has been debate around the relative meanings of the words "problem" and "incident," with the ITIL version only recently becoming widely accepted.
9. (CIO Magazine 2004)
10. (Greenspan 2005)
11. Assuming that current software engineering bottlenecks in exploiting hardware capacity are overcome, for example, making multiprocessing architectures more usable for mainstream developers.
12. (Carr 2003)
13. (Carr 2004), p. 108
14. (Lientz and Lee 2004)
15. (Standish Group 2004)
16. (Glass 1998)
17. See in particular the excellent work of Steve McConnell (e.g., McConnell 1996, 1998, and 1999).
18. (Brooks 1995)
19. (Remenyi, Money et al. 2000), p. 98
20. (Lutchen 2004)
21. Actually, transistor density on microprocessors, but this has been transformed in the popular press into an analogue of computing power. Limits of energy density and computational usability (e.g., commercial software support for multiprocessor architectures) are presenting significant challenges.
22. (Maizlish and Handler 2005), p. 12
23. (Kaplan 2005)
24. (Carr 2004), p. 113

25. (Rummler and Brache 1995), p. 2

26. *The American Heritage Dictionary of the English Language*, 4th edition. (2000). Houghton Mifflin.

27. (CIO Magazine 2004)

28. (IBM Corporation 1980)

29. It is almost certainly an essentially contested concept in the Galliean sense (Gallie 1956).

30. (IT Governance Institute 2003)

31. (Nolan and McFarlan 2005)

32. (McFarlan 1981)

33. (Office of Government Commerce 2004), p. 60

34. (Weill and Ross 2004), p. 30

35. (Clinger-Cohen 1996)

36. (Lutchen 2004), p. 134

37. (Remenyi, Money et al. 2000), p. 85

38. (Maizlish and Handler 2005)

39. (Schrage 2005)

40. See, for example, the article "Prune IT Systems, Not Budgets" in *CIO Magazine* (Schrage 2005).

41. (Bahadur, Desment et al. 2006)

42. (Hammer 2005)

43. (Rummler and Brache 1995)

44. (Schmidt and Lyle 2005)

45. (Microsoft Corporation 2005)

46. For example, references to individuals' participation in previous CASE Data Interchange Format (CDIF) standards activities are periodically seen on internal Object Management Group email lists and in the individuals' curriculum vitae. This might be an interesting area of IT historical research.

47. (Royce 1970)

48. (Carr 2004), p. 46

49. (Office of Government Commerce 2004), pp. 39–40

50. (Carr 2004), p. xiii

51. (Kaplan 2005)

52. (Porter 1998)

53. At this writing available for free download at *www.isaca.org*.

54. *www.sei.cmu.edu/cmmi/general/general.html*, accessed March 11, 2006.

55. The critique in Bach (1994) is significant and still relevant, as are his pointers to further resources and authors critical of CMMI.

56. Not to say that CMMI, Agile, and Rational Unified Process (RUP) are mutually exclusive; their relationship is more nuanced. It is possible to tailor RUP in an Agile fashion, and either RUP or Agile can be used to demonstrate CMMI maturity—CMMI arguably being more concerned (à la ISO 9000) that the organization is "documenting what it does and doing what it documents."

57. (Cazemier, Overbeek et al. 1999; Office of Government Commerce 2000; Office of Government Commerce 2001; Office of Government Commerce 2002a; Office of Government Commerce 2002b; Office of Government Commerce 2002c; Office of Government Commerce 2003; Office of Government Commerce 2004; Office of Government Commerce 2006). The final *Business Perspective* volume (Office of Government Commerce 2006) is forthcoming.

58. This is a subject of some controversy; ITIL considers the *Service Support* and *Service Delivery* volumes to be the "IT service management" volumes. However, this restriction is not reflected in other ITSM work—such as that by van Bon (2002), which takes a broader view.

59. (IBM Corporation 1980)

60. (van Bon 2002), p. xiii

61. (van Herwaarden and Grift 2002)

62. In the United Kingdom, project management is handled by the Prince2 method and systems development by SSADM; these, in conjunction with ITIL, might be seen as approaching a complete framework, but they would still be weak in IT portfolio management.

63. (van Bon 2002), p. 220

64. (Sharp and McDermott 2001)

65. (Sharp and McDermott 2001), p. 54

66. (Rummler and Brache 1995)

67. (Kaplan 2005)

68. (Rummler and Brache 1995)

69. (Porter 1998)

70. (Harmon 2003), p. 58

71. (Brache 2002), p. 10

72. (Porter 1998)

73. I take sole credit for coining this but don't intend to trademark it or anything obnoxious like that.

74. The concept of considering IT as a business within a business was conceived as early as (International Business Machines 1980).

75. (Porter 1998)
76. (Office of Government Commerce 2004), vol. 1
77. (Lientz and Lee 2004)
78. A rich framework to help position IT-generated demand is seen in Henderson and Venkatraman (1993), who distinguish among IT as an investment, profit, cost, or service center. This approach would help determine the acceptability of IT-driven demand.
79. (Royce 1970)
80. Yes, we are talking about the requirements of supporting requirements management. Stay with me.
81. (McClure 1989; Spurr and Layzell 1990). Also, Microsoft (2005) makes a strong if tendentious statement on the failures of first-generation CASE.
82. For example, the Object Management Group's model-driven architecture proposes a three-layer stack of computation-independent model, platform-independent model, and platform-specific model (Frankel 2003; Object Management Group 2002a; Object Management Group 2002b).
83. (Microsoft Corporation 2005)
84. (Office of Government Commerce 2000), p. 204
85. See Office of Government Commerce (2000), p. 187, section 8.5.9. This section clearly indicates that RFC authorization precedes software construction and even controls it. "Change management has a coordination role...to ensure that these activities are both resources and also completed to schedule." In this book's framework, those responsibilities are housed in "manage demand" and "develop solutions."
86. (Office of Government Commerce 2000). Contrast the discussions on pages 169 and 173.
87. (Office of Government Commerce 2000), p. 187, section 8.5.9
88. It's assumed that one reason for the ITIL approach is to ensure that new construction activities are fully publicized to all stakeholders; this is a critically important principle, and the terminology debate here does not negate that requirement.

    The ITIL Change concept might be equated with entire primary value chain.
89. (Lutchen 2004)
90. (Canfora and Di Penta 2006)
91. (Office of Government Commerce 2000), p. 169
92. (Office of Government Commerce 2000), p. 173

93. (Office of Government Commerce 2000), p. 105

94. *http://en.wikiquote.org/wiki/Napoleon_Bonaparte*, accessed August 6, 2006.

95. For example, this is seen in the value chain discussion by Office of Government Commerce (2004), which derives from Gibert (2006).

96. (McFarlan 1981)

97. (Benson, Bugnitz et al. 2004; Kaplan 2005; Maizlish and Handler 2005)

98. Wikipedia contributors, "Account," Wikipedia: The Free Encyclopedia, *en.wikipedia.org/wiki/Account* (accessed January 28, 2006).

99. Wikipedia contributors, "Portfolio (Finance)," Wikipedia: The Free Encyclopedia, *en.wikipedia.org/wiki/Portfolio_%28finance%29* (accessed January 28, 2006). (Emphasis added.)

100. Credit to Kaplan (2005).

101. The first segmentation example is from Benson, Bugnitz et al. (2004), and the latter two are a graphical representation of how Maizlish and Handler (2005) view it.

102. (Kaplan 2005)

103. (Benson, Bugnitz et al. 2004), p. 123

104. (Remenyi 1999; Remenyi, Money et al. 2000)

105. Capacity management in ITIL is somewhat of a grab bag, "poorly cohesive" in software engineering terms.

106. (Office of Government Commerce 2001), p. 129

107. (Waters 2003)

108. (Carr 2004)

109. (Carr 2004). To be completely accurate, his message is mixed. In some passages, he calls for more centralized IT governance to better manage risks, yet he predicts that IT will become as pervasive as electricity and that CIOs' goals should be to work themselves out of a job. This implies considerably more IT control vesting into the hands of consumers or individual corporate organizations at least.

110. (Office of Government Commerce 2002a)

111. (Office of Government Commerce 2001), p. 27

112. A comprehensive discussion of data stewardship can be found in English (1999).

113. "Information architecture" has two meanings—one related to data architecture (the COBIT use), the other more concerned with the user experience and "flow" made possible through the user interface at the application layer (personal correspondence to Charles Betz from Sean Goggins, April 29, 2006).

114. (Benson, Bugnitz et al. 2004), p. 84

115. (Dugmore 2002)

116. Jeffrey Kaplan places considerable emphasis on the discipline of cost accounting and argues that it is highly immature in IT environments (Kaplan 2005).

117. See discussions especially in the Office of Government Commerce (2001) "IT Financial Management" chapter and Aitken (2003), pp. 34–35 and 64–77.

118. (Patton 2006)

119. For an in-depth discussion of this see the ITIL *ICT Infrastructure Management* volume (Office of Government Commerce 2002b).

120. A related example of this can be seen in the ITIL *Application Management* volume (Office of Government Commerce 2002a), which treats application development as a primary value chain and the ITIL operational and tactical processes as supporting. It also analyzes the resulting conceptual matrix as a framework for that volume, resulting in interesting insights into developing applications for optimal service management results.

121. Adapted from Hertroys and van Rooijen (2002), Ruijs and Schotanus (2002), and van den Elskamp, Kuiper et al. (2002).

122. (Office of Government Commerce 2000)

123. (Rummler and Brache 1995)

124. (Lutchen 2004; Sturm 2005)

125. (van Bon 2002)

126. Again, see Henderson and Venkatraman (1993) for a useful in-depth framework relevant to these issues.

127. (Henderson and Venkatraman 1993)

128. (Kaplan 2005)

129. (Office of Government Commerce 2000), p. 47

130. (Kaplan 2005)

131. Comment by the CEO of Siebel Systems regarding its 2005 acquisition by Oracle (emphasis added).

132. (Burlton 2001)

133. (Hammer 2005)

134. (Drucker 1993)

135. Other "next generation" enterprise resources include brands, intellectual property, and relationships.

136. *http://en.wikiquote.org/wiki/Oliver_Wendell_Holmes,_Jr.,* accessed August 6, 2006.

137.   For further information on potential IT industry metric standardization, investigate the IT Process Institute *(www.itpi.org)*, the IT Service Management Forum *(www.itsmf.org)*, and the work of Dr. Steve Huchendorf at the University of Minnesota. Aitken (2003) is critical of attempting to make IT metrics "benchmarkable."

138.   (IT Governance Institute 2006)

139.   (Kimball 1998), p. 100

140.   (Sharp and McDermott 2001), p. 275, emphasis added.

141.   This book subscribes to the "UML as sketch" pattern proposed by Martin Fowler. Notational rigor is not an objective; communication is.

142.   The verb phrases in this problem domain often wind up being fairly generic, such as "contains" and "depends on." The simplified notation is generated in a UML tool, but graphically nesting subtypes is not idiomatic UML. I chose to do this as a nod to data modeling thought leaders such as Dave Hay and Len Silverston, whose significant intellectual contributions are documented in an Oracle Designer entity or relationship syntax that uses such nesting. (Dave and Len would probably fault the modeling here for not naming the relationships—sorry guys.)

143.   (Office of Government Commerce 2000)

144.   For further information on the ACID model see, for example, Bernstein and Newcomer (1997).

145.   (Office of Government Commerce 2000)

146.   (Office of Government Commerce 2000)

147.   (Office of Government Commerce 2000)

148.   I have had conversations with colleagues who distinguish between a "business RFC" and a standard one, seeing the business RFC as equivalent to an idea and/or demand request.

149.   (Office of Government Commerce 2000), pp. 169–170

150.   (Benson, Bugnitz et al. 2004; Kaplan 2005; Maizlish and Handler 2005)

151.   The ITIL discussion of change in terms of change control is world-class industry guidance. It just overreaches in my opinion.

152.   (Office of Government Commerce 2000), section 4.1.13, p. 34

153.   See Luckham (2002). Events are any occurrence with real or potential management significance. The field of business activity monitoring is concerned with events and has major research activities on such topics as stream-based queries.

154. (Office of Government Commerce 2000)

155. (Office of Government Commerce 2000)

156. (Office of Government Commerce 2000)

157. Note that the main model does not directly link incident to RFC; this is purely for visual simplicity.

158. (Office of Government Commerce 2000)

159. (Carr 2004), p. 108

160. Wikipedia contributors, "Account," Wikipedia: The Free Encyclopedia, *en.wikipedia.org/wiki/Account* (accessed January 28, 2006).

161. (Office of Government Commerce 2001)

162. (Kaplan 2005)

163. (Office of Government Commerce 2000), p. 175

164. (Office of Government Commerce 2000)

165. (Office of Government Commerce 2000)

166. (Office of Government Commerce 2001)

167. You might say that the question of whether or not metadata is a CI cannot be decided within the bounds of this framework.

168. See the OMG's MetaObject Facility specification (Office of Government Commerce 2002d), the academic work of Jean Bezivin, and anything else under the general heading of "reflexive metamodeling."

169. (Office of Government Commerce 2001)

170. (Object Management Group 2002a; Poole, Chang et al. 2002; Poole, Chang et al. 2003)

171. (Kaplan 2005)

172. (Object Management Group 2002a), Foundation package, Software Deployment Metamodel.

173. IT services may include processes, which are repeatable and event driven and therefore controllable in terms of cost. Including IT functions as services is more problematic due to ambiguity, and the model does not support this (which may be controversial; feedback is welcomed). See the discussion in Appendix A on process, function, and organization.

174. Technically, what raises an event on behalf of a datastore would be the RDBMS, which is itself a deployed software system. But there is a long-standing practice of conceptually combining the database catalog with the RDBMS software service that helps simplify this critical area.

175. (Hammer 2005)

176. (Office of Government Commerce 2000)

177. See Sturm, Morris et al. (2000) for a good discussion of end-to-end transaction management.

178. (Office of Government Commerce 2004)

179. (Office of Government Commerce 2002a)

180. (Office of Government Commerce 2001), p. 33

181. For example, the DMTF standards.

182. See Object Management Group (2002a), in particular the subsection on software deployment.

183. Naming the entity Definitive Software Library Entry was considered but rejected because of the previously discussed need to also handle hardware and software–hardware combined products. It also would be a clumsy name from a data modeling perspective.

184. Technically, all code has an interface, or at least an entry point for the operating system to start executing it.

185. Credit to Gordon Everest for introducing me to this term.

186. See, for example, Ambler and Sadalage (2006); however, if this is being done in a configuration management framework, the refactoring will be more of a logical challenge.

187. For the definitive sources on this sort of matrix analysis, see Spewak and Hill (1993) and Martin (1989).

188. (Benson, Bugnitz et al. 2004), p. 152

189. (Drucker 1963)

190. Object-oriented frameworks and databases sometimes allow direct implementation of many-to-many relationships. However, the logical issue does not go away; the means by which the relationship is maintained is just as important as how the base entities are maintained.

191. See Oracle's CONNECT BY operator.

192. See *www.dcml.org* and *www.w3.org/2001/sw/*. The Semantic Web is neither relational nor object oriented; it is yet another fundamental data representation paradigm being introduced to an industry still struggling to reconcile the first two. This gives pause in terms of staffing and talent management.

193. (Office of Government Commerce 2000)

194. (Kaplan 2005)

195. (Yourdon and Constantine 1979)

196. Contrary to Forrester Research.

197. (Office of Government Commerce 2001), p. 128

198. This book is an example!

199. For example, CA Argis.

200. As noted in Software Engineering Institute (2004). "Other authors have attempted to make finer-grained distinctions between different classes of CASE tools along a number of dimensions. The most common distinctions are the following:

   ▶ Between those tools that are interactive in nature (such as a design method support tool) and those that are not (such as a compiler). The former class is sometimes called CASE tools, and the latter class is called development tools.

   ▶ Between those tools that support activities early in the life cycle of a software project (such as requirements and design support tools) and those that are used later in the life cycle (such as compilers and test support tools). The former class is sometimes called front-end CASE tools, and the latter is called back-end CASE tools.

   ▶ Between those tools that are specific to a particular life cycle step or domain (such as a requirements tool or a coding tool) and those that are common across a number of life cycle steps or domains (such as a documentation tool or a configuration management tool). The former class is sometimes called vertical CASE tools, and the latter class is called horizontal CASE tools."

   Unfortunately, all these distinctions are problematic.

201. (Frankel 2003)

202. (Microsoft Corporation 2005)

203. In an earlier draft of this book this class of system was termed "release management," and that remains a focus in this discussion. It's not clear that there is actually a sensible "release management system" type.

204. (IBM Corporation 2005)

205. (Sturm, Morris et al. 2000)

206. See Sturm, Morris et al. (2000) for an excellent, in-depth discussion of this and related issues beyond the scope of this book.

207. See Date and Darwen (2000) for object and relational theory. Native support for inheritance, direct many-to-many associations, and recursive queries are major differentiators of object databases and relational databases.

208. Canfora and Di Penta (2006) address the problems of testing dynamically bound systems, a discussion relevant to configuration management. Also see the Fundamentals of Integration Metadata series on *www.erp4it.com.*

209. Again, see Canfora and Di Penta (2006).

210. For example, Telelogic's Systems Architect and Adaptive's IT Portfolio Management.

211. (Kimball 1998) p. 100

212. Wikipedia contributors, "Design Pattern (Computer Science)," Wikipedia: The Free Encyclopedia, *en.wikipedia.org/wiki/Design_pattern_%28 computer_science%29* (accessed July 17, 2006).

213. (Alexander, Ishikawa et al. 1977)

214. In this sense, the material is at the same level as some of the antipatterns work (see "Further Reading" at the end of Chapter 5). It's perhaps ironic that only negative "antipatterns" have been identified for IT management, and no positive pattern literature at this level is apparent. (Hopefully, this book will stimulate further work in this area.)

  Integrated IT management is an emerging field, and this book takes some liberty in using the term "pattern," which typically implies known uses. Some of these patterns are known to be used, but I do not wish to identify the companies—there would be many complications in doing so. Others are inferred from considering the various requirements implicit in industry process frameworks and literature. In time, a more refined and well-documented set of patterns hopefully will emerge—this is only an early attempt.

215. (Rummler and Brache 1995)

216. (Burlton 2001)

217. (Hertroys and van Rooijen 2002)

218. However, as Richard Soley notes, "One of the tenets of MDA is that one cannot (permanently) reduce the complexity of the software environment. Events such as business line changes, business integration changes, and mergers and acquisitions will always complicate the stack you're stuck with. The best you can do is reduce the complexity of an abstraction of your software environment, and drive integration from there" (personal correspondence to Charles Betz, February 27, 2006).

219. (van den Elskamp, Kuiper et al. 2002)

220. The Fundamentals of Integration Metadata series on the *www.erp4it.com* site goes into a great detail on enterprise application integration configuration management.

221. (Canfora and Di Penta 2006)

222. (van den Elskamp, Kuiper et al. 2002)

223. (van den Elskamp, Kuiper et al. 2002)

224. See, for example, van den Elskamp, Kuiper et al. (2002).

225. (Microsoft Corporation 2005)

226. Alternatively this could be considered a Configuration Audit process. ITIL is unclear here.

227. Precisely: party is an abstract class, and Chris is actually an instance of individual. Simplify things for clarity.

228. At this writing I am not aware of any vendor product providing this functionality, which I have seen emerge organically in three different organizations all trying to solve the same problem.

229. (Schmidt and Lyle 2005)

230. (Hohpe and Woolf 2003)

231. (Kern, Galup et al. 2000), p. 60

232. (Kern, Schiesser et al. 2004)

233. (Benson, Bugnitz et al. 2004)

234. (Office of Government Commerce 2000), p. 143

235. (Office of Government Commerce 2002a), p. 21

236. Wikipedia contributors, "Depreciation," Wikipedia: The Free Encyclopedia, *en.wikipedia.org/wiki/Depreciation* (accessed July 17, 2006).

237. (Aitken 2003), p. 168

238. It is perplexing that no IT portfolio management literature that I have seen details such techniques.

239. A related and sobering case study is presented in Sturm, Morris et al. (2000), p. 73.

240. (Gibson 2003)

241. (Carr 2004)

242. (Brooks 1995)

243. *http://www.ireland-information.com/irishmusic/partingglass.shtml*, accessed August 6, 2006.

244. (Spewak and Hill 1993)

245. (DeMarco 1979, Yourdon 1989)

246. Programmers today still build from the bottom up, but hopefully they have a higher-level design or at least know that somewhere there is an architect who may come by and annoy them.

247. (Finkelstein 1989 and Martin 1989)

248. (Spewak and Hill 1993)

249. However, object orientation (through its Unified Modeling Language and related specifications) is well suited to building a *metamodel* that can underpin such analysis.

250. Some UML tools have started to support matrixing, but you will not see it used in the major methodology books, nor is a matrix a recognized OMG diagram type.

251. Patterns, though, are not necessarily represented in object-oriented semantics. This book may have patterns represented as data models, system interaction diagrams, and/or process and function models, including RASI matrices.

252. (Fowler 1997)

253. (Lopez 2005)

254. (Burlton 2001)

255. (Sharp and McDermott 2001)

References

MARQUEE CREDIT IS DUE TO Michael Porter, the preeminent management systems theorist, for the concept of value chain introduced in his landmark *Competitive Advantage* (1998), a staple of MBA programs worldwide.

How do we assess the validity of a framework's claim to help us understand "IT process"?

The value chain is supported by the business process, and "process frameworks" are proliferating. How do we assess the validity of a framework's claim to help us understand "IT process"? A key volume on BPM is *Improving performance* by Geary Rummler and Alan Brache (1995). Much of modern consulting and business practice is based on principles first articulated therein. *Business Process Change: A Manager's Guide to Improving, Redesigning, and Automating Processes* by Paul Harmon (2003) and *Business Process Management: Profiting from Process* by Roger Burlton (2001) are further BPM references, as is Alec Sharp and Patrick McDermott's *Workflow Modeling: Tools for Process Improvement and Application Development* (2001).

This is not a book about crafting IT decision rights; it is a book about enabling them using a well-integrated architecture.

A widely cited work by MIT professors Jeanne Ross and Peter Weill is *IT Governance: How Top Performers Manage IT Decision Rights for Superior Results* (2004). Ross and Weill focus on the allocation and realization of decision rights at the highest levels of the enterprise—governance in the strictest sense, with comparisons of various centralized and decentralized models. This book complements Ross and Weill by discussing the architectures that *enable* IT governance. This is not a book about crafting decision rights; it is a book about how those decision rights can be enabled through a supporting infrastructure that provides the command, information, and control feedback necessary for decision effectiveness.

Robert Handler and Bryan Maizlish's *IT Portfolio Management Step-By-Step: Unlocking the Business Value of Technology* (2005) focuses on the concept of interlocking IT portfolios serving as major structuring mechanisms for managing enterprise IT in the large. Jeffrey Kaplan's *Strategic IT Portfolio Management: Governing Enterprise Transformation* (2005) is another compelling yet different take on the subject, more oriented toward the financial and project aspects of the topic.

My goal in this book has been to complement Kaplan, Handler, and Maizlish by drilling much deeper into the specifics of the business processes, data structures, and applications needed to pervasively implement and support portfolio management throughout a large IT organization.

Mark Lutchen's *Managing IT as a Business* (2004) provides a wealth of case studies (some quite sobering) and is firmly targeted to the CEO and business audience. As with Weill and Ross, this book seeks to show the *how* of enabling what Lutchen calls for.

We have no shortage of excellent point material discussing IT, but what is lacking is cross-functional analysis.

ITSM as a whole is an important influence, although I do not share the view that ITSM encompasses all aspects of IT management. ITIL and ITSM are strongest in IT operations, and when it comes to the planning and building aspects of IT management, ITSM must be reconciled with practice areas such as enterprise architecture, software development, and portfolio management that are coherent in their own right and not currently aligned with ITSM and its ITIL expression.

The *Guide to IT Service Management* (van Bon 2002) is an exhaustive compendium of much industry-leading thought on all aspects of large-scale IT management. This 800-page tome features 50 in-depth articles and case studies on issues such as service life cycle management, conceptual IT frameworks, and organizational and process issues. It is one of the most comprehensive and concentrated collections of practitioner-focused, high-quality IT management writings available in a field somewhat diffuse and hard to research.

The eight currently available volumes of the Information Technology Infrastructure Library (ITIL) are also primary sources. This massive work is detailed, rigorous, and extensive; it is one of the most important influences in contemporary IT management. However, it has some weaknesses and idiosyncrasies, which are addressed here, along with its considerable strengths.

Harris Kern's Enterprise Computing Institute has published a variety of worthwhile books by various authors covering enterprise IT, such as *Managing IT as an Investment, IT Problem Management, IT Production Services, IT Organization, IT Services,* and *Enterprise Architecture Toolkit.* This book complements the Kern material by tying the various threads together from a single authorial perspective; we have no shortage of point material discussing IT, but what is lacking is cross-functional analysis.

There is also continuous work emerging from the major research providers such as Gartner, Forrester Research, and AMR Research. Their research is necessarily time-sensitive and abbreviated, as it is targeted at senior decision makers and tracks fast-moving market forces. This book dives more deeply into the drivers and issues underlying product evolution in this segment, and it will enable you to interpret the research firms' publications in a broader context.

Where all of these publications talk about the "what," the intent of this book is to open up the question of "how."

Where all of these publications talk about the "what," including implementation plans and practical road maps, the intent of this book has been to open up the question of "how" from the perspective of the architect and systems analyst.

Agile Alliance (2001). Agile manifesto. *http://agilemanifesto.org/principles.html*

Aitken, I. (2003). *Value-driven IT management.* D. Remenyi, Computer weekly professional series. Oxford, Butterworth-Heinemann.

Alexander, C., S. Ishikawa, et al. (1977). *A pattern language: towns, buildings, construction.* New York, Oxford University Press.

Ambler, S. W., and P. J. Sadalage (2006). *Refactoring databases: evolutionary database design.* Indianapolis, Addison-Wesley Professional.

ASL Foundation (2005a). Application Services Library. *http://www.aslfoundation.org/*

ASL Foundation (2005b). ASL in the forest of models. *http://www.aslfoundation.org/*

Bach, J. (1994). "The immaturity of CMM." *American Programmer* (September 1994).

Bahadur, K., D. Desment, et al. (2006). "Smart IT spending: Insights from European banks." *McKinsey Quarterly* (January 2006).

Beck, K. (1999). "Embracing change with extreme programming." *IEEE Computer* **32**(10) (October 1999): 70–77.

Benson, R. J., T. L. Bugnitz, et al. (2004). *From business strategy to IT action: right decisions for a better bottom line.* Hoboken, NJ, John Wiley & Sons.

Bernstein, P. A., and E. Newcomer (1997). *Principles of transaction processing.* Morgan Kaufmann series in data management systems. San Francisco, Morgan Kaufmann.

Brache, A. P. (2002). *How organizations work: taking a holistic approach to enterprise health.* New York, John Wiley & Sons.

Brooks, F. P. (1995). *The mythical man-month: essays on software engineering.* Reading, MA, Addison-Wesley.

Brooks, P. (2006). *Metrics for IT service management.* The Netherlands, Van Haren.

Brown, W. J. (1998). *Antipatterns: refactoring software, architectures, and projects in crisis.* New York, John Wiley & Sons.

Brown, W. J., H. W. McCormick, et al. (1999). *Antipatterns and patterns in software configuration management.* New York, John Wiley & Sons.

Brown, W. J., H. W. McCormick, et al. (2000). *Antipatterns in project management.* New York, John Wiley & Sons.

Bumpus, W. (2000). *Common information model: implementing the object model for enterprise management.* New York, John Wiley & Sons.

Burlton, R. (2001). *Business process management: profiting from process.* Indianapolis, Sams.

Buschmann, F. (1996). *Pattern-oriented software architecture: a system of patterns.* Chichester, England; New York, John Wiley & Sons.

Canfora, G., and M. Di Penta (2006). "Testing services and service-centric systems: challenges and opportunities." *IEEE IT Professional* (March/April 2006).

Carbone, J. A. (2004). *IT architecture toolkit.* Enterprise computing series. Professional Technical Reference. Upper Saddle River, NJ, Prentice Hall.

Carlis, J. V., and J. D. Maguire (2001). *Mastering data modeling: a user-driven approach.* Boston, Addison-Wesley.

Carr, N. (2003). "IT doesn't matter." *Harvard Business Review* (May 2003): 5–12.

Carr, N. G. (2004). *Does IT matter? Information technology and the corrosion of competitive advantage.* Boston, Harvard Business School Press.

Cazemier, J. A., P. L. Overbeek, et al. (1999). *Security management.* OGC, ITIL Managing IT Services (Information Technology Infrastructure Library). London, The Stationary Office.

Central Computer and Telecommunications Agency (1994). *Data management.* Information Management Library (ITIL Back Catalog). London, The Stationery Office.

CIO Magazine (2004). "Special report: How to run IT like a business." *CIO Magazine* (May 2004).

Clements, P. (2003). *Documenting software architectures: views and beyond.* SEI series in software engineering. Boston, Addison-Wesley.

Clinger-Cohen (1996). Information Technology Management Reform Act (a.k.a. the Clinger-Cohen Act). *http://www.cio.gov/documents/it_management_reform_act_feb_1996.html*

CMMI Product Team (2001). Capability Maturity Model Integration (CMMI), version 1.1. Pittsburgh, Software Engineering Institute, Carnegie Mellon University.

Cook, M. A. (1996). *Building enterprise information architectures: reengineering information systems.* Hewlett-Packard professional books. Upper Saddle River, NJ, Prentice Hall.

Curley, M. (2004). *Managing information technology for business value: practical strategies for IT and business managers.* Hillsboro, OR, Intel Press.

Data Management Association International (2000). *Implementing data resource management.* DAMA International.

Date, C. J., and H. Darwen (2000). *Foundation for future database systems: the third manifesto.* A detailed study of the impact of type theory on the relational model of data, including a comprehensive model of type inheritance. Reading, MA, Addison-Wesley Professional.

DeMarco, T. (1979). *Structured analysis and system specification.* Englewood Cliffs, NJ, Yourdon Press.

Distributed Management Task Force (2000). Common information model (CIM) core model. *http://www.dmtf.org*

Distributed Management Task Force (2002a). CIM database model white paper 2003. *http://www.dmtf.org/standards/documents/CIM/DSP0133.pdf*

Distributed Management Task Force (2002b). Specification for the representation of CIM in XML. *http://www.dmtf.org/standards/documents/WBEM/DSP201.html*

Distributed Management Task Force (2003). Common information model schema. *http://www.dmtf.org*

Drucker, Peter F. (1963). "Managing for business effectiveness," *Harvard Business Review* May–June.

Dudney, B. (2003). *J2EE antipatterns.* Indianapolis, John Wiley & Sons.

Dugmore, J. (2002). "A standard for IT service management." *The guide to IT service management.* J. van Bon, ed. London, Addison-Wesley: 97–115.

English, L. P. (1999). *Improving data warehouse and business information quality: methods for reducing costs and increasing profits.* New York, John Wiley & Sons.

Finkelstein, C. (1989). *An introduction to information engineering: from strategic planning to information systems.* Reading, MA, Addison-Wesley.

Fowler, M. (1997). *Analysis patterns: reusable object models.* Menlo Park, CA, Addison-Wesley.

Fowler, M. (2003). *Patterns of enterprise application architecture.* Addison-Wesley signature series. Boston, Addison-Wesley.

Frankel, D. S. (2003). *Model-driven architecture: applying MDA to enterprise computing.* New York, John Wiley & Sons.

Gallie, W. B. (1956). "Essentially Contested Concepts." *Proceedings of the Aristotelian Society* **56**:167–198.

Gamma, E. (1995). *Design patterns: elements of reusable object-oriented software.* Reading, MA, Addison-Wesley.

Gibert, J. (2006). IT physician, heal thyself. *http://www.bita-center.com*

Gibson, W. (2003). *Burning chrome.* New York, HarperCollins.

Glass, R. L. (1998). *Software runaways.* Professional Technical Reference. Upper Saddle River, NJ, Prentice Hall.

Goldberg, H. (2004). "Unleashing the Power of Data." *DB2 Magazine* **9**(2). *http://www.db2mag.com/story/showArticle.jhtml?articleID=18901174*

Greenspan, A. (2005). Economic flexibility. Speech before the National Italian American Foundation, Washington, DC.

Halpin, T. A. (2001). *Information modeling and relational databases: from conceptual analysis to logical design.* San Francisco, Morgan Kaufman.

Hammer, M. (2005). "CIO Evolution." *CIO Magazine* (August 1, 2005).

Harmon, P. (2003). *Business process change: a manager's guide to improving, redesigning, and automating processes.* Amsterdam, Elsevier.

Hay, D. C. (1996). *Data model patterns: conventions of thought.* New York, Dorset House.

Hay, D. C. (2006). *Data model patterns: a metadata map.* Morgan Kaufmann series in data management systems. Amsterdam, Morgan Kaufman.

Hedeman, B., H. Frederiksz, et al. (2005). *Project management based on Prince2: an introduction.* The Netherlands, Van Haren.

Heffner, R. (2005). *Does SOA make applications obsolete?* Forrester Research.

Henderson, J. C., and N. Venkatraman (1993). "Strategic Alignment: Leveraging Information Technology for Transforming Organizations." *IBM Systems Journal* **32**(1): 4–16.

Hertroys, P., and B. van Rooijen (2002). "Information technology process model." *The guide to IT service management.* J. van Bon, ed. London, Addison-Wesley: 151–157.

Hohpe, G., and B. Woolf (2003). *Enterprise integration patterns: designing, building, and deploying messaging solutions.* Boston, Addison-Wesley.

Humphrey, W. S. (1989). *Managing the software process.* Reading, MA, Addison-Wesley.

IBM Corporation (1980). *A management system for the information business.* White Plains, NY, International Business Machines.

IBM Corporation (2005). *An architectural blueprint for autonomic computing,* 3rd edition. White Plains, NY, International Business Machines.

Institute of Electrical and Electronics Engineers (2005). *Guide to the software engineering body of knowledge: 2004 version.* Los Alamitos, CA, IEEE Computer Society Press.

IT Governance Institute (2006). *Control objectives for Information Technology 4.0. http://www.itgi.org*

Kaplan, J. D. (2005). *Strategic IT portfolio management: governing enterprise transformation.* Boston, Pittiglio Rabin Todd & McGrath.

Kern, H., S. Galup, et al. (2000). *IT organization: building a world-class infrastructure.* Professional Technical Reference. Upper Saddle River, NJ, Prentice Hall.

Kern, H., R. Schiesser, et al. (2004). *IT production services.* Professional Technical Reference. Upper Saddle River, NJ, Prentice Hall.

Kimball, R. (1998). *The data warehouse life cycle toolkit: expert methods for designing, developing, and deploying data warehouses.* New York, Wiley Computer.

Kimball, R., and M. Ross (2002). *The data warehouse toolkit: the complete guide to dimensional modeling.* New York, John Wiley & Sons.

Krutch, J. W. (1959). "The nemesis of power." *Human nature and the human condition.* Greenwood Press Reprint (April 24, 1979).

Laplante, P. A., and C. J. Neill (2005). *Antipatterns: identification, refactoring, and management.* Boca Raton, FL, Taylor & Francis.

Lientz, B. P., and L. Lee (2004). *Manage IT as a business: how to achieve alignment and add value to the company.* Amsterdam, Elsevier/Butterworth-Heinemann.

Linthicum, D. S. (2004). *Next generation application integration: from simple information to Web services.* Addison-Wesley information technology series. Boston, Addison-Wesley.

Lopez, Karen. (2005). "Re: Function and process." *http://groups.yahoo.com/group/dm-discuss/message/11646,* accessed July 30, 2006. (Free registration required to access URL.)

Luckham, D. C. (2002). *The power of events: an introduction to complex event processing in distributed enterprise systems.* Boston, Addison-Wesley.

Lutchen, M. (2004). *Managing IT as a business: a survival guide for CEOs.* Hoboken, NJ, John Wiley & Sons.

Maizlish, B., and R. Handler (2005). *IT portfolio management step-by-step: unlocking the business value of technology.* Hoboken, NJ, John Wiley & Sons.

Marco, D. (2000). *Building and managing the meta data repository: a full lifecycle guide.* New York, John Wiley & Sons.

Marco, D. (2003). "Meta data repository: a system that manages our systems." *The Data Administration Newsletter* (#23). *http://www.tdan.com*

Marco, D., and M. Jennings (2004). *Universal meta data models.* Indianapolis, John Wiley & Sons.

Martin, J. (1989). *Information engineering book II: planning & analysis.* Englewood Cliffs, NJ, Prentice Hall.

McClure, C. (1989). *CASE is software automation.* Englewood Cliffs NJ, Prentice Hall.

McConnell, S. (1996). *Rapid development: taming wild software schedules.* Redmond, WA, Microsoft Press.

McConnell, S. (1998). *Software project survival guide.* Redmond, WA, Microsoft Press.

McConnell, S. (1999). *After the gold rush: creating a true profession of software engineering.* Redmond, WA, Microsoft Press.

McFarlan, F. W. (1981). "Portfolio approach to information systems." *Harvard Business Review* (September–October 1981): 142–150.

Microsoft Corporation (2005). Visual Studio 2005 team system modeling strategy and FAQ. *http://msdn.microsoft.com/vstudio/default.aspx?pull=/library/en-us/dnvs05/html/vstsmodel.asp*

Narayan, R. (1988). *Data dictionary: implementation, use, and maintenance.* Prentice Hall mainframe software series. Englewood Cliffs, NJ, Prentice Hall.

Nolan, R. (1973). "Managing the computer resource: a stage hypothesis." *Communications of the ACM* 16(7) (July 1973): 399–405.

Nolan, R., and F. W. McFarlan (2005). "Information technology and the board of directors." *Harvard Business Review* (October 2005).

Object Management Group (2002a). Common Warehouse Metamodel (CWM) specification. *www.omg.org*

Object Management Group (2002b). MetaObject Facility (MOF) specification, Version 1.4. *www.omg.org*

Office of Government Commerce (2000). *Service support: service desk and the process of incident management, problem management, configuration management, change management and release management.* OGC, ITIL Managing IT Services (Information Technology Infrastructure Library). London, The Stationery Office.

Office of Government Commerce (2001). *Service delivery: capacity management, availability management, service level management, IT service continuity, financial management for IT services and customer relationship management.* OGC, ITIL Managing IT Services (Information Technology Infrastructure Library). London, The Stationery Office.

Office of Government Commerce (2002a). *Application management.* OGC, ITIL Managing IT Services (Information Technology Infrastructure Library). London, The Stationery Office.

Office of Government Commerce (2002b). *ICT infrastructure management.* OGC, ITIL Managing IT Services (Information Technology Infrastructure Library). London, The Stationery Office.

Office of Government Commerce (2002c). *Planning to implement IT service management.* OGC, ITIL Managing IT Services (Information Technology Infrastructure Library). London, The Stationery Office.

Office of Government Commerce (2003). *Software asset management.* OGC, ITIL Managing IT Services (Information Technology Infrastructure Library). London, The Stationery Office.

Office of Government Commerce (2004). *Business perspective: the IS view on delivering services to the business.* OGC, ITIL Managing IT Services (Information Technology Infrastructure Library). London, The Stationery Office.

Office of Government Commerce (2006). *Business perspective: the business view.* OGC, ITIL Managing IT Services (Information Technology Infrastructure Library). London, The Stationery Office.

Open Group (2002). The Open Group Architectural Framework (TOGAF), version 8. *www.opengroup.org*

Patton, S. (2006). "Beating the Boomer Brain Drain Blues." *CIO Magazine* (January 15, 2006).

Poole, J., D. Chang, et al. (2002). *Common warehouse metamodel: an introduction to the standard for data warehouse integration.* New York, John Wiley & Sons.

Poole, J., D. Chang, et al. (2003). *Common warehouse metamodel: developer's guide.* New York, John Wiley & Sons.

Porter, M. E. (1998). *Competitive advantage: creating and sustaining superior performance (with a new introduction).* New York, Free Press.

Project Management Institute (2004). *A guide to the project management body of knowledge (PMBOK guide).* Newtown Square, PA, Project Management Institute.

Reingruber, M., and W. W. Gregory (1994). *The data modeling handbook: a best-practice approach to building quality data models.* New York, John Wiley & Sons.

Remenyi, D. (1999). *IT investment: making a business case.* Computer weekly professional series. Oxford; Boston, Butterworth-Heinemann.

Remenyi, D., A. H. Money, et al. (2000). *The effective measurement and management of IT costs and benefits.* Computer weekly professional series. Oxford; Boston, Butterworth-Heinemann.

Royce, W. (1970). Managing the development of large software systems. IEEE Wescon, Institute of Electrical and Electronics Engineers.

Ruijs, L., and A. Schotanus (2002). "Managing the delivery of business information." *The guide to IT service management.* J. van Bon, ed. London, Addison-Wesley: 165–177.

Ruiz, F., M. Piattini, et al. (2002). "An integrated environment for managing software maintenance projects." *The guide to IT service management.* J. van Bon, ed. London, Addison-Wesley: 460–477.

Rummler, G. A., and A. P. Brache (1995). *Improving performance: how to manage the white space on the organization chart.* Jossey-Bass management series. San Francisco, CA, Jossey-Bass.

Schmidt, J., and D. Lyle (2005). *Integration competency center: an implementation methodology.* Informatica.

Schrage, M. (2005). "Prune IT Systems, Not Budgets." *CIO Magazine* (January 15, 2005).

Sharp, A., and P. McDermott (2001). *Workflow modeling: tools for process improvement and application development.* Boston, Artech House.

Simsion, G. C., and G. C. Witt (2005). *Data modeling essentials.* Amsterdam; Boston, Morgan Kaufmann.

Snopes.com (2006). Boiled beef. *http://www.uga.edu/srel/ecoview11-18-02.htm*

Software Engineering Institute (2004). What is a CASE environment? *http://www.sei.cmu.edu/legacy/case/case_whatis.html*

Spewak, S. H., and S. C. Hill (1993). *Enterprise architecture planning: developing a blueprint for data, applications, and technology.* Boston, QED Publishing Group.

Spurr, K., and P. Layzell, eds. (1990). *CASE on trial.* Chichester, England, John Wiley & Sons.

Standish Group (2004). CHAOS report. *http://www.standishgroup.com*

Sturm, R. (2005). *IT life cycle management: from theory to practice.* White Plains, NY, International Business Machines.

Sturm, R., and W. Bumpus (1999). *Foundations of application management.* New York, John Wiley & Sons.

Sturm, R., L. Erickson-Harris, et al. (2002). *SLM solutions: a buyer's guide.* Boulder, CO, Enterprise Management Associates.

Sturm, R., W. Morris, et al. (2000). *Foundations of service level management.* Indianapolis, Sams.

Tannenbaum, A. (1994). *Implementing a corporate repository: the models meet reality.* New York, John Wiley & Sons.

Tannenbaum, A. (2002). *Metadata solutions: using metamodels, repositories, XML, and enterprise portals to generate information on demand.* Boston, Addison-Wesley.

Teorey, T. J. (1994). *Database modeling & design: the fundamental principles.* San Francisco, CA, Morgan Kaufmann.

Tsykin, M. (2002). "Service level measurement: checkpoint 2000." *The guide to IT service management.* J. van Bon, ed. London, Addison-Wesley: 97–115.

van Bon, J., ed. (2002). *The guide to IT service management 2002.* London; Boston, Addison-Wesley.

van Bon, J., G. Kemmerling, et al. (2002). *IT service management: an introduction.* itSMF-Canada.

van den Elskamp, H., W. J. J. Kuiper, et al. (2002). "Integrated service management (ISM)." *The guide to IT service management.* J. van Bon, ed. London, Addison-Wesley: 116–130.

van Herwaarden, H., and F. Grift (2002). "IPW and the IPW stadia model (IPWSM)." *The guide to IT service management.* J. van Bon, ed. London, Addison-Wesley: 97–115.

Verhoef, C. (2002). "Quantitative IT portfolio management." *Science of Computer Programming* **45**:1–96.

Walker, G., and Harris Kern's Enterprise Computing Institute. (2001). *IT problem management.* Professional Technical Reference. Upper Saddle River, NJ, Prentice Hall.

Waters, R. (2003). "Corporate computing tries to find a new path." *Financial Times.*

Weill, P., and J. W. Ross (2004). *IT governance: how top performers manage IT decision rights for superior results.* Boston, Harvard Business School Press.

Wertz, C. J. (1989). *The data dictionary: concepts and uses.* Wellesley, MA, QED Information Sciences.

Yourdon, E. (1989). *Modern structured analysis.* Englewood Cliffs, NJ, Yourdon Press.

Yourdon, E., and L. L. Constantine (1979). *Structured design: fundamentals of a discipline of computer program and systems design.* Englewood Cliffs, NJ, Prentice Hall.

Index

Page numbers in boldface indicate where terms are defined.

About the Author

CHARLES BETZ IS A SENIOR enterprise architect and the chief architect for IT service management strategy for a U.S.-based Fortune 50 enterprise. Previously, he was the head of Enterprise Repository Services for the specialty electronics retailer Best Buy. He is Foundation Certified in ITIL (Information Technology Infrastructure Library).

He has held architect and capability lead positions for Best Buy, Target, and Accenture, specializing in metadata, configuration management, enterprise application integration, and IT governance. He holds a *summa cum laude* B.A. in Political Science and a Master of Science in Software Engineering, both from the University of Minnesota.

He is an active member of the professional community, belonging to the IT Service Management Forum, Institute of Electrical and Electronics Engineers, Association for Computing Machinery, and Data Management Association. He presents frequently both locally and nationally to professional associations and conferences.

He is the sole author of the popular *www.erp4it.com* weblog.

Charlie lives in Minneapolis, Minnesota, with his wife Sue and son Keane. His interests include writing, music, and cooking.